Social Change in Contemporary China and the Theory of Social Contradictions – The Social Class and Interest Group Analysis in Contemporary China

Wang Weiguang
Translated by Huang Yusheng

Paths International Ltd

中国社会科学出版社
CHINA SOCIAL SCIENCES PRESS

This book is published with financial support

from Innovation Project of CASS

Acknowledgements

We sincerely appreciate the input of China Social Sciences Press' s President Zhao Jianying and Deputy Chief editor Cao Hongju' s support for this project and Zhao Shixiong, Xia Xia, Li Haiying, Yang Yang, Wang Yue in the department of international Cooperation & Publishing at CSSP served as the editors, making the proof-reading. They have done much work in arranging the preparation of the English version.

We also sincerely appreciate the hard work of the translator, Mr. Huang Yusheng and the final proof reader, Miss Jane Yang. Without their diligent work this English version would not exist.

Finally we especially appreciate the financial support in the publication of this book from CASS Innovation Translation Fund.

August 2014

Preface to the Second Edition

This book is the second edition of my book *Efficiency, Equality and Harmony: On Contradictions among the People in the New Era and Socialist Harmonious Society* (published by People's Publishing House, Dec. 2006). During the four years after the publication of the book, various new developments at home and abroad have proved that, many views I expressed in the book are correct, including views on the two types of contradictions differing in nature, contradictions among the people, the existence and intensification of class struggle in certain limits, the differentiation of classes, strata and interest groups. They have also proved that it is absolutely necessary to take the theory of contradictions among the people as a guide in our work. The new developments in the short period of four years call for new theoretical explanations and guidance. Hence the book is revised and reprinted. For the selling of the book, at the suggestion of the editor, the above mentioned title was usedin the first edition. In this second edition, its present and also original title is used. The materials and data cited in the first edition are all from sources published before 2005. In order to ensure the consistence of the arguments with the facts and data, and also to test my views, in this revision, I did not add new facts or data, but only made some necessary editorial changes.

Since more than three decades of reform and opening up, on the one hand, the great achievements of our socialist modernization have attracted worldwide attention; on the other, many contradictions and problems have accumulated, the intensification and evolution of which, in terms of human relations, find their expressions mainly as intricate contradictions among the people and, in some cases, as contradictions among the people and the enemy in certain limits that take a non-dominant position. The frequent mass incidents and occasional vicious violent incidents are all the typical demonstrations of intensification of contradictions among the people, or the entwining of contradictions among the people and contradictions between ourselves and the enemy, andsome even tangled with class struggle. In the year 2009 only, there happened several large-scale incidents, including the March 23rd GanchengIncident in Hainan Province, the May 19th Huining Incident in Gansu Province, the June 10th Haiyuan Incident in the Ningxia Hui Autonomous Region, the June 17th Shishou Incident in Hubei Province, the July 24th Jilin TonghuaIron and Steel Plant Incident in Jilin Province, and particularly, the July 5th Urumqi Incident in Xinjiang Uygur Autonomous Region. 2010 also saw not a few mass incidents. These incidents differed in nature, and their participants mostly were ordinary people, but there might be some saboteurs or hostile elements behind the scenes. It shows that, at the present stage of our society, there are a large number of contradictions among the people and contradictions between ourselves and the enemy in certain limits; and there are large numbers of contradictions among the people of both class and non-class struggle nature, and evencontradictions between ourselves and the enemy. All these contradictions entwine and twist together, forming a very tricky and intricate situation. The brewing, evolution and outbreak of these social contradictions have a severe negative impact on the harmony and stability of our society and our endeavor of building socialism with Chinese characteristics.

It is obvious that, the in-depth examining and analyzing the roots of these contradictions, the correct distinguishing and handling the two types of contradictions differing in nature and the correct understanding and resolving of the numerous and outstanding contradictions among the people is a major political issue having a bearing on the long-term governance of our party, long-term peace and stability of our society and the development of socialism with Chinese characteristics. And the strengthening of the ability of our party as the party exercising the power, especially the ability of our leading cadres in correctly distinguishing and handling these two types of contradictions is also an important part of building up the governing capacity of the Party.

One tendency often conceals another. When correcting one incorrect tendency, we must pay attention to preventing another. Sincethe Third Plenary Session of the Eleventh Central Committee of our party held in 1978, we determinedly have abandoned the wrong line of "taking class struggle as the key link," and reaffirmed the scientific judgment that "Class struggle is no longer the principal contradiction in our society, but it will exist for a long time in certain limits." Experience since then tells us that, under the condition that class contradiction and class struggle is the principal contradiction of the society, we should always be aware of not expanding contradictions between ourselves and the enemy and not confusing the two types of contradictions differing in nature; on the other hand, under the condition that contradictions among the people constitute the principal type of contradictions in our society, while correctly handling these contradictions, we need to keep full vigilance against contradictions with class struggle nature in certain limits and correctly distinguish between and handle the two types of contradictions. In the first edition of this book, I wrote: "...though the exploiting classes as a whole no long exist in our country, various domestic and foreign hostile elements and forces as well as the exploiting elements associated with the exploiting system and classes are far from been eliminated, and class struggle between the people and these forces, elements and classes will exist in a certain scope, which even can intensify under certain conditions due to the following reasons: (1) China is still in a complex international environment, and foreign hostile forces have not given up their wild ambition to subjugate China by doing everything possible from peaceful evolution, political subversion to sabotage, corruption, etc.; (2) In the regions that adopt the policy of "one country two systems" and that has not yet achieved unification with the mainland, there are still exploiting classes, though most of which are patriotic, a few hostile elements among them are hostile to and try to interrupt China's socialist cause; (3) There are still remnants of the exploiting classes who are hostile to socialist China, criminals who disrupt socialist order, and reactionaries who are hostile to socialist system, etc., they will resort to every possible means to undermine China's socialist construction; (4) China is still at the primary stage of socialism with lots of economic, political, ideological, cultural remnants of the old society, coupled with the immaturity and imperfection of its socialist system, which will give birth to new criminals, new corrupt elements and new hostile elements." This judgment was confirmed by the history and the current situation and the developmental trends both at home and abroad. The March 14th Lhasa Incident in Tibet and the July 5th Urumqi Incident in Xinjiang are irrefutable evidence of it. To a certain extent, there were factorsof class struggle, which sometimes may be very violent, behind these two vicious incidents. Take Dalai Lama for example. He himself is the representative of the reactionary exploiting serf-owner class, who, under the cloaks of "human rights," "religion" and "universal values," attempts actually to restore the old social order and their lost interests. And the Western reactionary capitalist forces are behind him. Besides, there are also some elements who do not belong to reactionary exploiting class, but at the bottom of their heart, they long for the Western capitalist system. So we should maintain high vigilance on them, otherwise our country might change political color.

In times of adversity we should see the bright side of things; whereas in favorable circumstances, we should keep vigilance on the bad side. At the present stage when China's society and economy are both at favorable circumstances of development, some of our comrades see but the bright side of the situation to the neglect of many latent risks and the class struggle at certain limits, and fail to see class struggle behind some ethnic, religious or mass incidents, so that the strategy and tactics they used are not effective and the measures they take cannot resolve the problems in fundamental, comprehensive, strategic and institutional ways. This is very dangerous.

In the current period, it is imperative to vigorously develop socialist market economy, and, under the premise of publicownership taking the dominant role, to encourage the development of other sectors of the economy, and to allow the existence of other forms of distribution with distribution according to work as the main form. All these are necessary for the promoting socialist productive forces. Otherwise, it is impossible for us to finish the fundamental task of developing socialist productive forces and to provide solid material conditions for the shaping of new social formation. On the other hand however, other problems will inevitably come up, including the possibility of widening gap between rich and poor, contradictions between labor and capital, the intensification of various social contradictions, the differentiation, antagonism and conflicts between classes, strata and interest groups, and so on. If our vigilance are relaxed against the emergence of these problems, or fail to take necessary measures to contain, minimize and resolve them, their negative impact that we don't wish to happen will crop up.

Historical dialectics tell us that, we, on the one side should see that the general trend of history isirresistible; on the other hand, we should see that temporary retrogression of history is possible. By saying so I do not mean to make sensation. The following words of the great writer Su Shi of the Song dynasty in his article "On Chao Cuo" should make us think over: " The most dangerous and most un thing in the world is that, apparently everything is peaceful, but in fact there are latent threats. If this is left unaddressed, they may become worse to the extent that they arc incorrigible. We should always keep this sense of crisis.

I append to the book my article"The global Financial Crisis and the Historical Destiny of Socialism and Marxism" published in *Qiushi*, no. 21, 2010, an analysis of the recent situation, which is consistent with views expressed in this book.

Written in the Division Building, CASS, Beijing

Wang Weiguang

Preface

The correct understanding and handling of contradictions among the people is a major practical and theoretical issue. About 50 years ago, after the completion of the "three socialist transformations," on the basis of summing up the experience and drawing the lessons of the Soviet Union in its socialist construction led by Stalin, and by criticizing Stalin's wrong views on domestic contradictions in socialist countries and analyzing the changes of basic contradictions, principal contradiction and contradictions among the people in socialist China, Comrade Mao Zedong put forth the scientific theory of contradictions among the people. Unfortunately, due to the constraints of complex subjective and objective conditions of the time, later on Comrade Mao himself gradually deviated from the correct theory both in practice and theory; instead, he tried to resolve contradictions and problems emerged in socialist construction and development with the method of class struggle, and put forward the wrong theory of "continued revolution under the dictatorship of the proletariat" and the Ultra-Leftist wrong line of "taking class struggle as the key link," which ultimately led to the tragedy of the "Cultural Revolution" and the grave setbacks of socialist construction and development.

In the Third Plenary Session of the Eleventh Central Committee of the Communist Party of China(CPC), under the leadership of Comrade Deng Xiaoping, our party set things right in ideological and political lines, restored the correct line of seeking truth from facts and the new political line of "one central task (of economic construction) and two basic points(of adhering to the four cardinal principles and the policy of reform and opening up)," thus ushering in the new era of building socialism with Chinese characteristics. Under the new historical conditions, the Party restored the correct theory of contradictions among the people put forward by Comrade Mao and determinately abandoned the practice of handling contradictions among the people with the method of class struggle. In the great endeavors of socialist reform and opening up and building socialism with Chinese characteristics, by correctly understanding and handling a series of contradictions among the people, it has upheld and enriched this theory in the new period. And the Party's third generation of collective leadership with Comrade Jiang Zemin at the core and its new

Central Committee with Comrade Hu Jintao as General Secretary have added much new content to the theory.

The practices and lessons of socialist construction in socialist countries tell us that, whether we can correctly understand and handle contradictions among the people has a bearing on the position of our party as the governing party, on the success of our socialist reform and construction and on the cause of socialism with Chinese characteristics. Whenever we do well in this respect, the position of the Party will be consolidated and our endeavors will flourish; otherwise, our socialist causes will encounter setbacks and the Party's position will be in danger. Therefore, we must properly solve this political issue of fundamental significance.

The Party's Sixteenth National Congress put forth the strategic task of building a harmonious society in China. It is precisely the existence of contradictions that we need to pursue harmony, and it is our pursuit of harmony that requires us to handle contradictions. To understand harmony, we must first of all have a better understanding of contradictions; and the precondition to build a socialist harmonious society is to resolve contradictions. Marxist dialectics tells us that contradictions exist ever and everywhere; the law of contradiction is a universal and fundamental law governing the existence of all things as well as their inner sources and driving forces of development. We should apply the law of the unity of opposites, that is, the law of contradiction to understand and handle all kinds of contradictions among the people that realistically exist in our country. With regard to contradictions, it is not a question of whether they exist or not, nor of whether they are good or bad. It is good for a contradiction to be resolved, vice versa. After the old contradictions are resolved, new contradictions will emerge. Things move forward in the process of ceaseless resolution of contradictions. By harmonious society we do not mean non-existence of contradiction in the society, but stress to pursue harmony and progress by resolving contradictions. The key to the building of a socialist harmonious society lies in balancing the interest relations of all sides and in resolving contradictions among the people.

I have been paying close attention to this issue of practical and theoretical importance early since the 1980s, when I was still a graduate student in the university. And I have made a long time and extensive investigation, research and empirical analyses on contradictions among the people and their changes in China and in other socialist countries; and I also made overall theoretical examination on the research of this subject both at home and abroad. As the outcome of these studies, I published a series of works on this issue, including *On Contradictions and Development Motives of Socialist Society* (co-compiler, published by Qiushi Publishing House, 1986), *Contradictions, Driving Forces and Reform of Socialism* (Heilongjiang People's Publishing House, 1988), *On Social Interests* (co-author, People's Publishing House, 1991), *Economic Interests, Political Order and Social Stability: A Deep Reflection on Contradictions in Socialist Society* (The Central Party School Publishing House, 1991), *Some Reflections on Contradictions among the People in the New Period* (co-author, The Central Party School Publishing House, 1994), *On Interests* (People's Publishing House, 2001). And I have also conducted three related National Social Science Fund Projects: "Research on the Driving Forces of Socialist Development," "Research on the Interest Relationships and Contradictions in the Primary Stage of Socialism" and "Research on Contradictions among People in the New Period." It is worth noted that, my doctoral dissertation published in 1987 entitled "A Study on Socialist Contradictions" is also about this issue.

I really believe that, in making scientific study, one should be well-grounded with the spirit of perseverance like the Chinese sayings of "sharpening a good sword for ten years," and valuable academic fruit can only grow on a deep-rooted tree of intensive study. The book presented here is the outcome of my learning, reflection, investigation and research for more than 20 years. I hope it has some value of reference to the readers. My sincere thanks should be given to Prof. Yang Chungui for granting my use of some of the ideas expressed in our co-authored book *Some Reflections on Contradictions among the People in the New Period,* and to my student Peng Jinsong, who proofread all text and references of the book.

Wang Weiguang

In the campus of the Party School of the Central Committee of CPC

September, 2005

Contents

PART ONE

A Theoretical Study of Contradictions among the People

Our party's theory of contradictions among the people was gradually formulated on the basis of drawing on the historical experience of socialist construction at home and abroad and enriched by summing up the fresh experience of building socialism with Chinese characteristics. The three generations of collective leadership of the Communist Party of China (CPC) made great contributions to the proposition, formulation, enrichment and advancement of this theory. The Party's first generation of central collective leadership with Comrade Mao Zedong at its core creatively put forward the doctrine of contradictions among the people, which points out that contradictions exist within socialist countries and these contradictions mostly and often times manifest themselves as contradictions among the people needing our correct understanding and handling. The Party's second generation of central collective leadership with Comrade Deng Xiaoping at its core, set things right and thoroughly repudiated the "Left" political line of "taking class struggle as the key link," and advocated correct understanding and handling contradictions among the people in the new era, which adhered to and developed the correct theory. The Party's third generation of collective leadership with Comrade Jiang Zemin as its representative and the new Central Committee with Comrade Hu Jintao as General Secretary, in the new practice of building socialism with Chinese characteristics, have further enriched and developed the theory. All the practice of socialist building and development shows that, the correct understanding and handling of contradictions among the people in the course of building a harmonious socialist society is one of the themes of the political life of socialism with Chinese characteristics.

Chapter 1

The Proposition of the Theory of Contradictions among the People and Its Main Content

The theory of contradictions among the people put forth by the CPC represents an important contribution to Marxism and to the theory of scientific socialism. Comrade Mao Zedong's article *On the Correct Handling of Contradictions among the People* published in 1957 is the representative work of this theory, which outlines the basic ideas and the main content of it, marking its formulation. It embodies the Party's collective wisdom, in which Comrade Mao Zedong played a decisive and historical role.

I. The Creation and Putting Forth of the Theory of Contradictions among the People

The historical practices of socialist countries shows that, after the establishment of the socialist system, how to understand and handle the internal contradictions in a socialist country is a major issue vital to the fate and future of the country.

It is a new issue in the socialist practice as how to correctly understand and handle the internal contradictions in a socialist country after the establishment of socialist system. Due to the limitations in practice, the Marxist classical writers could not provide a definite answer to this question. But their expositions in this regard have an important guiding significance for us to correctly understand and handle these contradictions, and they also lay an ideological foundation for us to correctly formulate the theory of contradictions among the people, including contradictions within the Party, between the leaders and the masses, between workers and farmers, among the classes within the united front and among the social strata, as well as contradictions in the first stage of communism, such as those between urban and rural areas, between workers and farmers, between brain labor and manual labor, etc. About social contradictions under socialist system, Lenin foresaw that, under socialist conditions, "Antagonism will disappear while the contradictions will continue to exist."① And he noted that the main content of

① *Collected Works of Lenin*, vol. 60, People's Publishing House, 1990, p. 282.

political life in socialist countries would change, and that "politics should be a matter of the people", and the center of struggle would shift "gradually to economy."① In his polemic with Trotsky, Lenin once used the concept of "non-class economic struggle". He also talks in many writings about how to deal with contradictions within the communist party, among the various forces in the united front, between the leaders and the masses, and so on. Before the Soviet Union declared its entrance into the socialist society, Stalin did some analyses of the contradictions in the society of the Soviet Union and used the concept of "internal contradictions" (referring to the conflict between the workers and farmers). But after the Soviet Union declared its entrance into socialist society, he for a long time confused the two different types of contradictions and made major mistakes, which are lessons for our party to correctly understand and handle contradictions among the people.

In the period of democratic revolution, as to how to correctly handle the relationship and contradictions within the people's army and the revolutionary bases, such as those between the Party and the government, between the Party and the masses, between military and political affairs, and those within the Party, the army, and among the masses, as well as the relationship and contradictions among different classes, social strata and political factions in the United Front, our party had formed a set of effective methods, including the formula "unity-criticism-unity", and the guideline of "learning from past mistakes to avoid future ones, and curing the sickness to save the patient." These ideas and experiences constitute a theoretical basis and experiential premise in this respect. Nonetheless, in the strict sense, how to handle the internal contradictions in a socialist country remained a major issue yet to be resolved in the development of Marxism before the CPC formulated the theory of correctly handling contradictions among the people.

The practice of the new democratic revolution led by the CPC gradually put the issue of handling contradictions among the people on an important place of the agenda. On the eve of the founding of New China, in many of our party's documents and Party leader's speeches, it was mentioned that democratic methods should be widely used to resolve the contradictions of right and wrong among the people. As early as in June 1949, in his article On the People's Democratic Dictatorship, Comrade Mao Zedong points out that, to solve the internal problems within the people, "the method we employ is democratic, the method of persuasion,

---

① *Collected Works of Lenin*, vol. 60, People's Publishing House, 1990, p. 308.

not of compulsion."[1] Since the establishment of the people's democratic dictatorship in China in 1949, as contradictions among the people were frequently and numerously encountered, our party began to shape the idea of the correct handling of them. In June 1950, Comrade Mao Zedong pointed out in a speech in the Second Political Consultative Conference: to the people we can only "use democratic methods to educate and persuade them, which is self-education within the people, and criticism and self-criticism are the basic methods of self-education." This is the first time the concept "among the people" was put forward and discussed theoretically. After the founding of New China, Comrade Liu Shaoqi for the first time expounded the methods of handling contradictions among the people, thus made an important contribution to the formation of the theory.

In 1951, in his articleInternal Contradictions in the State-owned Factories and the Basic Tasks of Trade Union Work, Liu Shaoqi clearly put forward the concept of contradictions among the people and made a preliminary theoretical discourse on it. He believed that, in our society, "it can be seen that in general contradictions fall into two categories: fundamentally antagonistic and irreconcilable and fundamentally non-antagonistic and therefore reconcilable." In that period, China's national economy had not yet recovered, and the principal contradiction in the society as a whole was that between the new government and the remnants of the "three big mountains." A controversy arouse within the Party about whether there were contradictions in the state-owned factories. In July 1950, in his Report to the Enlarged Meeting of the Preparatory Committee of the Federation of Trade Union of Central-South China, concerning the phenomenon that some trade unions in the state-owned factories divorced from the masses in handling contradictions between the workers and management, Deng Zihui, then Third Secretary of the Central-South Bureau of the CPC Central Committee, raised the issue of stand of the trade union workers. He held that, basically speaking, the stand of the trade union workers and the management of the enterprises and government officials were identical. But their attitudes towards specific matters should be different due to the differences of their work positions. Only in this way were the trade unions needed by the workers and thus had their mass base and could play their role. After this article was published, Gao Gang, then First Secretary of Northeast Bureau of the CPC Central Committee,

---

① *Selected Readings from the Works of Comrade Mao Zedong*, vol. 2, People's Publishing House, 1986, p. 683.

disagreed with these views. In April 1951, he organized an article entitled "On the Identity of the Stand of the Management and Trade Union in State-owned Factories", which was submitted to the CPC Central Committee and Comrade Mao Zedong. Gao believed that there was only identity of interests in state-owned enterprises between the workers and the management and the two must be completely identical in all issues, without any difference. The debate was fierce. Comrade Liu Shaoqi, who was in charge of the work of trade union in the Central Committee at the time, viewing to properly resolve the debated issue, studied in details the arguments of both sides and wrote an article as long as more than 8000 Chinese characters entitled "Notes Made When Reading the Two Articles Written Respectively by Comrades Deng Zihui and Gao Gang" (it was later included in the *Selected Works of Liu Shaoqi*, vol. II, with the title "The Internal Contradictions in State-owned Factories and the Basic Tasks of the Trade Union Work".) It not only affirms the correct points of Comrade Deng Zihui on trade union work, but also analyzes philosophically the essence of the issue debated, in which he preliminary put forward and expounded the notion of contradictions among the people, with the main points as follows:

First, proceeding from the universality of contradictions, he demonstrates that there are contradictions in state-owned factories. He wrote: "Since everything is composed of contradictions, the state factory inevitably is a structure of contradictions, too." The basic contradictions in these factories "are contradictions between the factory administration and the workers, between the public interests and the private interests." These "are undeniable, true contradictions and exist as objective reality. It will take a long time and serious effort for us to readjust and cope with these contradictions."① He believes that there are no longer any class and class struggle in the state factories. When the factories were owned by the capitalists, the relations between labor and management within the factories are of class contradiction nature; when the factories are nationalized, class antagonisms no longer exist and the basic contradictions in these factories are contradictions between the management and the workers. This judgment, in a thorough dialectical thinking and scientific way, gives answer to the question of whether there are contradictions in state-owned factories after the establishment of socialist system. Although he discusses the issue within the scope of state-owned factories, the methods he used in studying this problem, without doubt, has a universal meaning. It opened up a new thinking for

① *Selected Works of Liu Shaoqi*, vol. 2, People's Publishing House, 1985, p. 93.

us to comprehensively study contradictions in socialist countries; and it also is a major breakaway from the long-established prevailing view in international communist movement that there is only political and moral identity but no contradictions in socialist countries.

It, proceeding from the particularity of contradictions, puts forth the initial concept of contradictions among the people. He points out that contradictions and relations in the state-owned factories "are those within the ranks of the working class and the people,"① "while sharing basically the same overall interests, they have contradictions stemming from individual or partial interests."② This shows that contradictions in the state-owned factories are mainly contradictions among the people, contradictions with a nature and characteristics "entirely different from the class antagonisms in capitalist factories, contradictions that are non-antagonistic in nature and can and ought to be reconciled or resolved through mediation."③ In the history of Marxism, its classical writers often mentioned contradictions inside party, contradictions between workers and farmers, contradictions between manual and mental workers, etc., none of them is like Comrade Liu Shaoqi, who made so creatively a summary of these contradictions with putting forth a new concept, the concept of "contradictions among the people," and made so correct a revelation of the connotation, nature and characteristics of it. Here, "non-antagonistic, reconcilable and through meditation" by no means implies that there is no struggle at all, but that these contradictions are different from class antagonisms, "while sharing basically the same overall interests, they have contradictions stemming from individual or partial interests,"④ so they can be resolved by adjusting and taking into consideration of the interests of both sides. This is precisely the idea later put forward by Comrade Mao Zedong that contradictions among the people, in general, are not antagonistic in nature.

Third, he dialectically points out that, when observing and analyzing social problems, we must distinguish between two different types of contradictions and he makes a theoretical generalization about them. He says: "In general contradictions fall into two categories: fundamentally antagonistic and therefore irreconcilable and fundamentally non-antagonistic and therefore reconcilable." "For instance, the

---

① *Selected Works of Liu Shaoqi*, vol. 2, People's Publishing House, 1985, p. 94.

② *Ibid.*, p. 96.

③ *Ibid.*, p. 93.

④ *Ibid.*, p. 96.

contradictions between the state factory administration and individual workers belong to the latter. "① Here, two different types of contradictions are actually referring to those in a wider scope, i. e., the whole society beyond factories, with those in factories only as examples.

Fourth, proceeding fromthe methods of resolving contradictions, he points out that "people from opposite standpoints will adopt opposing principles and policies" of resolving contradictions among the people. " On one side are the counter-revolutionaries, enemies of the working class and the people. Opposing the working class and other people, taking advantage of the antagonistic features of contradictions and of every weakness they can find in the two opposites, they sow dissension and stir up struggle and disunity, so as to facilitate their counter-revolutionary sabotage. On the other side are the communists, politically awakened members of the working class and other people. Standing with the workers and the people, they take advantage of the unity of opposites and every strong point of each of the opposites to promote reconciliation and compromise (through proper struggle). In this way the two opposites achieve unity and combine their efforts for production. "② This differentiation has great significance both in theory and practice. According to Comrade Liu, to correctly handle contradictions among the people, we first of all must stand with the working class and the people, "take advantage of the unity of opposites and every strong point of each of the opposites." This unity is the fundamental identity of interests within the ranks of the people, demonstrating all the advantages of the opposites that fundamentally are identical with the interests of the people. This identity is the basic premise for the correct handling of contradictions among the people. Any ignorance of or departure from this premise will necessarily undermine the foundation of the unity of the people. Secondly, in dealing with the contradictions of partial and temporary interests among the people, the principle of reconciliation and compromise should be adopted. Reconciliation and compromise means that interests of all sides should be considered rather than sacrifice or deprive the interests of one side for the interests of the other side. He says: "This method conforms to the policy proposed by Comrade Mao Zedong of considering both public and private interests in state-owned factories. "③ Thirdly, reconciliation and comprise

---

① *Selected Works of Liu Shaoqi,* vol. 2, People's Publishing House, 1985, p. 94.

② *Ibid.*, p. 94.

③ Ibid., pp. 94 – 95.

should go "through proper struggle". In other words, they should be governed by principles instead of in an unprincipled way. That is, when the overall interests contradict with individual or partial interests, "the latter should be subordinate to the former."① These contradictions should be correctly settled by readjustment of material interests and ideological education. Lastly, in handling contradictions among the people, we should prevent the enemies from taking advantage of the contradictions to sow dissension or stir up disunity within the people.

Fifth, from the perspective of transformation of contradictions he discusses the intensification of contradictions among the people and the methods for preventing it. He foresees that contradictions among the people may intensify, and "friction, conflict may occur and even strikers and a slowdown in production may occur."② He philosophically analyzes reasons: "Because cooperation and reconciliation in all contradictions are mutual and conditional, whereas accelerating conflict in a contradiction needs only the effort of one side and is thus unconditional and absolute."③ Therefore, "reconcilable contradictions might change into antagonistic ones for a period of time if either of the two opposites should fail to handle the conflicts appropriately." That is to say, efforts of both sides are needed in correctly handling contradictions among the people. As for state-owned factories, if conflicts occur between the managerial staff and workers, they should be settled in a realistic manner "by meeting the workers' rational demands that can be met and persuading the workers politically." If either of the two points is neglected, the contradictions cannot be solved properly. He further points out: "Worse still, when counter-revolutionaries and bad elements succeed in sowing dissension among them, the situation may become serious."④ Therefore, in the process of dealing with contradictions among the people, vigilance against the sabotage of the enemy should never be relaxed.

In short, although Comrade Liu Shaoqi's analysis of the internal contradictions in the state-owned factories in the early years of new China is within the scope of enterprises of the public ownership rather than that in socialist countries in general, since the contradictions it discussed belong to contradictions among the people, it has an overall significance. It constitutes the embryo form of the theory of

---

① *Selected Works of Liu Shaoqi,* vol. 2, People's Publishing House, 1985, p. 96.

② *Ibid.*, p. 96.

③ *Ibid.*, p. 96.

④ *Ibid.*, p. 95.

contradictions among the people.

If in the periods of recovery of national economy and socialist transformation, our party had been faced with many contradictions among the people, then, it is no doubt that, after the completion of socialist transformation, the question of how to handle contradictions among the people would become a question that must be answered by it in the practice of socialist construction. After the founding of New China, the property of the bureaucratic-capitalist class was expropriated and based on it the state-owned factories were established. Since the socialist economic system was first built up here, so was unavoidably the emergence of contradictions among the people. With the basic completion of socialist transformation of means of production and the set-up of socialist relations of production nationwide, contradictions among the people would inevitably become more outstanding in the whole society.

II. The Formation of the Theory of Contradictions among the People

From Comrade Liu Shaoqi's exposition we can see the embryo form ofthe theory of contradictions among the people. But it is only an initial one discussing the contradictions in the state-owned factories without taking them as an overall issue in the political life of socialist countries.

With the basic completion of socialist transformation of means of production andthe set-up of socialist relations of production nationwide, contradictions among the people inevitably became more outstanding in the whole society. Therefore our party's understanding of the issue was deepened. In his article On the Ten Major Relationships published on 2nd April, 1956, Comrade Mao Zedong points out that we must correctly deal with ten major relationships, i. e., the relationship between heavy industry on the one hand and light industry and agriculture on the other, the relationship between industry in the coastal regions and industry in the interior, the relationship between economic construction and defense construction, the relationship between the state, the units of production and the producers, the relationship between the central and the local authorities, the relationship between the Han and other ethnic groups, the relationship between Party and non-Party, the relationship between revolution and counter-revolution, the relationship between right and wrong, and the relationship between China and other countries. The ten major relations are also ten major contradictions. He suggests that the basic policy for handling these contradictions is to mobilize all positive factors, internal and external, to serve the cause of socialism. And he also elaborates the correct methods for dealing with them. This understanding already contains many of the ideas put forward later in his article On the Correct Handling of Contradictions among the People. On 4th December, 1956, in his letter to Mr. Huang Yanpei, Mao explicitly says: "Class contradictions in China have basically been resolved... but problems within the people will emerge one after another."①

At the same time, problems in international communist movement also set our party to pay more attention on contradictions among the people. In the Twentieth Congress of the CPSU (The Communist Party of the Soviet Union) held in 1956, Khrushchev made a secret report criticizing Stalin, which caused a great ideological turbulence in socialist countries; and especially the social unrests broke out in Poland and Hungary fully exposed the internal and external contradictions facing socialist countries. From the winter of 1956 to the spring of 1957, the impact of the chaos in international communist movement spread over to China, causing ideological confusion among some people. In addition, due to the short history of our socialist system, our lack of experience and our insufficient understanding in the respect, many challenges appeared, including issues of distribution, material benefits, pricing, housing, education, problems of employment, bureaucratic style of work in state personnel, etc. Worse still, because of the improper handling of these problems, there occurred a series incidents in which a small number of people created disturbances. More than ten thousand workers and ten thousand students made strikes throughout the country. Our party was fully alerted by the situation both at home and abroad. It had imposed the important theoretical task on our party to have a deeper understanding of contradictions among the people and reveal the universal law governing socialist system by summing up various and experiences and lessons.

The internal and external situation urged the Party to answer the questions of how to correctly handle the contradictions between ourselves and the enemy and those among the people. As Comrade Mao Zedong put it in his talk at the Conference of Secretaries of Provincial, Municipal and Autonomous Region Party Committees on 27th January 1957: "How to handle the contradictions between the people and the

① *Selected Letters of Mao Zedong*, Central Party Literature Press, 1983, pp. 514–515.

enemy and those among the people in socialist society is a branch of science worthy of careful study."[①] In September 1956, in the Eighth National Party Congress presided over by Comrade Mao, an important analysis of the principal domestic contradictions was made. In November 1956, in a speech in the Second Plenary Session of the Eighth Central Committee, Comrade Mao clearly claimed that, the class contradictions in China had been basically resolved, and that for resolving contradictions among the people and inside the Party, democratic method should be used. On December 29, 1956, in the article More on the Historical Experience of the Dictatorship of the Proletariat with Comrade Mao Zedong as the chief author, Stalin's mistakes in his later years is noted, the experiences of Poland and Hungry is summed up and the concepts of contradictions between ourselves and the enemy and contradictions among the people are put forth. In January 1957, also in his talk at the Conference of Secretaries of Provincial, Municipal and Autonomous Region Party Committees Comrade Mao Zedong pointed out that, in the revolutionary period, there were fewer struggles within the ranks of the people, because our attention was focused on class struggle; whereas in the construction period, although the class struggle partly remained, conflicts within the ranks of the people, that is, contradictions among the people would become the most commonly type of contradictions. He proposed that we should carefully study how to understand and handle them.

During this period, comrade Mao Zedongwas thinking over an issue, that is, the general subject of the correct handling of contradictions among the people after the class struggle in the main came to an end. He proposed that in handling contradictions among the people, we should use the method of criticism and education rather than class struggle; we should further develop socialist democracy and fully arouse the socialist enthusiasm of the people to boost economic development. After careful deliberation, on February 27, 1957, in the Eleventh Session (Enlarged) of the Supreme State Conference, Comrade Mao made a speech entitled On the Correct Handling of Contradictions among the People, which clearly put forward the theory of contradictions among the people, marking the formation of our party of this theory. Before and after this speech, in many talks and writings, Comrade Mao expounded the basic ideas contained in the theory. In January 1957, when reading and revising a document of the CPC Central Committee about dealing

① *Selected Letters of Mao Zedong,* Central Party Literature Press, 1983, pp. 514 – 515.

with strikes of workers and students, he criticized the erroneous guidelines and methods adopted many leaders in handling the incidents, because they often confused the two types of contradictions of different nature and used the same way to settle them. They failed to realize that the main cause of these incidents was bureaucracy. The fundamental approach to prevent the incidents such as strike from happening is to strengthen education and expand democracy. In mid March 1957, when Comrade Mao made inspections around the country, the theme of the meetings of cadres he presided over was also how to understand and handle contradictions among the people. He criticized the "Left" dogmatic attitude and methods in this regard. On April 27, 1957, the CPC Central Committee issued the decision on the rectification movement. The decision made it clear that the rectification movement took the correct handling of contradictions among the people as its theme. Seeing from his train of thought around the publication of the article, it is clear that, at least during the period before the Anti-Rightist Campaign was launched, Mao's dominant idea was on the study and handling of contradictions among the people. This is the process of creation, proposition and formation of the theory of contradictions among the people.

III. Further Elucidation of the Theory of Contradictions among the People

After the publication of the article "On the Correct Handling of contradictions among the people, " along with the enthusiasm of study, a variety of questions were raised. Keeping these questions in mind, Comrade Liu Shaoqi made an extensive investigation and research to Hebei, Henan, Hubei, Hunan and Guangdong provinces. On April 27, 1957, at an assembly of Party members and cadres, he made a speech entitled "How to Correctly Handle Contradictions among People", further publicizing Comrade Mao's basic ideas and answering questions raised by the cadres and ordinary people based on the first hand materials gathered in his survey. In fact, this speech constitutes a further theoretical development of the theory, which contains at least the following valuable ideas:

First, he pointed out thatthe principal type of contradiction in China is contradictions among the people.

In discussing the speech of Comrade Mao, many people were not very clear about whatis the principal contradiction in China. Some people said it was the contradiction between the proletarian and non-proletarian ideologies; some said it was the contradiction between workers and farmers; others said it was the contradiction between the working class and the bourgeoisie; still others said it was the contradiction between the superstructure and the economic base, between the relations of production and the productive forces, and between the advanced and the backward; and also some others said it was the contradiction between the masses and the leaders, and so on. Comrade Liu Shaoqi answered them by making specific analyses. He believed that, before the establishment of the People's Republic of China, the principal contradiction in China was one between the Chinese people on the one side and imperialism, feudalism and bureaucratic capitalism on the other; after the founding of New China, especially after the land reform, the principal contradiction had changed into one between the proletariat and bourgeoisie. And after the joint state-private ownership, this contradiction was in the main resolved. "Now the principal contradiction is one among the people."[①] He pointed out that currently there were two different types of contradictions differing in nature needing our correct handling in our society. Now the class struggle in China had in the main come to an end, so they were all incorrect understandings which believed that the principal domestic contradiction was between the proletarian and non-proletarian ideologies, or between the working class and the farmers, between the working class and the bourgeoisie, between the advanced and the backward, and so on. The only principal contradiction in China was the one among the people. He also specifically analyzed the relationship between these various contradictions and contradictions among the people. About the contradiction between the proletarian and non-proletarian ideologies, he said, after the imperialism had been driven out of China, the landlord class had been eliminated and the bourgeoisie had been in the main eliminated, this contradiction "found its expression mainly among the people", including inside the Party and in the ranks of Party cadres, specifically on their subjectivism, bureaucracy, sectarianism, selfish departmentalism, individualism, and so on, which are all manifestations of the ideology of the exploiting classes and the petty-bourgeoisie among the people. About the contradiction between the superstructure and the economic base, between the relations of production and the productive forces, and between the advanced and backward, he said, these contradictions in the past all manifested themselves as the contradictions between

---

① *Selected Works of Liu Shaoqi*, vol. 2, People's Publishing House, 1985, vol. 2, p. 296.

ourselves and the enemy, because the superstructure was of reactionary nature, and so was the relations of production; and the reactionary classes represented the backward forces while the revolutionary classes represented the advanced forces. But now that the situation has changed, in which the superstructure is the state under the leadership of the CPC, including the politics, law and culture. The relations of production are those of public ownership and distribution according to work, "these contradictions find expression among the people, not between the reactionary and revolutionary"... Therefore, these contradictions have become ones among the people." As to the contradiction between the people and the bureaucrats, "it generally belongs to contradictions among the people. By 'generally' I mean that, except for a small number of very bad, obdurate or anti-people bureaucrats, the contradictions between those who have made bureaucratic mistakes and the people come under the category of contradiction among the people."① As to the contradiction between the working class and the farmers, it without doubt is the contradiction among the people.

Second, he pointed out that there are two different types of contradictions in China, and we must correctly handle them.

Comrade Liu Shaoqi criticized and corrected the "Left" mistake of confusing the two different types of contradiction over the past few years.

Firstly, he explicitly pointed out: "Our main mistake over the years has been to handle contradictions among the people the way we coped with contradictions between ourselves and the enemy." In another talk in April of the same year, he said more bluntly that the public security organs had committed the "Left" mistake, and when drawing on lessons, we must raise this problem; if these practices were not corrected, we would certainly go wrong. He made it clear that the "Left" mistake had been reflected in "mistaking our own people for the enemy and attacking too many of them". For example, education through labor, a method designed to handle problems involving the people, was turned into one similar to the method used against the enemy; there should be a strict time limit of administrative detention, but many people were unlawfully detained for as long as that for prisoners; some department even detained and reformed people through labor, which is unlawful and impermissible; some leading members of Party and government departments authorized arrest at will in utter disregard of public security bureau and procuratorate. "Trying to cope with problems among the people... by

① *Selected Works of Liu Shaoqi*, vol. 2, People's Publishing House, 1985, vol. 2, p. 299.

antagonistic means will not resolve contradictions. On the contrary, it will aggravate those contradictions and even cause a split among the ranks of the people or the Party. "① He said: "It is utterly wrong to deal with the problems of our people and the problems of the working people the way we exercise dictatorship over the enemy. "② He even sternly pointed out that this is expression of the KMT style in our Party and government.

Secondly, he pointed out creatively thatthe dictatorship organs, "with regard to the people, they should also handle contradictions among them". There is no doubt that the public security organs, procuratorates and courts are dictatorship organs with regard to the enemy. But are they meant to handle problems involving only the enemy and not the people? Comrade Liu Shaoqi said: "This idea should be carefully studied." This thinking is quite profound and very important for guiding practical work. Because most of our laws, including civil law, economic laws, marriage law, administrative law, and so on, are for adjusting the economic and social relations among the people, if some one among the people violates the law, the dictatorship organs of course must handle it. However, these problems do not necessarily become contradictions between ourselves and the enemy just because they have been handled by dictatorship organs. Although the criminal law are mainly for punishing the criminals, a considerable number of the criminals belong to the category of the people, and if having violated the law, they will be imprisoned or even be sentenced to death. However, just as Comrade Mao Zedong put it: "but this is different in principle from the exercise of dictatorship to suppress enemies of the people." Only by clarifying this can the dictatorship organs in practical work carefully and consciously distinguish between the nature of different contradictions rather than use the way against the enemy to deal with some of the people who have broken the law. In addition, the dictatorship organs also have the responsibility for publicizing the legal system, so that the people can know the law, abide by the law and combat illegal behavior. Comrade Liu Shaoqi said: "Under the dictatorship of the proletariat, the state is also an educational institution. To enable the people to become communists, we should not merely depend only on education in. Being instruments of dictatorship, public security, procuratorial and judicial organs are also charged with the task of educating the people and handling contradictions among them."

---

① *Selected Works of Liu Shaoqi*, vol. 2, People's Publishing House, 1985, vol. 2, p. 451.

② *Ibid.*, p. 450.

Lastly, he stressed the need of improving the socialist legal system and ensuring people's democratic rights. "The legal system of the proletariat is the people's democratic legal system or socialist legal system. A legal system does not necessarily mean dictatorship. There must be legal system among the people; government functionaries and the masses must act within the bounds of public rules and regulations."[①] As to the lack of legal awareness of some Party members, particularly some leading cadres, he specially pointed out that we must correctly handle the relationships between the public security, procuratorial and judicial organs and the Party committees at all levels, "It is not a proper statement that the public security, procuratorial and judicial organs must absolutely obey the Party committees at all levels." Because, according to the Constitution, all legislative, judicial and administrative powers are under the control of the National People's Congress and its Standing Committee; under its leadership and supervision, people's courts exercise judicial power independently; people's procuratorates exercise their procuratorial power independently; the government independent exercise its executive power. The Communist Party of China is the governing party and the force at the core that leads the Chinese people. But this leadership refers to political, ideological, principles and policies rather than arranging everything and monopolizing everything. The Party conducts its activities within the framework of the Constitution and the law and Party members must take the lead in abiding by the law. And he clearly pointed out: "If decisions of a local Party committee are at variance with the law and policies of the Central Committee, which should be obeyed? In that event, one should obey the law and the policies of the Central Committee." And that "It is the right of the court to judge cases independently, and this is prescribed by the Constitution. No Party committee and government department should interfere with the court in this connection." "The procuratorate should combat all violations of law and discipline, no matter what organs or individuals are involved."

Third, he pointed out thatcontradictions among the people find expression mainly in the contradictions between the leaders and the masses and between the bureaucracy and the masses.

He believed "most of contradictions among the people boil down to the contradictions between the masses and their leaders, or, to be more specific,

---

① *Selected Works of Liu Shaoqi*, vol. 2, People's Publishing House, 1985, vol. 2, p. 452.

between the masses and bureaucracy on the part of the leaders."[1] This is a very important judgment. Among the many contradictions among the people, the contradiction between the leaders and the masses has a specifically important position. Firstly, our party is the governing party of our socialist country and our cadres at all levels are leaders in the country's political, economic and cultural life. So all the victories and achievements are closely related with our leaders, so do all the problems and mistakes. "We should assume responsibility for all that is irrational in society and for all the things we have failed to do well. People will also criticize the leaders of the state, the Party, the government and the economic departments for these matters."[2] Secondly, many major contradictions among the people, such as the material interest contradictions among the state, the collective and the individuals, the political contradictions between democracy and centralism, between freedom and discipline, etc., all find direct expression in the contradiction between the leaders and the masses. Thirdly, some contradictions among the people does not find direct expression as the one between the leaders and the masses, such as the contradictions within the working class, within the farmers, between the workers and the farmers, and between the workers and farmers on the one side and the intellectuals on the other, which need to be handled by the leaders at all levels. If not handled properly, they will eventually turn into the contradiction between the leaders and the masses. Therefore, the contradiction between the leaders and the masses, with its especially important position among contradictions among the people, will exist for a long instead of a short term. The correct handling of it is extremely important for the lasting unity, stability and peace of our country, for the mobilization of the initiative of the people in socialist building and for the accomplishment of the goals of our party and the country. Thirdly, the contradiction between the leaders and the masses finds its expression in the bureaucracy of the leaders. He held that if the leading organs overcome bureaucracy, problems can be solved and the contradictions can be eased. "Even if there some people who have wrong ideas and make irrational or excessive demands, the contradiction will not be sharpened if the leaders, free from bureaucracy, explain things clearly."[3] Therefore, whether this kind of contradiction can be resolved depends on whether we can overcome bureaucracy that divorces the

---

① *Selected Works of Liu Shaoqi*, vol. 2, People's Publishing House, 1985, vol. 2, p. 303.

② *Ibid.*, p. 303.

③ *Ibid.*, p. 303.

leaders from the masses and reality.

Fourthly, he pointed out that contradictions among the people also find expression in contribution.

This idea isComrade Liu Shaoqi's another important contribution to the theory of contradictions among the people. Although mentioned this issue in On the Correct Handling of Contradictions among the People, Comrade Mao Zedong focuses mainly on the political and ideological contradictions among the people, while Comrade Liu put the contradiction of material interests on a more important place in his discussion. Firstly, he highlighted the importance of this issue from the basic contradiction of socialist society, that is, the contradiction between the relations of production and the productive forces, and believed that these contradictions "are manifested mostly in distribution." He gave a number of examples: Farmers complain that workers receive more than they do; so are the of the primary school teachers; others complain that some people have lots of living space while they themselves have none at all, and that some others have got a promotion, while they haven't. "All these are related to distribution." "The relations of production must correspond to the growth of the productive forces." And as for the whole country, how much of state revenue should go respectively to accumulation, consumption, national defense, administrative expenses, culture, education, various industrial departments, people engaged in production and those not, primary school teachers, young workers, cadres and so on, all these questions involve the issue of distribution. "If we implement the principle (of distribution according to work) well, everyone will be satisfied and the development of the productive forces will be promoted."① Therefore he suggested that "comrades make a careful study of the question of distribution. Secondly, he pointed out that, the principles of "distribution according work" and "fairness and reasonableness" must be applied in the distribution of consumer goods. Regarding the fact that a few people want to get more from the enterprises and undertakings owned by all the people, he pointed out that everybody will oppose it if someone get more than he deserves, because under such ownership property is owned and shared by all the people, hence people dare to speak and have the right to voice their opinions on distribution. "The masses concerned about how socialist democracy is being practiced not only in political

---

① *Selected Works of Liu Shaoqi*, vol. 2, People's Publishing House, 1985, vol. 2, pp. 303 – 304.

affairs, but also in economic matters and production."① Lastly, he noted in particular that the in distribution, we should overcome and prevent the style and mentality of privilege of some of our leading cadres. For instance, some of them have got too big shares, too many material benefits and too luxurious houses; some took use of their position to record more work days for themselves, get larger bonuses, or bring their relatives and friends into the factories, etc., who had gravely divorced themselves from the masses and caused dissatisfaction of the masses. In some places even there was "a type of hierarchy." He warned: "Those whose scramble for too many material benefits are bound to trip and fall."②

Fifth, he pointed out that the intensification of contradictions among the people may cause disturbances.

Comrade Liu Shaoqi pointed out that disturbances may occur when contradictions among the people become acute. It is likely that counter-revolutionaries will joint the masses in creating disturbances. However, they can incite the masses only by taking advantage of their immediate economic demands and of the political and ideological problems weighing on their minds, not with counter-revolutionary programs or slogans. So when disturbances occur, we should deal with them as a problem among the people, even if some counter-revolutionaries lurk in their ranks. We should improve the method of political and ideological education and make self-criticism. About the reasons for the disturbances, he pointed out, firstly, most of them are related to the immediate economic interests of the masses and are reasonable, only a few are unreasonable; secondly, there are many political and ideological problems among the people, which we fail to discover and solve them; and ideological education in some localities is criticizing and punishing the masses, creating dislike among the masses. Thirdly, some counter-revolutionaries "incite the masses by taking advantage of their immediate economic demands and of the political and ideological problems weighing on their minds." And finally, it is the bureaucracy in the part of the leading organs. He said that, usually people do not create a disturbance all of a sudden, but follow these steps: people voice their opinions and raise demands first, and then they send representatives to negotiate with the people concerned. People do not create a disturbance until all other efforts have failed owing to the indifference of the bureaucrats, and the problems of the masses

---

① *Selected Works of Liu Shaoqi*, vol. 2, People's Publishing House, 1985, vol. 2, p. 304.

② *Ibid.*, p. 305.

can not be resolved over a period of time. About the method of dealing with the disturbances, he pointed out: we should analyze the economic demands of the masses so as to meet the reasonable ones that can be met and make clear explanation about the unreasonable part that cannot be satisfied. For ideological and political problems among the masses, we should strengthen education and improve our method of education. In the case of the counter-revolutionaries inciting the masses to create disturbance, we should first solve the problems of the masses, setting their minds at rest, before dealing with the counter-revolutionaries. " Otherwise, counter-revolutionaries cannot be eliminated." On the side of the leadership, we must overcome bureaucracy and listen to the complaints of the people, that is, to allow the practice of "small democracy," "if we do not allow small democracy, ' great democracy' is bound to come."①

Sixth, he pointed outsome wrong approaches in handling contradictions among the people.

Liu Shaoqi pointed out, on the matterof handling contradictions among the people, the basic approaches of some comrades are wrong. "Firstly, they put themselves above the people." Such leaders do not regard themselves as one among the people, but place themselves in opposition to them; not as the servants of the people, but as the overlords of them. "I am your boss and you are my subordinates; you should listen to me and I needn't listen to you; I have the right to order you about and you haven't such a right."② He said that the attitude of being above the people is not that of the proletariat and the masses but that of the exploiting classes and bureaucrats. With this attitude, the leaders will not regard masses as the same as themselves, and in handling matters among the people they will not treat ordinary workers, farmers and students the same way they treat Party members and cadres, so they cannot win the faith of the masses and thus cannot correctly handle various contradictions among the people.

"Second, some comrades draw a distinction between right and wrong only for the masses, not for themselves."③ And their conclusion is: the masses are always in the wrong and they are always in the right. So they always criticize and blame the masses. We should draw a distinction between right and wrong of the leaders as well

---

① *Selected Works of Liu Shaoqi*, vol. 2, People's Publishing House, 1985, vol. 2, p. 306.

② *Ibid.*, p. 307.

③ *Ibid.*.

as that of the masses. "As leaders, they should draw a distinction between their own right and wrong and examine their own mistakes before dong the same for the masses. They should recognize not only the wrong but also the right of the masses. Only in this way can the masses be convinced."① Thinking themselves as infallible and not allowing others to criticize their mistakes can only result in the opposition of the masses to the leaders and the irreconcilable contradictions.

"Third, instead of convincing people through reasoning, some leaders use coercive methods to deal with problems among the masses."② Even if some of the masses are in the wrong side, we should correct them by method of persuasion to raise their understanding. The use of coercive methods will only sharpen the contradictions.

"Fourth, some leaders handle contradictionsamong the people the way they deal with contradictions between the people and the enemy."③ This is totally wrong. Such leaders actually place themselves in opposition to the people. "As a matter of course, some among the people may go too far with regard to those who have made bureaucratic mistakes." With people who have made bureaucratic mistakes, they are also belong to the category of the people and should start with a desire for unity and arrive at a new unity through criticism.

Comrade Liu Shaoqi'stheoretical understanding of contradictions among the people represents the collective achievements of our party in understanding this issue.

VI. Main Points of the Theory of Contradictions among the People

The theory of contradictions among the people was systematically put forward by Comrade Mao Zedong and represents the collective wisdom of the whole Party. The main points of this theory can be summarized as follows:

First, it examines the socialist society by using the law of the unity of opposites, and for the first time in the history of socialist cognition asserts that contradictions exist within socialist countries, and clearly points out that basic contradictions still

① *Selected Works of Liu Shaoqi*, vol. 2, People's Publishing House, 1985, vol. 2, p. 308.

② *Ibid.*, p. 308.

③ *Ibid.*.

exist within socialist countries and within the ranks of the people.

Comrade Mao Zedong said: "... the law of the unity of opposites is the fundamental law of the universe. This law operates universally, whether in the natural world, in human society, or in man's thinking...But for many people it is one thing to accept this law and quite another to apply it in examining and dealing with problems. "① "Socialist society is likewise a unity of opposites. "② He said that the idea that contradictions can be found in socialist society was also wrong, "The point is not that there are contradictions to be found, but that it teems with contradictions. There is no place where contradictions do not exist. "③ In an editorial published in *People's Daily* on April 5, 1956 entitled "On the Historical Experience of the Dictatorship of the Proletariat" that had been discussed by the enlarged conference of the Political Bureau of the CPC, it was explicitly pointed out that socialist society also develops in the movement of contradictions between the productive forces and the relations of production. Society at all times, including communist society in the future, develops through continual contradictions. There will still be contradictions and struggle among people, albeit their nature and forms will be different from those in class societies. In his view, the basic contradictions of socialist society are manifested in the dialectical process of movement of the correspondence as well as contradictions between the relations of production and productive forces and between the superstructure and economic base. After a period of ideological preparation, Comrade Mao formally set forth the theory of basic contradictions in socialist society, which holds that the socialist society teems with contradictions, and the contradictions exist also within the ranks of the people, and that it is these contradictions that promote the progress of socialist society. These ideas of Mao's constitute a major theoretical breakthrough and innovation.

Second, it analyzes the concrete contradictions in socialist countries by using the principle of particularity of contradiction, suggesting that we need to correctly distinguish two different types of social contradiction.

It is not enough to admit that contradictions exist in socialist countries; it is needed to make concrete analysis of the contradictions in socialist society so as to identify their specific characteristics. He pointed out that, the basic contradictions of

---

① *Selected Readings from Works of Comrade Mao Zedong*, vol. 2, Peoples' Publishing House, 1986, p. 766.

② Mao Zedong, "Talks at a Conference of Secretaries of Provincial, Municipal and Autonomous Region Party Committees."

③ Mao Zedong, "A Dialectical Approach to Inner Party Unity."

socialist society usually do not find expression in acute antagonisms, conflicts, or sharp class struggle, but in contradictions among the people. The theory of contradictions among the people suggests that the internal contradictions in socialist countries can be divided into two categories: one is the contradictions between ourselves and the enemy, the other is among the people. Comrade Mao said: "We are confronted with two types of social contradictions—those between ourselves and the enemy and those among the people. The two are totally different in nature."①

Firstly, Comrade Maomade a scientific exposition of the concepts of people and enemy, pointing out that they are concrete and historical nature, that is, they vary in content in different countries and in different periods of history in a given country. After analyzing their content and category during anti-Japanese War and the War of Liberation, he said: "At the present stage, the period of building socialism, the classes, strata and social groups which favour, support and work for the cause of socialist construction all come within the category of the people, while the social forces and groups which resist the socialist revolution and are hostile to or sabotage socialist construction are all enemies of the people."② Specifically speaking, the contradictions within the ranks of the people comprise the contradictions within the classes, strata and groups of the people, and the interpersonal contradictions within these classes, strata and groups; the contradictions between the People's Government and the people, including the contradictions between the interests of the state and the interests of the collective on the one hand and the interests of the individual on the other, between democracy and centralism, between the leadership and the led; in addition to contradictions between Party and non-Party and that among ethnic groups and so on.

Secondly, Comrade Mao discussed thedifferences in nature of contradictions among the people and the contradictions between ourselves and the enemy, and their mutual transformation under certain conditions. The contradiction between ourselves and the enemy are antagonistic, meaning that they opposing and conflicting in interests like fire and water, in which the realization of interests of one side must take the expense of the interests of the other side as the prerequisite. Contradictions among the People are different in nature. Generally speaking, the fundamental identity of the people's interests underlies contradictions among the people. That is to

① *Selected Readings from the Works of Mao Zedong*, vol. 2, People's Publishing House, 1986, p. 757.

② *Ibid.*, pp. 757 – 758.

say, they are identical in the fundamental interests, the contradictions are partial and temporary, and are interdependent and mutually penetrate and transform in terms of nature, in which the realization of interests of any side may promote the realization of interests of the other side or provide necessary preparations for its realization. However, this distinction between antagonistic and non-antagonistic is relative, not absolute, and no unbridgeable gap between them. Under certain conditions, for example, if they are not handled properly; if we relax our vigilance and lower our guard; if they are stirred up by the enemy, and so on, contradictions among the people can become antagonistic. Although a development of this kind is usually only a localized and temporary phenomenon, it cannot be neglected, because improper handling of them may cause them to become intensified and antagonistic. Particular vigilance must be maintained to prevent a handful of counter-revolutionaries from using contradictions among the people to foment dissension or stir up disorder.

Third, using the law of transformation of contradiction, he asserts that contradictions among the people are the theme of socialist political life and the principal contradiction in the human relationship in socialist countries.

The theory of contradictions among the people correctly reflects the change after the basic completion of socialist transformation in China, and correctly points out that in the period of socialist construction, contradictions among the people will replace the class contradictions to become the principal contradictions in the human relationships. In the very beginning of the article, Comrade Mao said: "Our general subject is the correct handling of contradictions among the people."① He elaborates the basic idea that contradictions among the people are the principal domestic contradictions in socialist countries.

Fourth, based on the law thateconomy determines politics, it discusses the contradictions of material interests within the ranks of the people, touching on the economical root of contradictions among the people.

InOn the Correct Handling of Contradictions among the People, in addition to elaborating the contradictions of right or wrong, Comrade Mao also analyzes the contradiction of interests among the people. He suggests that we should properly handle the interest relationships among the state, the collective and the individuals. Interest relationship means interest contradictions. He wrote: "To resolve these

---

① *Selected Readings from the Works of Mao Zedong*, vol. 2, People's Publishing House, 1986, p. 756.

contradictions we must pay constant attention to the problems of production and distribution. "[1] Comrade Liu Shaoqi pointed out more explicitly that a large number of contradictions among the people find expression in distribution. Their analyses of contradictions among the people in distribution area had touched on the root cause of contradictions among the people.

Fifth, using the principle of resolving contradictions of different nature with different methods, it has elaborated a series of correct guide lines and measures for correctly handling contradictions among the people.

As to the methods of resolving the basic contradictions in socialist society, Comrade Mao held that, differing from those in capitalist society which can only be resolved by socialist revolution, contradictions in socialist society can be resolved by socialist system itself. As to the measures of resolution of contradictions among the people, Mao pointed out that, two different methods, one dictatorial and the other democratic, should be used to resolve the two types of contradictions differing in nature—those between ourselves and the enemy and those among the people. "To put it briefly, the former entail drawing a clear distinction between ourselves and the enemy, while the latter, between right and wrong." In terms of ideology, based on the historical experience of our Party, Comrade Mao Zedong epitomized the methods of resolving contradictions among the people into a formula "unity-criticism-unity," [2]that means starting from the desire for unity, resolving contradictions through criticism or struggle, and arriving at a new unity on a new basis. In other words, it is a method of "learn from past mistakes to avoid future ones and cure the sickness to save the patient," a method of democracy, discussion, criticism, education and persuasion, which is fundamentally different from the method of "ruthless struggle and merciless blows" resorted by the "Left" dogmatists in inner-Party struggle during the period of democratic revolution. Comrade Mao Zedong also proposed using the method of over-all consideration to coordinate the contradictions of interests among the people with the interests of the state and collective on the one hand and the interests of individuals on the other; adhering to the policy of "Let a hundred flowers blossom, let a hundred schools of thought contend" to correctly handle contradictions among the people in scientific and cultural fields; adhering to the policy of "long-term coexistence, mutual supervision" to deal with the relations with the democratic

---

① *Selected Readings from the Works of Mao Zedong*, vol. 2, People's Publishing House, 1986, p. 775.
② *Ibid.*, p. 759.

parties and democratic personages, besides a series of other guidelines and policies, such as uniting with and educating the intellectuals, improving the relationship between the Han and other ethnic groups, and so on.

With regard tocorrectly understanding and handling contradictions among the people, Comrade Mao discussed it as follows:

1. The question of the industrialists and businessmen. He said that, through the socialist transformation of private industry and commerce, members of the bourgeoisie had become administrative personnel in joint state-private enterprises and were being transformed from exploiters into working people living by their own labor; During the past few years, most of them had been willing to study and had made marked progress. But on the other hand, since they still got a fixed rate of interest on their capital, they had not yet cut themselves loose from the roots of exploitation. Between them and the working class there was still a considerable gap in ideology, sentiments and habits of life. They still had the task of studying and of remoulding themselves; they should regard the enterprises as the chief places in which to remould themselves to change some of their old views through study. Such study should be on a voluntary basis.

2. The question of the intellectuals. Mao pointed out that, the several million intellectuals who worked for the old society had come to serve the new society, and the question that now arose was how they could fit in with the needs of the new society and how we could help them to do so. This, too, was a contradiction among the people. Most of our intellectuals had made marked progress during the last seven years. They had shown they were in favor of the socialist system. Many were diligently studying Marxism, and some had become communists. "We should trust those who are really willing to serve the cause of socialism and should radically improve our relations with them and help them solve the problems requiring solution, so that they can give full play to their talents. Many of our comrades are not good at uniting with intellectuals. They are stiff in their attitude towards them, lack respect for their work and interfere in certain scientific and cultural matters where interference is unwarranted. We must do away with all such shortcomings."① At the same time, he said, the intellectuals must continue to remould themselves, gradually shed their bourgeois world outlook and acquire the proletarian, communist world outlook. Since our country's social system had changed, not only was it imperative

① *Selected Readings from the Works of Mao Zedong*, vol. 2, People's Publishing House, 1986, p. 779.

for large numbers of our intellectuals to change their world outlook, but it was also possible for them to do so. But a thorough change in world outlook takes a very long time, and we should spare no pains in helping them and must not be impatient.

3. The question of ethnic groups. He pointed out that it is imperative to foster good relation between the Han people and other ethnic groups. The key to this question lies in overcoming Han chauvinism. At the same time, efforts should also be made to overcome ethnic minority chauvinism. Both Han chauvinism and ethnic minority chauvinism are harmful to the unity of the nation; they represent one kind of contradiction among the people which should be resolved.

4. Thepolicy of "Let a hundred flowers blossom, let a hundred schools of thought contend" and "long-term coexistence and mutual supervision". Here Comrade Mao concentratedly discussed the ideological contradictions, contradictions among parties and the correct policies of handling them. He pointed out that the slogans were put forward "in the light of recognition of the continued existence of various kinds of contradictions in socialist society and in response to the country's urgent need to speed up its economic and cultural development."[①] "Letting a hundred flowers blossom and a hundred schools of thought contend" is the policy for promoting progress in the arts and sciences and a flourishing socialist culture in our land. Different forms and styles in art should develop freely and different schools in science should contend freely. Questions of right and wrong in the arts and science should be settled through free discussion in artistic and scientific circles and through practical work in these fields, rather than through administrative or coercive measures, because a period of trial is often needed to determine whether something is right or wrong. Some new and correct things at the outset often failed to win recognition from the majority of people and had to develop by twists and turns through struggle. "It is therefore necessary to be careful about questions of right and wrong in the arts and sciences, to encourage free discussion and avoid hasty conclusions."[②] He believes that what is correct invariably develops in the course of struggle with what is wrong. This is the law of development of truth and, naturally, of Marxism.

As to the struggle with wrong ideologies, he points out: "Ideological struggle differs from other forms of struggle, since the only method used is painstaking

---

① *Selected Readings from the Works of Mao Zedong*, vol. 2, People's Publishing House, 1986, p. 783.

② *Ibid.*, p. 784.

reasoning, and not crude coercion." "It is not only futile but very harmful to use crude methods in dealing with ideological questions among the people, with questions about man's mental world. You may ban the expression of wrong ideas, but the ideas will still be there. On the other hand, if correct ideas are pampered in hothouses and never exposed to the elements and immunized against disease, they will not win out against erroneous ones. Therefore, it is only by employing the method of discussion, criticism and reasoning that we can really foster correct ideas and overcome wrong ones, and that we can really settle issues."① As to the slogan of "long-term coexistence and mutual supervision," Comrade Mao Zedong holds that, it is a product of China's specific historical conditions. The democratic parties in China have a long history of cooperation with the working class party, and have made important contributions to the cause of liberation of the Chinese people; after the basic completion of the socialist transformation, they devoted to the task of uniting the people for the cause of socialism, we have no reason for not adopting the policy of long-term coexistence. Mutual supervision means advising and criticizing each other. It is obviously not a one-sided matter; it means that the Communist Party can exercise supervision over the democratic parties, and vice versa.

5. The question of farmers. Comrade Mao paid close attention to the question of farmers. He said: "We have a rural population of over 500 million, so how our farmers fare has a most important bearing on the development of our economy and the consolidation of our state power."② There are certain contradictions that remain to be resolved, such as those between the state and the co-operatives and those in and between the co-operatives themselves. Based on the understanding then, he pointed out that, the co-operative economy must be subject to the unified economic planning of the state, while retaining a certain flexibility and independence that do not run counter to the state's unified plan or its policies, laws and regulations. At the same time, every household id a co-operative must comply with the over-all plan of the co-operative or production team to which it belongs, though it may make its own appropriate plans in regard to land allotted for personal needs and to other individually operated economic undertakings. On the question of distribution, we must take the interests of the state, the collective and the individual into account. Accumulation is essential for both the state and the co-operative, but in neither case

---

① *Selected Readings from the Works of Mao Zedong*, vol. 2, People's Publishing House, 1986, pp. 786 – 787.
② *Ibid.*, p. 773.

should it be excessive. We should do everything possible to enable the farmers in normal years to raise their personal incomes annually through increased production.

In his article "On the Ten Major Relationship", he points out that theSoviet Union had adopted measures which squeezed the farmers very hard. It took away too much from the farmers at too low a price through its system of so-called obligatory sales and other measures. This method of capital accumulation had seriously dampened the farmers' enthusiasm for production. Our policies towards the farmers differ from these, because we take into account the interests of both the state and the farmers. Our agricultural tax has always been relatively low. In the exchange of industrial and agricultural products we follow a policy of narrowing the price scissors, a policy of exchanging equal or roughly equal values. So our relations with the farmers have always been good, but we did make a mistake on the question of grain. In 1954 floods caused a decrease in production in some parts of our country, and yet we purchased 7,000 million more catties of grain. The farmers were disgruntled. This lesson the whole Party must bear in mind.

6. The question of China's population of 600 million. As to the population of 600 million, Comrade Mao proposed that we should take a policy of over-all consideration and proper arrangement. He said: "In drawing up plans, handling affairs or thinking over problems, we must proceed from the fact that China has a population of 600 million."① Because the fundamental identity of the people's interests underlies contradictions among the people, in resolving them, we should keep our eyes on bringing every positive factor into play, on uniting with everyone who can be united with, and on doing everything possible to turn negative factors into positive ones so as to serve the great cause of building a socialist society. Whatever the problem—whether it concerns food, natural calamities, employment, education, the intellectuals, the united front of all patriotic forces, the minority nationalities, or anything else—we must always proceed from the standpoint of over-all consideration, which embraces the whole people, and must make the proper arrangement, after consultation with all the circles concerned, in the light of what is feasible at a particular time and place. On no account should we complain that there are too many people, that others are backward, that things are troublesome and hard to handle, and close the door on them.

Lastly Comrade Mao also emphasized that, to resolve these contradictions, we

---

① *Selected Readings from the Works of Mao Zedong*, vol. 2, People's Publishing House, 1986, p. 782.

need to strengthen ourideological and political work, and keep to the two most important principles of keep to the socialist path and the leadership of the Party. We should oppose both dogmatism and the tendency of asking for a two-party system and absolute democracy and absolute freedom.

Sixth, based on the principle that contradictions constitute the source of development of everything, it elaborated the causes of the intensification of contradictions among the people and its solutions.

Comrade Maofirmly stated that the basic contradictions, contradictions among the people provide the driving forces for promoting the development of socialism. Contradictions among the people usually are non-antagonistic. But in some conditions they may become intensified into antagonistic forms. In 1956, small numbers of workers or students in certain places went on strike; in the same year, in some agricultural co-operatives there were also disturbances created by a few of their members. He analyzed the causes of them: The immediate cause of these disturbances was the failure to satisfy some of their demands for material benefits, of which some should and could have been met, while others were out of place or excessive and therefore could not be met for the time being. But a more important cause was bureaucracy on the part of the leadership. In some cases, the responsibility for such bureaucratic mistakes fell on the higher authorities, and those at the lower levels were not to blame. Another cause of these disturbances was lack of ideological and political education among the workers and students.

Asto the prevention of contradictions among the people from intensification and methods of handling the disturbances, he suggested: (1) In order to root out the causes of disturbances, we must resolutely overcome bureaucracy, greatly improve ideological and political education, and deal with all contradictions properly. Because bureaucracy ignore the reasonable demands of some people, leading to the dissatisfaction of them; and their lack of timely in-depth and meticulous ideological and political work about the unreasonable demands of the masses made the contradictions remain unsolved for a long time, resulting in their intensification. To the masses, it is a question of education. Because among the masses some are prone to pay attention to immediate, partial and personal interests and do not understand, or do not sufficiently understand, long-range, national and collective interests. Quite a number of young people cannot readily see the contrast between the old China and the new, and it is not easy for them thoroughly to comprehend the hardships our people went through in the struggle to free themselves from the oppression of the imperialists and Kuomintang reactionaries, or the long years of hard work needed before a fine socialist society can be established. We must constantly carry on lively and effective political education among the masses and should always tell them the truth about the difficulties that crop up and discuss with them how to surmount these difficulties. (2) When disturbances do occur as a result of poor work on our part, then we should guide those involved onto the correct path, use the disturbances as a special means for improving our work and educating the cadres and the masses, and find solutions to those problems which were previously left unsolved. That is, turn bad things into good things. He said: "Disturbances by the masses are bad, and we do not approve of them. But when disturbances do occur, they enable us to learn lessons, to overcome bureaucracy and to educate the cadres and the masses. In this sense, bad things can be turned into good things."[①] So in handling any disturbance, we should take pains and not use over-simple methods, or hastily declare the matter closed. The ringleaders in disturbances should not be summarily expelled, except for those who have committed criminal offences or are active counter-revolutionaries and have to be punished by law. (3) As to a small number of individuals in our society who, flouting the public interest, wilfully break the law and commit crimes. They are apt to take advantage of our policies and distort them, and deliberately put forward unreasonable demands in order to incite the masses, or deliberately spread rumors to create trouble and disrupt public order, proper legal action must be taken against them. Punishing them is the demand of the masses, and it would run counter to the popular will if they were not punished.

---

① *Selected Readings from the Works of Mao Zedong*, vol. 2, People's Publishing House, 1986, p. 793.

Chapter 2

The Enrichment and Development of the Theory of Contradictions among the People under the New Historical Conditions

The Third Plenary Sessionof the Eleventh Central Committee of the CPC held 1978 is a major turning point in China's socialist development. Under the new historical conditions, the Party's second generation of central collective leadership with Comrade Deng Xiaoping at the core led the whole Party in emancipating the mind, seeking truth from facts and keep pace with the times, corrected the mistakes of confusing the two different types of contradictions made by Comrade Mao Zedong in his later years, restored the theory of correct handling of contradictions among the people, and has enriched and developed the theory in the practice of the new era of socialist reform and opening up. Since the Third Plenary Session of the Fourteenth Central Committee of the CPC, the Party's third generation of central collective leadership with Comrade Jiang Zemin at the core, based on the enrichment and development of the Party's second generation of central collective leadership, further enrich and developed the theory by summing up the new experience of building socialism with Chinese characteristics. Since the Sixteenth National Congress of the Party, the Central Committee of the CPC with Comrade Hu Jintao as general secretary, proceeding from the new reality, actively explored effective methods of resolving contradictions among the people in the new era and their long-term mechanism of resolution, strived to build a harmonious socialist society and has advanced the innovations of the theory.

I. Historical Experience of Correct Handling of Contradictions among the People

The theory ofthe correct handling of contradictions among the people, as a creative Marxist theory, has a history of more than forty years since it was first put forward. Both the experience and lessons of socialist construction prove that this theory has correctly summarized the laws and characteristics of contradictions among people in socialist countries and thus has a scientific guiding significance. And it also shows that the theory needs to be constantly enriched and developed. In the new historical period, whether adhere to and develop the theory of contradictions among the people is an important issue having a bearing on the success or failure of the great historic task of building socialism with Chinese characteristics.

For the enrichment of the theory of contradictions among the people, what are the major issues in the more than 50 years of practice of socialist construction that need our summarization and discussion? During the 20 years from 1957 when we expanded the anti-Rightist struggle up until to the Cultural Revolution, our party sharply deviated from the correct theory of contradictions among the people and made the serious mistake of broadening the scope of class struggle. In 1957, we made the mistake of expanding the anti-Rightist struggle; we mistakenly launched the campaign against "' Right' deviation" in 1959; the socialist education movement and the class struggle in the ideological fields conducted in the 1960s hurt a large number of cadres and intellectuals; let alone the decade long Cultural Revolution, which seriously confused the two types of contradictions differing in nature, causing nationwide domestic chaos. A review of the 20 years history shows that a lot of lessons and experience merit our serious summarization, which concerns the problem of our not applying the correct theory and shortcomings of the theory itself as well. Therefore, a reexamination of contradictions among the people on the basis of historical experience is needed for the adherence to and development of the theory.

First, the question of how to understand the principal social contradiction after the socialist transformation basically completed in China.

Now that the correct theory of contradictions among the people had been established and the effective principles and methods of handling contradictions among the people had been set up, why then, was in practice, had the correct theory not really been applied, and what led to the occurrence of a long-term, nationwide social turmoil like the Cultural Revolution that confused the two types of contradictions differing in nature? One of the important reasons for these is the misjudgment of the principal contradiction. But in fact the issue of the principal contradiction had been settled in the Eighth National Congress of the CPC. The Resolution of the Congress declares that the decisive victory has already been won in this socialist transformation. This means that the contradiction between the proletariat and the bourgeoisie has been basically resolved. "The principal contradiction within the country… is the one between the demand of the people for rapid economic and cultural development and the existing state of our economy and culture which fell short of the needs of the people." To solve this principal contradiction, it is necessary to clearly and strictly distinguish the contradictions between ourselves and the enemy from contradictions among the people and to correctly handle the latter, in order to rally the people of all ethnic groups in the "war against the natural world." Therefore, the correct handling of contradictions among the people had become the theme of the country's political life, with class contradiction becoming the secondary one. In the Speech at the Chinese Communist Party's National Conference on Propaganda Work, March 1957, Comrade Mao explicitly pointed out that quite a lot of our comrades wanted to make clear whether it was the internal contradictions among the people or class struggle as the primary, as if they would feel at ease with the class struggle as the primary, or they would feel uneasy. But I just wanted to change their places. An article published on May 2, 1957, *People's Daily*, entitled "Why Must We Carry Out the Rectification Movement?", which was revised by Mao, reads that, "The principle contradiction in the country…is the one between the people's needs for rapid social-economic development and the reality which fell short of the needs." And this contradiction "… in real life will necessarily be manifested as interpersonal contradictions, only that these contradictions have changed from those between the opposing classes into contradictions among people." "Contradiction between ourselves and the enemy still exists… but because it has become of secondary importance, and contradictions among the people come to the center stage." That is to say, the conclusion made in the Eighth National Congress of the Party about the principal contradiction is consistent with the judgment that contradictions among people had become principal type of contradictions in the country.

However, afterthe anti-Rightist struggle began in 1957, many comrades within the Party exaggerated the situation of class struggle at the time, who regarded the intensification of class struggle in a certain period and scope as the universal and long-term acuteness of it. Because Comrade Mao Zedong overestimated the severity of the situation of class struggle and he himself didn't have a thorough theoretical understanding of this issue, in the revised edition of On the Correct Handling of Contradictions among the People published on June 9, 1957, he added something inconsistent with the theory of contradictions among the people, declaring that the question of who would win — socialism or capitalism — had not yet been really settled. Having changed his correct theory, so in the concluding remarks at the Third Session of the Eighth Central Committee of the CPC, Comrade Mao said: "Now it is clear-cut: the main (or fundamental) contradiction is the contradiction between the proletariat and the bourgeoisie, between socialism and capitalism." And he publicly criticized the statement of the Eighth National Congress of the CPC on contradictions "is incorrect". This provided a theoretical basis for the expansion of the anti-Rightist struggle and the subsequent "Left" error of "taking class struggle as the key link." Although the general subject of correct handling of contradictions among the people had been explicitly put forward, it had not been applied in the following years; instead, class struggle had been taken as the key link. We can see from this that, one of the important cognitive roots of the long-term confusion of the two types of contradictions differing in nature is that class struggle was exaggerated, which is a bitter lesson of history that must never be forgotten.

Second, Comrade Mao Zedong's personal theoretical mistake is an important cause for our party's confusion of two types of contradictions differing in nature in practice.

Why then, did Comrade Mao Zedong's personal theoretical mistake lead to the Party's making of such serious historical mistakes in handling contradictions among the people? How can we prevent personal mistakes from harming the Party's endeavors? Comrade Mao Zedong had actually once been aware of this problem. He believes that Stalin's mistake of expanding the purge of counter-revolutionaries could not happen in developed capitalist countries such as Britain and the U. S. But it happened in a socialist country. One reason for this is that the relatively complete bourgeois political system can prevent the thinking and acts of a few individuals in the bourgeois ruling regime from harming the overall interests of the whole bourgeoisie. And we have yet to establish and improve the socialist political system to stop the leader's personal mistake from spreading to the whole Party and harming the cause of the Party. Although Comrade Mao Zedong recognized the importance of institutions, he himself could not go beyond the constraints of history. After building the basic system of socialism, we had not established a sound system that can ensure the implementation of correct lines and to guarantee the overall interests of the people. So today, we must integrate the correct handling of contradictions among the people with socialist political restructuring, so as to establish complete socialist political institutions as the guarantee for the correct handling of contradictions among the people. It is an issue of how to understand the relationship between contradictions among the people and social institutions and of what institutions that can ensure the correct handling the contradictions.

Thirdly, will the intensification of contradictions among the people lead to the domestic conflicts or crisis? In other words, can contradictions among people develop into antagonistic ones?

Comrade Mao Zedongbelieves that, in ordinary circumstances, contradictions among the people are non-antagonistic. But if they are not handled properly, antagonism may arise. Comrade Liu Shaoqi holds that, contradictions among the people could intensify into mass disturbances and temporary antagonism. These expositions show that, if not properly handled, contradictions among the people could change into antagonism. But in the international communist movement, there had long been an opinion denying the existence of antagonistic contradictions in socialist countries. For example, Mikhail Andreyevich Suslov, Secretary of the Communist Party of the Soviet Union in charge of ideological work, in an article entitled "The Great Ten Years" published in 1967, denies that the antagonistic nature of contradictions in socialist countries, although recognizing their existence. This situation was not changed until the 1980s. When the social unrest in Poland triggered an extensive debate over the nature of contradictions in socialist societies among theorists in the Soviet Union and Eastern Europe, some people explicitly believed that, in certain circumstances, antagonistic contradictions can occur in socialist society. But there are still others denying the existence of antagonistic contradictions in socialist countries. They believe that, there are remnants of forces, influence and elements of the old society, so there do exist such antagonistic contradictions as those between ourselves and the enemy. But it is unacceptable for them to admit that there are still antagonistic phenomena among the people in socialist society. Therefore, in examining the nature of domestic contradictions in socialist countries and in discussing whether there is antagonism in socialist countries, the key lies in the deep exploration of problems of whether there is antagonism among the people and political conflicts and crises in socialist countries.

Fourth, what are the economic roots ofoccurrence, development and solution of contradictions among the people?

In"On the Correct Handling of Contradictions among the People", in addition to stressing the political and ideological contradictions among the people and methods for resolving them, Comrade Mao also talks about material interests, emphasizing that this type of contradictions should be settled through production and distribution.

But due to the limitations of historical conditions, he does not lay particular stress on analyzing contradictions among the people from their profound socio-economic roots. For a long time, some of our comrades, influenced by this theoretical shortcomings, understand contradictions among the people in an oversimplified way, believing that contradictions among people concerns only questions of political or ideological right and wrong, rather than economic and interest conflicts. So, it is impossible from them to recognize the profound economic roots of contradictions among the people. This is one of the important cognitive causes that make us commit the "Left" or "Right" mistakes in handling contradictions among the people. Therefore, correctly recognizing contradictions of interests among the people, the leading position of this type of contradictions and their economic causes is another important part for adhering to and developing the theory of contradictions among the people.

Fifth, the issue of how to handle contradictions of right and wrong among the people.

The way to settle the contradictions of right and wrong among the people is by democratic method, the method of discussion, criticism, persuasion and education, and not by method of dictatorship, coercion or repression. This is a general principle. To implement this principle, a series of issue of understanding need further clarification.

Firstly, can the principle of resolving contradictions of right and wrong among the people through democratic method be applied in settling political issues? In fact, this seemingly undisputable question has not been completely settled yet. It appears that discussions could be done and different opinions could be expressed only on academic issues, while political issues are considered as taboo. This evidently shows that our democratic life is abnormal. In fact, the democratic rights of the people first of all should be embodied in democratic rights, that is, the people have the rights to speak, to make decisions, to supervise and to criticize on state policies and principles. This is the hallmark of socialist democracy. On the premises that the fundamental political stance is identical and on the basis of upholding the Four Cardinal Principles, it is completely normal to express different views in political life; and these differences can only be settled through democratic methods and discussions. Just as Comrade Deng Xiaoping put it: "In political life within the Party and among the people, we must use democratic means and not resort to coercion or attack."① Of course, this kind of democratic

① *Selected Works of Deng Xiaoping*, vol. 2, People's Publishing House, 1994, p. 144.

discussions should follow certain disciplines and keep in a certain scope. It is discussions that help solve the problems, unified our thinking and advance the development of the theories. In the process of discussions, there may be wrong ideas, but as long as these views are not contrary to the Constitution, the laws, the organizational principles or disciplines, they should be allowed to express. Through debate, right and wrong can be distinguished, wrong opinions can be corrected, and correct opinions can be maintained and fostered. In the contrary, coercive means usually gives rise to unconvincing result, errors cannot be corrected, and ideological unity cannot be really achieved; moreover, sometimes a correct thing may be considered to be wrong. In fact, the direct purpose of Comrade Mao Zedong's proposition of the formula "unity-criticism-unity" is to resolve contradictions inside the Party, "that is, to resolve the contradictions between the dogmatists and the great majority of the membership, and between dogmatism and Marxism."[①] And these contradictions first of all are manifested as the contradictions of right and wrong in political line. From this we can see that, contradictions of right and wrong among the people that should be resolved by democratic methods include not only contradictions of right and wrong in work, in understanding and in academic fields, but also those in political life. Without firmly establishing this basic point of view, it is impossible to create a political situation of liveliness and to achieve the goal of establishing a high degree of socialist democracy.

Secondly, when democratic means are used to resolve contradictions of right and wrong among the people, should we adhere to the principle of "everyone is equal before the truth?" The absurd phenomenon that "Power means truth, more power means more truth" once ran rampant in China and the statement that everyone is equal before the truth was violently criticized as bourgeois slogan. But in fact, posts and power belong to the category of politics while truth comes under the category of epistemology. There is no necessary relationship between them. Posts can give people power, but not necessarily wisdom. Everyone is equal before the truth essentially means that, whether the words of someone is truth must be tested in practice, no matter what post he holds and how big his power is. On the path of seeking truth, everyone should be equal and free in discussion and consultation, instead of oppressing others by power of position. Comrade Mao was once very cautious in dealing with some academic debates. For instance, at the end of 1955, a scholar from the Soviet Union, when having conversations with accompanying staff

---

① *Selected Readings from Works of Mao Zedong*, People's Publishing House, 1986, p. 763.

from Chinese side, said that he disagreed with Comrade Mao on Dr. Sun Yat-sen's world outlook. Some people believed that this kind of talk had negative bearing on the prestige of our leading cadre, and suggested reporting it to the relevant authorities of the Soviet Union. About this case, Comrade Mao wrote in a letter that, this kind of free talk should not be banned; different opinions on academic issues could be expressed by anyone, it had nothing to do with prestige. ① Another example is the debate in Chinese academic circles on dialectics and formal logic. In 1958, one of the participants of the debate Comrade Zhou Gucheng wrote to Comrade Mao, asking him to write a preface to the forthcoming book *Formal Logic and Dialectics,* Mao wrote in reply that he didn't do much study on logic, so couldn't make remarks about it; in addition, the debate was still going on, so it was impropriate for him to have a hand in it, therefore he couldn't write the preface. These examples show that Comrade Mao advocated free and equal discussions in academic field. Unfortunately, he didn't thoroughly implement his own correct ideas in his latter years. Given the historical lessons, the Guiding Principles for Inner-Party Political Life adopted in the Fifth Plenary Session of the Party's Eleventh Central Committee clearly states: "We must uphold the principles that everyone is equal before the truth and all Party members are equal before Party discipline and the law." "All leading cadres must treat others as equals; they should not think that all their words, right or wrong, must be obeyed." It is fundamentally wrong for anyone to use power, administrative means or political decisions to resolve academic or ideological contradictions of right and wrong among the people, because it will result only in stopping up criticisms and suggestions, choking off the truth and leading to rigid thinking.

Thirdly, what is the relationship between resolving contradictionns of right and wrong by democratic methods and by class analysis? This is another issue that has been thrown into total confusion. As early as in the 1950s, some people put the label of class struggle everywhere. They even said that Western medicine belonged to capitalist category and traditional Chinese medicine was feudal; and Thomas Hunt Morgan and Gregor Mendel were bourgeois, Lysenko and Michurin were socialists. This apparently created class struggle in pure academic sphere. This "Left" thinking went to an extremely absurd extent in the Cultural Revolution period: it was believed that "everything is related to principles or ideological line"; "new trends of class struggle" were watched out for everywhere; class struggle and class analysis were

① See *Selected Letters of Mao Zedong,* Central Party Literature Press, 1983.

widened and pushed to the extreme; class struggle in ideological realm was wildly exaggerated; contradictions between ourselves and the enemy and that among the people were total confused; and the normal democratic life and free academic discussions were stifled by the so called "total dictatorship" to a lamentably lifeless state. Actually, as a method for studying problems, class analysis is applicable only to class struggle. And even in a class society, it is not the only method, because many purely academic problems and different views on daily work have nothing to do with class struggle. Since class struggle will continue to exist within a certain scope and the ideological influence of the exploiting classes is impossible to be cleaned up at one stroke in a socialist country, the method of class analysis is not outdated yet. But it must be noted that a large number of social contradictions do not fall within the scope of class struggle. Just as is pointed out in the Resolution on Certain Questions in the History of Our Party since the Founding of the People's Republic of China adopted by the Sixth Plenary Session of the Eleventh Central Committee of the CPC: "We must correctly understand that there are diverse social contradictions in Chinese society which do not fall within the scope of class struggle and that methods other than class struggle must be used for their appropriate resolution. " Therefore, to stick to democratic methods in settling contradictions of right and wrong among the people, we must not only clearly distinguish the contradictions between ourselves and the enemy from those among the people, but also distinguish class contradictions from non-class contradictions and distinguish manifestations of class struggle from that of non-class struggle, so as to completely eliminate the "Left" influence of "class struggle as the key link" and the abuse of class analysis. Only in this way can people put down their mental burdens and emancipate their minds.

Sixth, the issue whether the formula "unity—criticism—unity" is the only approach to resolution of contradictions among the people.

For a long time, many people understand contradictions among the people in a oversimplified way, as though contradictions among the people are contradictions of right and wrong only, and therefore the only method of their resolution is "unity—criticism—unity, " or democratic means. Such understanding not only is inconsistent with the original meaning of Comrade Mao Zedong's writings, but also does not correspond to objective facts.

In On the Correct Handling of Contradictions among the people, in addition to paying special attention to contradictions of right and wrong among the people, Comrade Mao also mentioned many other contradictions, especially contradictions of material interests. For example, he said: "There are certain contradictions that remain to be resolved, such as those between the state and the co-operatives and those in and between the co-operatives themselves." "To resolve these contradictions we must pay constant attention to the problems of production and distribution."① Here what he talked about is precise contradictions of material interests among the people, and he stressed that we should properly handle these contradictions with economic means. He also pointed out in this article and in On the Ten Major Relationships: To resolve the contradictions of material interests among all levels in rural and urban areas and those between the state and the collective on the one side and the individual on the other, we must take the principle of "overall consideration and proper arrangement", "To give consideration to only one side, whichever it may be, is harmful to socialism and to the dictatorship of the proletariat." As to the relationship between the state and the workers, "we have always advocated plain living and hard work and opposed putting personal material benefits above everything else; at the same time we have always advocated concern for the livelihood of the masses and opposed bureaucracy, which is callous to their well-being. With the growth of our economy as a whole, wages should be appropriately adjusted." As to the relationship between the state and the farmers, "In the exchange of industrial and agricultural products we follow a policy of narrowing the price scissors, a policy of exchanging equal or roughly equal values". This was different from those of the Soviet Union that "adopted measures so-called obligatory sales and other measures", "which squeeze the farmers very hard." As to the relationship between the state and the factories, he said: "it's not right, I'm afraid, to place everything in the hands of the central or the provincial and municipal authorities without leaving the factories any power of their own, any room for independent action, any benefits." "Every unit of production must enjoy independence as the correlative of centralization if it is to develop more vigorously."

Comrade Liu Shaoqi in his article How to Correctly Handle Contradictions among the People stressed that, contradictions among the people "are manifested mostly in distribution," and that "I suggest that comrades make careful study of the question of distribution."② Comrade Deng Xiaoping also pointed out in 1979: "We must adjust the relations between these various types of interests in accordance with

---

① *Selected Readings from Works of Mao Zedong*, vol. 2, People's Publishing House, 1986, p. 775.

② *Selected Works of Liu Shaoqi*, vol. 2, People's Publishing House, 1985, p. 303.

the principle of taking them all into proper consideration. Were we to do the opposite and pursue personal, local or immediate interests at the expense of the others, both sets of interests would inevitably suffer."[1] It is obvious here that, contradictions among the people include not only ideological contradictions of right and wrong, but also contradictions of gains and losses or much and less of material benefits. In the past, due to our narrow-minded and one-sided understanding and the influence of the "Left" thinking of "give prominence to political ideas," oversimplification in practical work was common, that is, whenever contradictions among the people arose, they were regarded without any analysis as ideological problems that should be dealt with the "unity—criticism—unity" approach. As a result, a lot of contradictions among the people that actually didn't fall into the category of ideological problem were covered up, and the correct handling of contradictions among the people from economic point was neglected totally, so that this kind of contradictions piled up to the extent of intensification and beyond resolution. Given this profound historical lesson, under the condition of socialist market economy, learning to correctly handle contradictions among the people from the perspective of economic interests has become a major pressing issue.

It should be noted that in terms of material interests, contradictions between theourselves and the enemy and those among the people are fundamentally different in nature and characteristics. The former are of fundamental in nature and thus are incompatibly antagonistic like fire and water, in which the realization of interests of one side must take the expense of the interests of the other side as the prerequisite. Therefore, to resolve the contradictions of material interests between ourselves and the enemy, the only way is to expropriate the expropriators, although the possibility of temporary compromises and concessions cannot be excluded. On the contrary, the fundamental identity of the people's interests, generally speaking, underlies the contradictions of material interests among the people, and this type of contradiction is local and temporary. And in terms of nature, the different interests among the people are interdependent, interpenetrating and can transform into each other, in which the realization of the interests of any side may contribute to or create necessary conditions for the realization of interests of other sides. Therefore, to resolve contradictions of interests among the people is by no means to ignore the relatively independent interests of any side, but rather to, under the condition of safeguarding

---

① *Selected Works of Deng Xiaoping*, vol. 2, People's Publishing House, 1994, pp. 175 – 176.

the fundamental interests of all the people, "take the interests of all sides into consideration and make proper arrangements" as much as possible, so that the interests of all sides can be promoted in a well-balanced way.

To resolve contradictions of material interests among the people, first of all, we should primarily and mainly adopt correct economic means, including correct economic policies and laws, among others. Our ongoing reform towards socialist market economy, in a sense, is to institutionally and economically adjust material interests among the people. The reason why the household contract responsibility system can greatly promote the initiative of the farmers is that it had correctly coordinated the interests of the individual, the collective and the state. It is essentially handling contradictions of interests among the people through economic means.

Of course, political and ideological work is necessary in handling contradictions of material interests among the people. Because contradictions of material interests are bound to be reflected in people's minds, which can be handled correctly by some people but cannot by others, hence arise contradictions of right and wrong in understanding and thinking. For instance, some people damage the interests of the state, the collective and others for their own or for local interests; some people always make upward comparison in terms of salary and bonus regardless of conditions and contributions; some people impose random fees and compulsory donations to affiliated units and individuals under the pretext of overall interests, which aggravating unreasonable burden on businesses and farmers, and so on. These incorrect ideas and actions should be addressed through effective ideological and political work, so that people have a correct understanding of the relationship between state interests and individual interests, long-term interests and immediate interests, local interests and overall interests, to consciously implement the correct economic policies of the state. This shows that necessary political and ideological work and correct economic measures are complementary to each other, the premise and basis of which is the introduction of correct economic policies. The solution of ideological problems can provide necessary conditions for the solution of problems of material interests, but cannot completely replace it. In the final analysis, contradictions of material interests among the people can only be resolved by economic means. Without correct economic policies, there will be no criterion of right and wrong for ideological education to base on. In the past when "Left" policies spread unchecked, we adopted the policy of expropriating the farmers by making unpaid-for appropriation of their interests and "transition in poverty to a higher stage"; on the other hand, we conducted the so-called "socialist education," which not only failed to arouse the enthusiasm of the farmers, but added fuel to the "Left" policies. We can never forget this lesson.

Seventh, the issue of how to resolve complex contradictions among the people.

Contradictions among the people constitute a complex system of contradictions, including ideological contradictions of right and wrong, material contradictions of gains and losses, contradictions of different schools and styles in scientific and artistic fields, as well as many other contradictions in practical work. So methods for resolving these various contradictions should also be diverse. There is no hard and fast formula or panacea for them. What is required is precisely the reverse: the concrete analysis of concrete conditions. Even for one specific kind of contradiction, due to its complex causes, more often than not it cannot be resolved by relying only on one particular method but a variety of methods should be adopted instead.

Take for example, the contradictions arising from the bureaucratic style of work of some of the state personnel in their relations with the masses. This is a kind of common contradictions among the people. The causes of them include the ideological problems of the personnel, the problems of our system of leadership and cadres, among others. Therefore, it is necessary to oppose bureaucracy and strengthen ideological education. And it is impossible to overcome the unhealthy ideological styles such as acting like overlords, abusing power for personal gains, seeking personal privileges and so on without eliminating the influence of feudalism, capitalism and conducting the education about the Party's principle of serving the people. This includes the implementation of the principle of "unity—criticism—unity" and restrictions of discipline and law. But this is far from enough. Just as Comrade Deng Xiaoping said, "It is true that the errors we made in the past were partly attributable to the way of thinking and style of work of some leaders. But they were even more attributable to the problems in our organizational and working systems. If these systems are sound, they can place restraints on the actions of bad people; if they are unsound, they may hamper the efforts of good people or indeed, in certain cases, may push them in the wrong direction."① First, the emergence of bureaucracy has much to do with the over-concentration of power in our economic and political systems. In the modern large-scale production, since the needs of

① *Selected Works of Deng Xiaoping*, vol. 2, People's Publishing House, 1994, p. 333.

society are very complex and ever-changing, the conditions of the production units vary, and the economic relations among regions, departments and enterprises are very complicated, any state institution cannot fully know and make quick response to them. But in our economic system in the past, the functions of the government and enterprises mixed up, state institutions directly operated and managed enterprises, and everything was included in the state plan and took on by the state: this inevitably gave birth to bureaucracy. Soon after the October Revolution, Lenin said: "A complete, integrated, real plan for us at present = 'a bureaucratic utopia.'"① So the restructuring of economic system is also an important approach to overcoming bureaucracy. Secondly, bureaucracy is closely connected with the political structure with over-concentrated power and inadequate democracy. If there is no separation between the Party work and that of the government, all power is concentrated in Party committees, and the power of the Party committees themselves is concentrated in the hands of a few secretaries, especially the first secretary, so that all important issues are decided by individuals; while these few individuals, conferred with unlimited power with their limited wisdom, have to take charge of many affairs that they should not or cannot handle or are unable handle efficiently. In such circumstances, how can bureaucracy not come into being? Other important root causes of bureaucracy include overstaffing, the lack in our cadre management of necessary systems of selection, evaluation, supervision, rewards and penalties, recall and so on. Unscientific method of leadership is another cause of bureaucracy. For example, collective leadership without individual responsibility, only tick off documents and no one is responsible for anything in particular., etc., make many things been long delayed, or even been shelved forever. Therefore, Comrade Deng Xiaoping said: "In order to overcome bureaucracy... we have to improve our methods of work as well."② In short, to combat bureaucracy, a wide range of work need to be done, including not only criticism and education, discipline and legal constraints, economic and political restructuring, but also the improvement of methods of leadership. Only by using diverse and comprehensive ways can we achieve effective result in our combat against bureaucracy.

Evensimple contradictions of right and wrong in understanding, including different views in academic and practical work, often cannot be resolved only by

---

① Quoted from "Decision of the CPC Central Committee on Reform of the Economic Structure".

② *Selected Works of Deng Xiaoping*, vol. 2, People's Publishing House, 1994, p. 282.

means of "unity-criticism-unity". This is because some academic differences often originate in insufficient appropriation of materials by the relevant sides, making it difficult to convince each other in a short period of time. In this case, criticism, debates, discussions or battle of words alone is ineffective. Thus continued practice and experiments, more widely information gathering, in-depth research, exploration and demonstration are necessary. In On the Correct Handling of Contradictions among the People, Comrade Mao said: "Questions of right and wrong in the arts and science should be settled through free discussion in artistic and scientific circles and through practical work in these fields. "① Here he mentioned two, rather than one, methods—discussion and practice—of resolving contradictions of right and wrong in understanding. In many scientific fields such as elementary particle physics, astrophysics, life sciences, among others, there exist many different, even opposite opinions. These contradictions of understanding are obviously contradictions among the people, which need to be resolved through academic criticism and discussions on the basis of the policy of "letting a hundred flowers blossom, a hundred schools of thought contend." But in the final analysis, the resolution of these contradictions relies on in-depth research in new practices and experiments. So do differences of opinion in practical work. In dealing with such contradictions, our party has always insisted on the following principles and methods: (1) Repeated deliberation should be carried out before every major decision is made. (2) In Party meetings, every party member is allowed to freely express his views or criticize anyone; he should be protected even if his views are wrong. (3) Any one is allowed to make mistakes and to correct them as long as he has done his utmost. (4) If he does not agree to principles and policies formulated by the Party Central Committee, any individual is permitted to reserve his opinion, as long as he strives to implement them and does not violate them. Practice has proven that they are correct and effective in resolving contradictions of different opinions on work inside Party. These principles and methods include methods of free discussion and criticism, principles of democratic centralism for upholding Party discipline, and also the principle of "permitting reservations" in order to gradually achieve consensus in practical work. It is because we adopted these methods and principles that we have made great successes in various fields such as economic reform. Take rural reform for instance. In the beginning many people had not straightened out their thinking in this respect. On the

① Selected Readings from Works of Mao Zedong, vol. 2, People's Publishing House, 1986, p. 784.

one hand, we insisted on patient and meticulous persuasion and education, we didn't put labels on people and didn't use a big stick; on the other hand, we had deepened people's understanding through practice of reform. As a result, many people who previously held a suspicious or even opposing opinion raised their consciousness and changed their attitude, and the consensus was reached. This process presented a precious experience of resolving disagreement on major policies inside the Party.

To sum up, the content of contradictions among the people is very rich, among which various contradictions have their own complexity and particularity. We should handle them in comprehensive and flexible ways based on the principles of making concrete analysis of concrete problems and seeking truth from facts, instead of resorting to oversimplified, fixed or rigid work methods.

II. The Restoration and Development of the Theory of Contradictions among the People in the New Era

Since the Third Plenary Session of the Eleventh Central Committee of the CPC, our Party, following the guidance of the ideological line of seeking truth from facts, began to set things right by completely getting rid of the influence of the ultra-Left line of "taking class struggle as the key link" and restored the correct theory of contradictions among the people. Based on historical experience and lessons, we put forward a series of policies and methods for strictly distinguishing and correctly handling contradictions between ourselves and the enemy and that among the people, thus have restored and developed the theory of contradictions among the people.

First, reestablishing the general principle of taking the correct handling of contradictions among the people as the main content of China's political life

Sinceanti-Rightist struggle in 1957, Comrade Mao Zedong himself and the whole Party ideologically had deviated from the correct theory of contradictions among the people. During the Cultural Revolution period in particular, Lin Biao and the Gang of Four misrepresented the philosophical ideas Comrade Mao expressed in On the Correct Handling of Contradictions among the People as "taking class struggle as the key link," and as the philosophical basis of the so-called theory of "continued revolution under the dictatorship of the proletariat." They partially exaggerated Comrade Mao's exposition of class struggle in the article, so that his idea of "Our general subject is the correct handling of contradictions among the people" was completely tampered with. The Chinese Communists with Comrade Deng Xiaoping as representative clarified the confusion and restored the ideological and theoretical order. In the speech in celebration of the 30th anniversary the founding of the PRC, Comrade Ye Jianying pointed out that, in On the Correct Handling of Contradictions among the People, Comrade Mao scientifically analyzed the domestic political and economic situations, proposed the theory of correctly handling and distinguishing between the two types of social contradictions differing in nature in a socialist society, which indicated that the correct handling of contradictions among the people to rally the people of the whole country to develop its economy and culture had become the main content of China's political life. In the Resolution on Certain Questions in the History of Our Party since the Founding of the People's Republic of China sponsored by Comrade Deng Xiaoping and adopted in 1981, it is reiterated: "In the spring of 1957, Comrade Mao Zedong stressed the necessity of correctly handling and distinguishing between the two types of social contradictions differing in nature in a socialist society, and made the correct handling of contradictions among the people the main content of the country's political life. "① It is stressed that "We must correctly understand that there are diverse social contradictions in Chinese society which do not fall within the scope of class struggle and that methods other than class struggle must be used for their appropriate resolution. " These conclusions are fully in line with Comrade Mao's original meaning in On the Correct Handling of Contradictions among the People and actual conditions in our country. In the periods of democratic revolution and socialist transformation, class struggle was the main social contradictions and therefore the main content of China's political life. During these periods, it is without doubt that our party also needed to handle numerous contradictions inside the Party and among the people, but since contradictions among the people took only the secondary and subordinate position, this handling was subject to the resolution of the primary type of contradiction, i. e. , class struggle. After the basic completion of socialist transformation and establishment of socialist system, the situation and conditions fundamentally had changed. Although class struggle will continue to exist within a certain scope for a long time, it is no longer the principal contradiction, and therefore is no longer the main content of China's political life, which has shifted to the correct handling of contradictions among the people, the full mobilization of enthusiasm and creativity of the people and the

---

① *Resolution on Certain Questions in the History of Our Party since the Founding of the People's Republic of China* (Annotated Edition), People's publishing House, 1986, pp. 21, 65.

endeavor of building China into a prosperous, democratic and culturally advanced modern socialist country. The departure from this general principle will inevitably lead to the broadening of the scope of class struggle, the confusing of two different types of contradiction, which will cause great detriment to our socialist construction and development. This has been proved by the practices of socialist construction in China and in other countries.

Second, a series of analyses scientifically made of the change of contradictions among the people in the new era

(1) It has been confirmed that the exploiting classes had already been liquidated, and we must distinguish between class struggle and the reflection of class struggle among the people. In On the Correct Handling of Contradictions among the People, Comrade Mao said: "In our country, the contradiction between the working class and the national bourgeoisie comes under the category of contradictions among the people. By and large, the class struggle between the two is a class struggle within the ranks of the people."① This statement conforms to the reality of the time. But now conditions have greatly changed. In his article The United Front and the Tasks of the Chinese People's Political Consultative Conference in the New Period published in 1979, Comrade Deng Xiaoping wrote: "The means of production formerly owned by the Chinese capitalist class came under state control long ago, and the payment of a fixed rate of interest ended 13 years ago. The overwhelming majority of the capitalists with the capacity to work have transformed themselves into working people who earn their own living in our socialist society." "Today, as working people, they are contributing their share to our socialist modernization."② Therefore, the "class struggle between the working class and bourgeoisie within the ranks of the people," namely, the contradictions between the two, no longer exist. On the other hand, the influence of the exploiting classes will inevitably finds their expression within ranks of the people, making some contradictions among the people have a certain nature of class struggle, about this we should have a full understanding. But the expression of class struggle within the ranks of the people and class struggle among the people belong to two different categories, which we should never confuse.

(2) It was explicitly declared that the intellectuals have become part of the

---

① Selected Readings from Works of Mao Zedong, vol. 2, People's Publishing House, 1986, p. 758.

② *Selected Works of Deng Xiaoping*, vol. 2, People's Publishing House, 1994, p. 186.

working class and basic force to be relied upon as the workers and farmers. Comrade Deng Xiaoping pointed out: Firstly, the mental workers are also workers. They differ from the manual workers only insofar as they perform different roles in the social division of labor. With the advance of modern science and technology, manual labor will steadily decrease while mental labor will constantly increase. This is a historical progress. Secondly, we must concretely analyze the class attribute of the mental workers in a class society. Some are wholly in the service of the reactionary ruling classes and thus stand in an antagonistic relationship to manual workers; while some scholars and technicians too were exploited by the capitalists, who are completely different from those politicians who racked their brains for expedients of direct service to the reactionary ruling classes. Thirdly, under the socialist system, the overwhelming majority of them constitute part of the working class itself and are socialist workers and basic force to be relied upon like the workers and farmers in our socialist cause. The report to the 14th National Congress of the CPC further points out: "The intellectuals are part of the working class that has a relatively more grasp of scientific and cultural knowledge and are the pioneers of advanced productive forces. They play an especially important role in our reform and opening up and modernization drive. Whether we can give full play to their talents to a great degree determines whether our nation can become prosperous and our modernization drive can be realized."① Therefore, the CPC Central Committee repeatedly stressed that we must respect knowledge and talented people, and must politically trust the intellectuals, give full play to their talents in work and take a good care of their lives.

(3) With regard to the relations among ethnic groups, it explicitly points out that contradictions among the ethnic groups essentially belong to contradictions among the working people of all ethnic groups. Under the condition that the exploiting classes had been eliminated in our country, contradictions among the ethnic groups constitute part of the contradictions among the people. Comrade Deng Xiaoping pointed out: "Through democratic reform and socialist transformation, all fraternal ethnic groups in China one after another have long since taken the socialist road, and they have formed a new, socialist type of relationship among themselves—a relationship of unity, fraternity, mutual assistance and co-operation. China's patriots, whatever their ethnic group and religion, have made considerable progress

---

① *Documents of the Fourteenth National Congress of the CPC*, People's Publishing House, 1994, p. 31.

along this road. In the course of bringing about the four modernizations, the ethnic groups will achieve an even greater degree of socialist unanimity and their unity will become stronger and stronger." In handling the relations among ethnic groups, the CPC Central Committee stresses that we must firmly establish the correct idea of "the ethnic groups of the Chinese nation are inseparable" and that it is necessary to combat against Han chauvinism and also local ethnic chauvinism; it stresses the integration of the common interests of all ethnic groups with the special interests of each one, the integration of socialist unanimity with ethnic diversity; it gives emphasis on regional ethnic autonomy, and actively helps ethnic groups develop their economies and cultures, and it pays great efforts to the training and promotion of ethnic minority cadres and the gradual elimination of de facto gap between ethnic groups, so as to achieve common prosperity.

(4) As regards the issue ofthe democratic parties, it clearly affirms that all the democratic parties are political forces serving socialism under the leadership of the CPC. Comrade Deng Xiaoping said, the democratic parties "now have become political alliances of those socialist working people and those patriots supporting socialism with whom these parties are respectively linked."① This indicates that the foundation of cooperation between the CPC and the democratic parties is more solid, and socialism and patriotism are more consistent. On this basis, the CPC's guideline towards the democratic parties has also further developed from the original "long-term coexistence and mutual supervision" to the principle of "long-term coexistence, mutual supervision, sincere treatment with each other and the sharing of weal or woe." In practical work, before making major decisions, the CPC always listen to the opinions and suggestions of non-Communist parties and non-party personages, which means that system of multi-party cooperation and political consultation under the leadership of the Communist Party has further improved.

(5) As regards the issue of united front, it emphasizes that in new period, the scope of the united front has expanded rather than diminished, and its objects has increased rather than decreased. Especially the implementation of the principle of "one country, two systems" has opened a new phase for the patriotic united front and formed a front of two parts, one is all the laborers and patriots in Mainland China with socialism as its political basis, the other is the compatriots in Taiwan, Hong Kong and Macao and the overseas Chinese who support the reunification of the

---

① *Selected Works of Deng Xiaoping*, People's Publishing House, 1994, p. 186.

motherland. Comrade Deng Xiaoping said: "The thoughts of our compatriots in Taiwan, Hong Kong and Macao and of Chinese nationals overseas turn with longing to the motherland, and their sense of patriotism has grown constantly stronger. They are playing an increasingly important and positive part in the effort to achieve the great goal of reunifying our motherland, in supporting the country's modernization and in strengthening the international struggle against hegemonism."① Therefore, the Draft Resolution on Guiding Principles for Building a Socialist Society with an Advanced Level of Culture and Ideology emphasizes: To "really get rid of the narrow-minded view ideas that has cause serious harm for a long time, to make the Communists and non-Communists, Marxists and non-Marxists, atheists and religious believers, domestic compatriots and overseas Chinese, in short, all laborers and patriots, unite closely and act energetically to strive for our common ideals."

Third, guidelines and methods of enriching and improving the correct handling of contradictions among the people in the new historical conditions.

Firstly, emphasis has been put on the use of democratic and legal means in handling contradictions among the people. On the basis of summing up historical experience and lessons, Comrade Deng Xiaoping and CPC Central Committee repeatedly stressed that we must integrate democracy and law, to institutionalize socialist democracy and give it legal sanction, and to resolve contradictions among the people by democratic and legal means. Comrade Deng Xiaoping said: "Socialist democracy and socialist legal system are inseparable." Both inside the Party and among the people, we must promote socialist democracy, carry out the policy of "letting a hundred flowers bloom, a hundred schools of thought contend," and the principle of the "three don'ts": don't pick on others for their faults, don't put labels on people, and don't use a big stick; as to different views, including wrong ones, we cannot deal with in a simple or crude way, or political movements, but use the method of education and persuasion, that is, democratic way. But democracy must be guaranteed by legal system. Without a sound socialist legal system, the people's democratic rights might be deprived at any time; there will be no political stability and unity and thus no true people's democracy. There is no doubt that in the environment of arbitrary rule by individuals, there is no democracy at all; but democracy does not exist in a turbulent environment, either. Therefore, the state should improve the legal system, all Party members and the people should also learn

① *Documents of the Fourteenth National Congress of the CPC,* People's Publishing House, 1994, p. 31.

to use legal weapons to protect their democratic rights. Precisely because of this, it was proposed by Comrade Deng Xiaoping and the CPC Central Committee and approved by the National People's Congress the provision concerning the rights of citizens to "speak out freely, air their views fully, hold great debates and put up big-character posters" was deleted from the Constitution. Long-term practice has proved that the "speak out freely, air their views fully, hold great debates and put up big-character posters" as a whole never played a positive role; instead, it is not conducive to promoting socialist democracy and resolving contradictions among the people; it can only undermine political stability and unity, lead to unrest, and is prone to be exploited by hostile forces.

In the process of handling contradictions among the people in democratic andlegal means, Comrade Deng Xiaoping and the Party Central Committee stressed the need to draw clear distinctions, such as distinctions among academic issues, ideological issues, political issues, line issues and counter-revolutionary issues. It is pointed out in the Guiding Principles for Inner-Party Political Life: "We should not take common errors or errors of ideological understanding as errors of political line, nor should we confuse the errors of political line of inner-Party struggle nature with attempts of counter-revolutionary nature that try to subvert our Party and state."① We must prohibit the erroneous practices in the past, such as magnifying academic problem to be a question of political stance or world outlook, and arbitrary putting political labels, taking work errors as errors of political line, and taking political issues as contradictions between ourselves and the enemy. To correctly handle contradictions among the people, we must also strictly distinguish what constitutes an offence from what does not. In the Decision of the CPC Central Committee and State Council on Combating Serious Criminal Activities in the Economic Field, it is pointed out that, wc must make distinctions between mistakes in the work and law-breaking, between economic malpractice and economic crime, between problems arising from the loopholes in our policy of opening to the outside world and stimulating the economy and smuggling, corruption, speculation and swindling. And in giving sentence, we must make distinction between graft or corruption and turning general benefits into small group benefits.② In case a distinction cannot be made for

① *Selected Important Documents since the Third Plenary Session of the Eleventh Central Committee of the Communist Party of China, vol.* 1, People's Publishing House, 1982, p. 429.

② Ibid., pp. 1245 – 1246.

the time being, it should be treated carefully and first be regarded as contradiction among the people. We can never deal with it like what we did in the past, that is, to "burn down" or "knock down" first and then to make "re-examination" or "rehabilitation" afterward, which resulted countless losses.

In order to correctly handle contradictions among the people, great importance should be attached toinvestigation and research to avoid arbitrariness. Given lessons learnt from the broadening scope of class struggle in the anti-Rightist struggle and other political movements, the CPC Central Committee stressed: in the future, with regard to major ideological trends and social thought in a certain period, the whole Party must make judgment conforming to reality by first of all doing in-depth investigation and careful analysis to find out their background and development, scope, fields, etc., and strictly resolve them within the scope where they are in. We can never arbitrarily make expansion, let alone the practice of 'one-size-fits-all', or large-scale political movement.[①] We especially must prevent and combat against such erroneous practices as arbitrarily setting indicators or progress, arbitrarily looking for objects of struggle, magnifying problems, etc., without any investigation or grasping actual conditions.[②]

Secondly, emphasis has been put on handling contradictions among the people through reform. Essentially speaking, socialist reform is to adjust relations among the people and handle contradictions among the people, in order to arouse the enthusiasm of hundreds of millions of people to complete the great cause of building socialism with Chinese characteristics. The reform towards socialist market economy involves the adjustment of interests among the people. The purpose of it is, following the law of resources allocation by the market and the general principle of being favorable to the liberation and growth of the productive forces, to reasonably and properly resolve the contradictions of interests among state-owned economy, private owned economy, individual owned economy, shareholding economy and mixed economy, and contradictions of interests among the groups of these different sectors of the economy, contradictions of interests among state, enterprises, individuals, contradictions of interests among departments, contradictions among regions, as well as contradictions among individual laborers. Contradictions of material interests

---

① *Selected Important Documents since the Third Plenary Session of the Eleventh Central Committee of the Communist Party of China, vol.* 1, People's Publishing House, 1982, p. 497.

② *Ibid.*, p. 1245.

among the people constitute an objective existence. We can only recognize them, take them as they are, and resolve them according to economic laws. In the past we considered material interests as taboo, equated the mention of them with "revisionist" material stimulation, and tried to cover them up with empty political persuasion. The only consequence of it is the intensification of contradictions and the dampening of people's socialist enthusiasm. Since reform and opening up, in terms of ownership, we have developed a pattern with the public ownership as the mainstay, allowing the development of different forms of ownership and management; in terms of distribution, with a goal of common prosperity, we keep to the system in which distribution according to work is primary and a variety of modes of distribution coexist, encouraging some people and some regions to get wealthy first through honest labor and lawful operation, which has greatly aroused the enthusiasm of the people and greatly liberated and developed the productive forces, and the lives of the people gradually have improved. And in turn the resolution of contradictions on the basis of fundamental identity of interests among the people contributes to the development of their fundamental interests.

Political reforminvolves the adjustment of political relations among the people. There exist a series of political contradictions among the people, such as that between the Party and the government on the one side and the people on the other, between democracy and centralism, between the leadership and the led, and the contradictions arising from the bureaucratic style of work of some of the state personnel in their relations with the masses. These contradictions, although had been pointed out by Comrade Mao Zedong long ago, and many measures had been taken to resolve them in the practical work, were less considered from the viewpoint of structural reform. For instance, as how to make democracy be institutionalized and written into law, we not only do not have a sound system, but also have not acted strictly in accordance with the law and the legal system. Another example is the problem of bureaucracy. In this regard, in the past we mostly focused on ideological education, or used the so-called "mass democracy" to solve it, with less or no consideration of the reform of state leadership system. Since the Third Plenary Session of the Eleventh Central Committee, our party step by step proposed that, we should, proceeding from political structure, reform our government institutions and cadre and personnel system, improve socialist democracy, establish social dialogue and consultation system, strengthen our socialist legal system, etc., with a view to establish a highly democratic socialist political system that is sound in legal system and is high efficiency and full of vitality. With the deepening of political reform, the political situation advocated by Chairman Mao Zedong that is characterized by both centralism and democracy, both discipline and freedom, both unity of will and personal ease of mind and liveliness, "will gradually come into being."

III. Further Enrichment and Development of the Theory of Contradictions among the People Based on the Profound Study under the New Conditions of Reform and Opening Up

Since the Fourth Plenary Session of the Thirteenth Central Committee of the CPC, inthe new development stage of socialist reform and opening up, facing complex new situations, new realities, new contradictions and new problems, it has become a major issue confronting our party as how to correctly handle contradictions among the people. The Party's third generation of central collective leadership, inheriting the theory of contradictions among the people which was founded by Comrade Mao Zedong and restored and developed by Comrade Deng Xiaoping, solved a series of contradictory problems among the people in the new period, creatively enriching and developing this theory in practice.

How to correctly understand and handle contradictions among the people in the new era has become a major issue for our party. Comrade Jiang Zemin made an important speech at the Fifth Plenary Session of the 14th CPC Central Committee, entitled Correctly Handle Certain Major Relationships in the Socialist Modernization Drive. In this speech, on the basis of comprehensively summarizing historical experience at home and abroad, he profoundly expounded twelve major relationships in China's modernization drive, namely twelve major contradictions, and put forward methods and guidelines for their solution. In 2001, in his Speech at the Meeting Celebrating the 80th Anniversary of the Founding of the Communist Party of China, he elaborated our party's analysis and understanding of the new of new social strata emerged in the course of our socialist reform and opening up, which further enriched and developed the theory of contradictions among the people.

First, from the perspective of political awareness, stress has been put on the fundamental importance of correctly understanding and handling contradictions among the people in the new era.

In the 1990s when China's reform and opening up entered a critical period, Comrade Jiang Zemin repeatedly exhorted the leading cadres of the Party at all levelsto carefully study Comrade Mao's theory of contradictions among the people by combining it with the new realities, pay careful attention to their new manifestations and new trends in the new situation, especially their new development originated in the change of interest patterns and relations since the reform and opening up, so as to properly handle them. He pointed out in the Second Plenary Session of the Fourteenth Central Committee of the CPC: In new situation of accelerating reform and opening up, to correctly understand and handle contradictions among the people, to mobilize all positive factors and to turn negative factors into positive ones are the themes of the political life of our country and important foundation for maintaining our social stability. He believed that leading cadres at all levels shoulder the arduous task of correct handling contradictions among the people. It is a major political issue for the whole Party to make leading cadres at all levels be able to correctly handle contradictions among the people, contradiction between the leadership and the masses, thereby to ensure the smooth progress of reform and opening up and our modernization drive; and the cadres should constantly improve their ability and level in this regard. He stressed in the Report to the Fifteenth National Congress of the CPC: "The Party committees and governments at all levels must work conscientiously, responsibly and enthusiastically to solve the people's practical problems in their life and work. With regard to contradictions among the people, we should go deep into the realities, carry out investigation and study and do ideological and political work well. As the circumstances may differ, we should properly use economic, administrative or legal means to tackle the contradictions and prevent them from becoming more acute." He pointed out in the Report to the Sixteenth National Congress of the CPC that "Party committees and governments at all levels...must carry out in-depth investigations and study, strengthen ideological and political work in light of different cases, and employ economic, administrative and legal means to handle the contradictions among the people properly, those involving their immediate interests in particular, so as to maintain stability and unity."

Second, scientific elaboration and correct understanding has been made about the changes and composition of changes of classes and strata within the ranks of the people in the new era. Correct analysis and understanding of the new changes of social classes and strata in the present stage is the premise of the correct understanding and handling of contradictions among the people. The more than two decades of reform and opening up and the gradual establishment of the socialist market economy have given birth to the major changes, combinations and differentiations of classes and social strata and a number of new social strata as well. How to correctly understand these new strata and the new developments has become a pressing major issue. After the establishment of the socialist system, exploiting class as a whole has ceased to exist. As the mainstay of the people, the working class is consisted of the working class, the farmer class and the intelligentsia as part of the working class. Since reform and opening up, with the formation of pattern of ownership in which public ownership is the dominant mainstay and diverse forms of ownership develop together, and the formation of distribution system with diverse models, in addition to the two major class of working class and farmer class, a series of new social strata have emerged. Along with it, the subjects of interests become more diverse. All this determines that contradictions among the people are more complex. The Party's scientific analysis of these changes has provided a policy basis for the correct handling of contradictions among the people.

Third, a series of new issues and new problems have been comprehensively analyzed. Comrade Jiang Zemin's Correctly Handle Certain Major Relationships in the Socialist Modernization Drive is a new development of Comrade Mao Zedong's On the Ten Major relationships. In the new historical period, with the gradual establishment of the socialist market economy, the various contradictions among become more complex. Comrade Jiang made a comprehensive analysis of a series of new conditions and new problems among the people in the new era and an in-depth and systematic deliberation on how to deal with a variety of major social contradictions and their new forms in China. It includes: the relationship between the public sector and other sectors of the economy, the relationship between the eastern region and the central and western regions, the relationship of income distribution between the state, enterprises and individuals, the relationship between central and local authorities, the relationship between material progress and moral and ethical progress; in the economic field, there are contradictions between the public sector and the individual-owned, private-owned and other sectors of the economy; contradictions within the public sectors between the state-owned, collective-owned, mixed-owned, share-holding and other forms of ownership, as well as those among different components of the same ownership; contradictions of imbalanced development between regions; contradictions between urban and rural areas and between the working class and the farmers; contradictions between different industries; contradictions between leaders and managers on the one side and the ordinary workers on the other side; contradictions between the self-employed, the private entrepreneurs and the employees; contradictions among subjects of interests due to the widening of income discrepancies between regions, between industries, between work units, and between laborers.

In terms of ideological understanding, there contradictions between the advanced and the backward, between science and superstition, between values and between ethical outlooks, etc., which arise from the significant changes brought about by reform and opening up and by of establishment of the socialist market economy. All these contradictions are manifested in human relations among the people. The proper handling and effective alleviating of them is very importance for the strengthening of reform, stability and development.

Fourth, the guidelines and methods for timely and effectively handling contradictions among the people were clearly put forth.

Firstly, the important thought of Three Represents is made as the guideline for correctly understand and handle contradictions among the people. All complex contradictions must be dealt with in light of the guideline. Secondly, correct handling of contradictions among the people is considered from the general interest of reform, development and stability. To solve China's problems, the most important prerequisite if stability. Without a stable environment, we can accomplish nothing and may even lose what we have gained. From the inherent relationship of reform, development and stability, Comrade Jiang Zemin demonstrated that the correct handling of contradictions among the people is the foundation for maintaining social stability. Thirdly, rule of law is taken as the basic guarantee for correct handling of contradictions among the people. In the report to the Fifth National Congress of the CPC, Comrade Jiang explicitly pointed out: "Rule of law is the basic strategy employed by the Party in leading the people in running the country. It is the objective demand of a socialist market economy, an important hallmark of social and cultural progress, and a vital guarantee for lasting political stability of the country." The strategy of rule of law provides a fundamental guarantee for resolving contradictions among the people within the legal system. And fourthly, apply the principles of "placing equal emphasis on both material progress and ethical cultural progress" and "material civilization, institutional civilization, and cultural and ethical civilization" in handling contradictions among the people.

The Party's third generation of collective leadership with Comrade Jiang Zemin at the core, following the principle of "placing equal emphasis on both material progress and ethical cultural progress" put forward by Comrade Deng Xiaoping, place Party building, anti-corruption and building an honest government, and socialist cultural and ethical progress on more prominent position. Only by raising the ideological, ethical, scientific and cultural qualities of the Chinese nation, can contradictions among the people be settled fundamentally. In the Sixteenth National Congress of the CPC, Comrade Jiang Zemin proposed the strategic measure of putting equal importance on "material, political and cultural and ethical progresses," in which socialist political progress was placed on an extremely important place. This has provided a basic political guarantee for the correct handling of contradictions among the people. And finally, a sound social security system that can meet the various and multi-level needs of the people provides a important way for handling contradictions among the people.

After the Sixteenth National Congress of the CPC, the new central committee of the Party with Comrade Hu Jintao as general secretary, proceeding from the new realities, further actively explored the effective solutions to contradictions among the people, to better accomplish the great task of handling contradictions among the people under new situations and circumstances. Comrade Hu paid great attention to contradictions among the people under the new situations, stressed that to correctly understand and handle them is fundamentally important to social stability, and required it should be taken as a major political task, and diligent efforts must be made to ensure its success. He said: "We must fully understand the essential importance of the correct handling of contradictions among the people and make efforts in a down-to-earth manner, because it plays a great role in consolidating the mass basis of the Party's governance and ensure the lasting political stability of the country."①

Heasserted that to correctly handle the contradictions among the people, we must take the important thought of Three Represents as the guideline. The important thought of "Three Represents", on the basis of the new practice of reform and opening up and our socialist construction, has thoroughly understood the profound changes in the social life and social structure of the country and scientifically makes a judgment on the forces on which our drive of building socialism with Chinese characteristics should rely. We must take the important thought of "Three Represents" as the guideline, uphold and implement the Scientific Outlook on

---

① Hu Jintao, "Speech at the Opening Ceremony of the Autumn semester of the CPC Party School, 2002".

Development, bring all positive factors into full play, properly handle relationships of various interests, ensure social stability, build a harmonious socialist society, so as to create a situation in which all people are well positioned, do their best and live in harmony, to gather the immense strength of advancing the development of socialism.

In accordance with the requirements of theimportant thought of "Three Represents," to correctly handle contradictions among the people in the new era, we must: Firstly, to establish and improve a regular and institutionalized mechanism for dealing with disputes in a timely manner, to as far as possible resolve the conflicts and hidden risks at the community level. This include: taking the establishment of a sound reflection mechanism that can timely and accurately report social conditions and public opinions as the of contradictions of properly handling contradictions among the people; taking the coordination of interest relations through policies as the an effective measure of properly handling contradictions among the people; taking the rule of law and the full play of function of laws as the guarantee of dealing with contradictions among the people; taking patient and meticulous ideological and political work and their fullest expression as an important means to solve contradictions among the people; taking the full play of the guiding role of publicity as a necessary way to solve contradictions among the people; taking the improvement of community-level Party organizations and political powers and their fullest roles in the this regard as the organizational guarantee for resolving contradictions among the people; and taking the advancement of socialist democracy and socialist political civilization as the political guarantee for correct handling of contradictions among the people.

Secondly, the key to resolving contradictions among the people is keeping in mind the vital interests of the people, working hard to solve practical problems in their work and daily life, and implement the policies of the Party and the state to the letter. For the interests of the people is the starting point and goal of all our party's work; we must always maintain the party's close ties with the people, exercise state power for the people, and always concern about the lives of the people and earnestly safeguard their. Only by doing so, can we fully mobilize the enthusiasm of the people and thus ensure the proper resolution of contradictions among the people. To this end, we must give an overall priority to taking good care of people's lives. People's interests are no small matters. We must go to the people in their neighborhoods and homes, listen to their views, care about their hardships and promptly attend to their grievances. In so doing, we are sure to alleviate all kinds of contradictions. We must: put the policies of the CPC Central Committee and State Council on social security and others to the letter to really settle the issues that most concern the public; make the best use of the circumstances and patiently and meticulously do ideological and political work well among the masses; firmly hold mass viewpoint, effectively change the style of work, and resolutely overcome bureaucracy to efficiently solve the pressing problems affecting people's life and production; pay attention to method of work and properly address problems or mass incidents affecting stability; and leading cadres at all levels should strictly observe discipline and maintain integrity to win the trust of the masses by playing exemplary roles.

Thirdly, we should build up the Party's governing capacity and improve the capability and level of our leading cadres in properly handling contradictions among the people. Whether contradictions among the people can be correctly handled has become an indication whether the governing party has a high capability in governance. Strengthening the capability to properly deal with various contradictions and relationships is an important part of the Party's governance capability building. Leading cadres at all levels should learn to correctly handle contradictions among the people and improve their capability in this respect under the new situation and learn to properly balance the interest relations of all sides.

Lastly, while emphasizing the correct handling of contradictions among the people, we should not lose our guard againstthe trouble-making and sabotage of hostile forces.

Comrade Hu Jintao pointed out: we must clearly see that international hostile forces did not and will not change their strategic plot of Westernizing and dividing China; they always try to throw our country into disorder by taking use of some factors of instability in our country to carry on agitation and create disturbances. So we should keep on guard against their attempts.

Chapter 3

Contradictions among the People Constitute the Primary Kind of Contradictions of Human Relations in Chinese Society at the Present Stage

The theory of contradictions among the people correctly reflects the changes of social relationsin our country after the basic completion of socialist transformation. It summarizes that in the period of socialist construction, contradictions among the people have become the main kind of contradictions of human relations, replacing contradictions between classes. In the primary stage of socialism and the new period of socialist reform and opening up, this kind of contradictions as the primary kind of contradictions of human relations, will manifest themselves massively, frequently and prominently in all fields and aspects of social life. To carefully study and correctly handle contradictions among the people in the new period is a major issue for our party to resolve.

I. The Correct Handling of Contradictions among the People Remains the Main Theme of Political Life in China at the Present Stage

In a class society, human relations, in essence, are manifested as class relations; class distinctions and class antagonism influence people's all social relations inclusion economic relations, political relations; and class contradictions and class struggle affect and constrain people's all social activities in political, economic, cultural and other areas. So contradictions, conflicts, clashes and struggle among classes constitute the theme of political life in a class society. Before the establishment of socialist system in China, the theme of its political life was class contradictions and class struggle, which determines that the primary task of the new democratic revolution carried out by the CPC and the people led by it is of the nature of revolutionary class struggle. During that period, class struggle was the principal social contradiction in the society, while contradictions among the people, although also existed, were in a subordinate position. After the establishment of the socialist system, the theme of the political life in the country fundamentally changed: the system of class exploitation has been abolished, the exploiting classes as a whole ceased to exist and class struggle is no longer the theme of the country's political life, although class distinctions and contradictions will exist in a fairly long historical period. Instead, how to correctly handle contradictions among the people in order to arouse the enthusiasm of building socialism of the people, to concentrate efforts on economic construction and to improve people's material and cultural life, has become the fundamental task of the Party and the theme of entire political life of our socialist country in the new period.

After the establishment of the socialist system, it has become an extremely significant practical and theoretical issue whether to recognize that there are contradictions in socialist countries, if any, what the contradictions are and how to handle them. There are two wrong ideas about this issue: the first one does not recognize the existence of contradictions in socialist countries; while the second one, although admitting that there are contradictions in socialist countries, expands the scope of these contradictions and takes every contradiction as the contradiction between ourselves and the enemy. Many socialist countries had learned bitter lessons in this problem and the Soviet Union under Stalin's leadership paid a heavy price for it. When the Soviet Union declared having entered into a socialist society, Stalin first believed that in the country "the relations of production completely correspond to the character of the productive forces."① And soon after it, he asserted that in the Soviet Union, "such motive forces as the moral and political unity of Soviet society, the mutual friendship of the nations of the U. S. S. R. and Soviet patriotism" had developed.② These are the well-known theory of "completely correspond" and theory of "power of unity". These views, in fact, are metaphysical, because the former denies the existence of contradictions and latter denies that contradiction is the internal power of the development of things. Stalin believed that there was no contradiction among the people and the political and moral unity were the internal power of its social development. But in reality, there were lots of social contradictions in the Soviet Union at that time. How to interpret these contradictions? Stalin had to theoretically consider all types of domestic

---

① *Selected Works of Stalin*, vol. 2, People's Publishing House, 1979, p. 449.

② *Collected Works of Stalin*(1934 – 1952), People's Publishing House, 1979, p. 263.

contradictions in the Soviet Union as contradictions between the people and the enemy brought about by external causes. He believed that there was no contradiction among the people in the Soviet Union, and if any, they were noting but contradictions between the people and the enemy brought about or aroused by external causes. These views of "external causes" and "contradictions between the people and the enemy" are also typical metaphysical ideas. Besides, he put forward the famous Leftist point of view: "the further forward we advance, the greater the successes we achieve, the greater will be the fury of the remnants of the defeated exploiting classes, the more ready will they be to resort to sharper forms of struggle." "One end of the class struggle operates within the frontiers of the U. S. S. R., but its other end stretches across the frontiers of the bourgeois states surrounding us."① All domestic contradictions in the Soviet Union were said to belong to the contradiction between the people and the enemy, and the causes of which were attributed to external causes, the impact of imperialists and the reactionaries, the encirclement of the bourgeois countries and the exploiting classes. Stalin's metaphysical views and extremely wrong theories greatly harmed the socialist development in the Soviet Union. In practice, due to his denial of contradictions in socialist society, Stalin and the Communist Party of the Soviet Union totally confused two different types of contradictions in the country's political life, which led to the mistake of expanding the Purge that severely disrupted the normal life of socialist democracy and legal system. In the economic and political sectors, due to their denial of the objective existence of social contradictions, they failed to find the real motive forces of social development, leading to the formation of a rigid economic and political system, choking the vitality of socialist economy and dampening people's enthusiasm. All of these are part of the deep-seated causes for the slow and stagnant social development in the Soviet Union, which ultimately resulted in the intensification of various contradictions and eventual disintegration of the socialist Soviet Union.

Historical experience of socialist construction in China also shows that, whenever we make a clear distinction between ourselves and the enemy and keep to the theme of correctly handling contradictions among the people, the socialist cause thrive; and vice versa. In the anti-Rightist struggle, the social education movement and the unrest of the Cultural Revolution, we severely confused the two different types of contradictions differing in nature, put many contradictions among the people

① *Collected Works of Stalin*(1934 – 1952), People's Publishing House, 1979, p. 129.

into the category of class contradictions and class struggle, even as contradictions between ourselves and the enemy, and took class struggle as the theme of the socialist political life, thus making the mistake of broadening the scope of class struggle, which inflicted great suffering upon the people and serious damage to the Party. Since the Third Plenary Session of the Eleventh of the CPC Central Committee, by setting things right theoretically, repudiating the erroneous theory of taking class struggle as the key link and correctly distinguishing between the two different types of contradictions, we have greatly aroused the enthusiasm of the people and achieved great success in socialist reform and opening up and construction. But in this process, we suffered disturbances both from the Right and "Left" thinking. On the one hand, some comrades, failed to recognize the objective existence of contradictions between ourselves and the enemy and the existence of class struggle within a limited scope, either relaxed their vigilance against or take a laissez-faire attitude towards the strategy of the Western hostile forces to Westernize and divide our country and the sabotage and disruptions of various hostile forces; or could not reveal the nature of the anti-Party and anti-socialist ideological trend of bourgeois liberalization, and did not unequivocally oppose it, but supported it instead to a certain degree. On the other hand, after the drastic changes in Eastern Europe and the disintegration of the Soviet Union occurred, and serious political disturbances of June 1989 happened in China, some people doubted the theory of the correct handling of contradictions among the people, advocating that we should take it as the central task to oppose the attempts of the Western hostile forces to Westernize and divide China and bring about peaceful evolution in China. These two tendencies had once brought damage to our socialist cause. Both positive and negative experiences repeatedly prove that, the correct understanding and handling of the two different types of contradictions and the keeping to the theme of correctly handling contradictions among the people is of great importance to our cause of socialism.

II. There Exist Two Types of Contradictions Differing in Nature in the Present Stage in Our Society

In the present stage in China there exist two different types of social contradictions, one is those among the people, the other is those between ourselves and the enemy.

1. The precondition of correctly handling contradictions among the people is the clear distinction between the two types of contradictions.

The people and the enemy are two historical categories, which vary in content and reference in different countries and different periods of history. There is no concept of the people that remains unchanged, so is the concept of the enemy. Specific times, places, and socio-economic, political and economic factors determine the scope and specific reference of the two concepts. Generally speaking, any class, stratum, group or individual favorable towards the development of social productive forces comes within the category of the people. The fundamental standard in judging whether one belongs to the category of the people or the enemy is whether his words and deeds are in favor of the development of social productive forces and social progress. But when using this standard, we must combine it with the historical conditions to exam the classes, strata and individuals within the specific economic and political relations.

What is the content of the category of the people and the enemy respectively in the historical conditions of socialism? In On the Correct Handling of Contradictions among the People, Mao Zedong pointed out that, the classes, strata and social groups which favor, support and work for the cause of socialist construction all come within the category of the people, while the social forces and groups which resist the socialist revolution and are hostile to or sabotage socialist construction are all enemies of the people. In the present historical conditions in China, workers, farmers, intellectuals and other socialist workers and builders, patriots who support socialism and the reunification of the motherland, all patriotic classes, strata and individuals, including patriotic bourgeoisie and other personages in Hong Kong, Macao and Taiwan, the owners of non-public enterprises that conduct legitimate business activities and other new emerging social strata, all belong to the category of the people. Among which, workers, farmers and intellectuals are the the mainstays.

Under socialist system, contradictions among the people are of non-antagonistic nature, which occur among the people and are identical in fundamental interests. The nature, characteristics, occurrence, movement and resolution of these contradictions are all determined by the basis of "identical in fundamental interests," which are the internal foundation of the movement of Contradictions among the people, which have the following features: (1) the economic nature of public ownership as the mainstay and political nature of the people as masters of the country determine that the fundamental interests of the people are identical, and that contradictions among the people on this basis are non-antagonistic. (2) a large number of contradictions among the people emerge in the process of socialist development itself, with a few non-dominant contradictions caused by the remnants of the old society; (3) contradictions among the people, in terms of root cause, are manifested as contradictions of interests among the people, which to some extent manifest themselves as political and ideological contradictions of right and wrong; (4) in real life, contradictions among the people are extensive and frequent in contrast to contradictions between ourselves and the enemy; (5) generally speaking, contradictions among the people are non-antagonistic and can be resolved with non-antagonistic methods. But if not properly handled, antagonism may arise, and they may change into contradictions between ourselves and the enemy.

Contradictions betweenthe ourselves and the enemy are antagonistic social contradictions between these two social forces on the basis of opposing fundamental interests, which determines the nature, characteristics, occurrence, movement and resolution of these contradictions. "Opposing fundamental interests" are the intrinsic nature of the movement of contradictions between the ourselves and the enemy, which, under socialist system have the following features: (1) Opposing fundamental economic interests underlie the occurrence and development of contradictions between ourselves and the enemy. Under socialist system, although the social basis of class exploitation has be eliminated, the remnants of economic basis and superstructure of the old society still exist, so do the demands of interests of the exploiting classes represented by the anti-socialist forces, thus the opposition between socialist economic base and superstructure and the those of the remnants of the old society, and opposition between the demands of interests of the exploiting classes and the demands of the people constitute the social basis of the existence of contradictions between ourselves and the enemy. (2) Although rooted in opposing economic relations and interests, contradictions between ourselves and the enemy find their expression mainly in their fundamentally antagonistic political and ideological relations and activities, including confrontations, conflicts, disputes, even fierce struggles in these two fields. In socialist political life, contradictions between ourselves and the enemy are adversarial and irreconcilable. (3) In the socialist stage, although contradictions between ourselves and the enemy exist, they are not inherent to socialist society in nature. The establishment of socialist system has eliminated the system of exploitation of man by man and the economic base of antagonism between the people and the enemy as well, whereas socialist system itself doesn't give birth to contradictions between ourselves and the enemy, which come from the outside of socialist system, that is, from the economic, political and ideological remnants of the old society and the subversion, sabotage and corruption of the external reactionary forces. These contradictions are generated outside but exist in socialist system. (4) Contradictions between ourselves and the enemy in socialist countries manifest themselves not as full-scale confrontations between antagonistic classes, but as antagonism and struggle between small numbers hostile elements and forces and the people. (5) Contradictions between ourselves and the enemy in socialist countries are sporadic in contrast to contradictions among the people, and both their scale and scope of influence are under the control of the socialist system; whereas in an exploitive society, when contradictions between the people and the enemy intensify to a certain degree, they are bound to expand to all areas of society and can only be resolved by ways of armed conflicts or seizure of power by force; under socialist system, however, they are mainly settled through legal means and people's democratic dictatorship, and some of them can even be handled as contradictions among the people by means of non-dictatorship. (6) Under certain conditions, contradictions between ourselves and the enemy can transform into contradictions among the people. (7) As socialism develops from primary to higher and more mature stages, the scope, scale and influence of contradictions between ourselves and the people will become smaller and smaller and eventually will cease exist, though the possibility of their temporary intensification and acuteness cannot be ruled out.

2. In primary stage of socialism in China, the two types of contradictions will coexist for a long time, and the contradictions between ourselves and the enemy may intensify in certain conditions

Whywill contradictions between ourselves and the enemy coexist in China for a long time? This is because, on the one hand, China's socialist economic and political system has been basically established, system of exploitation has been overthrown, and except for Taiwan, Hong Kong, Macau, the exploiting classes as a whole have been eradicated. All this determines that contradictions between ourselves and the enemy and class struggle as well are no longer the principal social contradiction in our society. On the other hand, however, though the exploiting classes as a whole no long exist, various domestic and foreign hostile elements and forces as well as the exploiting elements associated with the exploiting system and classes are far from been eliminated, and class struggle between the people and these forces, elements and classes will exist in a certain scope, which even can intensify under certain conditions due to the following reasons: (1) China is still in a complex international environment, and foreign hostile forces have not given up their wild ambition to subjugate China by doing everything possible from peaceful evolution, political subversion to sabotage, corruption, etc.; (2) In the regions that adopt the policy of "one country two systems" and that has not yet achieved unification with the mainland, there are still exploiting classes, though most which are patriotic, a few hostile elements among them are hostile to and try to interrupt China's socialist cause; (3) There are still remnants of the exploiting classes who are hostile to socialist China, criminals who disrupt socialist order, and reactionaries who are hostile to socialist system, etc., they will resort to every possible means to undermine China's socialist construction; (4) China is still at the primary stage of socialism with lots of economic, political, ideological, cultural remnants of the old society, coupled with the immaturity and imperfection of its socialist system, which will give birth to new criminals, new corrupt elements and new hostile elements.

Whythen, will contradictions among the people exist for a long time in our country? This is because, on the one hand, with the establishment of China's public ownership of means of production and people's democratic dictatorship, the social position of the previously exploited working class, including workers, farmers and handicraftsmen, have fundamentally changed to become masters of the means of production and the country with the intellectuals also becoming part of the working class. The new social strata emerged in the process of socialist reform and opening up, such as private entrepreneurs, etc., are the builders of the socialist cause. In short, all social strata and forces that support our socialism and the reunification of the motherland are members of the big family of socialist China. Their fundamental interests are identical rather than conflicting. On the other hand, because China is currently in the primary stage of socialism, the relative backwardness of its social productivity and shortage of material and cultural wealth cannot fully meet the people's growing needs, making the contradictions of material interests among the people become particularly prominent, such as contradictions and interest differences between urban residents and rural residents, between workers and farmers. Since the features of the old type of division and separation of labor still remain, there are still significant class and other differences, such as big social, class and interest differences between urban and rural areas, between the workers and the farmers, between manual and mental workers, between working class and farmers class, between those work in the field of education and the manual workers in enterprises and tertiary industry, between different social strata and interest groups, and so on; since the production relations in the primary stage of socialism are far from developed and perfect, and there are also different forms of ownership with public ownership as the mainstay, different realization forms of public ownership and diverse sectors of the economy such as joint ventures, joint-stock enterprises, enterprises of mixed ownership and so on. Besides, there are also different distribution systems with distribution according to work as the main form. All this gives rise to complex contradictions among interest groups within the ranks of the people. For instance, there are certain income differences and interest contradictions between workers in state-owned enterprises and those in collective owned enterprises or joint ventures, between owners of foreign capital and private enterprises and their employees, and among managers, technical personnel and ordinary workers in the enterprises of the same ownership.

Sincethe market economy is an inevitable stage of the development of socialist economy, we must vigorously develop the socialist market economy, in which some contradictions are inherent. For example, there are competitions, frictions or conflicts between plan and market, between markets in different areas and regions, between resources allocation in the market, among commodity producers, among producers, sellers and consumers, and so on. All these conflicts and competitions will inevitably find expression in contradictions of human relations. Since our superstructure, democracy and legal system are not sound enough, contradictions will inevitably exist between the leadership and the masses, between higher and lower levels, between inside and outside the Party, between government and farmers, etc. Because our socialist society is still in its primary stage and has the birthmark of the old society in political, ideological, cultural and moral sectors, and the political and ideological consciousness, moral standards and quality of our social members cannot go beyond the limitations of history, contradictions will necessarily exist in political, ideological and ethical areas, which will find expression in people's social behaviors, influence and intensify contradictions of human relations. As to the contradictions of right and wrong arising from differences in stands, viewpoints and methods, in experience, in scientific and cultural level, and in perspectives, etc., they without doubt will exist forever. In short, these profound social and historical factors determine that, in the primary stage of socialism in China, a lot of contradictions among the people will inevitably exist.

III. Contradictions among the People Is the Basic One among All Types of Contradictions at the Present Stage in China

In the primary stageof socialism and the period of reform and opening up in China, class contradictions, class struggle and contradictions between ourselves and the enemy will continue to exist within certain limits. In certain conditions, contradictions between ourselves and the enemy may become acute, and an intricate political situation may also arise in which the two types of contradictions interweave. Nevertheless, among all types of contradictions, contradictions among the people are still the most outstanding, most frequent and most ordinary type taking the basic position among social and contradictions of human relations. The reasons are as follows.

First, after the establishment of socialist system, social relations in the society will fundamentally change, and contradictions among the people will replace class contradictions to become the basic contradictions in human relations in a socialist country.

In a class society, human relations are essentially manifested as class relations, so class contradictions and class struggle become the theme in the political life in the society and thus become the basic contradictions in human relations. After the establishment of socialist system, the exploiting system as a whole no longer exists, so does the exploiting class. Along with it, human relations within the country will fundamentally change, so does the theme of the country's political life. Although class differences and class contradictions will continue to exist for a fairly long time, class struggle is not longer the theme of the country's political life; likewise, class contradictions are no longer the primary type of contradictions in human relations. Since China is still in the primary stage of socialism, the deep-rooted social and historical factors in political, economic, cultural and other areas lead inevitably to the existence of large amounts of contradictions among the people. This type of contradictions is the basic ones in human relations at the present stage, and the correct handling of them is the primary theme of political life in present China.

Second, the nature andcharacters of basic contradictions at the present stage of socialism in China determines that contradictions among the people take the primary position among all social contradictions.

Inreal social life, basic social contradictions will necessarily manifest themselves in human relations. In other words, basic social contradictions will necessarily manifest themselves as contradictions of human relations. In a class society, whether it is slave society, feudal society or capitalist society, the contradiction between the private ownership of the means of production and social productivity is antagonistic and irreconcilable. This determines that the existence of fierce contradictions and conflicts of interests among people is inevitable, and that the basic social contradictions manifest themselves largely and mainly in class relations in forms of class contradictions and class struggle. After the establishment of socialist system in China, its relations of production basically conform to the development of its productive forces, so does its superstructure to economic base, except for some aspects and links. On the one hand, because the basic contradictions in socialist society are non-antagonistic, they can be resolved through conscious adjustment and reform. After more than twenty years of reform and opening up, a basic economic system for the primary stage of socialism is established and socialist market economy has come into being, which have greatly released and developed socialist productive forces; and we have timely and accordingly carried out political restructuring, gradually established the basic political institutions of the primary stage of socialism and strengthened the construction of socialist legal system and democracy, which have greatly aroused the enthusiasm of the people. On the other hand, however, China's socialist reform still has long way to go in that the basic socialist economic-political system and its corresponding economic-political system needs to be further improved; at the same time, even if the basic socialist economic-political system and its corresponding economic-political system be in place, with the development of social productivity and society, new inconformity and imperfection will emerge. Therefore, the contradictions of both conformity and inconformity between socialist economic base and superstructure and between the relations of production and productivity will exist for a long time, and the basic contradictions in socialist society are impossible to disappear. In the present stage of our society, the basic social contradictions are manifested as the inconformity of specific form of relations of production, i. e., the economic structure with the development of productivity, and inconformity of the concrete form of superstructure, i. e., the political structure with the economic base. In the current stage, the feature of relationship between the productive forces and relations of production and between superstructure and economic base is that conformity and inconformity coexist, and there are certain non-antagonistic contradictions on the premise of basic conformity. This determines that, there are no antagonistic contradictions and conflicts among the people, and the basic contradictions largely and mainly manifest themselves as contradictions among the people.

Third, at the current stage, the principal contradiction determines that largely, frequently and prominently manifest themselves as contradictions among the people.

In the whole system of contradiction in socialist society, basic social contradictions are at the first level, while the principal contradiction is at the second level. Principal contradiction here refers to the contradiction that plays the dominant and leading role in the complex course of social development (not exclusively concerning human relations) at a certain stage of a certain form of society. It is pointed out in the Report to the Thirteenth National Congress of the CPC that, the principal contradiction in our society is one between the ever-growing material and cultural needs of the people and the backwardness of social production. As to human relations specifically, at the primary stage of socialism, this principal contradiction mainly manifest themselves as contradictions among the people: on the one hand, the relatively backward social production can only provide a limited material and cultural wealth; on the other, the material and cultural needs of the people are ever growing, which cannot be met by the limited production. This gives rise to the extraordinary prominence of the contradictions in interest distribution. The principal contradiction at the primary stage of socialism determines that contradictions among the people occupy the dominant position in the system of contradictions in human relations.

Fourth, in the new conditions of socialist reform and opening up and the process of shifting towards socialist market economy, the transformation of the old structures to the new ones and the change of pattern of interest distribution determines that contradictions among the people are extraordinarily complex.

Reform and opening up, while having boosted the economy and improved people' life, also made the interest contradictions among the people more outstanding and widespread, because the diverse forms of ownership and modes of distribution made the differences and contradictions among different interest groups bigger. The development of the market economy makes the economic relations become more complicated, patterns of distribution more diversified and social contradictions multi-tiered. Contradictions in economic area in turn give rise to contradictions in political and intellectual areas. And changes in economic, political and intellectual areas all together make human relations among the people more complicated, which add new forms and content to contradictions among the people.

The above factors determines that, in the new historical period, contradictions among the people become more complex, more diversified and more outstanding, and become the theme of the political life of our socialist country.

In social life, contradictory phenomena of society will be manifested through behaviors of men as the subjects of social life in contradictions of human relations. In a society of class antagonism, basic social contradictions are manifested as class struggle. The fundamental driving force of the development in a class society is class struggle, and its locomotive of social development is social revolution. In a socialist country, what, then, is the direct driving force of social development in place of class struggle? It is no other than contradictions among the people. In a socialist country, productive forces basically conform to production relations, so do superstructure to economic base. But there are also some contradictions and inconformity between them, which manifest themselves as contradictions among the people, or as struggles and contradictions between advanced and backward, between right and wrong within the ranks of the people. Production competition and labor emulation in economic area, competitions between different ownerships in socialist market economy, competitions within the economic area, make the socialist economy full of vitality and constantly move forward. Political contradictions and contradictions in thinking among the people are mainly manifested as the contradictions between advanced and backward and between right and wrong. For instance, struggle of the people against bureaucracy and corruption that run counter to the interests of the people, struggle for overcoming backward phenomena within themselves through criticism and self-criticism, etc. Generally speaking, thc advanced elements of the people and the right ideas, the true, the good and the beautiful things among the people reflect and represent the interests of the people and are in accordance with and contribute to the development of social productive forces. On the contrary, the backward elements and erroneous ideas and ugly things among the people are against people's interests and thus are detrimental to the development of social productive forces. When some links in the socialist economic base and superstructure that do not fit and hinder the development of social productive forces, the advanced elements within the ranks of the people, who represent the fundamental interests of the society, will mobilize, persuade and lead the people in carrying out socialist reform. In the course of reform, struggles between advanced and backward and between right and wrong are unavoidable. It is precisely these struggles that push forward the cause of socialist reform. So, we say that contradictions among the people constitute the direct driving force promoting the advance of socialism. In socialist countries, especially in the primary stage of socialism, class struggle will continue to exist within certain limits. Revolutionary class struggle is necessary for defeating the decadent and backward social factors and remnants of the old society, and also is one of the motive forces promoting the progress of China's society. But compared with the position of contradictions among the people, it is secondary, and along with the development of socialism, its historical role will keep declining until it ultimately disappeared.

In the new historical conditions of socialist reformand opening up, particularly in the reform towards socialist market economy, the content and forms of contradictions among the people are much more complex than when our party first raised this issue. Many economic, political and interest relationships need to be adjusted and many new contradictions will arise. The whole Party must attach great importance to, earnestly study and properly handle various contradictions among the people, so as to mobilize the enthusiasm of the people and to accelerate reform and opening up in order to complete the building of a moderately prosperous society in all respects and a strong socialist country.

Chapter 4

Correctly Understanding and Handling Interest Contradictions among the People in the New Era

Contradictions of human relationsconstitute the main part of contradictions among the people at this stage in our society, while interest contradictions are the root cause of all other contradictions among the people. So correctly understanding and handling interest contradictions among the people is the key to the handling of contradictions among the people in general.

I. Interest contradictions are the material and economic causes of emergence and change of contradictions among the people

InOn the Correct Handling of Contradictions among the People, in addition to analyzing political and ideological contradictions among the people and methods for resolving them, Comrade Mao Zedong also talks about various interest contradictions. But due to the limitations of historical conditions, he didn't pay enough attention to economic causes of contradictions among the people in his analysis. In fact, interest contradictions are the material and the economic causes of and factors affecting the development of various contradictions among the people. Only by making in-depth analysis from material aspect can interest contradictions among the people be correctly understood and handled. And only by profoundly understanding the interest contradictions among the people can contradictions among the people in general be correctly understood and handled.

To correctly understand the interest contradictions among the people, we must firstof all have a clear understanding of what interests are. To understand interests, we must first get a clear understanding what need is. What is need? Marx and Engels pointed out: "Life involves before everything else eating and drinking, a habitation, clothing and many other things. The first historical act is thus the production of the means to satisfy these needs, the production of material life itself."① That is to say,

① *Selected Works of Marx and Engels*, vol. 1, People's Publishing House, 1995, p. 79.

needs are the expression and inexorable requirements of human life activities, which lead to the first historical activity of man—production. The essence of man's needs his objective dependency on conditions for material and intellectual life, which are manifested as his initiative orientation toward and pursuit of the objects on which his material and intellectual needs depend. It reflects the desire of man as subject of needs for social conditions of life as the object of needs, and are the internalization of the initiatives of the subjects toward the objects (the external world). Needs can be divided into conscious part and unconscious part, such as instinct of love. The content of needs is objective, but their forms are subjective. Needs are the internal motivation of man's historical activities and the basic driving force for the development of social production. Nothing but human social needs constitute the basis of interests.

Human needs themselves are not interests, and distinctions should be made between them. The differences between needs and interests are: Firstly, needs reflect man's direct desires for the objects, while interests are higher-level and rational desires of man for objects, reflecting his rational concern, interest and understanding of objects of needs. Secondly, needs are directly manifested as the dependency of the subjects of needs on objects of needs; while interests, through these dependency, manifest themselves as the relationship originated in the subjects' direct desires for the objects, that is, as the distributive relationship between man and the objects of needs. Therefore, needs represent the direct dependency of man on the objects of needs. For needs to be transformed into interests, role of the relations of production is indispensable. In a specific social form, human needs are manifested as interests in certain economic relations, which are the reflection of needs in economic relations. Interests cannot be understood outside real socio-economic relations. Man's need for food, for example, is his most fundamental material need. But to fulfill this need, he must first of all own the means of production, and then through certain form of social distribution to get it. So, man's needs for material conditions of production and for materials are manifested as the interest relationship between human beings. From this we can see that, the direct needs of human beings for objects are manifested, through the intermediary of economic relations, as interest relationship between them. The social essence of interests is a kind of social and economic relationship. In the primary stage of socialism, especially in the process of reform toward the socialist market economy, the realistic social and economic conditions determine that there exist various complex interest contradictions within the ranks of the people.

First, in the primary stage of socialism, the less developed market economy and relatively backward productive forces make the relative insufficiency of people's living materials, resulting in further prominence of interest contradictions among the people in distribution. Ours is a primary stage socialist country built on a basis of relatively backward material conditions, whose limited production of material means of life can not fully meet the needs of the people; on the other hand, the politically and economically liberated working people are in an urgent need of greater improvement of living conditions both in the material and cultural living conditions. In these circumstances, if the distribution is unreasonable, the interest contradictions among the people will become more outstanding.

Second, in the primary stage of socialism, the diverse forms of ownership determine that the interest contradictions among the people are also diverse. In this stage, along with public economic sector, there are also individual or private as well as other forms of economic sectors, such as the mixed ownership, joint ventures, share-holding enterprises. This determines the variety of interest contradictions among the people. For example, contradictions between workers in the public sectors and individual laborers and managers or employers in private sectors, contradictions between employers and employees in private enterprises, contradictions between individual laborers and private managers on the one side and the consumers on the other, etc. Under socialist conditions, the individual laborers are self-employed workers, whose productive activities are not exploitative, and whose existence is an integral part of the economy of primary stage of socialism. In general, interest contradictions between individual producers or traders and workers in public enterprises are non-antagonistic. However, because the means of production and products of labor in the individual sector of the economy are privately owned by individuals, and individual economy represents the personal interests of the individual workers, it in some degree is contradictory to the state interests of socialist country as a whole. In the primary stage of socialism, individual economy is a component of the whole economy, and its existence and development is helpful for economic growth, for creating job opportunities, for invigorating the market, and for better meeting the various needs of the people. But it must be seen that the private economy will inevitably has its negative sides. Firstly, the nature of its employment determines that the relations between the employers and employees are that of wage-labor. Secondly, because of its private nature, it is possible that, driven by profit-seeking, private economy may engage in profiteering activities that can disrupt the market and harm the overall and long-term economic interests of socialism. Within sector of the private economy itself, there are interest contradictions between the employees and employers; interest contradictions among different entities, and interest contradictions between the private economy and the state-owned economy.

Third, the diversity ofrealization of economic interests in the primary stage of socialism further exacerbates the interest contradictions among the people. The diverse forms of ownership determine the diversity of its distribution forms. In this stage, in addition to distribution according to work as the main form of distribution, there are also other distribution forms. For example, there is distribution according to needs in form of social welfare, distribution according to production factors in form of unearned income, and so on. This determines that, interest contradictions exist among the state, the collective and the individuals; among groups of different incomes; between employers and employees. The diverse forms of distribution determine the complexity of forms of interest realization, and make the interest contradictions among the people more complicated.

Fourth, the complicated economic relations in the primary stage of socialist market economy determine the existence of intricate contradictions of economic interests among the people. For example, in this stage, the public economy as themainstay coexists with non-public sectors of the economy. This structure determines that there exist interest contradictions reflecting these economic relations. In the relations of market economy in this stage, the intertwined contradictions between the social labor of the public sector of the economy and individual labor, and that between the social labor of the non-public sectors of the economy and individual labor leads to the extreme complexity of contradictions among the people. Other interest contradictions include those in resources allocation, market segmentation, those among commodity producers, those between commodity producers and business operators in the circulation links, and those between the producers and operators on the one side and the direct consumers on the other. All these intricate interest contradictions determine the existence of complexity and development of interest contradictions among the people.

Fifth, in the primary stage of socialism, there are still remnants of the old economic base, old superstructure and old social elements, making the interest contradictions among the people interweave with those between the people and the enemy. This contributes to the acuteness of the interest contradictions in this stage.

The existing remnants of old economic base and superstructure and their negative impact on interest contradictions in the primary stage of socialism makes it possible that non-antagonistic interest contradictions become antagonistic. Meanwhile, due to historical, realistic and international and other reasons, there are still hostile elements, new-born hostile elements, secret agents, counter-revolutionaries, etc., who represent the private interests of a small group of the old exploiting classes and the anti-socialist forces. Their contradictions with the people are of antagonistic nature, which sometimes take the forms of fierce class struggles. The interweaving of these two interest contradictions of different nature is bound to make the interest contradictions among the people more acute, more intricate and more difficult to be correctly handled with.

Sixth, the specific forms of economic base of primary stage of socialism are immature and unsound, so are its specific forms of superstructure. This makes the interest contradictions among the people more outstanding. In this stage, socialist public ownership is not a public ownership in complete sense in that there are differences as well as contradictions between state-owned economy and collective economy, and the relative independence of different economic entities must also be recognized. In this stage, due to the relative low level of market economy and unbalanced development, there are tremendous differences between the state-owned economy and collectively economy in terms of possession of means of production, sale conditions, quality of workers, environment of profitability, etc., which exacerbate the existing interest contradictions. From the point view of counter reaction of superstructure on economic base, the immatureness of the superstructure, especially the drawbacks and defects in political field in the primary stage of socialism, aggravate the already outstanding interest contradictions. For instance, when the interests of the people are seriously damaged by the bureaucratic style of work, the people cannot effectively stop it immediately due to the unsoundness of the socialist democracy. In this case, contradictions among the people can change into fierce conflicts of interests.

Seventh, the relative low level of cultural and moral standards in the primary stage of socialism aggravates the existing differences of interests and contradictions among the people. In China's primary stage of socialism, people's ideological, moral and cultural standards are not high enough, which adds to the acuteness of interest contradictions among the people.

In summary, after the establishment of the socialist system in China, the deep-seated and complex economic, political, cultural, ethical causes in the primary stage of socialism determine that, in the different classes, strata and interest groups, contradictions exist not only among individuals or specific interests, but also between individuals or specific interests and the common interests of the whole society. Interest contradictions among the people are the root causes of existence and development of contradictions among the people.

II. The Position, Forms, Nature and Features of Interest Contradictions among the People

Contradictions among the people constitute a complex system composed of many contradictions, including contradictions between ethnic groups, contradictions between regions, contradictions among collective units, contradictions between enterprises, contradictions within the ranks of the working class, contradictions within the farmer class, contradictions within the intelligentsia, contradictions within individual labors, contradiction within private economic operators, contradictions between the working class on the one hand and the farmer class and other working classes on the other, contradictions between the governing party and the government on the one hand and the people on the other, contradictions between the leadership and the masses, contradictions between the higher levels and lower levels, contradictions between Party and non-Party, contradictions within the Party, contradictions among the state, the collectives and the individuals, contradictions among individuals, contradictions among social strata, contradiction among interest groups, and so on. These contradictions are manifested in economic, political, ideological and other fields, among which, the interest contradictions among the people are the material and economic roots of the emergence, existence, development and intensification of all other contradictions among the people, and are the dominant type of contradictions constraining the development of other types of contradictions.

In contemporary China, although the social system for the existence of antagonistic interest contradictions among classes is abolished after the establishment of socialist system, the remnants of the old relations of production and the old division of labor remain, and in particular, there are different forms of ownerships. Therefore, there are still interest contradictions of non-class antagonism nature within the ranks of the people. In the primary stage of socialism, the existence of remnants of the old society and anti-socialist elements determines that some the interest contradictions among the people are inevitably antagonistic, but this type of contradictions is not in the dominant position.

Althoughinterest contradictions exist both in societies of class exploitation and socialist society, the interest contradictions among the people in the primary stage of socialism in China are distinctive in features.

First of all, the nature of the interest contradictions is different. The interest contradictions in societies of class exploitation are class antagonism in nature, while those in the primary stage of socialism are non-antagonistic because of fundamental identity of interests of the people. Here "fundamental identity" means that, in the primary stage of socialism, every member of the working people have the same status in possessing the means of production and in realizing their own interests through their own labor. So there is no fundamental antagonistic interest contradiction among them; on the contrary, they have the same interest aspirations and sources, therefore, these contradictions exist only within the ranks of the people. In this stage of socialism, the interest contradictions between the employers and employees within the non-public sectors of the economy are also different from those between the exploiting and the exploited classes in the old society, for they usually are non-antagonistic in nature either because of their subjection to the restrictions of socialist system. The fundamental identity of interests of the people determines that, the interest contradictions among the people are non-antagonistic. Here non-antagonism refers to its nature, in that neither of the two contradictory sides take completely negating or excluding the other side as the necessary conditions for proving or realizing its own interests. That is to say, fundamentally and generally speaking, these contradictions are non-antagonistic, although it does not exclude the possibility of local or temporary conflicts between them.

Secondly, the interest contradictions are manifested in different areas. In a society of class exploitation, interest contradictions are outstanding already in production. In the process of capitalist production, through their ownership of and control over the means of production, the capitalists appropriate or occupy the fruits of labor of the workers, whose amount of labor is in inverse proportion to the amount of material interests their gained, suggesting that in capitalist society, interest contradictions occur already in the process of production. In the socialist society, in contrast, because the social basis of class exploitation and opposition is basically eliminated, workers in the production area are working for themselves, for their own interests and for the overall interests of society that are closely related to their own interests, and there is no interest relations of class opposition among the workers or between the workers and the managers. Therefore, in the primary stage of socialism, the interest contradictions among workers are mainly manifested in distribution. This is because the system of distribution according to work brings about the de facto differences of distribution, which in turn results in the differences of distribution of means of subsistence and production.

Thirdly, the methods of solving interest contradictions are different. In the primary stage of socialism, the non-antagonistic natureof interest contradictions among the people determines that, in resolving these contradictions, as precondition, we can neither change socialist economic or political system nor eliminate or negate any side of the contradictions. In short, these contradictions cannot be solved through social revolution or by force. Instead, they can only be resolved through the self-improvement and self-reform of socialist system, through the establishment of appropriate economic and political structures, and through the development of productive forces, that is say, through socialist system itself, by economic means, political and ideological work, criticism and self-criticism, and by adjustment and coordination of interests.

Apart from the above mentioned features, in the current period of the primary stage of socialism in China, the interest contradictions among the people also show the following new developments.

First, the interest contradictions among the people are more outstanding. In the primary stage of socialism, due to the backwardness of productive forces and the underdevelopment of commodity economy, as well as the shortage of material wealth, the material means of livelihood are far from enough; in addition, our distribution policy and social security system are not reasonable or sound enough, making interest contradictions among the people more acute and sharper.

Second, contradictions among the people mostly and frequently occur in distribution and mainly manifested in income gaps and contradictions by it. This is because the diversity of forms of ownership and modes of distribution as well as the shortcomings of the current institutions and policies highlight the income gaps among the people.

Third, interest contradictions among the people often find expression in forms of direct conflicts, which, if not handled properly, can invite a certain degree of social unrest. In the primary stage of socialism, contradictions among the people often find expression of face to face conflicts. For example, some people may take way of direct confrontation, such as strike, collective petition, demonstration, assault on government bodies because of dissatisfactions arising from housing, wages, prices, land demolition etc. ; and among the masses, fierce disputes, even violent conflicts, may occur because of property disputes, asset allocation, land use and other. If they are not properly handled, these problems may lead to greater social unrest, affecting the political stability of socialist society.

Fourth, interest contradictions among the people often find their expression in the cadre-mass relations. A considerable section of the masses make the direct local or unit leaders as targets in expressing their grievances or in conflicts.

Fifth, boundaries of groups between the contradictory sides are clear-cut in interest contradictions among the people. In the primary stage of socialism, the interest groups within the ranks of the people show acomplex pattern. The boundaries between groups, the interest demands of different groups and the contradictions among them are all clear-cut.

Inreal social life, the interest contradictions among the people in human relations in China are manifested as follows:

First, interest contradictions between all workers and a section of workers and those between different sections of workers. State interests represent the interests of all workers, while enterprises and groups represent the interests of some sections of workers. Therefore, contradictions between state interests and group interests are directly manifested as contradictions between all workers and some sections of the workers. Different enterprises and different groups, respectively representing the interests of their own, request the increment of their interests. So the contradictions between the interests groups are directly manifested as interest contradictions among different sections of the workers. Since in the primary stage of socialism, we must recognize and respect the personal interests of the workers, interest contradictions will occur among individual workers due to the differences of their interests.

Second, interest contradictions between leaders, administrators on theone side and the ordinary people on the other. In the primary stage of socialism, Party and government leading cadres and administrative personnel at all levels and all economic units, are the representatives of state or collective interests. They decide the orientation of state or collective interests through exercising administrative or operational power. In this context, the interest contradictions among the people are manifested as contradictions between the leading cadres or administrators at the higher level and those at the lower level, between different levels of leaders and administrators, and between leaders and administrators at different levels on the one side and the workers on the other. The interest contradictions between leaders and administrators at different levels on the one side and the workers on the other has two implications: one is that, the leaders and administrators are not the subject of their own interests but as representatives of the state or collective interests, so their contradictions with the ordinary workers are those among the state, the collectives the individuals; the other is that, the leaders and administrators also have their own individual interests, so the interest contradictions between them as subjects of individual interests and the working people, belong to, in fact, contradictions of individual interests. So if a leader or administrator imposes unreasonable personal interest demands on the overall interests, it will be in contradiction to the interests of the masses and other leaders or administrators who uphold the overall interests.

Third, interest contradictions between operators in non-public sectors of the economy such as private economy and individual economy on the one side and the state leaders, administrators and workers in public economy on the other side; interest contradictions between laborers in non-public economy and workers in state-owned and collective economy; and interest contradictions within the operators of non-public economy. Under socialist conditions, the non-public sectors of the economy and state-owned and collective economy come under different types of ownership, there will certainly exist interest differences between the operators of the former and the leaders, administrators and workers in the latter. And because of the differences of income distribution between the laborers in the former and those in the latter, there will also exist interest contradictions between them. And there will be interest contradictions among the different operators of non-public economy because the law of the market economy. On the other hand, the operators of the non-public economies, including the private economy and individual economy as integral components of the economy of the primary stage of socialism, are also citizens of the country. Therefore, there are certain interest contradictions between them and the state leaders and administrators.

Fourth, the ongoing reformtoward the socialist market economy has given rise to some new situations in the contradictions among the people. Firstly, the reform, on the one hand has made the socialist economy more vigorous, on the other, it has made the interest contradictions among the people more outstanding. The reform of state-owned enterprises is a good example of it. By plunging the enterprises to compete in the market, it has mobilized the initiatives of them and made them establish broader horizontal economic links, but at the same time it has made the social and economic relationships more complicated, in which the enterprises may focus only on their own performances and profits so that the contradictions in the production and distribution links become more obvious and intricate. Another example is the market. The gradual emergence of various kinds of market as the mechanism of economic regulators, while invigorating the socialist economy, makes the socialist market relations and contradictions become more complex. Secondly, the socialist economic reform requires the corresponding political reform. As a result, the various relationships and contradictions in political life, including the handling of relationship between the government and the Party, between the government and enterprises, between central and local governments, etc., become more outstanding than ever before. Thirdly, the market-oriented economic reform has profoundly changed people's ideas as well as the structure of human relations, making relations among the people more complex and multi-leveled. In short, our reform toward socialist market economy has brought about profound changes in our social life and thus given new content and forms to interest contradictions among the people.

Because of the combined interaction between the domestic and foreign factors, interest contradictions among the people often interweave with contradictions between ourselves and the enemy and with class struggle existing in certain limits, making the interest contradictions among the people find intricate expressions.

III. Different Subjects of Interests, Different Interest Groups, and Contradictions among Them

Interest contradictions among the people unfold themselves as the contradictions among different subjects and different interest groups.

Subjects of interests refer to those who engage in production and other social activities in certain economic conditions and bearers, pursuers, realizers and receivers of interests. Subjects of interests can basically be divided into two major levels: individuals and groups. Only through certain social relations can individuals realize their own interests, because an interest group have more advantages in pursuing and safeguarding the interests of their members and is far more competitive and powerful in facing up conflicts of and struggles for interests; individuals usually participate in interest competition and realization by identifying themselves with interest groups. Interest groups refer to groups based on certain social conditions and consisted of individuals having similar interest demands and attitudes. Different interest groups have different and even conflicting interest demands, and contradictions among them constitute the mainstream of social interest contradictions.

The concept of "interest group" varies in content in different period of history. The earliest interest groups of human beings were primitive communities formed on blood relationship and habitat, such as clans, tribes or tribal confederacies. With the development of social division of labor and private ownership, society was divided into classes, which further subdivided into different social strata. Classes and social strata are the most stable interest groups in class society. And based on common interest demands, larger interest groups are formed among these classes, strata and interest groups through horizontal social relationship, such as families, nations, economic entities (enterprises, consortia, companies, etc.), states, international organizations (like Association of South East Asian Nations, European Union, etc.). In the broad sense, interest groups refer to all interest communities including classes, strata, ethnic groups, economic entities. In the narrow sense, interest groups refer to interest communities smaller than classes and strata. In socialist countries, the exploiting classes as such have been eliminated, with class contradictions demoting to a secondary place. So it is extremely significant to properly understand and handle contradictions among different interest groups on the premise of properly identifying classes and strata.

Under socialist system, the contradictory relationship among individuals, collectives and the state as interest subjects are vertically linked. Individuals are the subjects of individual interests that can be divided from different angles: from the angle of ownership, they can be divided into individual interests of workers in state-owned economy, farmers in collective economy, workers in mixed economy, workers in individual economy, workers in private sector of the economy, etc.; from the angle of division of labor or occupation, they can be divided into individual interests of the manual workers, mental workers, teachers, civil servants etc.; from the angle of employment, they can be divided into individual interests of the employed workers, the unemployed, the retirees, etc. A collective is the subject of the common interests of its members. Households, enterprises, government and public bodies, regions, social groups, social strata, classes, ethnic groups, etc., are all communities of certain interests. In a socialist country, households are not only consumption but also production and other business units (such as individual commercial households, specialized households, contract households, etc., in rural areas), and the interests of households as the main undertakers of economic and consumption interests have direct bearing on the individual interests of their members. In socialist economic activities, households are links as well as intermediaries between the interests of individuals and the state. The economic interests of collectives of enterprises in a socialist country can also be divided from different angles: the interests of state-owned enterprises, the interests of collectively owned enterprises, the interests of limited liability companies, the interests of different sectors of production in state-owned enterprises, and so on. In a socialist country, each government department, each public institution and each region also has its own relatively independent common interests. So do different social groups, strata, ethnic groups, such as the common interests of the intelligentsia, the farmer class, the working class, etc. In socialist economic life, enterprises (including state-owned, collective-owned, mixed-owned and private-owned enterprises), as the economic entities and the elementary cells with relatively independent status in socialist market economy, are collectives with most salient economic significance. They are at a higher place in terms of economic interests relative to individuals or households, and clearer economic interests relative to units, regions, classes, strata and ethnic groups in a socialist country.

Due to various social and historical causes, under the condition of the socialist market economy, there exist differences, economic differences in particular, among individuals and collectives (ethnic groups, classes, strata, regions, enterprises, departments and units) , which will necessarily give rise to horizontal contradictory relationship among them. For instance, because of differences of income and economic status and treatment, there exist certain economic differences and interest contradictions in public-owned enterprise between the managers and workers, between engineering and technical personnel and manual workers, among engineering and technical personnel themselves, and among manual workers themselves; so do among workers in different working positions (such as between cadres and ordinary workers, between intellectuals and manual workers, among soldiers, teachers, artists, sports workers, doctors, nurses, workers in service industries, etc.) Within socialist countries, differences and contradictions will emerge between ethnic groups and between regions due to differences in economic development; so do among working class, the farmer class, the intelligentsia, the newly emerged social strata, and among enterprises, sectors and units of different social division of labor due to economic conditions, environments and benefits.

All interest contradictions among the people, whether contradictions among interest individuals or among interest groups, or contradictions concerning vertical or horizontal interests, are closely around and subject to the main line of the contradiction between the common interests and specific interests of the society. The reasons are as follows: Firstly, the common interests of the society are the result of the interactions among its specific interests, with the two constituting the main relationship in the system of social interests. Secondly, any individual or specific interest is only a part of the common interests, with the functioning mechanism of the former on the constraint and influence of the latter. For example, if the nation is faced with a crisis, the contradictions between specific interests within the nation will relatively ease off and subject to the interests of the nation as a whole. Thirdly, the existence, development and resolution of horizontal contradictions among individual or specific interests is subject to and constrained by the existence, development and resolution of the contradiction between the specific interest and common interests. Fourthly, the contradiction between the common interests and the specific interests can exist at all levels of their realization. There are contradictions between common interests and specific interests within an enterprise; similarly, in the enterprise at a higher level, there are also similar contradictions between the specific interests (such as interests of constituent corporations, etc.) and common interests (such as parent company), and so on. Relative to national common interests, collective interests, group interests, and individual interests are specific interests; likewise, individual interests are specific interests relative to collective interests. Contradictions between specific interests and common interests, as a universal type of contradiction, exist at all levels and sectors of social life.

The contradiction between specific interests and common interestsspecifically demonstrate itself as follows:

First, the contradiction between long-term interests and immediate interests. An example is the contradiction between production and need. Their relationship is unity of opposites: the purpose of production is to meet the needs of the people; to meet the growing needs of the people requires the development of production, which, in turn requires that, rather than eating and dividing everything up, we must proportionately restrict the immediate needs of the people, in order to appropriately expand reproduction. This will give rise to the contradiction between developing production and meeting the needs of the people, which is highlighted in the ratio between accumulation and consumption. Over-emphasis on consumption will only lead to the impediment of expansion of reproduction and exhaustion of resources; on the other hand, if stress is placed only on accumulation, the interests and enthusiasm of the consumers will be damaged, which in turn will affect accumulation in the long run. Only by appropriately balancing the relationship between accumulation and consumption can the contradiction between production and needs be properly resolved. For by expanding production through proper accumulation, the needs of the people can be better met, and the expansion of consumption will promote the development of production. If we consume everything up without restraint in a short-sighted manner, the long-tern interests of the people will be jeopardized. On the other side, if we focus only on production and accumulation by neglecting the needs of the people and consumption, the enthusiasm of the people will be affected. Relative to collectives and individuals, the interests of the state represent the common and long-term interests. So the state should both uphold the fundamental interests and pay attention to the immediate interests of the people, so that they can consider the long-term interests while enjoying the immediate ones. The contradiction between the common interests and specific interests in socialist countries is inevitably expressed as the contradiction between long-term interests and immediate interests.

Second, the contradiction between local interests and overall interests. Common interests refer to the overall or entire interests of all the members in a social community (enterprise, ethnic group, stratum, class, state, etc.); the interests of any part or member in a community fall into the category of local or individual interests of specific individuals or collectives. Relative to collectives and individuals, the state represents the overall interests; while relative to individuals, the collectives represent the overall interests. The contradiction between local interests and overall interests is mainly reflected on the relationship among the individuals, the collectives and the state. In the economic life of socialist countries, the relationship between the state and the enterprises constitute the main line of the contradictory relationship between the overall interests and the local interests. In a socialist country, the state represents the fundamental interests of the people and entire society, while enterprises, as the elementary cells of economic life of the state, are subordinate to the state. Enterprises as a part of the state must take the overall interests of the state into consideration and fulfill the tasks assigned by the state. At the same time, as relatively independent economic entities, they should have their own independence to fully display their own initiatives. The overall situation cannot be active without the initiatives of the locals. Thus the contradiction between the common interests and specific interests in a socialist country finds their expression in the contradictions between the overall interests and the local (or specific) interests.

Third, the contradiction between the gained interests and future interests. A gained interest refers to any interest that has been obtained or realized; any interest that needs yet to be obtained or realized after certain efforts is future interest. These two kinds of interests are both united and contradictory. The unity of them lies in the fact that, the gained interests are the premise and basis for the realization and accomplishment of future interests, and there will be no future interests without the gained interests. In a class society, gained interests and future interests are completely separated from and antagonistic to each other, whose contradiction is demonstrated as class contradictions. Under socialist conditions, productive forces basically conform to relations of production and the interests of the people are fundamentally identical. This determines that the gained and future interests of the people are identical. But because of the differences of interests and the interest groups, there are also some discrepancy and contradictions between them, which are specifically manifested in the following: some people abandon the future interests of the society for their gained interest; some leaders seek special interests by abusing power. Both are in conflicted with the fundamental and long-term interests of the people. The contradiction between socialist common interests and special interests will inevitably find their expressions mostly in the contradiction of gained interests and future interests.

IV. Measures for Handling Interest Contradictions among the People

To correctly handle interest contradictions among the people, we first of all must analyze the nature ofthe contradictions to distinguish contradictions among the people from contradictions between ourselves and the enemy, and accordingly to properly handle them in different ways. In his On the Correct Handling of Contradictions among the People, Comrade Mao Zedong proposed the use of economic measures to address interest contradictions among the people. In 1979, Comrade Deng Xiaoping pointed out: "We must adjust the relations between this various types of interests in accordance with the principle of taking them all into proper consideration. Were we to do the opposite and pursue personal, local or immediate interests at the expense of the others, both sets of interests would inevitably suffer."① Economic approach serves as the major method for solving interest contradictions among the people, and "make overall plans and take all factors into consideration" on the basis of "care for personal interests" are the two fundamental principles in handling interest contradictions among the people.

Not directly relying on enthusiasm, but aided by the enthusiasm engendered by the great revolution, and on the basis of personal interest, personal incentive and business principles, we must first set to work in this small peasant country to build solid gangways to socialism by way of state capitalism. "Care for personal interests" is an important principle in correctly handling interest contradictions among the people. Lenin once explicitly pointed out that "Personal incentives can step up production." And socialist construction cannot "directly relying on enthusiasm," but on the basis of personal interest, personal incentive and business principles. "Otherwise we shall never get to communism, we shall never bring scores of millions of people to communism." "We must not count on going straight to communism. We must build on the basis of peasants' personal incentive." "We say that every important branch of the economy must be built up on the principle of personal incentive. There must be collective discussion, but individual responsibility. At every step we suffer from our inability to apply this principle."② After the victory of the socialist revolution, the basic interest contradictions of society are no longer those between the exploiting and the exploited classes, but rather the non-antagonistic ones among the individuals and groups within the ranks of the people. The realistic interest demand of the people is no longer to get rid of their exploited and oppressed social status, but to improve their material and cultural life. Under these new conditions, we should mobilize the enthusiasm of the people by giving full play to their concern about their material interests to build socialism in the process of constantly meet their material interests and demands. In the primary stage of socialism, affirmation of people's concern over their interests means the affirmation of their concern over the outcome of their labor. By doing so, people's pursuit of personal interests can be channeled into the

---

① *Selected Works of Deng Xiaoping*, vol. 2, People's Publishing House, 1994, pp. 175 – 176.

② *Collected Works of Lenin*, vol. 42, People's Publishing House, 1987, pp. 176, 190 – 191.

direction of increasing income through work. This can both promote the development of socialist economy and help resolve the interest contradictions among the people.

First, establishing a primary stage socialist political-social system that conforms to the complex interest pattern, can give full play to the impetus of interests and can arouse the enthusiasm of different interest groups. Interest relations, in fact, are no other than the relations among the interest subjects. The reasonable and specific interests of each individual laborer and each interest group, which are the motives for their work, should be taken into full account. On the other hand, however, the specific and individual interests of each group and individual must be subordinated to interests of the state as a whole, because specific interests without constraints will have a negative impact on the society. In the primary stage of socialist market economy, we must take into full account of the interests of the individual, the collective and the state. At the same time, we must also take full consideration of the interests of all the subjects of different sectors of the economy, on this basis, to establish a distribution system with diverse forms and correct policies of distribution, and an effective macro regulation system to take full advantage of the market mechanism. The complexity of interest groups in society will inevitably lead to the complexity and diversity in ideological and political fields. This requires that we should further improve socialist democracy at the primary stage of socialism, improve Party leadership, strengthen socialist legal system, expand the scope and channel of all strata of society to participate in political activities, in order to effectively carry out the ideological and intellectual work in all aspects and at all levels. Therefore, we should build an effective social, economic and political system in which the interests of all groups can be properly taken into consideration and all the people can joint hands to give full play to their enthusiasm.

Second, maintaining a good socialist market order so as to create a competitive environment that can provide fair and equal opportunities to all interest groups. In the market activities in the primary stage of socialism, all individuals and groups evaluate their economic performance by the returns the get, they all want to get a maximum income at minimum pay, which requires that the product of labor be distributed through the law of value of the market economy in its normal sense. But in the current economic life in China, the foundation of our market economy is relatively weak and the market is not mature enough and is full of loopholes, which provides opportunities for speculative activities, leading to the unreasonable interest distribution. This requires us to further regulate the economic order, develop a market economy and improve the market system with law as its safeguard, so as to maintain a good market order and provide a fair starting line for different interest groups.

Third, establishing a reasonable distribution system, forming a reasonable pattern of distribution and social structure. Both the interest distribution pattern of equalitarianism and disparity are not conducive to social stability and harmonious development. A "gourd-shaped" social structure of polarization nature is detrimental to social harmony. A harmonious society requires a reasonable social structure in two aspects:

One isa reasonable interest distribution structure. In the first place, we should ensure that every social member has the equal access to conditions and opportunities of interest competition, and attention should be paid not only on the fairness of results, but also on fairness of starting points, conditions and opportunities. People accept those who make their fortunes through honest business activities and hard work, but extremely hate the income gap and disparity caused by inequity of opportunities or injustice, especially gray income, illegal income, or income from corruption. So we should establish a good market order and distribution order, to provide for each member of society a fair starting line of competition and environment of interest competition. In the second place, we should ensure the equality of each social member in interest distribution. We should establish a rational distribution system, in which distribution according to work is primary and a variety of modes of distribution coexist and which is adaptable to the market economy and combines incentive, efficiency as well as a sound social security system.

The other isthe formation of a reasonable social structure comprising classes, strata and various interest groups. In line with the reasonable interest distribution pattern, we should increase the income of low-income group and expand the proportion of the medium-income earners, so as to form a social structure with common prosperity as the goal and both ends being small and the middle being large, that is, the middle class makes up the largest proportion in the population. In this structure, classes, strata and interest groups mutually benefit, that is, the increase of benefits of those in the higher position improve also the increase of those in a lower position rather than to the prejudice of each other's interests; in spite of differences, they cooperate together to promote their common prosperity with their enthusiasm being fully aroused; they open to each other, which means that every group has equal access to upward social mobility; and they share in the fruits of development.

Accordingly, we should establish an economic-socio system adaptable to the market economy in the primary stage of socialism that is conducive to the adjustment of interest relations among all sides, conducive to the mobilization of enthusiasm of different social members and conducive to strengthening social harmony and stability. In this stage, we must keep a good balance between individual, collective and national interests by fully taking into account of the interests of different social members, classes, strata and interest groups as well as various interest relations of the people, so as to form an institutional security that can balance the interest relations all sides, can mobilize their enthusiasm and promote their benefits.

Fourth, strengthening the study of different interest groups among the people, to base the settling of interest contradictions among the groups on scientific analyses. We must carry out in-depth research and wide survey to get a clear grasp of the interest groups within the ranks of the people, and get a full understanding of the conditions and causes of their formation, their sense of community and demands, the features of relations among the groups and the basic law governing the development of the contradictions, to formulate the correct measures for handling inter-group conflicts.

Fifth, comprehensively using policy, legal, ideological, cultural and moral measures and strengthening our education to properly coordinate and reasonably adjust relations and resolve contradictions among the interest groups. In the primary stage of socialism, there are considerably large interest differences among individuals and among interest groups within the ranks of the people. Some of these differences will produce negative influence on the society and mental imbalance of some groups, which will dampen their spirits, or exacerbate their negative consumption mentality and behavior of comparing with others, eventually leading to complaints, frictions even conflicts between groups. Although some of these phenomena are not unusual in the process of reform, some of the unreasonable differences, if not properly adjusted, will affect people's enthusiasm in the long run. Some reasonable differences should also be adjusted through measures of policy, laws, and intellectual and moral measures. We should develop and adopt proper economic and political policies, use such economic means as taxes and finance, take advantage of the political strength of our party and state and all kinds of administrative disciplinary measures, strengthen ideological and political work and the building of socialist political, material and cultural civilizations, to gradually alleviate and ultimately solve the interest problems, to ensure that our interest structure in the primary stage of socialism is always in the best state.

Chapter 5

Correctly Understand and Handle Ideological Contradictionsamong the People in the New Era

Economic and political contradictions among the people in socialist society will necessarily find their expression in ideological and cultural fields. In a socialist country, with the establishment of socialist economic and political systems, the principal contradiction is no longer confrontation of class interests or class struggle, and the fundamental economic and political interests of the people are identical, in spite of the existing differences and conflicts of classes. This determines that, the principal ideological contradiction among the people in socialist countries is the contradiction of right and wrong on the basis of fundamental identity of interests. At the present stage, the contradiction between right and wrong among the people is the dominant contradiction in ideological field needing our correct understanding and handling. This is an important part under the general subject of correct handling of ideological contradictions among the people.

I. Ideological Contradictions among the People and Their Roots

Socialideology is the reflection of the social process of people's material and spiritual life. It is the summation of views, ideas, cultures and theories about social life and social relationship formed in social practice and social mentality reflected in people's feelings, emotions, customs, and so on. Different from individual daily social consciousness reflecting individual things and the simple sum total of individual consciousness, social ideology is the ideology of a social class or group, and constrains the individual consciousness of the social class or group. It is the reflection of social being. The expressions of social ideology are diverse, including political ideology, legal thinking, ethics, culture, arts, science, philosophy, religion, and such social mentality as social feelings, emotions and customs, etc. Contradictions in social practice will inevitably be reflected in social ideology and social mentality, demonstrated as contradictions in the field of social ideology.

In a class society, social ideology, as the reflection of social being, has a class nature. The summation of a class's viewpoints ofpolitical ideology, legal thinking, ethics, culture, arts, science, philosophy, religion and others constitute the ideology of the class. The differences of people's class status and class interests determine the differences of their class consciousness, and their different, even the fundamentally antagonistic, ideologies. Class contradictions and class struggle in economic and political fields are bound to be manifested, through social consciousness, especially through social ideology, as class contradictions and class struggle in ideological and cultural fronts.

In the primary stage of socialism in China, in the ideological field, namely the ideological and cultural fronts, there exist two types of contradictiondiffering in nature: one is the contradiction and class struggle between the fundamentally antagonistic class interests andclass positions, that is, the contradiction and struggle between the socialist ideology of the working class and the decadent and backward ideology of the bourgeoisie and other exploiting classes; the other is the non-antagonistic differences and struggle among social members with fundamentallyidentical interests, that is, ideological contradictions among the working class, the laborers and all the social members who love socialism, love China and support the Party. In interpersonal relationship, these two types of contradiction of two fundamentally different natures are manifested respectively as ideological contradictions between ourselves and the enemy and as ideological contradictions among the people.

In China, the establishment of the socialist system marked the elimination of the exploiting class system in Chinese mainland. However, China is still in the primary stage of socialism with much economic, political, ideological and cultural remnants of the old society; internationally, there is still contest between socialism and capitalism; socialism is still under the international environment affected by capitalist economy, politics, military and culture, and overseas hostile elements have always been trying to restore capitalism in China through ideological penetration; in some of China's territories where socialist system has not yet been established, there are hostile elements who stubbornly oppose socialism and the CPC and who always hope to restore the old social order through "peaceful evolution" in the mainland of China; and internally there are still forces extremely hostile to socialism and representing either the overthrown or the newborn exploiting classes, who, in collusion with international hostile forces, make ideological contest with us by using every opportunity, including our mistakes, in an attempt to overthrow our socialist system.

In fact, ever since the establishment of socialism in China's mainland, the hostile forces at home and abroad have never given uptheir attempt to defeat the CPC and socialism and to restore capitalist system. Since China adopted the opening up policy in the 1980s, the international and domestic hostile forces have beentaking use of opportunity to open a breach by intensifying ideological infiltration and by making contests between socialist system and the exploiting systems and between the working class and the bourgeoisie. In short, in the primary stage of socialism, there always exists class struggle in our ideological field. In our country, we once exaggerated class struggle in the realm of ideology and confused the contradictions among the people with those between ourselves and the enemy thus launched a series of movements of class struggle, during which a large number of cadres and people suffered. That was completely wrong. In spite of it, we cannot ignore the objective existence of class struggle in ideological sphere, or fail to perceive the "peace evolution" conspiracy of the anti-socialist elements at home and abroad through ideological contest. The victory Chinese revolution after World War II had greatly changed the situation of the world; In 1950, John Foster Dulles explicitly declared a "war of ideology" against communism.

Class struggle in the realm of ideology first of all is saliently reflected in ideological and political aspects and the confrontation and struggle of viewpoints of political theories. Politically, the confrontation and struggle between adherence to the Four Cardinal Principles and the ideological trend in favour of bourgeois liberalization is the concentrated expression of contest and struggle between socialism and capitalism and between working class and bourgeoisie. A few people at home and abroad obstinately hold their viewpoints of bourgeois liberation, by using mass media, direct their spearhead at Marxism and Leninism, stigmatizing them as "out of date" and "propagated" theories; and they attack against China's socialist system as feudalism far worse than capitalism and attack against the CPC, intending to replace the theory of scientific socialism with the theory of capitalist democracy.

In the current primary stage of socialism in China, despite the existence of class struggle in the realm of ideology and contradictions between ourselves and the enemy, most of the ideological contradictions are still ideological and cultural contradictions of right and wrong among the people. The establishment of socialist system has eliminated the exploiting class as a whole. Along with it, class confrontation no longer exists and class struggle is no longer the principal contradiction. So does the classstruggle in the realm of ideology and the confrontation between ourselves and the enemy on the cultural and ideological fronts. The numerous and frequent contradictions in ideological and cultural fields are those right and wrong among the people.

Ideological and cultural contradictions among the people can be divided into two parts, one is those of the nature of class struggle and the other is those not. Within the ranks of the people, there is a part of the ideological and cultural contradictions that is of the nature of the class struggle, this is because:

First, China is in the primary stage of socialism, with many economic, political, ideological, and cultural remnants and vestiges of the old society, which will inevitably be reflected in people's minds and ideological realm. Therefore, this realm is full of ideological contradictions and struggles between the new, socialist and working class ideology and that of the old, capitalist and other exploiting classes. Compared with social existence and economic base, ideology is relatively independent, which is manifested not only in fact that changes in ideology lags behind changes in social existence, but also in the fact that advanced ideology can in varying degree foresee the trends of social existence, thus has predictability be forward looking to a certain extent. In general, ideology will ultimately change with the social existence, but the change is not immediate. Instead, it will keep its influence for a long time. Although the socialist revolution has eliminated the exploiting society, system and exploiting class as a whole, their ideology will continue to exist for a period, and the old traditions, ideology, culture and social mentality as a huge conservative force will exist for a long time. Since China is a country with a long history of feudalism, despite the protracted struggle led by the Party has completely eliminated the feudal system, the ideological and cultural legacy and backward customs of the feudal society will not disappear automatically with the change of society; therefore, to develop socialist ideology and culture, we must continuously criticize and overcome a variety of ideologies of exploiting classes and non- working class. Just because of this, the contradictions and struggles between the working class, socialist and new ideology with that of the exploiting class, capitalist and old society in the ideological field are bound to exist for a long time; so do the ideological contradictions of the nature of class struggle within the ranks of the people.

Second, as a socialist country, China is in an international circumstance where socialist and capitalist systems, and the working class and the exploited class ideologies coexist, so it will be inevitably affected by the ideologies of the bourgeoisie and other exploiting classes unavoidably spread in. The anti-socialist forces abroad and the forces outside Chinese mainland that are hostile to socialism are likely to take advantage of various opportunities to infiltrate the corrupt, backward ideas, ideologies and cultures into the country. Especially since the reform and opening up, the decadent ideology of the exploiting class come in along with it, resulted in existence of class struggle in the ideological and cultural fields in our socialist country. This class struggle will necessarily find their expression within the ranks of the people, making part of ideological and cultural struggle among the people is of the nature of the class struggle to a certain degree. For example, a few years ago some missionaries from the Holy See sent secret instructions to incite a few followers in coastal areas of China to be faithful to the "underground churches" of the Holy See and to conduct reactionary religious activities, challengingthe Chinese Patriotic Catholic Association. In the coastal areas only the underground churches had developed a large number of followers. The religious ideas with reactionary political attitudes spread by the underground churches are in opposition to the patriotic religious ideas, and antagonistic relationship with socialist thought is of the nature of class struggle. This opposition and struggle are manifested as the ideological and cultural contradictions with a nature of class struggle. Ideological contradictions among the people with a nature of class struggle represent the contradictions and struggle between the ideologies of the opposing classes. This kind of contradictions are mostly fall into the category of contradictions among the people, except for a few elements who politically stick to their reactionary stands to spread anti-Party and anti-socialist opinions or those who disseminate the capitalist poisonous ideas that corrupt our adolescents in conducting hooliganism or criminal activities.

In short, in the primary stage of socialism in our country, class struggle in the ideological field, though not being the principal contradiction, will exist for a long time. This struggle will necessarily find its expressions in the ideological and cultural exchanges within the people and determines the existence of ideological and cultural contradictions and struggles with the nature of the class struggle.

In the current socialist stage in China, there is another type of ideological and cultural contradictions among the people that are not of class struggle nature, which refers to the ideological and cultural conflicts or confrontations not representing fundamentally opposing class interests, class stands or class antagonism. This is because:

First, in the current stage of our society, due to complex economic reasons, there are different classes, strata and interest groups within the ranks of the people, which will bring about differences among them. These differences are bound to find their expressions in the ideological field and manifested themselves as the differences and contradictions among different interest subjects. For example, ethnic differences and cultural differences to some extent represent themselves as the ideological and cultural contradictions among the people.

Second, our reform toward socialist market economy makes the interest subjects in our society become diverse, which intensifies their interest consciousness and competition in economic and political activities. This has caused changes in people's conception of right or wrong, merits or demerits, gains or losses, noble orhumble and other values, and at the same time changed people's lifestyles, mentality, cultural activities, ways of thinking and ideas, resulting in the diversity and variety of social and cultural awareness and eventually the corresponding complexity and diversity of ideology and culture among the people.

Third, the existence of traditional and old ideas, moral standards and forces of habit determines the ideological and cultural contradictions and struggle between new and old, conservative and innovation, tradition and modern as well as progressive and backward among the people. The reform of the old and traditional system first of all is the impact on the old and traditional ideas. The contradictions between emancipation of minds and the renewal of ideas and conservatism and rigid thinking, and those between the "left" and right tendencies are frequent existence in the period of socialist reform and opening up.

Fourth, the differences of civilization level, cultural circumstance, social conditions, etc., will bring about the differences and contradictions in people's ideas, religions, social mentality, arts and culture, habits and other aspects. For example, between the Han and other ethnic groups, between ethnic groups themselves, even between different regions of the Han and between different communities within the same ethnic group, there are different customs, religious beliefs, cultural lives, and etc. The conflicts between different kinds of consciousness of ethnic groups will necessarily be manifested as the ideological and cultural conflicts among the people.

Fifth, both the nature and human society are complex, so do the subjective understanding of human beings either as individuals or as groups. This determines the existence of differences and contradictions in sciences and ideas between the people, between the masses and between different schools of thought. For example, in the field of social sciences, as to a particular social phenomenon, due to various objective and subjective differences, different scholars tend to have different understanding, which, reflected in academic point of view, will arise the disputes between different academic views, opinions, style, genres and schools, which belong to the differences and contradictions of thinking and understanding among the people, and are not class struggle in nature.

To sum up, ideological and cultural contradictions of not being class struggle in nature among the people numerously and frequently manifest themselves as the dominant contradictions in the realm of ideology.

Historical experience shows that, to correctly understand and handle ideological contradictions among the people is an important aspect under the general subject of correctly understanding and handling contradictions among the people. In this regard, we have both painful lessons and successful experience to learn from. On the one hand, within the socialist countries, the ideology and values of bourgeoisie and other exploiting classes do has considerable influence, even has their traditional advantages in some fields; internationally, the reactionary forces, backing up their military and economic strengths, are intensifying the implementation of their "peaceful evolution" strategy, especially their activities of corruption and infiltration through various ideological channels; whereas socialist ideology, although the most advanced on in human history, is still young and need a long-term process of strengthening and improving compared with the ideology of bourgeoisie and other exploiting classes in terms of maturity, history as well as dissemination media and tools. Therefore, the class struggle of fundamental opposition in the realm of ideology will exist for a long period, and it is wrong to neglect this struggle. But on the other hand, the unlimited expansion of the class struggle in the ideological field will cause serious damage for the development of socialism. In this regard, we must strictly distinguish ideological contradictions and struggles of class struggle nature from those of non-class struggle nature; and in interpersonal relationships, we must strictly distinguish the ideological contradictions between ourselves and the enemy from those among the people, and strictly distinguish ideological contradictions among the people of class struggle nature from those of non-class struggle nature. Historically, we had committed "leftist" mistakes. We took class struggle as the central task, expanded the class struggle in the ideological field, seriously confused ideological and cultural contradictions of class struggle nature with those of non-class struggle nature, seriously confused the contradictions between ourselves and the enemy with those among the people, and mistakenly took lot of ideological and cultural contradictions among the people of non-class struggle nature as ones of class struggle nature, even as those between ourselves and the enemy. These mistakes had hurt the masses and brought great harm to our socialist construction. Since Third Plenary Session of the Eleventh Central Committee of the Party, we have correctly handle the class struggle in the ideological field, correctly handled the two different types of contradictions of different nature in the field, and correctly distinguished and handled the ideological contradictions among the people of class struggle nature from those of non-class struggle nature, which has liberated a large number of cadres and the masses from the yoke of ultra-left trend of thought, mobilized the enthusiasm of the cadres and masses, and promoted the prosperity and development of socialist ideology, culture, economy and society. But in recent years, some of our comrades emphasized material progress while neglecting the ideological sphere, being weak and lax in the fight against the bourgeois liberalization and ideologies and cultures of capitalism and other exploiting classes, and lacking proper vigilance against ideological class struggle. This is also wrong. We must correctly understand and handle the ideological contradictions among the people by seriously learning from our lessons and experience in handling the two types of ideological contradictions.

Ⅱ. The Manifestations of Ideological and Cultural Contradictions among the People

The ideological and cultural contradictions among the people on the basis of fundamental identity of interests constitute the dominant ones in the realm of socialist ideology. They manifest themselves as the conflicts between right and wrong, new and old, advanced and backward, innovation and conservatism and between scientific and superstitious, i. e., ideological contradictions of right and wrong among the people.

First, the ideological contradictions of right and wrong among the people in a socialist country can manifest themselves as the contradictions between the correct and wrong ideas. Correct ideas refer to the theories, lines, principles and policies, academic points of view and other understandings that accord with the essence of things and objective laws of development; and vice versa. Under socialist conditions, the scope and extent of ideological and cultural contradictions of class struggle nature will gradually reduce and finally die out, while the ideological contradictions of right and wrong among the people will become increasingly outstanding and extensively, massively and frequently find expressions in the different understandings of various phenomena in all areas, aspects, things, phenomena of social life, and in the ideological confrontations and struggles within the Party, between higher and lower levels, between leadership and the masses, and between different interest groups within the people. For example, in socialist construction, there is the contradiction and struggle between the correct and wrong roads; in the process of socialist reform and opening up, there are contradictions and struggles between the right and wrong ideas of reform; in social sciences research, there are also debates between the right and wrong academic points. How to judge whether an idea is right or wrong? The sole criterion is practice. All that which has been proved wrong through practice should be resolutely corrected. But in the struggle between the correct and wrong ideas, some understanding cannot been identified immediately; it takes time and needs longer period of practice of test, therefore, the policy of "Let a hundred flowers blossom and let a hundred schools of thought contend" should be introduced to advance sciences, to find truth and to correct the wrong things.

The ideological contradictions of right and wrong among the people in a socialist country also find expression in the contradictions between new and old ideas. New ideas represent the requirements of development of productive forces and economic, political and social progress, represent the trend of social and historicalprogress, and represent the thoughts, ideas, moral standards and lifestyle of the advanced classes and interest groups; whereas old ideas, representing the requirements of backward production relations and economic base, and the needs of the backward social classes and forces, are backward thoughts, ideas, moral standards and lifestyles not suitable to the trends of social and historical development. Although some of the ideological contradictions of right and wrong among the people belong to class struggle in nature, most of them are not. China is a country with deep-rooted feudal traditions; in socialist China that was born out of the semi-colonial and semi-feudal society, there are inevitably a lot of old traditional ideological and cultural ideas. Although the socialist revolution overthrew the old system of exploitation and wiped out the feudal land system, the bourgeois ideology, the pernicious influence of feudal ideas and the backward feudal customs and habits will exist for a long time. As powerful conservative forces, they not only reside in the minds of the older generations, but also will be passed down to the next several generations. On the other hand, the new ideas, new cultures, new traditions, new concepts, new moral standards and new trends representing the advanced productive forces, the working class and socialism are emerging and developing, showing a strong vitality and the trend of defeating and replacing the old ones. Thus, great conflicts occur between the new ideas and values and the old ones, which constitute the ideological contradictions of right and wrong in terms of new and old ideas among the people. For example, the spirit of socialist collectivism and the working class qualities, such as putting public before self interest, sacrificing oneself for others, constitute sharp contrast and moral, ethical and value conflicts with the old, selfish ideas such as "birds die in pursuit of food, and human beings, of wealth". Other examples include the conflict between the long-term legacy of the ancestral relationship with the new socialist ideas, the serious conflict between the idea of "more sons, more blessings" and tendency of early marriage and early child-bearing in the rural areas with the socialist concept of family planning. There are also great conflicts between the new lifestyle with the outmoded regulations and bad habits left over by the old, even the feudal society. Since reform and opening up, with the gradual establishment of a socialist market economy, people's ideas of planned economy and the corresponding ideas, values, moral standards, ways of thinking, etc., have been gravely impacted. People began to re-examine traditional things from a new perspective. It is necessary as well as inevitable to emancipate our minds, update our ideas to completely clean up the old traditional system of idea, culture, values and moral standards. Reform toward socialist market economy brings with it a great change of ideas. In a sense, in the new era of socialist reform and construction, The ideological contradictions of right and wrong among the people are more violent and more outstanding. Of course, there are many precious ideas, values and morals formed in the history of mankind and the Chinese nation that do not belong to the category of old ideas; on the contrary, they should be carried on and developed. The fundamental orientation in correctly handling the ideological contradictions of right and wrong in terms of old and new ideas among the people is to eradicate the old ideas and establish the new ones, that is, to criticize the old, to establish the new, to carry on the fine and to discard the bad.

The ideological and cultural contradictions among the people in socialist countries, also find expression in the contradictions between the advanced and backward ideology and culture. These contradictions actually belong to the category of ideological and cultural contradictions between old and new, only that they are narrower in scope. In socialist countries, advanced ideas and culture refer to theories and views that are conducive to the development of social productive forces and socialism, such as patriotism, collectivism, world outlook of the working class, socialist view of life and values, socialist moral standards; the backward ideas and cultures can be divided into two parts. One part includes that are harmful to the development of socialist productive forces and socialist ideological and theoretical views, including: the old world outlook, values, views on life; the old ethical system left over by the old society comprising old moral standards, decadent ideals, old sentiments and so on; the backward cultural system hampering the development of productive forces, such as feudal world outlook and moral standards, ideology ofsmall peasants, decadent bourgeois ethics , individualism, egoism , etc. is not conducive to the development of social productive forces backward cultural system. These ideological and cultural conflicts to some extent and within a certain range and certain period of time have a class nature. For instance, the antagonism and struggle between the ideology of the working class and that of the exploiting class, to a certain extent, has a class character. But this kind of struggles, which occurs and exists on the basis of the fundamental identity of the people's interests, and is the reflection of the ideology of the exploiting classes within the ranks of the people, belongs to the question of right and wrong among the people with a class character. The other part is the ideological contradictions of right and wrong concerning the advanced and the backward, which has no class character. For example, the conflict between the opinion of maintaining the planned economy and the rigid economic system of the past with the opinion of developing a brand new socialist market economy, is not necessarily the ideological struggle with a nature of class struggle; they are in general the ideological struggle between the advanced and the backward, which will be more frequent and outstanding with the development of socialist society. The ideological and moral differences between the advanced and the backward persons, for instance, will take up a growing share in social ideological field.

The question of right and wrong within the ranks of the people also manifests itself as the contradiction between the innovative and conservative ideas. In a sense, this contradiction is one aspect of the ideological and cultural contradictions between the new and the old, the advanced and the backward. Innovative ideas are the reflection of socialist newborn things and development trends in people's minds, which support and protect the new things, be keen in innovation and have an enterprising spirit. Conservative ideas are the reflection and their impact on people'sminds of things that have stepped off the historical stage in the process of development of socialism, these idea are rigid, conservative and slavishly adhere to things of the past. In general, innovative ideas represent the long-term, fundamental and overall interests of the people of socialist society, whereas the conservative ideas represent the tendency of some people the immediate, vested and individual interests at the expense of the long-term, fundamental and overall interests of the people. (There are, of course, differences in understanding; but in the final analysis these difference are influenced by differences in interests). The causes of contradictions between innovative and conservative ideas are mainly as follows: (1) In some period of socialist society, there will emerge the situation where some links or aspects of the production relations are not in correspondence with the productive forces, so are the superstructure and the economic base. Therefore, reforms and adjustments are constantly needed, which, will necessarily affect the interest relations among people. The differences of interests because of them will make people keep different understanding and attitude toward reform, which will be largely manifested as the ideological contradiction between the innovative and conservative ideas. (2) Socialist reform represents a great systematic project that will necessarily influence the economic, political, cultural and social and other areas of life and people's lifestyles and ways of thinking, causing the growth of new things and the decline of the old in all areas. In people's minds, these influence and changes are manifested as the contradictions between the innovative and the conservative thinking. (3) In socialist society born out of the old society, there are a lot of remnants of things and ideas of the old society, which will inevitably conflict with new things and new ideas of the new society and manifest themselves as the ideological contradictions between the innovative and conservative ideas. These kind of contradictions, under socialist conditions, still belongs to ideological question of right and wrong among the people.

Some ideological questions of right and wrong among the people represent themselves as the ideological contradiction and struggle between science and superstition. In socialist countries, scientific thinking include materialist atheism, emphasis on knowledge, culture and education, cognitive line and way of thinking of seeking truth from facts, emancipating the minds and keeping pace with the times, etc; while superstitious beliefs include the idealist theologism, paying little attention to knowledge, culture and education, believing only in books or higher authorities, personal cult, etc. The contradictions between these kinds of cognitive line and way of thinking constitute the basic content of the ideological contradictions between science and superstition among the people in socialist countries. In carrying out socialist reform and construction, we must rely on knowledge and science, and adhere to ideological line of emancipating the mind, seeking truth from facts and keeping pace with times; whereas the superstitious beliefs are serious obstacle severely hampering the development process of socialism with Chinese characteristics. To resolve this kind of contradictions, we cannot force people to give up their superstitious beliefs; instead, we can only use the methods of persuasion, education, criticism and self-criticism, science education and publicity through mass media to finally make the masses gradually get rid of the shackles of superstitions.

Right and wrong, old and new, advanced and backward, innovative and conservative, science and superstition: these are main manifestations of the ideological contradictions or right and wrong among the people in socialist countries, which are non-antagonistic contradictions among the people on the basis of fundamental identity in politics, ideology and culture. Seeing from the broad sense they belong to the question of right and wrong between correct and wrong ideas.

In anticipating the social situation of communist society, Marxist-Leninist classic writers point out, there would be ideological contradictions of right and wrong between correct and erroneous, innovative and conservative, backward and advanced, etc. If so, what are their differences from those in the socialist society?

The differences are: ideological and cultural contradictions in socialist society are mingled with, constrained and influenced by the conflicts between and the socialist consciousness and those of exploiting classes, whereas the ideological contradictions in communist society are out of these conflicts. In the primary stage of socialism, the ideological remnants of exploiting classes are common phenomena, and the remnants of feudalism, the decadent ideas of capitalism, small producers, etc., will stubbornly exist in ideological and cultural fields. Thus, in the primary stage of socialism, the conflicts between socialist ideology and ideological remnants of the exploiting classes, especially the feudalism, will be very sharp sometimes. Some of them will be demonstrated as ideological contradictions or struggle between the people and enemy; but most of them are manifested as the questions of right and wrong among the people; and so do the contradictions between the socialist ideology and old ideology, such as the ideology of small producers, which sometimes are also outstanding. The complexity of the ideological contradictions among people in the primary stage of socialism lies in the fact that, the contradictions between socialist ideas and the remnants of ideas of the old society (the remnants of the exploiting classes and small producers) intermingle with and take up a certain proportion in the ideological contradictions of right and wrong between correct and erroneous, old and new, advanced and backward, innovative and conservative, scientific and superstitious. This determines that, in the primary stage of socialism, the ideological contradictions of right and the wrong among the people, to some certain extent, have a nature of class antagonism, which can transform into the ideological contradictions between ourselves and the enemy. Another factor determines the complexity of the ideological contradictions among the people in the primary stage of socialism is that, the ideological contradictions between socialist ideas and the remnants of the old society inevitably will find their expression with the ranks of the Party and intermingle with the contradictions of right and wrong within the Party. Therefore, in the primary stage of socialism, to solve the ideological contradictions of right and wrong among the people, we must correctly handle the contradictions between socialist ideas and the decadent ideas of capitalist ideology and the remnants of feudal ideology, contradictions between socialist ideas and those of the small producers; must correctly distinguish between and handle the ideological contradictions between ourselves and the people and those among the people; correctly distinguish between the ideological contradictions of right and wrong among the people with a class struggle nature and those without and correctly handle them. We must try as far as possible to prevent the ideological conflicts among the people from intensifying and to avoid committing the "Left" mistakes. On the other hand, it goes without saying that we cannot blindly accommodate the backward, wrong negative, or even the reactionary ideas, but rather take a tit-for-tat struggle against them and to conquer the erroneous ideas by using correct ones.

Given the fact that, China is a country with a deep-rooted traditional ideas of feudalism, and that in the primary stage of socialism in China the ideological question of right and wrong among the people to some extent manifest themselves as the contradictions between the socialist new ideas, new concepts and new customs and the old, even feudal ideas, concepts, culture and customs; and that feudal ideology have seriously hampered the development of China's socialist market economy and socialist productive forces as well the development of socialist science and culture, currently it constitutes an important ideological task to resolutely carry out the struggle against feudalism.

III. Correctly Handle Ideological Contradictions among the People

The fundamental thing in correct handling the ideological contradictions among the people is to develop the socialist productive forces. We should promote socialist modernization and the emancipation of productive forces through reform and opening up, that is, to promote socialist cultural and ethical progress through socialist material progress; at the same time we should improve socialist democracy, legal system andthe rule of law, and ensure socialist cultural and ethical improvement through the improvement of socialist political civilizations, so as to greatly advance socialist ideology and culture to continuously meet people's increasing spiritual and cultural needs, to create a good social and cultural atmosphere, to ensure social stability, to build a harmonious society and an ideological and political situation in which everybody enjoys ease of mind.

Since Third Plenary Session of the Eleventh Central Committee when our Party has shifted its focus of work to economic development and a new situation of reform and opening up has been formed, Comrade Deng Xiaoping, in view of the trend of thought in the society and within our Party which is sceptical of or opposed to the Four Cardinal Principles, repeatedly emphasized the extreme importance of upholding the Four Cardinal principles. Reform and opening-up are the only way to realize modernization in China and the Four Cardinal Principles are the political guarantee for it. It constitutes the political program in unifying the whole Party and all the people in our great cause of socialist construction and reform, the basis for us to keep political and ideological coherence, and the ideological weapon for us in criticizing and winning out against various reactionary, decadent, backward and conservative ideologies. Whether in economic or political and ideological field, as long as we always keep to the socialist road, uphold the people's democratic dictatorship, uphold leadership by the Communist Party and uphold Marxism-Leninism and Mao Zedong Thought, Deng Xiaoping Theory and the important thought of "Three Represents", we can always rally the whole Party and all the people in promoting our economic and ideological work and in mobilizing people's enthusiasm for political activities and production.

First, giving full play to the guiding and educative role of Marxism in ideological field .

To do better in ideological work and correctly handle the ideological contradictions among the people, we must give full play to the guiding role of Marxism, and to unified the thinking of whole Party and all the people with Marxism-Leninism, Mao Zedong Thought, Deng Xiaoping Theory and the important thought of Three Represents.

Marxism is the world outlook and ideology of the proletariat, the most advanced class in history. The scientific nature of Marxism is line with the development trend of history and with its class nature. Under the condition of existence of class, ideology, in essence, is the theoretical expression of interests of a certain class, so it has a class nature. Marxism represents the development direction of the advanced productive forces and the fundamental interests of the representatives of new productive forces—the working class; it is the world outlook and guiding ideology of the working class in their practice of revolution and construction, and also the guiding ideology of socialist reform and opening up. Mao Zedong Thought is the first theoretical achievement in adapting Marxist tenets to China's conditions; Deng Xiaoping Theory is the theory of socialism with Chinese characteristics formulated in the new historical period by the Chinese Communists with Comrade Deng Xiaoping as the representative, which is an creative contribution of the Chinese Communists to Marxism, the adherence to and the development of Mao Zedong Thought and the theoretical basis guiding our work in the new era; Our Party's third generation of collective leadership with Comrade Jiang Zemin at the core, adhering and developing Deng Xiaoping Theory, put forward the important thought of Three Represents, which is an innovative achievement in adapting Marxism to China's realities. In the new world situation and new stage, to strengthen the guiding role of Marxism, we must arm the whole Party and educate the people with Deng Xiaoping Theory and important thought Three Represents. In ideological field, as long as we give full play to the guiding role of Marxism, we can correctly grasp and adjust various relationships and contradictions among the people and thus do a better job in ideological field.

Second, making vigorous efforts to promote socialist cultural and ethical progress to improve the ideological and cultural quality of the whole nation

In the primary stage of socialism in China, one of the most important reasons for the existence and development of ideological contradictions among the people is that our intellectual production are relatively backward, the people's intellectual and cultural life are relatively meager and intellectual products are relatively inadequate, which cannot meet the increasing needs of people's intellectual and cultural life. The key method is to promote the cultural and ethical progress, including vigorously to develop socialist intellectual productivity, to enrich socialist intellectual and cultural life, to enhance socialist cultural building, to advocate socialist new ideas, new culture, new moral standards and new style, and to produce more excellent intellectual products, so as to meet the growing ideological and cultural needs of the people and to better handle the ideological contradictions among the people. To greatly promote socialist cultural and ethical progress, we must:

(1) Vigorously develop socialist education to improve the basic quality of the whole nation and bring up a new generation with socialist consciousness. People are the subjects of creative activities in socialist society. To develop socialist productive forces, it is necessary to improve the quality of the whole nation by improving socialist education and the workers' scientific, cultural knowledge and broadening their mental horizon. (2) Promote socialist science and culture. (3) Cultivate the correct sense of market economy and democracy of the members in socialist society, so that they are adaptable to the needs of socialist market economy and socialist democracy. To develop socialist market economy and democracy requires that people should have the sense of competitiveness, value orientation and moral standards compatible with modern market economy and a strong sense and values of democracy adaptable to the development of socialist democracy. China's thousands of years of feudal tradition, the ten-year turmoil of the "Cultural Revolution" and influence of the "Leftist" mistakes have left many decadent ideas on people's minds that are at variance with the development of market economy and democracy. Therefore it is highly necessary to cultivate people's senses of market economy and democracy to meet the needs of the development. (4) Intensify education for all citizens in socialist ideals and moral standards. Since in socialist countries individual interests are recognized, and the principle of distribution according to work and so on are applied, which are prone to the tendency of spontaneous blindness and fetish of

money. In this context, it is more necessary to educate all the people in lofty ideals and socialist moral standards, to make them firmly implant in minds the thinking that they are masters of the country with high socialist integrity, and to encourage them to work for the country and the collectives. (5) Carry forward and cultivate the national spirit. National spirit is the moral force and kingpin on which a nation relies for survival and development, and also the most essential and most profound expression of national culture. With a strong and inspiring nation spirit and noble national character, when faced with complicated ideological and cultural interactions and contradictions world-wide, a nation will always be filled with an enterprising spirit. (6) Carry out educational work among the masses in the principles, line and policies of the Party and the government, as well as in socialist laws. The development of socialist productive forces requires a sustained stability, and the development of socialist market economy also needs an orderly conditions. So we should create a social environment in which everyone abides by the law and stability and unity are maintained. If people's qualities are poor in this regard, the line, policies and laws, no matter how correct or complete they are, will serve no purpose. We must carry out publicity and education in the Party's line and program, the laws and regulations of the state, to guide the people in forming the habits of observing the disciplines and laws and consciously creating, maintaining good work, production and public order. (7) Carry out correctly ideological struggles among the people to guide them in getting rid of decadent, backward or ignorant old ideas, morals, cultures and habits. (8) Intensify among the cadres and the masses education in Marxist theory. The lofty goals of socialism can only be realized through the conscious activities led by the Party. Because whether people's understanding is in accordance with the objective law is greatly important in their transforming the objective world, people need the guidance of Marxist theory to correct understand the development law and the great future of socialism, so as to work hard toward the set goals by combining individual interests with those of long-term interests of the nation. (9) Establish an ideological system compatible with socialist economic base and an effective system of ideological and political work. The fundamental purpose of extensive socialist democracy is to create an ideological and political situation in which everybody speak out freely and has ease of mind, and "a hundred flowers blossom and a hundred schools of thought contend". This requires us to make reform of ideological institutions and improvement of political work. Since the founding of New China, although our ideological and political work has made some achievements, under the influence of "leftist" ideology, in line with the rigid economic-political institutions, our ideological and political institutions were also rigid, along with the "leftist" ideological and political work system and methods, which to some extent affected the emancipation of socialist minds and the prosperity of culture and science. Therefore, institutional issues must be addressed to ensure the socialist cultural and ethical progress.

Fundamentally speaking, to promote socialist cultural and ethical progress is to raise the qualities of members of socialist society, such as ideological, theoretical, cultural, moral levels, creativity. Only by bringing up a new socialist generation of all-round development, can we avoid the intensification of all possible social contradictions, correctly handle all kinds of contradictions and do a better work in ideological field.

Third, Thoroughly Implement the Principle of Letting A Hundred Flowers Blossom and Let A Hundred Schools of Thought Contend

The principle of letting a hundred flowers blossom and a hundred schools of thought contend reflects the features and laws governing the development of science and culture, and represent the Party's respect for knowledge and talents; it not only is a basic policy of our party for developing science, culture and arts, but also an important principle for up to correctly handle ideological contradictions of right and wrong among the people. In following the principle, we must, under the premise of adhering to Marxism as the fundamental guiding ideology, promote research on social science, develop social undertakings in the fields of culture, science and technology, education and so on; we must improve democracy and guarantee academic freedom; we should encourage emancipating the minds, exploration, innovation, promote and encourage free and equal discussions, promote and encourage free and equal discussion and development of different academic and artistic opinions, styles, schools, and during which, we should strictly stick to the doctrine of "three don'ts": don't use a big stick, don't put labels on people and don't pick on others for their faults; when carrying on academic criticism, we should aim at helping those criticized by presenting the facts and reasoning things out; we should make clear distinctions by not arbitrarily taking problems derived from understanding or different views as problems of political orientation. In short, we should create a atmosphere and environment of unity, democracy, harmony to promote the development of science and culture. The past practices of resolving different opinions and disputes in ideological field, i. e., mass criticism or class struggle, cannot help the resolution of contradictions among the people; on the contrary, they will only intensify contradictions and destroy science and culture.

The only way to settle questions of an ideological nature among the people is by the democratic method and the method of persuasion. Ideological and political work is our party's advantage; it is the fine tradition of our party to, through ideological and political work, mobilize, guide, unite and inspire the people to strive for realizing their own interests. In the new historical era, to correctly handle ideological contradictions of right and wrong among the people, and to mobilize the enthusiasm of the masses, we must, through our ideological and political work, publicize and implement the Party's theories, lines and policies, publicize Deng Xiaoping Theory and important thoughts of Three Represents as well as theories of socialist market economy. In view of the changes of various interests derived from policy reasons, we should do well in coordinating all interest groups and respects, to guide the people in correctly understanding and facing various complex issues and interest adjustment, to help the people in their proper handling of interest relationship between immediate and long-term, partial and overall, collective and individual. We should actively and correctly guide people in dealing with their changes of minds deriving from market economy and opening up, to help them raise their consciousness on competition, efficiency, equality, laws, etc., and renew their ideas and knowledge. We should guide people in cultivating correct ideals, beliefs, values, views on life, in promoting good morals and social conducts and in resisting decadent and ugly things. We should vigorously promote patriotism, collectivism and socialism, to further strengthen the cohesion of our party, state and nation, and the cohesiveness of our cadres and the masses. We should strive to produce more excellent cultural products and make our socialist advanced culture more prosperous, so as to meet people's needs for cultural products of higher taste and their needs for more healthy and colorful cultural life. In short, we should correctly handle ideological contradictions between right and wrong among the people by effective ideological, political and publicity work.

Chapter 6

Correct Understanding and Handling of the Contradiction between the Leaders and the Masses in the New Era

Under the condition of our partyas the governing party, especially in the new situation of reform and opening up and development of the socialist market economy, the contradiction between the leaders and the masses is showing many new features and manifestation of expression both in content and form. Correct understanding and handling the contradiction in the new situation, keeping a close ties between our party and its cadres and the masses, maintaining the flesh-and-blood ties between the Party and the people are the keys to the success of building socialism with Chinese characteristics as well as the fundamental guarantee for the success of the socialist reform and opening up and modernization drive. Comrade Deng Xiaoping pointed out that, among the Party's three fine styles of work, "What is most important is to maintain close ties with the masses". In his speech "The Leading Cadres Must Stress Political Awareness," Comrade Jiang Zemin pointed out: "What is political awareness? Fundamentally speaking, political awareness is mainly about our attitude toward the people and our ties with them." We must take Marxism, Leninism, Mao Zedong Thought, Deng Xiaoping Theory and the important thought of Three Represents as the guide, carefully study new situations, sum up new experiences and solve new problems, so as to ensure that our party always keeps flesh-and-blood ties with the people. By doing so, we are sure to be able to withstand all trials and tribulations, and no matter how the international situation changes and how many difficulties and obstacles on our road ahead, we will always put ourselves in a invincible position and will realize the great goal of building a moderately prosperous society in all respects and win new victories in our advancing the great endeavor of building socialism with Chinese characteristics.

I. The Contradiction between the leaders and the masses is an Important Manifestation of Contradictions among the People

In general, the contradiction between the leaders and the masses plays an extremely important role among the various types of contradictions among the people and is an important expression of them. Comrade Liu Shaoqi said: "Contradictions among the people are now in many cases manifest themselves as the contradictions between the masses of the people and the leaders."① This judgment is undoubtedly correct and accords with the actual conditions in our country. The reasons are as follows:

First, most of the major social contradictions in our socialist country in many cases find their expression in the contradictory relations between the leaders and the masses. For example, the basic contradiction of socialism will find its expression in the contradictory relations between the leaders as managers and executives of economic and political functions and the masses as factors of the productive forces. In the primary stage of socialism, the contradiction between the relatively backward social production and the increasing material and cultural needs of the people is saliently reflected in the insufficient supply of consumer goods in meeting people's needs. So it is the unshirkable duty of the leaders at all levels to solve the shortage of consumer goods. Especially facing severe economic difficulties when consumer goods are scarce, the leaders has become the focus of all social contradictions, and the contradiction between them will become a concentrated expression of all social contradictions .

Second, in the political life of our socialist country, because our party is the governing party, its leaders at all levels are in the leading positions in political, economic, cultural and other social areas. The success or failure of the entire socialist cause is closely related to the leaders, so do all the problems and mistakes. As the leaders of the masses, on the one hand, they shoulder the duty of guiding, educating, organizing and mobilizing the people; on the other, they should rely on and subordinate to the masses, receive the supervision of them and avoid divorcing from them. This determines that the relations between the leaders and the masses constitute the principal human relations in our country and the contradictions

① *Selected Works of Liu Shaoqi*, People's Publishing House, 1985, p. 303.

between them become an important expression of the contradictions among the people.

Generally speaking, under our socialist system, the contradiction between the leaders and the masses is non-antagonistic. However, it can become acute and antagonistic in the following cases, among others: when the major policy or decision mistakes of the leaders damage the people's legitimate interests; when the serious bureaucratic style of work of the leaders jeopardize the reasonable interests or demands of the people; when the degenerate or corrupt elements among ranks of the leaders embezzle people's property or seriously damage people's interests; when some of the masses fail to recognize the necessity of sacrificing the partial or immediate for the whole or long-term interests and therefore show their discontent about it; when the unreasonable requests of some people are rejected and then taken use by some scoundrels to stir up troubles, which are not dealt with timely, resolutely or correctly by the leaders.

In the contradictionbetween the leaders and the masses, the primary aspect is the leaders. Just as Comrade Liu Shaoqi put it, "The leadership is responsible for every mistake and everything unreasonable in our society. The people will call the leaders in the state, the Party or government, including departments in charge of economic affairs, to account, and we are accountable[①] for them." In a contradiction between the leaders and the masses, if the leaders are in the wrong side while the masses in correct side, then the primary aspect of the contradiction in no doubt leaders, and the resolution of it depends whether the leaders can correct their mistakes and secure the forgiveness of the masses; On the other hand, if leaders are correct and the masses are wrong, the primary aspect of the contradiction is still the leaders, for the resolution of the contradiction depends whether the leaders can correctly handle it by educating and persuading the masses. For example, when some of the masses ask unreasonable demands in distribution and make troubles, the key to it is whether the leaders can make effective efforts to persuade, educate and guide the masses. Therefore, usually the leaders constitute the primary aspect and the dominant side in the contradiction between them and the masses. Of course, we cannot blame all the contradictions or problems appeared in the masses on the leadership. When we say that the leaders constitute the primary aspect in the contradictions between the leaders and the masses, we refer to the responsibility or

① *Selected Works of Liu Shaoqi,* People's Publishing House, 1985, p. 303.

work of them, not simply about right or wrong.

Contradictions among the people frequently find their expression in the contradictionbetween the leaders and the masses, "more exactly, in the contradiction between the bureaucracy of the leadership and people."[①] Since the primary aspect of the contradiction is the leadership, the contradictions between bureaucracy, corruptions and other malpractices of the leadership and the masses constitute important manifestations of it.

When talking about bureaucracy, we must make clearly distinguish the concepts of bureaucrats, bureaucracy, bureaucratic system and bureaucratic style of thinking. Bureaucrats are officials in the exploiting class society, who were fostered by and served the ruling class to oppress the ordinary people. Bureaucracy refers to a kind of political system that is bureaucratized. Bureaucratic system refers to the specific institution of the bureaucratic political system; whereas bureaucratic style of thinking refers to the manifestation of bureaucratic system in ideology or style. The establishment of the socialist system had fundamentally eradicated the bureaucratic system, so bureaucrats, except for some individuals of them, as a social stratum of the ruling classes in the old society no longer exist. However, our current social administrative system still have some shortcomings left over by the bureaucratic system, and some of the personnel in our government still have the bureaucratic style of thinking, sometimes even serious. When we talk about bureaucracy, we refer to the bureaucratic style of thinking, including those having serious bureaucratic style of work, and bureaucratic drawbacks in our system. Bureaucracy is fundamentally against the interests of the people, divorced from the masses and from practice, which harms the people's fundamental interests. If bureaucracy is rampant, the contradictions among the people that could have been resolved properly will become intensified. When the masses put forward reasonable demands and rise up against the bureaucracy that are unconcerned about the people's welfare and undermines national interests, the contradiction between bureaucracy and the masses constitute the mainstay of the contradiction between the leaders and the masses; when some of the masses made unreasonable demands, display erroneous tendencies or take excesses, the bureaucratic style of leadership will make the wrong tendencies or behaviors become more acute, further aggravating the contradictions. In this case, the contradictions between the bureaucracy of the leadership and the masses will become

① *Selected Works of Liu Shaoqi,* People's Publishing House, 1985, p. 303.

the mainstay of the contradiction between the leaders and the masses. On the other hand, the residue left over by the old society, combined with the shortcomings in our institutions, gives rise to the considerable corruption in the personnel of the Party and government organizations, which are serious detrimental and sharply contradictory to people's interests. If left widespread without control, these contradictions with an antagonistic nature will eventually aggravate into conflicts and incidents, making latent antagonism develop into real confrontations, and then transform into contradictions between the people and the enemy. So, for the resolution of the contradiction between the leaders and the masses, it is important to combat against bureaucracy, corruption and unhealthy styles institutionally, politically, ideologically in the Party and government bodies.

II. The Contradiction between the Leaders and the Masses in the New Era and Their Conspicuous Manifestations

The nature, purpose and guiding ideology of our party and state determine that the leading organs at all levels of the Party and the government and their leaders represent the interests of the people and for the service of the masses. Comrade Deng Xiaoping said: "Leadership means service." This statement profoundly sums up the essence of the relationship between the leadership and masses. This, without doubt, doesn't means that there is no contradiction between the leaders and the masses. Contradictions exist everywhere and it is not in accordance with reality and dialectics to think otherwise. In fact, many contradictions among the people, including contradictions of interests, of right and wrong, find their expression in the contradictions between the leadership and masses. Our task is to correctly understand and resolve these contradictions in order to continuously strengthen the flesh-and-blood ties between our party and leadership with the masses.

The major manifestations of thecontradiction between the leaders and the masses are as follows:

First, in economic life, there exist contradictions of interestsbetween the leaders and the masses. Firstly, it is the interest contradictions among the state, the collective and the individuals. On the one hand, the leading organs and leading cadres should base themselves on the overall interests of the work of the entire Party and the whole country, take the interests of all sides into account and make overall arrangements, rather than simply consider one side at the expense of others. On the other hand, the masses, in looking for and protect their individual or partial interests, should consciously safeguard and subordinate to the collective and overall interests. Either for the leadership or for the masses, any over-emphasis on the interests of one side at the expense or even the denial of the other side, will damage the interests of the masses and lead to the intensification of the contradiction between the leaders and the masses. Secondly, there are certain contradictions of personal interests between the leaders and the masses. Within the ranks of our party members and cadres, due to the influence of the ideology of the exploiting classes, some elements abuse the power entrusted by the people for their personal gains, violate and prejudice the interests of the masses and even become degenerated and corrupt, causing strong resentment among the masses and thus intensifying the contradiction between the leaders and the masses.

Second, in political life, there are contradiction of democracy and centralism and that of freedom and discipline between the leaders and the masses. Centralism without democracy is by no means centralism but rather arbitrariness, while democracy without democracy is by no means democracy but anarchy. Similarly, without freedom, there can be no discipline, and vice versa. Only the unity of them can bring about the situation with both liveliness and unity of will and action. The relationship between the leadership and masses will become tense if the leaders separate the two sides by one-sidedly over-emphasizing discipline or centralism in a patriarchal or dictatorial way at the expense of democracy and freedom; or if some of the masses one-sidedly over-emphasize democracy and freedom in a way of decentralism or anarchy by ignoring centralism and discipline.

Third, there are contradictions of right and wrongbetween the leaders and the masses in terms of thinking and understanding. The correct decisions of the leaders will surely get support from the masses, but a process of publicity and education is also needed to gain their acceptance; the wrong decisions of the leaders jeopardizing the interests and going against the wills of the masses will surely meet the resistance and opposition from the masses. If the leaders act in a severely bureaucratic, subjective or authoritarian way, or a few of the masses stubbornly stick to their wrong ideas, or refuse to accept education, or even stir up unreasonable troubles, the contradiction between the leaders and the masses will become tense, even very acute.

Fourth, in addition to the above mentioned direct contradictionsbetween the leaders and the masses, there are also indirect ones between them. For the contradictions among the people of different classes, strata, groups, regions, departments, individuals and so on often need the leaders to deal with. If they are handled well, the people will be satisfied; otherwise, they may cause the dissatisfaction of the masses, which possibly be expressed in form of contradiction between the leadership and masses. The leaders of our party and government at all levels are serving the people, so they are attributed to all the good things in the society; at the same time, they are also responsible for all the bad things, which demonstrate that they are not doing well, so the people have the right to bring them to account.

In short, contradictions among the people find their expression as the contradiction between the leaders and masses as the focus and mainstay. The handling of them has a bearing on the consolidation of the governing position of our party, the unity and long-term stability of our country, and the success of socialism with Chinese characteristics. So we must attach great importance to the study and proper handling of them. The resolution depends on the leaders. As long as they keep close contact with the masses, it is not difficult to solve, even if the problem lies in some of the masses, such as wrong ideas, unreasonable demands or improper behaviors. But once the leaders divorce themselves from the masses, the contradictions will become acute and intensified.

In condition that our party is governing party in China, especially in the new situation of reform and opening up andestablishment of a socialist market economy, the contradiction between the leaders and the masses has become the focus of contradictions among the people. In recent years, the tension of the contradiction between the leaders and the masses is mainly manifested in the following three main aspects:

Firstly, a few of our cadres are divorced from the masses by seeking privilege, profits and extravagant life, even become corrupt and degenerated, which fundamentally jeopardize the interests of the people and thus arise their strong resentment. The malpractices of these cadres include: abuse power for personal profits, trading power for money, racketeering, embezzlement and corrupt practices, violating the law while in charge of its enforcement, seeking private gains at the expense of public interests, extravagance, cronyism, forming cliques and ganging up, and so on. Although these are the conducts of only a few Party members and cadres, they have influence on the image and prestige of the Party and the government and the social conduct, making the relationship between the leaders and the masses that ought to be like that between fish-and-water become separated from each other like "oil and water," or even become incompatible like "fire and water." In the Decision of the Central Committee of the Communist Party of China on Strengthening the Ties between the Party and of the People, it is pointed out that, "If corruption spread unchecked, our party will face the risk of heading for self-destruction." So we must "unswervingly strive to build a clean and honest government, carry forward the spirit of working hard, to overcome corruption and other misconducts. These are strategic measures to improve the relations between our party and masses and to guarantee for the invincible status of our cause."①

Secondly, in ideological style and work style, some of our leading cadres are seriously alienated from the masses. Bureaucracy, subjectivism, authoritarianism, arbitrary decision-making, etc., which are against the interests of the masses, are widespread. Comrade Deng Xiaoping said: "Bureaucracy remains a major and widespread problem in the political life of our Party and state."② Its harmful manifestations include the following: standing high above the masses; abusing power; divorcing oneself from reality and the masses; spending a lot of time and effort to put up an impressive front; indulging in empty talk; sticking to a rigid way of thinking; being hidebound by convention; overstaffing administrative organs; being dilatory, inefficient and irresponsible; failing to keep one's word; circulating documents endlessly without solving problems; shifting responsibility to others; and even assuming the airs of a mandarin, reprimanding other people at every turn, vindictively attacking others, suppressing democracy, deceiving superiors and subordinates, being arbitrary and despotic, practising favouritism, offering bribes, participating in corrupt practices in violation of the law, and so on. Such things have reached intolerable dimensions both in our domestic affairs and in our contacts with other countries." Our Party is the party in power, which both gives us the opportunity to serve the people and make some of our comrades prone to be tainted with bureaucracy. Just as what Lenin said: "If anything will destroy us, it is this."③

Thirdly, there are contradictions between the correct leadership and some backward elements of the masses. For instance, contradictions will occur between

---

① *Selected Important Documents since the Thirteenth National Congress of the CPC,* vol. 2, People's Publishing House, 1991, p. 933.

② *Selected Works of Deng Xiaoping,* vol. 2, People's Publishing House, 1994, p. 327.

③ *Collected Works of Lenin,* vol. 52., People's Publishing House, 1988, p. 300.

some backward elements who haven't have their interests satisfied or don't have a correct understanding and the leaders who uphold the fundamental interests of the masses and maintain correct opinions.

Among the three major causes worsening the relations between the cadres and the masses, the first two are the chief ones.

III. Adhering to the Mass Line of the Party: the Fundamental Principle and Method in the Correct Handling of Contradictions between the Leaders and the Masses

Adhering to the Party's mass line is a fundamental principle and method in the correct handling of the contradictions between the leaders and the masses. This is a scientific summary of long-term experience proved by history.

1. "Serve the interests of the masses in everything we do" is the fundamental purpose of our Party

Our party's mass line is to serve the interests of the masses and rely on them in everything we do, "from the masses, to the masses." The premise and foundation of this line is "to serve the interests of the masses in doing everything," which is also the fundamental purpose of our party. Without this, "to rely on the masses" is out of the question, nor is "from the masses, to the masses." Comrade Mao Zedong said: "All of our work cadres, regardless their high or low position, are the people's servants, and everything we do is to serve the people."① This is the starting point and goal of every statement and every action of our leading organs and leading cadres. They have only the obligation to serve the interests of the people, and never have the right of acting against them. Historical experience shows that, to ensure that "everything we do is to serve the people", we must correctly handle the following three relationships:

First, correct handling the relationship between people's fundamental interests and immediate interests. The important thought of Three Represents, in the final analysis, is representing the people's fundamental interests. Two points are important here. One is representing the interests of the overwhelming majority of the people,

---

① "Our Tasks in 1945", in Jiefang Daily, December, 26th 1944.

not a few people; another is representing their fundamental interests rather than ignoring them or paying attention only to their immediate interests. This guiding thought, reflected in the Party's program, line and all actions, is that the Party's program and line must represent the fundamental interests of the masses, and never forget the long-term goal and program. Otherwise, it would be against or damage people's fundamental interests. The ultimate goal of the Party is the realization of Communism. To achieve this goal, we should formulate and realize different specific programs and lines in different historical stages. At the present stage, the fundamental interest of the Chinese people is to build socialism with Chinese characteristics, to liberate and develop the productive forces and to improve people's material and cultural lives. The Party's basic line of "one central task (of economic construction) and two basic points (of adhering to the four cardinal principles and the policy of reform and opening up)" are the basic guarantee for building socialism with Chinese characteristics, which represent the fundamental interests of the Chinese people. Therefore, the Party and government leading cadres at all levels must unswervingly adhere to this line. Any vacillation in and departure from—whether because the influence of the right or the "Left" side—can only undermine the fundamental interests of the Chinese people. Anyone who attempts to change the line would not be countenanced by the people; he would be toppled. The Party and government leading cadres at all levels must be highly conscious and determined in this issue. It is a test whether a leading cadre represents the fundamental interests of the people.

The stress on representing the fundamental interests of the people doesn't mean that we can ignorespecific problems of the immediate concern of the people. The two of them are inseparable. If we ignore the immediate concern of the people, the fundamental interests of them will become a castle in the air, and it is impossible for people through their personal experience to realize that the Party and the government represent their fundamental interests, and thus it is impossible for them to consciously strive for the realization of the Party's basic line. In the practice of implementing the important thought of Three Represents and the Party's basic line, we must earnestly try hard to do useful and good things for the tangible material benefits of the people. At present, some of our leading cadres are eager to build ostentatious "image" or "performance projects", which, in fact are projects harming the interests of the people; some formalistic in work style, indulging in empty talk, pursuing vanity instead of pragmatism; some are slack in their work and do nothing to care about the hardships and problems of the masses and bring no improvement to the places where they have worked for years; some leading cadres even commit corruption that seriously undermine people's interests. The masses are very discontented with these phenomena, so we must take great determination to change them.

In the issueof representing and ensuring the interests of the masses, "first of all we must ensure our policies and their implementation are in accord with the interests of the people."① Although the Party's basic line, principles and policies since the Third Plenary Session of the Eleventh Party Central Committee are correct and get the support of the masses, there are still defects or errors in our specific work or measures. For example, in recent years there occurred some cases of violating the interests of the farmers; in a period of time, price scissors in the exchange of industrial products for agricultural products has expanded; burdens on farmers are excessive, income growth of farmers is slow, etc., which have caused the dissatisfaction of farmers. These derived both from the shortcomings of our policy-making and from the ineffective implementation of our correct policies. Another example is the certain degree of confusion in our economic work, which arose both from our deep-seated institutional problems and ineffective macro-control as well as some localities, departments or units disregarding of the orders and prohibitions of the central government. The important condition to ensure the rapid and steady economic development and to safeguard the interests of the people, is that, among others, we should correctly handle the relationships between overall and partial, and between long-term and immediate interests, and should make decision according to economic laws and thoroughly implement them under the principle of taking all-round consideration and subordinating to the general interest.

Second, correct handling the relationship between being responsible to the people and to higher authorities. Since the Party's organizational principle is democratic centralism, the leading organs and cadres at the lower levels must subordinate to the higher authorities and resolutely implement their instructions and decisions. This is what being responsibility to higher authorities means. Any anarchy or decentralism is strictly prohibited. However, responsibility to the higher authorities cannot be set in opposition to responsibility to the people. Lower

---

① *Selected Important Documents since the Thirteenth National Congress of the CPC*, vol. 2, People's Publishing House, 1991, p. 929.

authorities must be responsible to the higher authorities, while the whole Party must be responsible to the people, just as what Comrade Mao Zedong said: "Our duty is to hold ourselves responsible to the people."[①] True responsibility to higher authorities refers to: Firstly, in carrying out the instructions of higher authorities, local conditions must be taken into consideration, and principles must be translated into actions to make them supported by the local people and implemented in practice; Secondly, if the instruction of the higher authorities is not correct or not completely correct, it must be, based on reality, the voice of the masses and the attitude of being responsible to the people, reported to the higher authorities, and suggestions are made to help the higher authorities revise the decision, or, in case of inability to revise the decision, to take initiative to minimize the loss. By doing so, we can ensure the consistency of responsibility to the leading bodies with responsibility to the people.

At present, responsibility to the higher authorities is set in opposition to responsibility to the people by some leading organs and cadres. Some of them, flaunting the banner of "being responsible to the people", seek gains for their own localities, departments or units by disregarding the instruction from the higher authorities; or take a utilitarian attitude toward it, even comply in public but oppose in private, or make misinterpretation and discount in fulfillment. These conducts are prohibited by Party and political disciplines and are also not responsible to the masses but undermine their interests. Some people, though clearly aware that the instruction or decision of the higher authorities does not suit the actual conditions or goes against the interests and arouses discontent of the people, still take a blind ear to the opinions of the masses and take coercive measures to force it under the cover of "being responsible to higher authorities", with a real motive to safeguarding their official posts. Both cases run counter to the Party and government's purpose of "everything we do is for the interests of the people," and are not the correct attitude of a Party member or public servant.

Third, correctly handling the relationship between personal interests of the leaders and that of the people. The purpose of "everything we do is for the interests of the people" is by no means denies the leaders' personal interests. Leaders also without exception need food, clothing and other material and cultural conditions. To the Party and the government, personal interests of the leaders constitute a part of

① *Selected Works of Mao Zedong*, vol. 4, People's Publishing House, 1991, p. 1128.

the interests of the people and their meeting can improve the conditions for the leader to better serve the people. However, the personal interests of leaders constitute only a small part of that of the people, which cannot be achieved without the realization of the interests of the overwhelming majority of the people. Therefore, "the interests of the people come before everything else" is the supreme principle for every Party member and cadre. For the leaders of the masses, "plan and worry ahead of the people, and enjoy the fruits after the people" is their bounden duty. When contradiction emerges between personal interests and the interests of the people, the leaders should consciously subordinate without reluctance his personal interests, even stop at no sacrifices, to the interests of the people. All those who seek only personal fame or gains, who commit misconducts of violating the law or disciplines such as abuse of power, bribery, embezzlement, moral degeneration, and who act as overlords and unconcern about welfare of the people, are opposed to the fundamental purpose of our Party and government. Dr. Sun Yat-sen once said: "One should aspire to do big things rather than become big man." All of our leading cadres should use their power to serve the people rather than seek their personal gains. Power can be used to make great contributions to the state and society, but also can make one become corrupt and degenerate. How to use their power is a severe test for every Party member and every cadre.

2. "Relying on the masses in everything we do" is the source of our party's strength

In addition to the problem of "everything we do is for the interests of the people," there is another problem of "how to work for the people", that is: should we mobilize and organize the masses and make the masses liberate themselves, or should we let a few "heroes" to boss the show like "saviors"? Our answers are as follows:

Firstly, inapplying the principle of relying on the masses, we first of all must have faith in them, respect and support their initiative. Historical activities are the cause of the masses. The destruction of the old world and the construction of a new world would be impossible without the participation of the masses. The wisdom and strength of any individuals, including outstanding ones, is limited. Only the wisdom and strength of the people that is boundless. The task of leaders is not to boss the show for the masses or to give charity to them, but to lead and unite them in striving for their interests. Is it to march at their head and lead them, to trail behind them, gesticulating and criticizing, or to stand in their way and oppose them? This is a question about the fundamental stance and attitude of a leader toward the masses. The views must be thoroughly criticized and out-and-out historical idealism against the people that set the leadership in opposition to the masses and that deny the role of the masses.

Secondly, inapplying the principle of fully relying on the masses, we should have a correct understanding of the role of the leaders and follow the method of combining the leadership with the masses. In a class society, the masses are divided into classes and classes are usually led by political parties, and parties are led by the leading group. To make the people recognize their mission and unite to fight for their own liberation, it is a must for leaders to make correct lines, principles and policies, and then, through informing, organizing and guiding the masses, to turn these into actions of the masses. Denying the role of leaders will make the masses become rudderless and cannot fully play role. Therefore, notions such as "labor movements will arise spontaneously," "mass movements are reasonable by nature," are all incorrect. Comrade Mao always stressed that, in all the practical work, we must employ the method of combining the leadership with the masses. "However active the leading group may be, its activity will amount to fruitless effort by a handful of people unless combined with the activity of the masses. On the other hand, if the masses alone are active without a strong leading group to organize their activity properly, such activity cannot be sustained for long, or carried forward in the right direction, or raised to a high level."①

Thirdly, in applying the principle of fully relying on the masses, we should oppose both authoritarianism and "tailism." All mass struggles should rely on the initiative and willingness of the masses themselves. The responsibility of our leaders is to inspire and raise the consciousness of the masses, and on a voluntary basis, to help them organize themselves to carry out all necessary struggles according to the circumstances. Even if a struggle is in need objectively, but subjectively the masses are not yet conscious of it, the leaders must patiently wait while actively carrying out ideological work until most of the masses have become conscious of the need. Comrade Mao Zedong said: "Commandism is wrong in any type of work, because in overstepping the level of political consciousness of the masses and violating the principle of voluntary mass action it reflects the disease of impetuosity."②This kind

---

① *Selected Works of Mao Zedong*, vol. 3, People's Publishing House, 1991, p. 898.

② *Ibid.*, p. 1095.

of work style is still serious in our leadership, especially in our community-level work. It is one of the important causes leading to tension of the relationship between the leaders and the masses, which must be effectively corrected. "Tailism" is also wrong because "in falling below the level of political consciousness of the masses and violating the principle of leading the masses forward it reflects the disease of dilatoriness."① Some of the opinions of the masses are correct and some are not so correct, another some even wrong. Respecting the masses doesn't mean that "we just follow what the masses want," instead, we should support the correct opinions while criticizing the wrong. Comrade Mao Zedong said: "We must heed the correct views and act upon them. The reason why the leadership of the Central Committee is correct is chiefly that it synthesizes the material, reports and correct views coming from different localities... Listen also to the mistaken views from below; it is wrong not to listen to them at all. Such views, however, are not to be acted upon but to be criticized."②

3. "From the masses, to the masses" is the basic method of leading the masses

To truly "serve the interests of the masses" and "rely on them in everything we do," we must also have correct method of leading the masses. Comrade Mao said: "Take the ideas of the masses and concentrate them, then go to the masses, persevere in the ideas and carry them through, so as to form correct ideas of leadership—such is the basic method of leadership."③ This method of leadership is the creative use of Marxist theory of knowledge. Knowledge originates in practice, while the subject of practice is the masses, and the practice of the millions of people is the fertile source of knowledge and objective criterion for testing the truth. The method of leadership of "from the masses, to the masses" is completely consistent to the process of cognition of "from practice, to practice."

Inpersisting in this method, we should do the following:

Firstly, humbly learn from the masses, become their pupil first then become their teacher. The masses, being in the forefront of practice, have extremely rich experience, wisdom and creativity that are much richer than that of the leaders that are comparatively narrow and limited. The leading organs are just like a processing

---

① *Selected Works of Mao Zedong*, vol. 3, People's Publishing House, 1991, p. 1095.

② *Ibid.*, pp. 1441 – 1442.

③ *Ibid.* p. 900.

factory with their raw materials or semi-finished products coming from people's practice. Only those who have personally participated and done research in the practice of the masses can know the actual conditions and facts and sum up useful experience to form correct ideas of leadership. Those who behave in a commandeering manner, and who "the moment they alight from the official carriage" make a hullabaloo and lecture the people, thinking they are clever than the masses, are impossible to put forward any insightful ideas. Comrade Deng Xiaoping said: "It was the farmers who invented the household contract responsibility system with remuneration linked to output. Many of the good ideas in rural reform came from people at the grass roots. We processed them and raised them to the level of guidelines for the whole country."① In his review on the draft of the Report to the Fourteenth National Congress of the Communist Party of China, he again pointed out: "Many things in the reform and opening up are summed up from the practice of the masses. When mentioning my contributions in the report, they must be considered within the scope of that of the collective leadership, for the new things did not come from my brain alone, but rather from the wisdom of the masses and the collective. My contribution is to sum up and promote them."② We should follow the example of Comrade Deng Xiaoping in respecting the creativity of the general public, consciously go to the masses to learn from them, sum up their experience and listen to their voices and opinions. This is particularly important in our exploration of the path of building socialism with Chinese characteristics.

Secondly, giving full scope to democracy and solicit correct opinions of the masses. It is stated in the Decision of the CPC Central Committee on Strengthening the Party's Ties with the People: "in the decision-making process, the Party committee must observe the principle of democratic centralism, give full play to democracy, carefully heed dissenting opinions and exercise correct centralism on the basis of democratic discussion" and "listen to opinions from all sides to make careful comparison, examination and evaluation."③ Comrade Mao Zedong asked us to be "resourceful and decisive." To be decisive, we first of all must be resourceful. To

---

① *See Deng Xiaoping's Philosophical Thinking,* compiled by the Philosophy Teaching and Research Department, the Party School of the Central Committee of the CPC. The Central Party School Publishing House, 1993, p. 261.

② *Ibid.*

③ *Selected Important Documents since the Thirteenth National Congress of the CPC,* vol. 2, People's Publishing House, 1991, p. 930.

be resourceful is to listen more carefully to the opinions of the masses, including opinions of the majority and the minority, cadres and masses, within the Party and outside the Party, positive and negative as well as opinions of leadership members, etc. After this and also analysis and synthesis, correct decision is made through democratic procedures. Only by doing so can we avoid one-sidedness and reduce mistakes. Some leading cadres have the patriarchal style of work to make the final say alone, and hear only views of praise, opinions from cadres or from within the Party while unwilling to listen to views of criticism, from the masses and from outside the Party. So it is not possible for them to make comprehensive and correct policies or decisions.

Thirdly, to implement, test, enrich and develop the views of the leadership in the practice of the masses. For the correct views of the leadershipto be formed by applying "from the masses" to become the power of changing the world, they must be brought back to the masses to be understood, grasped and translated into conscious actions of the masses. Comrade Mao Zedong said: "To be good at translating the Party's policy into action of the masses, to be good at getting not only the leading cadres but also the broad masses to understand and master every movement and every struggle we launch—this is an art of Marxist-Leninist leadership. It is also the dividing line that determines whether or not we make mistakes in our work. "① This requires us to inform the masses, educate the masses and to raise the policy consciousness and understanding of the masses. If the Party's policy is knew only by a few people who act on the behalf the masses, our work is necessarily inactive and not only the Party's policy cannot be implemented, but also opposition may occur between the leaders and the masses due to the misunderstanding of the masses. The process of "to the masses" is also a process of testing, because opinion formed by applying "from the masses" has not been tested before it is practiced. And only the practice of millions of people is the sole criterion for testing truth. If a view is found wrong in practice, it must be corrected immediately, or improved if needed. And a correct view need also to be enriched and developed based on new experience. In short, the rich and live practice of the masses is the source of understanding of the leaders. "from the masses, to the masses, " "Then once again concentrate ideas from the masses and once again go to the masses so that the ideas are persevered in and carried through, " This form repeats itself in endless cycles, which change both the

① *Selected Works of Mao Zedong,* vol. 4, People's Publishing House, 1991, pp. 1319 – 1320.

objective and subjective world, and improve the understanding of both the leaders the masses—this is the basic method of the Party in leading the masses.

IV. Improving the Leadership System and Socialist Political Civilization: The Basic Guarantee for Strengthening the Ties between the Leaders and the Masses

Strengthening ties between the leaders and the masses is a systematic project involving many aspects, among which ideological education is the basis. We must conduct education among our leading cadres at all levels in the important thought of Three Represents, in mass viewpoint and mass line, in the purpose of serving the people wholeheartedly, in hard working, and in Marxist scientific world outlook and methodology. At the same time we must provide the masses with education in patriotism, socialism, collectivism as well as ideals, morality, science and culture. "He will win whose army is animated by the same spirit throughout all its ranks." Only with one heart and one mind can we unite to fight for our common goal.

However, ideological education alone is not enough. Comrade Deng Xiaoping said: "It is true that the errors we made in the past were partly attributable to the way of thinking and style of work of some leaders. But they were even more attributable to the problems in our organizational and working systems. If these systems are sound, they can place restraints on the actions of bad people; if they are unsound, they may hamper the efforts of good people or indeed, in certain cases, may push them in the wrong direction."[①] Therefore, on the basis of ideological education, we must pay attention to the improvement of our systems, proceeding from the improvement of Party and state leadership system to strengthen the construction of socialist political civilization, so as to fundamentally overcome corruption, bureaucracy and other undesirable phenomena in some of our leading organs and leaders. In other words, we must guarantee the close relations between the leadership with the masses by improving our fundamental system.

First, reforming the highly centralized political system and strengthening socialist democracy. In addition to sharing some common features with the old types of bureaucracy, bureaucracy in our socialist system has its distinctive characteristics. It is closely connected with our high centralism in economic, political, cultural and social

---

① *Selected Works of Deng Xiaoping*, vol. 2, People's Publishing House, 1994, p. 333.

fields, which we have long regarded as essential for socialist system. Firstly, our leading organs at various levels have taken charge of many matters which they should not and cannot handle, or cannot handle efficiently. These matters could have been easily handled by the enterprises, institutions and communities at the community level, provided we had proper rules and regulations and they acted according to the principles of democratic centralism. But in the past they were all concentrated to the Party and state organs, resulting in low efficiency, even wrong decisions, which seriously dampened the enthusiasm of the masses in all aspects. We should clearly define the scope of functions and powers among the Party, government, economic and mass organizations, to make centralization or decentralization as is needed with neither "going beyond their scope." Second, inside the leading organs, power was inappropriately and indiscriminately concentrated in the hands of an individual or a few people. When major issues were discussed inside the Party, very often there was insufficient democratic deliberation. Hasty decisions were made by one or a few individuals when they should had been made under the principle of majority rule. This led to the emergence of a number of patriarchal personages with unlimited power, to whom everyone else had be absolutely obedient and even personally attached. Given these lessons, democratic centralism must be strictly exercised in the leading organs of the Party and government at all levels. Major issues must be full discussed following the democratic procedures and decided in accordance with the principle of majority rule. Subordination of the lower Party organizations to the higher means that a lower organization must implement the decisions and instructions from the higher one. This does not, however, preclude relations of equality among Party comrades. Comrades at the higher levels should not imperiously order about those at lower levels, and they certainly must not make them do anything in violation of the Party Constitution or the country's laws; No one should fawn on his superiors or be obedient and "loyal" to them in an unprincipled way. The relationship between a superior and a subordinate must not be the one between cat and mouse. Nor should it be like the relations in the old society between monarch and subject, or father and son, or the leader of a faction and his followers.

Second, formulating and improving administrativelaws and regulations and establishing the system of individual responsibility. For a long time we have had no strict administrative rules or regulations and no system of individual responsibility from top to bottom. We also lacked strict and explicit terms of reference for each organization and post so that there are no rules to go by and most people are often unable to handle independently and responsibly the matters, big or small, which they should handle. They can only keep busy all day long making reports to higher levels, seeking instructions from them, writing comments on documents and passing them around. Some people are seriously afflicted with selfish departmentalism: They are always ducking responsibility, jockeying for power and wrangling with others, thinking only of the interests of their own unit. This is another important cause of bureaucracy. So we must establish and improve from top to bottom administrative laws and regulations and individual responsibility, so that every one has his own task and responsibility, and those who neglect their duties should be penalized. By doing we aim to fundamentally overcoming the lax situation in which everybody seems responsible but no one takes responsibility.

Third, establishing and improvingregular methods for recruiting, rewarding and punishing cadres or for their retirement, resignation or removal. Cadres should not always be recruited and promoted to higher positions. They may be demoted and should always be ready for either a higher or a lower post. Clear distinction should be made between those who work and those do not, between those who work hard and those do little, and between those who work well and those do not. Overstaffing and too many administrative levels and deputy and nominal posts, low efficiency, serious bureaucracy, etc. are all have direct relationship with the defects of our personnel management system. We should improve our election and appointment system to truly elect people on their merits; we should improve the system of rewards and penalties to award the diligent and punish the lazy and select the superior and remove the inferior; and we should strictly implement retirement system and reform the system of life tenure in leading posts.

Fourth, establishing and improving the system of effective oversight to combat corruption and uphold integrity. It is no doubt that the self-restraint of leading cadres and being strict with them are important. However, to prevent the abuse of power and corruption, an effective supervisory mechanism is absolutely necessary. It is pointed out in the Decision of the CPC Central Committee on Strengthening the Party's Ties with the People that "Supervision over leading organs and cadres at all levels must be strengthened. We should improve supervision both within and outside the Party, both top-down and bottom-up."[①] Those who abuse their power or those who neglect their duties must be criticized and educated; and serious offenders must

---

① *Selected Important Documents since the Thirteenth National Congress of the CPC,* vol. 2, People's Publishing House, 1991, p. 935.

be punished in accordance with the law or Party discipline. No one who violates Party or political discipline, or laws, regardless of his post, should go unpunished. We must strengthen supervision of the people in particular. The people have the right to report and file charges over anyone who violates law and discipline, impeach, replace or recall him and ask his economic compensation. We should give full play to the role of public opinion to expose those who abuse power or derelict their duties, in order to create a strong social pressure, so their bad behaviors can go nowhere, to an extent that even if some officials intend to shield each other by using relationships, they can do nothing of the kind.

Fifth, upholding rule of law andstrictly observing the law. The law is not only the weapon in handling contradictions between ourselves and the enemy, but also instrument in solving contradictions among the people. Leaders must act in accordance with the law; when handling various contradictions and disputes of the masses, the law must be strictly observed and the phenomenon that power overshadows law must be eliminated. Whoever does violate the law must be subjected to investigation by the public security organs and brought to justice by the judicial organs according to law. The masses should also learn to protect their rights and benefits by using the law, and cannot do whatever they like although when they are in the right. All citizens, no matter leading cadres or ordinary people, are equal before the law. No one is allowed to interfere with law enforcement, and no one who breaks the law should go unpunished.

Chapter 7

Actively Preventing and Correctly Handling the Intensification of Contradictions among the People

In the primary stage of socialism in China, due to complex domestic and internationalreasons, confrontation, conflict, and even mass incident and social unrest may occur among the people. The correct understanding and handling of the problems is of high significance for social stability and long-term peace and order in our country and for the consolidation and development of socialism.

I. The Antagonistic Side and Intensification of Contradictions among the People

Generally speaking, contradictions between ourselves and the enemy are antagonistic in nature, while those among the people are not. But if we confuse the two different types of contradiction, lose vigilance or handle them improperly, contradictions among the people can become intensified or transformed, leading to serious confrontation or social conflicts.

To understand the antagonistic side andthe intensification of contradictions among the people, we must first of all be clear about what the antagonistic contradiction is and what the non-antagonistic contradiction is.

Comrade Mao Zedongpointed out in On Contradiction that: "... antagonism is one form, but not the only form, of the struggle of opposites. "① Based on this view, we can consider antagonism as form in which the opposites resort to open conflict to resolve it when the contradiction develops to a certain degree. Contradiction is universal, while antagonism is a particular form of its solution. A contradiction is antagonistic only when opposites are fundamentally opposed to each other in nature and have to resort to open conflict or antagonism as its solution; If its opposites are fundamentally identical in nature, even if it ultimately has to be resolved by open conflict, the contradiction is still non-antagonistic.

---

① Selected Works of Mao Zedong, vol. 1, People's Publishing House, 1991, p. 334.

We mustdistinguish the antagonistic nature from antagonistic phenomena of contradictions, distinguish entire antagonism of society from individual antagonism, and distinguish class antagonism from non-class antagonism. The antagonistic nature of a contradiction refers to the antagonism of opposites of a contradiction because they essentially antagonistic; while the antagonistic form of a contradiction refers to the resolution of a contradiction in the form of open conflict derived from the specific circumstances. If the opposites of a contradiction are fundamentally antagonistic in nature and the contradiction is resolved by open conflict, this contradiction is antagonistic. By contrast, if the opposites of a contradiction are not fundamentally antagonistic, although open conflict occur between them, this contradiction is not antagonistic, only that it occasionally or temporarily manifests itself in the form of conflict, which is only an antagonistic phenomenon of a contradiction. Entire antagonism of society refers to the antagonism among major classes or forces of a society, which is originated from the living conditions of the society. Individual antagonism refers to the antagonism among individual elements or groups of society. Since the socialist system is a non-antagonistic system, there is only antagonism between individuals rather than between classes, such as contradictions between working people and the remnants of the old society, occasional contradictions among individuals within the working people, contradictions between the new social elements and those of the old society. Class antagonism originates from interest contradictions between fundamentally antagonistic classes caused by private ownership of means of production. In comparison, non-class conflicts have nothing to do with class antagonism. For example, the war between tribes in primitive society is not class conflict. If antagonism is believed to happen only between classes, then antagonism or conflict among the people in non-class society and socialist society is hardly understandable.

Second, after making the above distinctions, we can now see clearly that, in the primary stage of socialism in our country, there exist conflicts or antagonism among the people and also the possibility of intensification and transformation of these contradictions. The reasons are as follows:

(1) There are isolated phenomena of antagonistic contradictions among the people. In the present stage in China, there are still economic, politic, ideological residue of the old society, in addition to the influence and subversion of external anti-socialist forces in economic, political, ideological and cultural fields, leading to the existence not only contradictions between ourselves and the enemy in a certain

scope, but also occasional antagonistic contradictions among the people. Take the relationship between the private and public economy for instance. These are two different economies in nature, and in the primary stage of socialism private economy is permitted to exist. Therefore, under certain conditions, contradictions between private and public economies manifest themselves in non-antagonistic form. So does the relationship between the private owners and their employees, contradictions belonging to the category of contradictions among the people. In political field, the contradictions between the people and elements left over from the old society, such as the feudalists, bourgeois, historical reactionaries, etc., are antagonistic in nature. However, as long as these elements no longer engage in anti-socialist political activities, honestly submit to socialist transformation and do things beneficial for the people, their contradictions with the people can be regarded and handled as contradictions among the people. Some antagonistic contradictions within the Party also belong to the category of contradictions among the people. Contradictions between the leaders and the masses are non-antagonistic in nature, but those between the severe bureaucrats in the leadership and the masses are antagonistic. In the realm of ideology, contradictions between socialist ideology and feudalist and capitalist ideologies are antagonistic, but the contradictions among the people arising from the influence of these two ideologies come under the category of contradictions among the people in general.

The above analysis shows that individual antagonistic contradictions among the people do exist. By "an individual antagonistic contradictions among the people" we mean: firstly, by saying that the opposites of a contradictions are antagonistic in nature, we refer to its nature, but not the occurrence of antagonistic phenomenon or its necessary resolution through open conflicts. Secondly, a contradiction of antagonistic nature cannot be equated with antagonistic state in reality; it is a latent antagonistic contradiction, which, if handled properly, can become non-antagonistic. And thirdly, an antagonistic contradiction is not equivalent to a contradiction between ourselves and the enemy. Also, in the entire system of contradictions among the people, contradictions of antagonistic nature among the people are few in number and secondary and subordinate in position. With the continuous development of socialism from primary to higher stages, the individual antagonistic contradictions among the people, which are transient in character, will decrease in number. Lastly, the non-antagonistic contradictions among the people, deriving from the basic and principal contradictions of socialist society, are endogenous and the dominant in feature and reflect the essential characteristics of socialism, while the individual antagonistic contradictions among the people are non-endogenous, subordinate ones not reflecting the essential characteristics of socialism.

(2) There are contradictions of class struggle nature among the people in a certain limits. Due to domestic and international factors, class struggle will continue to exist within certain limits in our socialist country, which will inevitably be reflected in the ranks of the people, causing the existence of contradictions with class struggle nature. In China, except for Hong Kong, Macao and Taiwan, class opposition and class struggle between the exploiting and the exploited classes exist only in a limited range, but they do no exist within the ranks of the people. The differences between the working class and peasantry do not manifest themselves as class struggle. And the contradictions prevailing within the ranks of the people are not antagonistic in nature and they do not fall within the category of class struggle. However, this does not exclude the fact that, some of the contradictions among the people have a nature of class struggle. For example, the combating against bourgeois liberalization; the fighting against corrosion of bourgeois ideology; the contradictions between the people and some persons who commit petty crime of endangering public security or social order: these contradictions, although having a nature of class struggle, are still belongs to the contradictions among the people.

(3) Non-antagonistic contradictions among the people can transform into antagonistic ones, and contradictions among the people can transform into contradictions between ourselves and the enemy. Facing complex factors at home and abroad and social contradictions, if we lose vigilance, confuse contradictions, make wrong decisions or handle improperly, a non-antagonistic contradiction among the people can transform into antagonistic one, and even a contradiction among the people can transform into that between ourselves and the enemy. If our policy is incorrect or our handling is improper, some contradictions among the people can intensify, even result in conflicts. For example, some incidents such as worker strikes, mass violent conflicts or incidents of bloodshed are caused by the improper handling of discontent of the masses over shortage or the increase of prices of consumer goods. In this kind of incidents, except for a few bad elements, the majority of those involved belong to the category of the people. Another example is the quarrel over means of production in rural areas. After the implementation of household contract responsibility system, disputes often happen between farmers over irrigation, land boundary and the like. If not handled timely and effectively, they

can develop into violent conflicts. On the other hand, antagonism is only one form of manifestations of contradictions among the people. It is neither the ultimate nor the only resolution. These phenomena, often as the result of insufficient vigilance or improper handling and usually temporary and local, do not represent the essence of contradictions among the people which are non-antagonistic in nature. These antagonistic phenomena do not mean that these contradictions are antagonistic in nature, because they are only temporary and individual form of manifestation of the contradictions.

(4) In reality, the two types of contradictions differing in nature intertwine, forming a complex situation, in which the class struggle in a limited range and the contradictions of no-class struggle in nature; the limited number of contradictions between ourselves and the enemy and the overwhelming majority of contradictions among the people; the antagonistic contradictions in the non-dominant position and the dominant no-antagonistic contradictions, etc., are often inextricably intertwined rather than clearly distinguishable from each other, thus forming a complex social situation. This is particularly true in the primary stage of socialism. Take the demonstration of some students, workers, farmers or ordinary citizens for example. Generally speaking, the majority of the masses are patriotic and their demonstration actions belong to the category of contradictions among the people. But the causes are very complex, including instigation of hostile forces, our mistakes in work, and so on. Among them contradictions between us and the evil elements hiding behind and deliberately making incitement and subversion belong to the contradictions between ourselves and the enemy.

Third, the prominent manifestations of intensification and antagonism of contradictions among the people are interest and social conflicts within the ranks of the people

Contradictions among the people are manifested as interest conflict in terms of dynamic behaviors of the subjects of interests. So recognizing interest contradictions among the people necessarily means recognizing the interest conflict among the subjects of interests within the ranks of the people. Under socialist system, interest conflicts can be divided into two categories: one is interest conflicts among the people and the other is those between ourselves and enemy. The majority of them belong to the first category as the dynamic manifestations of their interest contradictions. In fact, interest conflicts among the people are not uncommon. Examples include opposition in emotion and conflict of action due to disputes between different subjects of interest, sabotage, go-slow, demonstrations, even large-scale conflict with the government. The prominent manifestations of intensification and antagonism of contradictions among the people are interest conflicts and social conflicts within the ranks of the people. Fundamentally speaking, this kind of conflicts in socialist countries is non-antagonistic in nature. But lack of vigilance against or incorrect handling of them will lead to antagonistic conflict of interests, which finally may make the relationship between the Party and government with the masses become worse and develop into political conflicts or unrest or social turmoil.

Interest conflicts within the people in socialist countries basically take two forms, i. e., direct conflict and indirect conflict. If the interest of one side of the opposites of the contradiction is infringed by the other side, it will lead to direct conflict. For example, in China's rural areas, simply because the crops of one side are destroyed or its water is cut away, head-on collision occurs, which, sometimes develop into bloodshed. Direct interest conflict means direct emotional or behavioral confrontation arising from direct interest disputes. Second, different from direct conflicts of interest that often originate in the economic sphere, indirect conflicts of interest generally occurs in the political and ideological fields. Indirect conflicts of interest, at the first glance, may seem unrelated to interests, but in fact, political or ideological conflicts represent the conflicts between different subjects of interests, only that they take the indirect and covert forms of political struggle. Indirect interest conflicts are the expansion, deepening and chain reaction of direct interest conflicts. If improperly handled, some direct interest conflicts will intensify into indirect interest conflicts, spreading from economic conflicts into political conflicts and from local conflicts into social conflicts.

Interest contradictions and social conflicts among the people can be basically divided into horizontal form and vertical form. Horizontally, they manifest themselves as contradictions and conflicts among individuals, among interest groups, strata, classes, and even between ethnic groups, between nations and between countries. Vertically, they manifest themselves as contradictions and conflicts among the three sides of individuals, the collectives and the state, which is specifically reflected in the relationship between individual workers with the leaders and managers of (state or collective-owned) enterprises and with leading cadres in the organization of the state. Examples of them include: contradictions and conflicts between the decisions and measures representing the overall interests made by the leaders and the unhealthy tendency of some of the masses who concern only immediate interest or pursue excessive personal benefits; contradictions and conflicts between the bureaucratic style of work of some leaders who are indifferent to the well-being of the masses and the justified demands of the masses; contradictions and conflicts between the corruption of some leaders and the struggle of some of the masses in safeguarding their own interests; contradictions and conflicts between the subjective mistakes made by some leaders that injure the interests of the masses and the discontent of the masses because of it; contradictions and conflicts between state leaders and leaders of enterprises, between central and local, between higher and lower level authorities, between centralization and decentralization, etc. In all these contradictions and conflicts, if the interest demands of the masses are justified, then the leaders constitute the principal aspect of the contradictions, whose resolution depends on the improvement of the leadership system, style of thinking and method of work of the leaders; even if they derive from the backwardness or unreasonable demands of the masses, their resolution depends also on the mass work of the leaders. In general, the leaders always constitute the dominant side in the contradictions between the leaders and masses. Also, among the horizontal and vertical interest conflicts within the ranks of the people, the contradiction between the leaders and the people plays a leading role.

Contradictions among the people may cause wider social conflicts, which, intertwined with the class struggle and contradictions between ourselves and the enemy in the primary stage of socialism and stimulated by the subjective mistakes of the leaders in handling them, will become further intensified and sharpened. This being the case, they will further lead to social unrests bringing about severe damage to the social order, political stability and economic development in socialist countries.

II. The Issue of the Correct Handling of Mass Incidents

In many cases, the intensification of contradictions among the people results in mass incidents. By a mass incident we mean a mass conflict happens in forms of petition, strike, demonstration and the like, which is triggered by local contradictions, conflicts or confrontations, or temporary economic difficulties, or when the demands of some of the masses have not been met, or when the bureaucratic or corruptive behaviors of some personnel in the Party or the government severely violate the interests of the people and have not been timely rectified, or when some of the masses having incorrect ideas are incited, and so on. Mass incidents are objective social phenomena reflecting the intensification of contradictions or conflicts among the people. They are different from the political conspiracies of a handful elements opposing to the Party and socialism, and from the criminal activities of rioting and looting; and the majority of the masses involved in these incidents are also different from those criminals who fish in troubled waters and make looting, rioting or other sabotage. Mass incidents can cause social unrest or instability to varying degrees, disrupt public order and economic development. Social contradictions can become sharper, even become antagonistic by mass incidents, besetting the society and economy of the country and directly endangering the power of the state. How to understand and deal with mass incidents constitutes an important part of the correct handling of the intensification of contradictions among the people. The experience and lessons of development of socialism in the world clearly tell us that, in socialist countries, there exist various contradictions among the people, and these contradictions can intensify into confrontations, mass incidents and other kinds of social conflicts, resulting in extreme political instability, even threatening the survival of the socialist countries. Take the Soviet Union for example. In his leading of the socialist construction of the country for as long as 28 years, Stalin made grave mistakes both in understanding and action. Under his leadership, the Soviet Union made severe political purges since 1930s, creating numerous unjust, false and wrong cases and a large number of innocent victims. The expansion of the purges undermined the socialist democracy and legal system of the Soviet Union, leading to many abnormal phenomena and gradual intensification of accumulated domestic contradictions. During the era of Khrushchev, mass demonstrations broke out in March 1956 in Tbilisi, capital of Georgia; in 1956 and 1959, large-scale strikes and demonstrations occurred, which were all suppressed by the authorities using armed forces, bring about large number of casualties. According to incomplete statistics of scholars from former Yugoslavia, from 1958 to August, 1969, there were a total of 1906 workers' strikes Yugoslavia.[①] In the summer of 1953, tens of thousands of workers took to the streets in former Democratic Republic of Germany, requesting improvement of their living conditions and fundamental political reform, and violent clashes happened between strikers and

① Naica Ivanov, *Worker Strikes in Socialist Federal Republic of Yugoslavia from* 1958 – 1969, Qunzhong Publishing House, 1964, p. 157.

the government. In the summer of 1956, large-scale workers unrests and clashes between the workers and the army happened in Poznan, Poland, causing serious bloodshed, the political crisis and major changes in the top leadership of Poland in the autumn of the same year. In the autumn of 1956, the Hungarian Incident shocking the whole socialist bloc broke out. At the end of the 1960s, numerous social crises happened in Poland. In August 1968, students took to the streets in Poland and major riots broke out across the country. Eleven years later, in Ddynia and Szczeciaski, two famous industrial cities in Poland, large-scale worker riots and bloodshed incidents took place, leading to the changes of top leaders of the party and government in Poland. In the middle 1970s, a number of large-scale workers' strikes broke out again in Poland. In the early 1980s, the movement of the Solidarity across the country brought the country into turmoil. The Prague Spring of 1968 in Czechoslovakia shocked not only the country but also the socialist movement around the world. In China, the unprecedented Cultural Revolution also fully exposed our domestic contradictions, so that the development of our socialism beset by an extremely dangerous crisis. The drastic changes in the former Soviet Union and Eastern Europe are the results of breaking out of the unsolved contradictions accumulated over the years, coupled with other domestic and international factors. The political turmoil on June 4, 1989 in China is essentially the result of intensification of various contradictions. The economic and political unrests arising from intensification of contradictions in socialist counties are bound to affect the stability and power security of the countries.

The direct causes of mass incidents are often serious economic difficulties, especiallysome wrong economic policies and measures that undermine the people's immediate interests, resulting in the relative decline of their living standards and their demands unsatisfied. These demands, except for a few, mostly are reasonable and resolvable. Among the causes of mass incidents, one factor merits attention, that is, the bureaucracy and corruption of some leaders. Because of bureaucratic style of work some leaders, the reasonable and resolvable demands of the masses are ignored; and no work has been done in rejecting the unreasonable demands of some of the masses. Especially with regard to the malpractices bitterly detested by the people, such as corruption, oppression, nepotism, etc., the leaders with a bureaucratic style of work take no effective effort to correct them; on the contrary, they sidestep them, even take a protective attitude toward them, so that the discontent of the masses accumulate and eventually erupt into mass incidents.

Another cause of mass incidents is that no sufficient efforts are made to educate and persuade the backward section of the masses, so that the masses are possessed by bigotry or erroneous views, resulting in radical words, emotions, behaviors and acts of some people to vent their dissatisfaction to the Party and government, or put forward unreasonable demands, and so on. In these circumstances, the main reason of the insufficient education of the masses is still the bureaucracy of the leaders. Yet another cause of mass incidents is that, the discontent and tendency of riot of the masses are made use by some domestic and external reactionary elements who spread feudal and capitalist ideas, political philosophy and rumors, sow discord and instigate troubles and incidents. The key to preventing the sabotage of a few bad elements lies also in the hands of the leaders. The factors of instability in the complex relations between different ethnic groups are also an important cause of mass incidents. Many socialist countries are multi-ethnic. Complex historical, religious, cultural and other social factors may bring about frictions and conflict between ethnic groups, which can develop into mass incidents. The mass incidents in some socialist countries are more or less associated with the defects in their institutions. After the establishment of socialist system, these countries copied in a different degree, the highly centralized government model of the Soviet Union and in a fairly long period of time ignored improving socialist legal system. Because their democracy and legal systems were not sound, some socialist countries even wrongly carried out inner-party struggles and political movements, which seriously violated democracy and the laws, giving birth to large numbers of unjust, false and wrong cases and strong resentment of the people. Lastly, in the process of socialist reform, the transition of the old system to the new and the adjustment of interest distribution will highlight the social contradictions, which, if not properly handled, will intensify and result in temporary mass incidents.

Somemass incidents actually reflect the contradictions between the bureaucracy of some of the leaders and the masses, in which the main participants are the masses, but their targets are often leading organs of the Party and government.

If werelax our vigilance against mass incidents or handle them incorrectly, the contradictions will further intensify even develop into serious political conflict or turmoil, which is possible to make the contradictions among the people transform into those between ourselves and the enemy, thus directly endanger the fate of the Party and the state. Therefore, in dealing with mass incidents, we must in the first place distinguish between the two different types of contradictions, because, except a handful of evil elements, most of the participants belong to the category of the people. We must resolutely guard against two erroneous tendencies: one is heaping of all the blame on the masses without any discrimination, which will encourage the bureaucracy of the leaders; the other is the failure in seeing the erroneous tendency of the masses, and thus relaxing vigilance against the evil elements. While meeting the reasonable demands of the masses, ideological education given to them must be strengthened. The small number of individuals who flout the public interests and wilfully break the law and commit crimes must receive legal sanction. Lessons must be drawn up to resolutely abolish various malpractices, corruption and bureaucracy; defects and mistakes of the leadership must be corrected in their relationship with the masses and in their properly handling of various contradictions. On the other hand, the fundamental way to resolve mass incidents is to, through socialist reform, promote the development of productive forces, vigorously improve socialist democracy, legal system and the socialist system itself, so as to uproot the latent risk of the social unrest, facilitate the growth and constantly improving people's lives.

III. Basic Measures for Preventing the Intensification of Contradictions and Occurrence of Social Unrest

At present, reform and opening up must be strengthened: our economic structure must be reformed to promote socialist productive forces and material civilization; our political structure must be reformed to develop socialist democracy and political civilization; and our cultural system must be reformed to facilitate socialist cultural and ethical progress. We should enhance the building of socialist material civilization, political civilization, cultural progress and harmonious society to provide a firmer institutional guarantee, making the handling of contradictions among the people based on procedures, laws and systems, so as to effectively resolve the contradictions among the people and prevent the intensification of contradictions, mass incidents and social unrest.

First, we must establisha economic-political system conducive to the development of social productive forces. The various expressions of contradictions among the people at the primary stage of socialism, in the final analysis, is due to the fact that the existing material and cultural level cannot meet the people's growing needs. In China, the root cause of contradictions among the people at the present stage is nothing but the contradiction between the backwardness of our social production and the growing needs of the people. Therefore, the only way to fundamentally solve the contradictions among the people is to unswervingly take the development of social productive forces and economy as our focus of work. So our attention in socialist reform should be paid into the establishment of a economic-political system favoring the development of social productivity and socialist market economy, which is the ultimate approach to resolving the contradictions among the people at the primary stage of socialism.

Second, we mustestablish a socio-economic-political system that can bring the initiative of the masses into full play. The most profound significance of the correct handling of the contradictions among the people lies in mobilizing the enthusiasm of the people. Suppressing or discouraging the enthusiasm will make the contradictions more acute. Comrade Mao Zedong pointed out in his On the Ten Major Relationships that if we are to promote socialist construction, we must bring the initiative of internal and external factors. The essential idea of making reform of socialist institutions is to better mobilize the enthusiasm of the masses. As a country at the primary stage of socialism, China is relatively in a low level of productive forces. In order to adapt to this reality, we should establish structures compatible with this reality in the systems of ownership, distribution and management, and in the links of production, circulation, exchange and distribution, to better resolve the economic and distributive contradictions among the people and coordinate interpersonal economic relationship. An incompatible economic system that discourages the initiative of enterprises and individuals is unfavorable to the resolution of various contradictions among the people. Stress should also be put on the reform of political structure by centering on the improvement of democracy and legal system, to institutionally guarantee people's right of participation and right to act on one's own in the political and economic life, so as political relations between individuals more rational. The reason why an unsuitable political structure affect the enthusiasm of the people is it is unfavorable for relieving political contradictions among the people. So, socialist reform must be focused on the correct handling of the contradictions among the people in economic and political life to mobilize their enthusiasm in production and politics.

Third, we must establisha socio-economic system in favorable to the resolution of contradictions of material interests among the people. Within the ranks of the people in socialist countries, there are different subject of interests with different interest demands. To reasonably meet these demands, the incomes representing the rational demands of the subjects of interest must be guaranteed. The differences of the incomes should at once reasonable and not too big. This requires the establishment of an economic-political system that can both effectively distribute incomes among different subjects of interests and reasonably cope with the differences.

Fourth, we must economically and politically establish and improve the socialist legal system, so that contradictions among the people can be handled in an institutionalized way and according to procedure and law. To handle the contradictions among the people by the rule of man will inevitably make the mistake of confusing the two different types of contradictions; only the legal system can provide guarantee for the correct handling of them. Thus, the improvement of socialist legal system to make it as the ordinary way of solving the contradictions among the people is of great significance.

Fifth, we must be good at correctly distinguish between two different types of contradictions, so as to timely and effectively resolve the contradictions of the people early before they become intensified. Prevention is the first priority in this regard, that is, we should by all means prevent them from happening. This requires that the Party committees and governments at all levels should always remain sober-minded, carefully observe the changes of domestic and international situation, to find any sign or tendency of intensification of the contradictions, so as to timely and effectively forestall the problems and resolve them in the bud. We can never take the bureaucratic attitude of waiting until problems pile up. On the other hand, once a problem does come up, we should not be panic, but rather be cool-minded to distinguish between the masses and bad elements, that is, using different methods to handle different types of contradictions.

In short, the institutional guarantee andbasic measure to correctly handle the contradictions among the people and to prevent the intensification of the contradictions, mass incidents and social unrests is to deepen reform, so as to build an economic and political system that can effectively resolve the various contradictions among the people, and can keep the socialist market economy, democracy and harmonious society all in good order.

Chapter 8

Basic Principles of and Methods for the Correct Handling of Contradictions among the People in the New Era

To correctly handle contradictions among the people, we first of all must clearly recognize that contradictions among the people and those between ourselves and the enemy are two types of contradiction differing in nature, which must be resolved by completely different methods. Comrade Mao Zedong pointed out: "How to handle the contradictions between the people and the enemy and those among the people in socialist society is a branch of science worthy of careful study."① The correct understanding of the two different types of contradictions is the premise for their resolution in a scientific way. But correct understanding doesn't necessarily mean the correct handling of them, for which purpose, different methods must be used.

I. Methods of Confrontation and Struggle, or Dictatorship Must Be Used in Handling Contradictions between Ourselves and the Enemy

In the primary stage of socialism in China, contradictions between ourselves and the enemy are contradictions that emerged on the basis of fundamental opposition of interests, and for their resolution, the method of confrontational struggle, that is, the method of dictatorship must be used in general. The method of confrontational struggle or dictatorship means that, under the leadership of the CPC, the state function of people's democratic dictatorship is exercised and legal power is used in resolving both domestic and international contradictions between ourselves and the enemy. Domestically, it is used to repress the social forces and groups opposing, undermining or being hostile to socialist construction; to repress various types of criminals and dregs of society, that means, they are not permitted to take part in

① Mao Zedong, "Speech At Conference Of Provincial And Municipal Committee Secretaries".

political activity and be compelled to obey the law, to engage in labor and, through such labor, be transformed into new men. Internationally, it defends our socialist motherland from subversion, sabotage and possible aggression of the imperialism and various anti-socialist forces.

In handlingcontradictions between ourselves and the enemy, we must pay attention to the following issues: First, we should use socialist legal system, i. e., through legal procedure to resolve the contradictions between ourselves and the enemy. During the revolutionary war years, we resolved the contradictions between the people and the enemy mainly through armed struggles. But after the establishment of socialist system with the people holding the power and the weapon of socialist legal system, this type of contradictions should be resolved through legal procedure. Second, we should properly handle the issue of class struggle. During the revolutionary war years, we resolved the contradictions between the people and the enemy mainly through large-scale, turbulent class struggles. But in socialist society, class struggle is still one of the forms, though not the principal one, of resolving contradictions between ourselves and the enemy. Of course, class struggle in socialist society are different from that in the class society in terms of object, scope, priority and role, and it mainly takes the form of people's democratic dictatorship, specifically, through legal process. Therefore, in solving contradictions between ourselves and the enemy, we must properly handle the issue of class struggle. We can neither expand class struggle, nor imagine that "class struggle has totally died out", nor launch class struggle of mass movement characteristic of the war years, nor completely abandon the form of class struggle. In this circumstance, the antagonistic contradictions between ourselves and the enemy should be resolved through form of class struggle within a certain bounds, in other words, through instrument of dictatorship, including legal system. Third, we should use different tactics and ways and handle them properly in terms of scope, limit, and timing to take a good use of different legal proceedings and different means of dictatorship.

II. Methods for Resolving Contradictions among the People Must Differ from Method for Resolving Contradictions between Ourselves and the Enemy

"Qualitatively different contradictions can only be resolved by qualitatively *different methods.*"[①] Therefore, methods for resolving contradictions among the people must differ from that for resolving contradictions between ourselves and the enemy.

First, economic means should be mainly used to resolve contradictions of material and economic interest among the people.

Second, democratic methods should mainly be used to resolve ideological contradictions among the people.

Mao Zedong pointed out: "The only way to settle questions of an ideological nature or controversial issues among the people is by the democratic method, the method of discussion, criticism, persuasion and education, and not by the method of coercion or repression." And he epitomized the democratic method into a formula "unity—criticism—unity." Comrade Deng Xiaoping also said: "In political life within the Party and among the people we must use democratic means and not resort to coercion or attack." So, democratic method is not only the basic way to solve the problem of right and wrong but also to solve contradictions in political life within the people.

How, then, can we use the principle and means of democracy to solve ideological contradictions among the people in ideological and political fields? First of all, we should improve and develop socialist democracy, which is the basic guideline in this regard. Ours is a democratic country with the people being the masters. Only by steadily carrying out political reform to truly realize extensive, comprehensive and sound socialist democracy and political civilization in political, economic, ideological and cultural life, and political life in particular, can we effectively prevent the leading bodies within the Party and the state from bureaucracy and corruption, strengthen the ties between the cadres and Party with the masses, so as to fundamentally mobilize the enthusiasm of the people, better coordinate relationships among ethnic groups, among classes, and among groups; relationships between the CPC and the democratic parties, between the Party and the masses; relationships within the Party, between the leadership and the masses, between superiors and subordinates, between central and local governments and so on, to ensure the stability and unity of our socialist country. Secondly, the basic measure for handling question of right and wrong within the people is to carry out effective ideological and political work and to use the approach of "unity—criticism—unity" to

---

① *Selected Works of Mao Zedong*, vol. 1 People's Publishing House, 1991, p. 311.

promote socialist cultural and ethical progress. Using democratic methods to solve the question of right and wrong among the people, in fact, is to carry out effective ideological and political work and correct ideological struggle through criticism, praise, education, explanation, persuasion, consultation, dialogue and so on, so as to promote socialist cultural and ethical progress, introduce correct ideas into the people and guide them to consciously distinguish right from wrong and resist wrong and backward ideological influence. Thirdly, to implement the principle "let a hundred flowers blossom and a hundred schools of thought contend," strengthen socialist cultural construction to resolve contradictions among the people in the fields of science and culture. In these fields, it is necessary to both adhere to the guidance of Marxism and advocate the free disputes among different academic schools and free development of different artistic styles and forms. The question of right and wrong in these fields should be resolved through practice and free discussions under the guidance of Marxism, The principle of "Let a hundred flowers blossom and a hundred schools of thought contend" is the embodiment of using democratic methods to solve contradictions among the people in the fields of science and culture. Fourthly, there also some contradictions among the people that must be resolved through compulsory administrative measures. With regard to the principal method of operation of trade union in the Soviet Union, Lenin pointed out that the main method is persuasion and education; but on the other hand, as participants in the exercise of state power they cannot refuse to share in coercion. For resolving contradictions among the people, democratic means is the main method; but against the phenomena of violating the law and disciplines among the people, compulsory administrative regulations and disciplines must be used in order to protect the order of work, study, production and life of the people. Democratic method and coercive method are complementary to each other. Lastly, the development and improvement of socialist legal system is the basic guarantee to solve ideological and political contradictions among the people. It is hard to avoid the error of confusing the two different types of contradictions to handle these contradictions by relying only on rule of man. Therefore we should develop and improve socialist legal system to provide legal and procedural guarantee for their solution.

Third, contradictions among the people are complex and versatile, so that comprehensive methods are needed to effectively resolve them.

The manifestations of contradictions among the people are very complex, which must be handled through different and overall methods. In the present stage, contradictions among the people are not isolated to each other but rather constitute a complex system of contradictions, within which external and internal factors are interlinked and interact. Therefore, in resolve these contradictions, there is no fixed formula or prescription for all disease, we cannot use a single method, but rather take different ways according to specific conditions. Take the relationship between the Communist Party and the democratic parties for example. We adopt the principle of "long-term coexistence, mutual supervision", and resolve problems between them through democratic consultations and dialogues under the political consultation system led by the Communist Party. Another example is the contradictions between the leaders and the masses, which "at a large extent find their expression in contradictions between the masses and the leaders, more specifically, in the bureaucracy of the leadership and the people." So the correct handling of the leadership and the mass depends on to a large extent our effective overcoming of bureaucracy. This is because bureaucracy divorce themselves from the masses and reality, leading contradictions among the people that could have been resolved in reasonable way become sharpened; even when the cause of the contradictions does not lie in the side of the leadership but in the unreasonable request or incorrect ideas of some of the masses, the leaders, if without the work style of bureaucracy, can and should make clear explanation and careful work so that the contradictions cannot become intensified.

How, then, can we overcome bureaucracy? Due the complexity of its causes, efforts in various aspects are needed. Firstly, we must strengthen ideological education, so that leading cadres at all levels firmly foster the idea of serving the people wholeheartedly. Comrade Mao Zedong once said that bureaucracy, "in terms of social origin, it reflects the survival in our party and government of the reactionary style of work (an anti-popular style of work, a Kuomintang style of work) of thc reactionary ruling classes in dealing with the people." Therefore, to overcome bureaucracy, we must resolutely resist and eliminate the ideological influence of feudalism and capitalism, overcome the malpractices such as "acting as overlords", abuse of power for personal gains, and mentality of privilege. Secondly, we must remove the soil for bureaucracy, i. e., defects in our systems. Comrade Deng Xiaoping said, "it is true that the errors we made in the past were partly attributable to the way of thinking and style of work of some leaders. But they were even more attributable to the problems in our organizational and working systems. If these systems are sound, they can place restraints on the actions of bad people; if they are unsound, they may hamper the efforts of good people or indeed, in certain cases, may push them in the wrong direction. This requires us to make reform in our leadership system to eliminate the malpractices such as over-concentration of power, overstaffing, and gradually improve systems of cadre selection, evaluation, supervision, rewards, penalties and dismissal, etc. Thirdly, the unscientific method of leadership is also one of the causes of bureaucracy. For example, the phenomena that there is collective leadership but without individual responsibility, official documents are endlessly routed around, many issues are put off protractedly even shelved forever, major decisions are made personally by violating the principle of collective leadership, and so on. For this, Comrade Deng Xiaoping said, "In order to overcome bureaucracy ... we have to improve our methods of work as well. "And the bureaucrats who have brought great loss to the Party and the people must be punished by the law and Party discipline. Another example is ethnic relations. In dealing with ethnic contradictions, we must firmly foster the idea that fundamentally identical interests underlie this type of contradictions among the people of different ethnic groups who cannot be separated from each other. We should integrate the common interests of all ethnic groups with that of specific ethnic groups and the conformity of socialist society with the diversity of ethnic groups, to practice ethnic regional autonomy system, and vigorously support and assist their economic and cultural development, so as to gradual eliminate the de facto gap between ethnic groups, realize the common prosperity of all ethnic groups and handle properly the contradictions between Han and other ethnic minorities.

Fourth, socialist reform and opening up and vigorous development of socialist productive forces are the institutional and material guarantees for the correct handling of contradictions among the people.

How can we ensure that we can correctly handlecontradictions among the people? We have bitter lessons in this regard. Now that we had established the theory of two different types of contradictions accompanied by a set of principles and methods in handling contradictions among the people, why in the past we didn't apply the correct theory in practice so that such social unrest as the decade long "cultural revolution" that completely confused the two types of contradictions differing in nature still took place? As known to all, due to historical limitations and a certain lack of thoroughness in theory, Comrade Mao Zedong violated the basic ideas of the theory of contradictions among the people. But another question is: why did the individual mistake of Comrade Mao Zedong lead to the serious historic mistake of the whole Party? How can we prevent individual mistakes from harming the cause of the Party? Actually Comrade Mao himself had been aware of this problem. He pointed out that Stalin's mistake of expanding the scope of purge was unlikely to happen in developed capitalist countries such as Britain and the U.S., but it happened in the Soviet Union. The reason is that in those countries a relatively complete bourgeois socio-economic and political system is in place, which can somehow prevent the individual in the bourgeois ruling group from harming the overall interests of bourgeoisie, and can to some extent coordinate their internal contradictions. And since our socialist economic and political system was far from sound, it could not effectively completely stop individual leaders from making mistakes that could harm the cause of the whole Party, and could not properly handle contradictions among the people from the perspective of institution. Although Comrade Mao was aware of the importance of institutions, he himself could not transcend the limitations of history. The fundamental cause for our party's mistake of confusing the two different types of contradictions lies in the institution. After the establishment of the basic system of socialism, we hadn't yet build up sound institutions to ensure the implementation of correct lines, to protect the overall interests of the people, and to keep the relationship of interests among people in proper order. Therefore, we must integrate the theory of correct handling the two different types of contradictions with the present reform of socialist political structure, to establish a sounder socialist economic-political system as a fundamental institutional guarantee for the handling of the two types of contradictions differing in nature.

Apart from political reform toward a complete set of social, economic and political institutions, a more important and more fundamental solution is to vigorously develop the socialist productive forces, to enhance the overall national strength of our socialist country and the improve the lives of the people. The principal contradiction in our society is still one between the ever-growing material and cultural needs of the people and the backwardness of our social production, which is the deep-rooted cause of the existence, complexity and prominence of contradictions among the people. Therefore, the most fundamental and important thing is to develop the economy. Only by doing this through socialist reform and opening up and liberating the productive forces can we resolve the contradiction between production and needs and thus fundamentally provide a guarantee for the resolution of contradictions among the people. It is in this sense we say that the development of the socialist productive forces is the material guarantee for our correct handling of contradictions among the people.

PART TWO

An Analysis of the Classes, Strata and Interest Groups and Their Relationships at the Primary Stage of Socialism in China

Since reform and opening up, with the development of the socialist market economy, the structure of social members in our country has undergone great changes. Differentiation and combination have occurred among the original classes and strata, and new strata and new interest groups have emerged. Therefore, a scientific understanding of the social structure and a correct analysis of the classes, strata, interest groups and their relationships in the current stage is an important part of the theory of contradictions among the people, an important premise for improving our social management and social construction in the new era and an important basis for our party to formulate line, principles and policies at the primary stage of socialism.

Chapter 9

Scientific Methodsfor Analyzing Social Classes, Strata and Interest Groups and Their Relationship

To correctly understand the social structure, that is, the composition of the classes, strata and interest groups and their relationships in the current stage of our society, we must, first of all, have a scientific analytic method.

I. The Study of Structure of Social Members and Its Significance

In human history, each specific social formation has its own patterned structure, known as social structure, which can be divided into social economic structure, political structure and cultural structure. Social economic structure mainly refers to the economic structure, including the structure ofrelations of production and structure of productive forces. Relations of production can be subdivided into relations of ownership, relations of distribution, etc., with the structure of ownership and distribution as the most important components. The structure of ownership determines the structure of distribution. In the final analysis, the structure of ownership is composed of the ownership of different nature, and the structure of distribution is composed of different modes of distribution. The structure of productive forces includes such specific components as means of production, labor, etc. The structure of productive forces determines the structure of relations of production.

Of the social economic, political and cultural structures, it is the economic structure that mainly determines the structure of social members of a society, which is academically called as structure of social classes or structure of social strata. According to Marxist viewpoints of social structure and social classes, the structure of social members refers to the way of existence, belonging, status and role of the individuals, their proportion and relationships. The structure of social members of human society since the emergence of class is mainly made up of classes, strata and interest groups. In other words, in the macro-level, members of a society can be divided into classes, strata and interest groups. In a class society and a society having classes, structure of social members refers mainly to the structure classes, strata and interest groups. A classless society has, without doubt, its own structure of social members. Under certain social and historical circumstances, the structure of the social members of a certain social formation in a certain stage of development is relatively stable. In this book, the author focuses mainly on the structure of classes, strata and interest groups in China in the primary stage of socialism in which classes exist.

The study of the structure of social members in our society in the current stage is the study of the structure of classes, strata and interest group in the primary stage of socialism. It involves the major issues having a bearing on the survival and development of our party and nation, and is an important basis on which we understand our national conditions and scientifically judge the development of China's social development and to make line, principles and policies. The scientific analysis and correct understanding of these issues is a precondition for us to correctly analyze, understand and handle all types of contradictions among the people and to coordinate the interests of all sides so as to mobilize the enthusiasm and creativity of all social members.

To analyze the structure ofsocial members means, by using scientific principles, standards and methods, to categorize the classes, strata and interest groups of the social members, in order to determine their social statuses, attitudes, ways of production and life, roles in the structure, as well as their modes of existence, proportions and mutual relationship, respectively. The correct analysis of it has always been an important basis for the CPC to make correct line, principles and policies both in the revolutionary war and in era of peaceful construction and reform and opening. In the democratic revolution period, Comrade Mao Zedong published his famous article "Analysis of the Classes in Chinese Society", which analyzed the classes in China in a scientific way and correctly answered the question of first importance of the revolution, that is, "Whom should we rely on? Whom should we unite with? Whom should we combat against?" and suggested the correct line, principles, policies and strategies for our party to carry out and win the new democratic revolution. Similar analysis is also necessary in the period of socialist construction and reform and opening up for the following reasons:

First, it is an important issue having a direct bearing upon the survival of our party and nation. Whether we can correctly understand the changes of the structure of members in our society is directly related to the issue whether we can consolidate the class basis and mass basis of our party as the governing party, and is extremely important for us to consolidate the position of our party and national strength of our socialist country.

Second, it is an important basis on which we have clear understanding of the nature of China's society and make a scientific judgment of our social conditions. The structure of social members is an important component of our national conditions and is thus one of the fundamental bases on which to determine at what stage our society is and what basic conditions it has. The correct understanding of the structure of our social members and the statuses, features of different classes, strata and interest groups as well as their relations, their development trends and the roles they play in our socialist modernization, will help us to have a deeper understanding of our basic national conditions.

Third, it is the basis on which our party and government scientifically make correct line, principles and policies. Under the new historical conditions, it is necessary for our party and government to conduct careful investigation, study and objective analysis of the changes in the members ofour society before formulating lines, principles and policies.

Fourth, it is a precondition for us to correctly analyze, understand and handle all types of contradictions among the people, to coordinate the interests of all sides and to maintain social stability and build socialist harmonious society.

II. Economic, Class, Interest and Stratum Analysis of the Structure of Social Members in Our Society

To have a correct understanding of the structure, classes, strata and interest groups of our society, scientific methods of analysis are necessary. Economic analysis, class analysis and interest analysis are the basic methods for us historical materialists to both analyze social phenomena and classes, strata and interest groups and their relations. Lenin said that it is "obliged to seek for the roots of social phenomena in production relations (and) obliged to reduce them to the *interests* of definite classes."① Economy constitutes the prerequisite to the existence and development of all societies, and economic relations are the bases of the existence

① Collected Works of Lenin, vol. 1, People's Publishing House, 1984, p. 464.

and development of social relations. In social life, economic relations inevitably demonstrate themselves as or find their expression in interest relations. In class societies, economic relations find their expression mainly in relations and interests of classes. Therefore, to understand social phenomena and structure of social members, it is important to make analysis from economic foundation of social existence, and the analysis of interest relations is imperative. In a class society, the economic and class analyses of social phenomena will inevitably lead to correct method of understanding, that is, class analysis. The three analyses are both consistent and different.

Stratification is an important sociological method of analyzing social structure, which, although different from the economic, class and interest analyses of historical materialism, has a degree of consistency and connections with them, so it can also be applied, under the guidance of historical materialism, to analyze social structure.

III. The Understanding of the Structure of Social Members Must Start with Economic Analysis

Historical materialism believes that it is man's social being that determines his social consciousness. Therefore, the ultimate cause of social development is material and economic factors, so are all social phenomena. Historical idealism, on the contrary, insists that social existence is determined by social consciousness, so the ultimate cause of social development is spiritual power, and all social phenomena are inevitably explained from this point of view. Explaining social and historical phenomena based on the material and economic factors fundamentally distinguishes historical materialism from historical idealism.

To reveal the general law of social development based on the characteristics of social history and to analyze complex social phenomena, the structure of social members and the classes, strata and interest groups and their relations, we should, on the one hand, understand the roles of ideological motives of social members and their relations; on the other, we should not stop here, but to find the material and economic reasons behind these motives.

Marx provided us with a good example of economic analysis. Marx of 1835-1841 was a firm revolutionary democrat politically, but largely a Hegelian idealist philosophically. During 1842-1843, after graduated from school to the society and cameinto contact with material interests, Marx turned from his philosophical and political criticism of society to the study of economics, shifting his focus to the material and economic relations in the then so-called "civil society," especially the analysis of economic structure of capitalism and the criticism of its political economy. Through economic analysis of social phenomena, Marx recognized the social significance of labor practice and found that, the production of material goods is the foundation of the existence and development of society, and productivity is the ultimate cause of social development, and relations of production is the most basic economic relations of social life. Proceeding from this, he revealed that mode of production of material life conditions the general process of social economic, political and intellectual life. He therefore scientifically resolved the fundamental problem of relations between social existence and social consciousness, thus established historical materialism. It is clear that economic analysis is the basic method used by Marx in creating the theory of historical materialism.

Given the fact that all material and economic factors are the bases of all social life and the decisive forces promoting social development, and all social problems are rooted in the most profound economic facts, and all social phenomena are ultimately conditioned and affected by certain economic reasons. So, to understand social problems, we must start from the analysis of economic issues, so does the analysis of structure of social members and the understanding of classes, strata and interest groups and their relations.

In making economic analysis, we must first of all adhere to the criterion of productive forces, which ultimately determine the social and historical development. Progress of human society, in the final analysis, is the result of the development of productive forces. This is a fundamental view of historical materialism, and also the basic starting point from which we understand and explain social and historical phenomena. In expounding Marxist historical materialism, Lenin pointed out: "... only the reduction of social relations to production relations and of the latter to the level of the productive forces, provided a firm basis for the conception that the development of formations of society is a process of natural history."① Later on, he explicitly mentioned that the development of productive forces is the "supreme criterion in judging social progress."② In the period of democratic revolution, Comrade Mao Zedong pointed out that, the criterion for testing the good or bad and big or small of the policies and role of all parties is to see whether they favor the

① *Selected Works of Lenin*, vol. 1, People's Publishing House, 1995, pp. 8-9.

② *Collected Works of Lenin, vol.* 16, People's Publishing House, 1988, p. 209.

development of productive forces. The report to the Thirteenth National Congress of the CPC Central Committee clearly put forward the concept of "the criterion of productive forces," and specifically states: "We should take it as the fundamental criterion and the starting point of all our work whether it is favorable toward promoting the growth of the productive forces." Comrade Deng Xiaoping clearly put forth the "three favorables," that is, whether it promotes the growth of the productive forces in a socialist society, increases the overall strength of the socialist state and raises the people's living standards, and at the same time, he pointed out that, the "three favorables," in the final analysis, can be boiled down to whether it is favorable toward the development of the productive forces. The criterion of productive forces, in fact, is to take whether it is favorable to the growth of the productive forces as the fundamental criterion for measuring social advancement and all our work and as the fundamental method of understand and explain social and historical issues. Taking the development of productive forces as the criterion in understanding social issues means that, it is the fundamental criterion for judging whether the relations of production, superstructure and specific institutions of a social formation meet the requirements; the chief criterion for determining the nature of a society, for measuring the stage of social development and for judging social progress; the supreme criterion for making distinction between good and bad and between success and failure of lines, principles, policies and measures of a political party; the basic criterion for judging between right and wrong of a person, a class, a political party. It is without doubt that, we must use this criterion in a scientific, comprehensive and proper way, and combine it with the balancing the relations between overall benefit and partial benefit, long-term benefit and short-term benefit, material benefit and intellectual benefits, and so on. And we must use it in a consistent way when taking it respectively as the fundamental, supreme, chief and basic criterion, to prevent from replacing other specific criteria with it. In practice, we cannot use it everywhere in an absolute, simplistic and vulgar manner. It is just a general principle and criterion for us to understand structure of social members, and understand classes, strata and interest groups and their relations.

In making economic analysis, we must adhere to the principles that material relations determine political and ideological relations, and economic relations determine non-economic relations, thus explain political and ideological relations on the basis of material and economic relations. In the process of social production, men establish relations not only with nature, but also among themselves. Marx said:

"They produce only by working together in a specified manner and reciprocally exchanging their activities. In order to produce, they enter into definite connections and relations to one another, and only within these social connections and relations does their influence upon nature operate – i. e., does production take place. "① The social relations established among people in the process of production are the relations of production, i. e., economic relations, which essentially are material relations. Relations of production consist of three dimensions: ownership relations, status of people in social production and their relations and the distribution relations of labor products, which exist throughout all the four links of production, exchange, distribution and consumption. Of these, ownership relations are the primary part and direct criterion for judging the nature and level of development of a society. In human social life, the relations of production of a society, that is, material and economic relations are the primary ones that determine all other social relations, including ethical, family, political and ideological relation, and determine also the superstructure and specific form of a society. Therefore, it is also an important way to analyze social phenomena starting from the relations of production on the basis of the productive forces.

To analyze the structure of social members and the changes of social classes, strata and interest groups from the point view of material and economic relations means that, we should take the nature and situation of relations of production as the criterion for measuring whether the superstructure corresponds to the economic base, as well as a direct indicator for determining the formation and stage of development of a society; take relations of production as the basis for analyzing the law of all changes of social relations; take the forms and amount of possession of means of production, the position and role of people in production and the forms of distribution of products as important criteria for judging a person, a social group and a political party in the structure of society, as well as their class nature, political attitudes, social behavior and ideological thinking.

In doing so, we should see to it that "economic factors" are not vulgarized as "the only decisive type of factors" and the economic analysis as the only means of analysis. Ideological relations are relatively independent to material relations and the former have a certain degree of counteraction to the latter, as are the relationships between political relations and economic relations, social consciousness and social

---

① Selected Works of Marx and Engels, vol. 1, People's Publishing House, 1995, p. 344.

existence, superstructure and economic base, relations of production and productive forces. Social life is extremely complex, so are factors affecting it. If we analyze society and structure of social members only from the angle of economic factors by denying the role of other social factors, we will fail to correctly explain the complex social and historical phenomena, structure of social members and social classes, strata and interest groups and their relations and changes.

IV. Class Analysis Is the Expansion of Economic Analysis of Structure of Social Members

Class analysis method refers to the application of Marxist theory of class and class struggle to analyze social and historical phenomena, structure of social members, as well as classes, strata and interest groups and their relations. This approach is the necessary expansion of the method of economic analysis, and application of dialectic method in social sector, which is a scientific method used by the proletariat and its party in analyzing social structure, classes, strata and interest groups.

The emergence of class is the result of development of productive forces, and private ownership is economic cause of society being divided into classes. And the class identification must be based on such basic economic criteria as people's possession of the means of production, position and role in the relations of production and distribution methods of getting products. Class struggle comes from confrontation and conflict in socio-economic relations. Using the method of economic analysis in the study of social and historical phenomena, one necessarily will come the following correct conclusions: class struggle exists in class societies; people can be divided into different classes; the social nature of human beings are mainly reflected in their class attributes; every kind of thinking without exception is stamped with the brand of class; and class struggle is the basic line and direct driving force of class societies. Faced with the complicated class relations in class societies and constant change of class struggle, "Marxism has provided the guidance—i. e., the theory of the class struggle—for the discovery of the laws governing this seeming maze and chaos."① The theory of class struggle is the fundamental method of analyzing historical phenomena of class societies and analyzing structure of social members.

---

① *Selected Works of Lenin*, vol. 2, People's Publishing House, 1995, p. 426.

To correct grasp and use the scientific method of class analysis, we must uphold materialist dialectics and oppose subjectivism and metaphysics.

First, we mustinsist on seeking truth from facts in class analysis. In class societies, the phenomenon of classes, although existing everywhere, is not the only or all-embracing one; although class relations are the basic relations between man and man, it does not mean that all social relations fall under the category of class relations; and class struggle, although being important, is not the only form of social practice. That is to say, we should, on the one hand, recognize the universality and importance of the method of class analysis, but on the other, must not go to extreme in applying it. We must maintain the "objectivity of observation", proceed from reality and seeking truth from facts, so that to recognize the objective class structures, class relations and class struggle as what they are, and not to turn a blind eye to the simple reality of the existence of class and class struggle. At the same time we can never ignore facts by arbitrarily categorizing the structure, relations or phenomena of non-class nature into class one.

Second, we must maintain an all-sided way and try to avoid one-sidedness. Class phenomena in society are extremely complicated and diverse. And class struggle finds its expression not only in economic struggle, but also in political and ideological struggle; not only in economic sector, but also in ideological, political, cultural and other sectors. Therefore, in applying the method of class analysis, we must grasp "the entire totality of the manifoldrelations of this thing to others,"① to maintain an all-sided way and avoid one-sidedness. That means that, we should both analyze class struggle in economic sector and not neglect class struggle in political, ideological, cultural and other sectors; analyze both the economic status and political attitudes of all social groups; analyze both the economic status, political attitudes and ideological tendency of each class and its relations with other classes, its social environmental changes and development, etc. In short, we should understand the complicated class relations and class struggle in a comprehensive, dialectical and development way, instead of in an isolated, static and one-sided way.

Third, we must, in making class analysis, to the principle of concrete analysis of concrete conditions, the living soul of Marxism. Class and class struggle will be different in forms and characters depending on time, place and conditions. Class structures, class fronts, class enemies, class friends, classes as reliable forces, as

① *Selected Works of Lenin*, vol. 2, People's Publishing House, 1995, p. 411.

well as the expression and features of class struggle will be different with the differences of formations of society, the differences of development stages of the same formation of society, the differences of countries at the same stage of the same formation of society, and even the differences of localities, ethnic groups and time span within the same country of the same stage of the same formation of society. This requires that we should grasp the change and special law of class struggle in different time, place and conditions. Take China for example. At the present primary stage of socialism, the exploiting class as a class has been eliminated, and class struggle is no longer the principal contradiction in our society and exists only within certain limits, so its targets, scope, scale and methods are different from those in the revolutionary war years. We are bound to make serious mistakes if we fail to keep to the living soul of Marxism of concrete analysis of concrete conditions, and maintain the out-dated attitude of the revolutionary wartime in viewing and handling the classes, strata and interest groups in the primary stage of socialism and the class struggle within certain limits. In the specific circumstances of today, we can neither make the mistake of magnifying class struggle by regarding it as the principal contradiction and taking it as the central task, nor can we neglect or deny the existence of class struggle in certain limits.

In short, the method of class analysis isa scientific and exact method, so we must, by applying material dialectics, make concrete, historical, realistic and all-round analysis of the existence of classes, class relations and class struggle. The indiscriminate application of this method with rigid thinking is opposite to the principle of class analysis of historical materialism.

V. The Special Significance of the Method of Interest Analysis in Analyzing Social Structure

Leninpointed out that "if you do not show the interests of which classes and which particular interests are dominant at the moment in determining the nature of the various parties and their politics, you are not really applying Marxism and have, *in fact*, rejected the theory of the class struggle."① Interests dominate people's social and historical activities, and certain economic relations are necessarily reflected in certain interests—this is an important principle of historical materialism. To

① *Collected Works of Lenin*, vol. 15, People's Publishing House, 1988, p. 375.

analyzing the complex economic, political, cultural, ideological and other social life and their relationships based on principle of interest is an important method to see through the mysteries of social history and to analyze social structure, classes, strata and interest groups and their relations.

Interest is an important category of historical materialism in observing society and history. By interest analysis, we mean that, according to the principle of interest, to unveil the interest motives underlying people's social activities and the relations of production on which the interest relations are reflected, and then proceeding from it, to explain various social relations and social and historical phenomena. In the methodological framework of historical materialism, economic analysis, class analysis and interest analysis are consistent and complementary to each other rather than mutually exclusive or opposed. Whether it is economic analysis, class analysis, or interest analysis, they are all built on the basis of the basic principle of historical materialism of "productive forces and the relations of production is the premise of whole society." Economic analysis advocates analyzing social and historical phenomena from the perspective of material production and their relations, while the method of class analysis is the concrete use of economic analysis in observing social life and social phenomena, and method of interest analysis is the further manifestation of economic analysis. In a class society, the method of interest analysis, although being consistent with the method of class analysis, has its own special significance by taking the interest relations, contradictions and conflicts as basic clues.

First, the method of interest analysis is more specific than the methods of economic analysis and class analysis. The former focuses on analyzing the root causes of social history fromthe angle of macroeconomics, while the later stresses on dividing classes and analyzing the basic clues of class struggle from the perspective of economic relations in class societies. In contrast, the method of interest analysis makes specific study on social problems by investigating human relations. In a class society, the relations of production manifest themselves as certain class relations, which in turn manifest themselves as class interests. Method of interest analysis is to analyze the social phenomena from more direct and specific interest relations.

Second, interest analysis can be taken as a supplement to class analysis. In a class society, neither all social phenomena fall into class struggle, nor all social relations belong to class relations. Therefore, method of interest analysis can be used in non-class struggle areas. In class societies, there are interest differences not only between classes, but also between different strata and interest groups within the same class, so interest analysis can be used in dividing strata and interest groups within the same class. In a non-class society, although class relations and class struggle do not exist, a degree of interest differences and contradictions do exist. For instance, there are interest contradictions and relations between tribes in the primitive society. In these circumstances, analysis method has a universal significance.

Lastly, the method of interest analysis has its special significance in the primary stage of socialism. In this stage, the exploiting class as a whole was eliminated, and class struggle and antagonistic class contradictions exist only in certain limits. Under the condition that class contradictions and class struggle no longer takes the dominant role, how should we understand the changes of relations between classes, social strata and interests, as well as the relations of contradiction among the people? To answer these questions, the method of interest analysis has its special methodological significance.

The key to doing interest analysis is to use it to scientifically divide the interest groups, and then to further examine the statuses and roles of these groups in the interest relations and their contradictions, so as to grasp the objective laws governing their development. An interest group refers to a group of people with similar interest demands and attitudes toward their common interests based on certain social relations. Different interest groups have different, even contradictory interest demands. An individual needs to gain his interests through certain social relations. An interest group is far more powerful than individuals in pursuing and maintaining the interests of its members, so individuals tend to engage in interest struggle and realize their interests by joining in interest groups.

Interest group is a historical category. Its content differs under different historical conditions. The earliest interest groups in human society are primitive community organized on the bases of kinship and common territory of activities, such as ethnic groups, tribes, tribal alliances, and so on. With the emergence of social division of labor and private property, classes appeared within the society, and a class is consisted of different social strata, which can be further divided into interest groups. Classes and social strata can also be considered as the most stable interest groups in a class society. Through horizontal social ties and based on certain common interest demands larger and relatively stable interest groups are formed among classes, social strata and various interest groups, such as clans, ethnic groups, various economic entities (businesses, companies, consortia, etc.), international organizations(such as the European Union, the United Nations). In the primary stage of socialism, on the premise that the exploiting class as a whole no longer exists, class contradictions are no longer dominant and class struggle exists only within certain limits, it has an extremely practical significance to get a correct understanding of the contradictions among different interest groups.

The key to scientifically analyzing interests and dividing interest groups lies in the criteria of identification. What, then, are the criteria?

First, to identify the basic characters of interest groups by the possession of means of production. The different positions and roles of people in the relations of ownership of social means of production determine that they belong to different economic interest groups. Therefore it is a premise to analyze interest groups from the relations of ownership.

Second, to identify interest groups from the perspective of relations of distribution and other economic relations. Different ways of distribution, interest realization and income will surely give rise to different interest groups. Therefore it is an important precondition to scientifically analyze interest groups from distributive and other economic relations.

Third, in the precondition of adhering to the criteria of economic factors in identifying interest groups, differences of division of labor and social statuses caused by other social reasons should also be taken into account.

To sum up, the criteria for identifying interest groups must base themselves on basic economic relations such as possession of means of production, roles in the process of production, incomes and so on, in addition to other social factors. The basic criteria for interest group identification show that, Marxist theory of class identification based on ownership of means of production is still important methodologically and is consistent with the criteria of class identification. The interest demands of different groups vary, so do their interest differences and contradictions, which are important clues in analyzing social phenomena, social members as well as classes, strata and interest groups.

Examiningsocial and historical phenomena by using the method of interest analysis by no means imply that we deny the basic methods of economic analysis or class analysis; on the contrary, we should, under the guidance of the scientific outlook of historical materialism, make a good combination of these three methods in observing, analyzing and explaining classes, strata and interest groups and their relations.

VI. The Sociological Theories of Social Stratification Can Be a Supplement to the Theoretical Method of Historical Materialism

The theory of social stratification is a sociological way of analysis. We can neither use it to deny or replace Marxist methods of economic analysis, class analysis and interest analysis, norshould we reject it with Marxist theory. We should rather take it as a supplementary analytical method to the method of historical materialism.

1. The sociological method of social stratification and its foreign representative theories

The term "stratification" is of geology origin, referring to the differentiation of layers in geological structure. It sociology, it refers to the classification of social members. Its theories and methods involve the ranking and analysis of people in a society based on their possession of social resources. The well-known Western sociologist Max Weber believed that there are three most important social resources, namely, material wealth (including money), social prestige and political power, approximately equivalent to *li* (interests), *ming* (prestige) and *quan* (power) respectively in Chinese. Sociological stratification analyzes hierarchical differences of social members due to differences of possession of social resources, capabilities and opportunities.

A new theory of social stratification is popular in the West in recent years, that is, the "new middle class" theory, which tries to replace class analysis of historical materialism. This theory constitutes a theoretical reflection of the changes of social classes and social strata in developed capitalist societies. Although still using the concept of class in a way, it in fact replaces the concept of class by the concept of social strata. Its main points include: taking non-productive labor and economic, political, ideological and other factors as the criteria for identifying new petty bourgeoisie; taking working conditions distinguishing from traditional working class as the criteria for identifying "new working class"; taking the dual functions of some people in the process of production as criteria for identifying "new middle class" or "middle-class", or "professional-managerial class."

The term of "new petty bourgeoisie" was put forwarded by the well-known Western sociologist, also a representative of "Structuralist Marxist," Nicos

Poulantzas. He is the proponent of the doctrine of multiple determinations of class division. He argued that, in social structure, the three elements of economy, politics and ideology in the division of classes is to some extent a unity, among which, the element of economy plays a decisive role, whereas politics and ideology also plays a very important role. He believes that the main criteria in identifying the "new petty bourgeoisie" are: first, taking the "non-productive labor workers" as the criterion for determining "the new petty bourgeoisie", so most of the salaried non-productive workers are categorized as "the new petty bourgeoisie distinguishing from both the working class and the petty bourgeoisie; second, not only economic status but also political and ideological attitudes being taken as important factors in determining people's class positions. Therefore, he categorized the workers who engage directly in material production and produce surplus value as the working class, while other waged and salaried workers as "the new petty bourgeoisie," including business employees, white-collar workers, service personnel, managerial personnel, scientific and technical personnel and other mental workers. He believed that the new petty bourgeoisie with technicians and managers as its main body are under the rule of capitalist class economically, politically and ideologically, but in terms of class relations they are in the position of ruling the working class, so they should be excluded from the working class.

The representatives of the theory of "the new working class" include left French theorists Serge Mallet, Andre Gorz, Alain Touraine, *et al.* They believe that after World War II, especially since the 1950s and 1960s on, tremendous changes occurred in Western capitalist societies in terms of economic development, application of science and technology and the improvement of social welfare, so that the absolute impoverishment of the working class basically disappear, the manual workers in the traditional sense are decreasing while white-collar workers increasing, which give rise to a new working class who make a living by selling their knowledge and skills with a medium level income. Correspondently, changes also occurred in the structure, qualities and demands within the working class. Thus, a new working class comes into being, which is different from traditional working class characteristic of manual work. The new working class consists of two parts, one is the professionals who are skilled in operating complicated equipment, the other include scientists, engineers, technicians and others who engage in invention and research and managerial personnel. The new working class is not only a part of the working class in developed countries, but also the vanguard of them, who potentially are more radical than the traditional blue-collar workers engaged in manual labor in that they struggle with the capitalists not on the issue of wage, but in the control of the business. The theory represents the theoretical changes of the working class in Western developed capitalist countries.

The representative of the theory of "new middle class" is Italian scholarGuglielmo Carchedi. He argues that in a capitalist society, those who are in the "contradictory class location" belong to the "new middle class" that are not in possession of means of production but perform both the function of capital and the function of workers, so they are both exploiters and the exploited, such as the administrators.

The representative proponents of the notion of "the professional-managerial class" are Barbara Ehrenreich and John Ehrenreich. They believe that in contemporary developed capitalist countries, a new class, the professional-managerial class, has come into being, which consists of such mental workers as middle-level administrators, engineers, academics, teachers, managers, nurses. They don't possess the means of production and their main function is to carry on the reproduction of capitalist culture and production; they, like the working class, abhor the capitalist class, but on the other hand, they position are above the working class.

2. We should both insist on the method of class analysis and develop, enrich and supplement it.

Some people hold that class analysis is outdated to analyze the classes and strata in the primary stage of socialism in China. They argue that, after entering the primary stage of socialism, the exploiting class as a whole has been eliminated, and classes and class struggles, although existing within certain limits, are no longer the principal contradiction in our society, as is the human relations of class antagonism nature, therefore, the method of class analysis is of no use. Some other people think that, after the establishment of the socialist system with the public sector playing a predominant role in the economy, the ownership of means of production as the criterion of class division is out of date, because the method of class analysis is applicable only to the analysis of private ownership society, not the primary stage of socialism with the public ownership being predominant. Still others believe that, with the emergence of multiple new strata and interest groups at the primary stage of socialism, the method of class analysis is hardly useful. It is obviously wrong to think that class analysis is outdated and not applicable in analyzing the structure of social members in the primary stage of socialism in China. The reasons are as follows. Firstly, in the primary stage of socialism, although class exploitation and class antagonism as a whole have been eliminated, it does not mean that class no longer exists in this stage; nor does it mean that a society without class exploitation is a classless society. In this stage, the working class and farmer class as the two major classes still exist, so do the differences between them. Besides, new social strata and interest groups will also emerge. Secondly, although currently there is no polarization in our society, class differences and contradictions still exist. And there is the possibility of polarization in the process of building the socialist market economy if we relax our vigilance against and control over it. So the social reality in the primary stage of socialism proves the fallacious of the view that class analysis is obsolete.

It is one-sided to indiscriminately say that the method of class analysis applies only class societies. The primary stage of socialism is a period in which public ownership is the leading factor and other forms of ownership coexist with it and classes exist in it, whereas the method of class analysis applies to the examination of not only the antagonistic or opposing class relationships, but also non-antagonistic or non-opposing class relationships.

On the other hand, however, it is undoubtedly not enough by simply copying Marxist theory of class analysis, or Comrade Mao Zedong's analyses of classes in Chinese society in the 1920s and 1930s, or our Party's analyses of the classes in Chinese society in early period after liberation. This is because, in the primary stage of socialism, with the deepening of reform and the development of the market economy, differentiation and combination have taken place among the original classes and strata, and new strata and interest have emerged in our society. Therefore, while using the method of class analysis, we should recognize that this method alone cannot cover the entire reality of social phenomena. To deepen our understanding of the structure of social classes, strata and interest groups in the primary stage of socialism, we should introduce new methods such as interest group analysis, sociological method of stratification, and so on, in addition to the method of class analysis. And we should have a viewpoint of development on it, that is, generally speaking it is suitable for analyzing the structure of social members in the primary stage of socialism in China today. It, without doubt, needs to be developed and improved to catch up with the times, reality and changes of relations between classes either under the socialist system or in the capitalist system.

3. From the Marxist point of view, class analysis and stratification are not clear-cut separated from, independent of or opposite to each other.

Comrade Mao Zedong's article "Analyses of the Classes in Chinese Society" is a classic writing using the Marxist method of class analysis. In this article, He did not put class analysis as opposed to analysis of strata. Instead, he took the method of class analysis as the primary one and premise in examining the structure of social members, on the basis of which, he further divided the classes into strata. Comrade Mao's framework of analyses is as follows. First, stratum analysis is subordinated to class analysis as the premise and framework of the theory of class analysis. Second, stratum analysis is taken as a supplement to class analysis. For instance, he analyzed lumpen-proletarians, who were outside any class yet could not constitute a stratum. And third, he took stratum analysis as a quantitative base of class analysis, upon which judgments on classes were made. Obviously it is metaphysical to think that class analysis and stratum analysis are absolutely opposite to each other. On the contrary, they are complementary to each other and can be integrated. The concepts of class and stratum are not necessarily opposite. It is an oversimplified judgment to consider that class analysis is Marxist and stratum analysis is bourgeois. On no account can we replace or negate class analysis with stratum analysis.

About class, in his letter to Joseph Weydemeyer on March 5, 1852, Marx gives a complete account of his view: "Now as for myself, I do not claim to have discovered either the existence of classes in modern society or the struggle between them. Long before me, bourgeois historians had described the historical development of this struggle between the classes, as had bourgeois economists their economic anatomy. My own contribution was (1) to show that the existence of classes is merely bound up with *certain historical phases in the development of production;* (2) that the class struggle necessarily leads to the dictatorship of the proletariat; (3) that this dictatorship itself constitutes no more than a transition to the abolition of all classes and to a classless society." According to Marx, Marxism is by no means in favor of class struggle, nor is it intended to sustain it. But later on some people misunderstood and misused Marxism, leading to a deviation which blindly makes a fetish of class struggle, ignores the reality by advocating "taking class struggle as the key link" and believes that "class struggle will sustain for thousands of years" and so on. This kind of left deviation has deep influence in our political life.

Class analysis is a method for examining the structure of social members from the perspective of Marxist materialism. Of course we can also make stratum analysis under the premise or framework of class analysis, in which the former, being subordinate to the latter, when used alone, is usually for examining the structure of social members from sociological perspective. The two methods do not exclude or oppose but rather complement to each other. We can neither over-simplistically say that the issue of class is about historical materialism while the issue of social stratification is of sociology; nor can we believe that class analysis is a Marxist method while stratum analysis are non-Marxist or anti-Marxist. Only the attempt to negate or replace class analysis with stratum analysis is non-Marxist or anti-Marxist. Class analysis and stratum analysis are two analytical methods of social structure from different perspectives. Classes are social stratification from nature or macro-level perspectives, whereas strata reflect qualitative or micro-level social stratification; class analysis mainly takes the ownership and distribution of means of production as its criterion, whereas stratum analysis takes a broader scope of possession of social resources, incomes, occupations, etc., as its criteria; class analysis bases itself on the fundamental criterion, whereas stratum analysis, on multiple criteria; classes reflect differences in quality between social hierarchies, whereas strata reflect difference of quantity between them; relations between classes include in them the relations between the exploiting class and exploited class that are fundamentally antagonistic, whereas relations between strata does not necessarily include them. Therefore, we can neither arbitrarily deny stratum analysis, nor can we simplistically say that class analysis is outdated and should be replaced with stratum analysis. On the other hand, however, it is also one-sided to advocate only class analysis and thus use it to absolutely deny stratum analysis or replace other academic analyses.

Some people believe that class analysis intrinsically includes stratum analysis, so stratum analysis is unnecessary; some others believe that stratum analysis is more comprehensive andmore specific than class analysis, so the former can replace the latter. Both views are one-sided. In terms of concept, they are different from each other, with the former being a concept of historical materialism in Marxist philosophy while the latter a sociological concept. But they are consistent to a degree and associated in the sense of application. Firstly, they study the same social subject, that is, both class and stratum are interest groups bound together by common interests, which, in a class society, can be divided as classes or strata. Secondly, they have the same object of study. Both study the differentiation and stratification of social members deriving from the development of the productive forces and division of labor. Thirdly, when used together, stratum is subordinate to class, for a class can be divided into different strata; a class contains strata, and in between classes there may be relevant strata. On the other hand, there are differences between them. The major criterion for class identification is economic relationship, that is, ownership of means of production, while the criterion for strata identification is the ownership of social resources in the broad sense; the criterion for class identification is unique and fundamental, while those for strata identification are changing and multiple. For example, we can divide strata based on property, incomes, occupations, social statuses, education, skills, etc.; while class division, in the final analysis is based on the ownership of means of production.

In the primary stage of socialism in China today, we can take sociological stratum analysis as a supplement to class analysis. But we can not negate or replace class analysis by stratum analysis. Some scholars advocate "moderately dilute the concept of class" and taking "the category of stratum as a diluted concept of class." "In sociology, the concept 'class' has been incorporated into the scope of strata and stratification, with strata being a generic concept and class subordinate to it." I do not agree with these arguments. In the present stage of socialism, although class struggle is no longer the principal contradiction, both the exploiting class and exploited class as a whole have ceased to exist, and in the process of reform toward socialist market economy some new strata and interest groups emerge, which cannot be readily distinguished by using the original concept of class, yet we by no means can deny the existence of classes, differences of classes, class contradictions and class struggle, as well as deny class viewpoints and the method of class analysis. Of course, in this precondition, it is also necessary to introduce sociological method of stratum analysis.

4. The scientific definition of class, stratum and interest group

When we use the method of class analysis while adopting other methods as supplement in examining the structure of social members in the primary stage of socialism, it is necessary to scientifically define the concepts of class, stratum and interest group.

Firstly, the concept of interest group. It can be understand by its broad and narrow sense. In the broad sense, an interest group refers to the community of people bound by common interests. Here interest group is a general concept, classes and strata can be regarded as interest groups, so can families, enterprises, nations, states, etc. In the narrow sense, an interest group refers to an interest community smaller than a class and a stratum. For instance, in the old China, the class of bourgeoisie can be subdivided into three strata of national bourgeoisie, bureaucrat-bourgeoisie and petty bourgeoisie; and national bourgeoisie can be further divided into different interest groups of commercial capitalists, financial capitalists, industrial capitalists, and so on.

Secondly, the concept of interest group applies both in class society and classless society. In a classless society, classes and strata cease to exist, therefore, the two concepts are no longer applicable; but differences of interest still exist, so do interest groups, thus the concept of interest group is still applicable. And it can be used to analyze interest groups both of class nature and non-class nature, because even in a class society, there are groups of non-class nature or marginalized groups; and it can be used to analyze the different interest groups within a non-exploiting class, such as those in the working class, an to analyze the interest groups within the exploiting class, such as those in the landlord class.

After the concept of interest group is clarified, we can then use the three concepts of class, stratum and interest group in two senses.

Firstly, class, stratum and interest group are concepts with same connotation but progressive levels, with class at the first level and stratum and interest groups at the second and third levels respectively. A class can be divided into different stratum, and a stratum into different interest groups. In the progressive conceptual structure, interest group in the narrow sense is at the third-level.

Secondly, class, stratum and interest group are conceptually independent, overlapping and mutually inclusive. Outside classes, there may be relatively independent and marginalized stratum; likewise, there may be relatively independent and marginalized interest groups outside stratum. For example, the private entrepreneurs in the primary stage of socialism constitute a relatively independent stratum, but we cannot say that the emergence of this stratum means the formation of a new bourgeoisie. Besides, interest groups can also be used as a concept in the broad sense.

Chapter 10

New Changes in Classes, Strata and Interest Groups in Present-day China

A correct understanding of the changes in the structure of social members, that is, the changes and features of classes, strata and interest groups in present China, is the precondition for the correct understanding and handling of them and their relations as well as contradictions among the people.

I. The history and status quo of the structure of social members in China

Since the Opium Wars, China has experienced three major social transformations. The first is the one brought about by the Revolution of 1911, which, although overthrew the feudal dynasty, was incomplete in terms of transformation. The second is the one brought about by the success of the democratic evolution, which is a complete one that gave birth to the establishment of the socialist system. The third is also a complete one toward the market economy, which is brought about by socialist reform and opening up. The structure of social members changed along with the social transformations. Apart from the transformation caused by the Revolution of 1911 that overthrew the feudal monarchy, since the founding of New China, Chinese society underwent two major changes The first change occurred during the 28 years from the founding of new China throughout the transitional period and the period of socialist transformation up until the Third Plenary Session of the Party's 11th Central Committee. In the early days of this historical period, that is, immediately after the founding of New China, the exploiting classes, including the landlord class and bureaucrat capitalists was deprived by the people of means of production, and the socialist transformation of the exploiters was carried out. But national bourgeoisie and elements of the petty bourgeoisie such as the self-employed still remained in the city; in the countryside, middle farmers still remained, while poor farmers and farm laborers were allocated some land and means of production to become individual agricultural laborers. The structure of social members in the early period of New China was composed of the working class, the farmer class, the national bourgeoisie, the urban and rural petty bourgeoisie. After the "three great socialist transformations" (the movement of socialist transformation of agriculture, handicrafts and capitalist industry and commerce), the national bourgeoisie became the joint-owners of joint state-private industrial and commercial enterprises with a fixed rate of interest on their capital; in the countryside, after the completion of collectivization, the former individual laborers become agricultural laborers of collective ownership; and most of the self-employed workers and individual laborers both in the city and the countryside has become workers in the collective-owned economy and the number of the remaining few was reducing. The structural pattern of social members was gradually formed, which was composed of "two classes, one stratum," that is, the working class, the farmer class and the stratum of intelligentsia within the working class, plus the industrialists with certain interest income from and businessmen and the individual workers in the city and the countryside.

The second changetook place since the Third Plenary Session of the Eleventh Central Committee of the CPC held in 1978. The structural pattern of Chinese social members significantly changed during this period. Although the structure of "two classes, one stratum" remains, its proportions and components have profoundly changed. Some new strata and interest groups have taken shape and restructuring occurred within the original classes and strata. The new structure becomes more diverse and complicated.

Theoretical summary of the structure of social members in present China, the representative views are as follows:

First, the notion of "two classes and one stratum", that is, the working class, the farmer class and the stratum of intelligentsia within the working class.

Second, the notion of "two classes and three strata," that is, the working class, the farmer class and the strata of intelligentsia, the self-employed and the private entrepreneurs.

Third, the notion of "two classes, several strata and several interest groups," which identifies, besides the working class, the farmer class and several strata, several interest groups within the classes and strata.

Fourth, the notion of "ten strata." The Institute of Sociology of Chinese Academy of Social Sciences (CASS) put forward a theoretical framework with occupational classification as its basis and the possession of organizational resources, economic resources and cultural and technical resources as its criteria of stratum division. Organizational resources include resources of administrative organization and political organization. The possession and disposal of organizational resources mainly refers to the power of disposing social resources (including human and material resources) based on the systems of national political organization and political party organization. The possession and disposal of economic resources mainly refers to the rights of possession, disposal, use and management of means of production. The ownership and disposal of cultural and technical resources refers to the possession (through certification and qualification) of knowledge and skills recognized by the society. The possession of these three kinds of resources determines the status and overall position of an individual in the entire structure of social members. According to this principle of social stratification, the Institute of Sociology of CASS divided the social members in China into ten strata: the stratum of state and society administrators, the stratum of managers, the stratum of private entrepreneurs, the stratum of professionals, the stratum of clerks, the stratum of the self-employed, the stratum of commercial service personnel, the stratum of industrial workers, the stratum of agricultural laborers, and the stratum of the jobless, unemployed, half-unemployed in urban and rural areas.

(1) The stratum of state and society administrators. This stratum is at the highest or higher social level and one of the dominant strata in social structure. Its proportion is 2. 1 percent in the whole society, 1. 5 percent at city level and 0. 5 percent in the areas below county level.

(2) The stratum of managers. This stratum is composed of managers of the state-owned economy and the collective economy, managers in the private sector and managers in foreign-funded enterprises. This stratum, currently accounting for 1. 5 percent of the entire membership of the society, is the promoters and innovators in the socialist market economy.

(3) The stratum of private entrepreneurs, accounts for 0. 6 percent of the entire membership of the society.

(4) The stratum of professional and technical personnel, whose proportion is 5. 1 percent of the entire membership of the society.

(5) The stratum of clerks, accounted for 4. 8 percent of the entire membership of the society.

(6) The stratum of the self-employed, referring to those who own a small amount of private capital and make a living by put the capital into operational

activitiesin such sectors as production, circulation, services, financial, accounting for 4.2 percent of the entire membership of the society.

(7) The stratum of the commercial service personnel, accounted for12 percent of the entire membership of the society.

(8) The stratum of industrial working class, accounted for 22.6 percent of the entire membership of the society, about 30 percent of which are migrant workers.

(9) The stratum of agricultural laborers, accounted for about 44 percent of the entire membership of the society.

(10) The stratum of the jobless, unemployed, half-unemployed in urban and rural areas, accounted for 31 percent of the entire membership of the society.

Fifth is the notion of "a number of interest groups," dividing the social members at the present stage in China into several interest groups.

Sixth, is notion of "five major strata." From the consumer perspective it believes that there are five strata in China, they are, the richest stratum, the upper middle stratum, the middle stratum, the poor strata and the poorest stratum.

Seventh is the notion of the emergence of a "newborn bourgeoisie." It holds that in addition to the already existing classes, a new class of bourgeoisie has come into being.

II. Causes of changes in the classes, strata and interest groups at the present stage in China

The structure of social members of a society is determinedultimately by its productive forces. At the present stage, the main causes of the changes in the structure of social members in our country, that is, the changes in classes, strata and interest groups, are determined by the development of the productive forces and factors that determined by this development, including the conditions of the market economy, industrial structure, ownership structure, distribution structure, employment structure, etc.

First, thechanges brought about by the development of productive forces and the rise of new industries in our society are the material causes of the changes in classes, strata and interest groups. In line with the rapid progress of high-tech and economic globalization, the productive forces in our society have undergone tremendous changes: the economy maintains a steadily fast growth, new industries are constantly emerging and growing, high-tech enterprises are on the upswing, the adjustment and upgrading of industrial structure is deepening, the proportions of the first, second and tertiary industries have changed profoundly, so do the allocation of resources of the productive forces and factors of production, and significant changes have occurred in the composition of capital—all these have given rise to the emergence of new careers and new jobs, as well as new requirements and changes of the workers. Under these circumstances, a considerable number of people have been dropped behind or knocked out because of their failure in adapting to these changes. On the other hand, many people have found new positions by enhancing their qualities to meet the requirements of modern industries. Some people stand out to become distinguished in their strata.

The development ofthe productive forces began to break China's urban-rural dual structure and brings about the mobility between classes, strata and interest groups. The urban-rural dual structure is a structural obstacle hindering social mobility and differentiation, which include the ownership, household registration system, differences between industries and sectors, resources allocation system, etc. With the development of the social productive forces and the gradual breaking down of urban-rural dual structure, the possibility of farmers moving to the urban areas has increased, and the gradual reform of the household registration system, its urban-rural integration in some regions and its loosening control in metropolitan cities have attracted the entrance of a large number of migrant workers, which also constitutes an important condition for the restructuring and differentiation of social members.

In short, changes in industrial structure and socio-economy have provided realistic basis and possibility for the structural changes of social members; along with it, social classes, strata and interest groups corresponding with the changes of modern industrial structure have also undergone profound changes.

Second, the transformation and completion toward socialist market economy is the structural reason for thechanges of social classes, strata and interest groups. The replacement of the planned economy by the market economy makes the structure of the original social classes, strata and interest groups previously under the planned economy differentiate and recombine, to gradually forming new ones suitable for the market economy. The deepening of the reform toward the socialist market economy has brought about tremendous changes to the structures of ownership, industry, employment and distribution, which have shaken the original structure of social members and accelerated the differentiation and mobility between them and changes of their identity, status, composition and proportional relations. This is more prominent in the following areas: First, differentiation between manual and non-manual workers; Second, differentiation between managerial personnel and non-managerial personnel; Third, differentiation between the high, middle and low income earners.

Reform toward the market economy itselfimplies the adjustment of interest pattern, with the old one being broken and the new one taking shape. This kind of adjustment will necessarily change the original structure of social classes, strata and interest groups, so that their income gaps widen, their economic and political status and their attitudes become diverse. The differences and contradictions among the people constitute an objective existence, upon which people with similar interest orientation form interest communities and further form different new strata and interest groups.

Third, changes in ownership structure are the economic reasons for the structural of social classes, strata and interest groups. After more than 30 years of socialist reform and opening up, the single ownership under the planned economy has been broken, forming a new pattern with the public sector remaining dominant and diverse sectors of the economy developing side by side, which is the first level of change in the ownership structure. At the level of realization form of public ownership, the two modes of public ownership, i. e., the state ownership and collective ownership have also been changed into the diverse forms of realization, including mixed ownership, share-holding ownership, cooperative ownership, partnership ownership, etc. Changes at the two levels have brought the structural changes of classes, strata and interest groups, which become increasingly complex and diverse, so do accordingly and profoundly the composition and features of the original working class, farmer class and the intelligentsia.

Fourth, the adjustment of mode and policy of distribution are the direct cause of structural changes in social classes, strata and interest groups. Since reform and opening up, China's income distribution system has significantly changed, which has a direct influence on the structural changes in social classes, strata and interest groups. The egalitarian practice of having everyone "eat from the same big pot" under the planned economy was discarded, andthe system under which distribution according to work is dominant and a variety of modes of distribution coexist has gradually developed and improved, which has greatly mobilized the people's enthusiasm. A person's income is directly linked with his economic benefit, his social contribution and labor intensity as well as the input of social production factors. As a result, the gap between personal incomes widened. All of these have a profound impact on the structural changes of social classes, strata and interest groups. And with the deepening of reform, such factors as capital, technology, managerial expertise have a share in income distribution, so that distribution according to work is organically combined with distribution according to production factors, making sources and forms of income more diverse and the distribution pattern more complex. Especially after some people, classes and interest groups get richer before others and there emerge the high, middle and low-income strata, the income gaps widened, so does the structural changes of social members.

Fifth, the adjustment and changes in the structures of urban and rural, industry and agriculture and mental labor and manual labor arethe deeper causes of structural changes in social classes, strata and interest groups. The development of the productive forces, the completion of the market economy, the adjustment of industrial structure and the changes in income distribution structure, etc., have led to the profound changes in structures of urban and rural, industry and agriculture, mental and manual labor, and so on. In addition, the changes are also generated by the acceleration of urbanization and industrialization and the development of tertiary industry, which have give birth to a large number of small towns and the incorporation of vast rural area into the urban areas, turning thousands of farmers into urban residents and workers, plus the growth up of new generations in large quantities of workers and intellectuals.

Sixth, the progress in education, science, democracy and culture, etc., are the social causes of structural changes in social class, strata and interest groups. The development of socialist culture, science and technology and education and the improvement of democracy have greatly raised the level of education, science and technology, culture of social members in general and have improved their political and moral consciousness, which have a deep influence on the changes in social classes, strata and interest groups. For example, the degree of education of a social member has an underlying influence on his occupation, status, prestige, income, and the improvement of his qualifications will significantly enhance his advantages in career, social status, income, etc.

In summary, since the Third Plenary Session of the Party's Eleventh Central Committee, various dynamic factors contribute to the structural differentiation and reorganization of social members and the emergence of new strata. The development of the productive forces has vigorously promoted the changes in social relations of production and the superstructure, which in turn leads to a series of structural changes of social members; the constant progress of the socialist market economy has given rise to the trends of marketization and diversification in Chinese society and the structure of its social members. China's accession to WTO, the integration of its economy into the international economic circulation in the process of globalization also constitutes factors prompting the reorganization and differentiation of the structure of Chinese social members. The reform and opening up, which has generated the continuous changes in its structures of ownership, distribution, industries and employment, has influenced the structural changes in its social members in a broader scope and at a higher level. The rising of personal ability and quality have a deeper impact on personal income, making the structural changes in its social members and its social classes, strata and interest groups more profound. The rank of the working class is continuously growing and its quality is constantly improving, leading to the emergence of new combination and differentiation; so does the farmer class, with more farmers joining in the working class. All these changes have generated many new social strata and interest groups.

III. Features of the structural changes in Chinese social members

In the present stage of our society, the working class, the farmer class and the intelligentsia are still the dominant classes or strata. However, under the new condition of reform and opening up, new changes can be found in the composition, status, roles and features of the classes, strata and interest groups due to the following factors, among others: The restraints and influence of the development of the productive forces, the gradual formation of the economic pattern in which the basic economic system in which public ownership is the mainstay of the economy and economic entities of diverse ownership develop together; The system of income distribution in which distribution according to work is the main form that coexists with other forms of distribution; the complex social, historical, political, economic, human, intellectual and other causes in this stage; and the influence of relations of production and superstructure. The features of the new changes can be summarized as follows:

First, social and economic organizationsand economic interest communities are complex and diversified.

With the deepening of reform towardthe socialist market economy, some of the social and economic organizations have transformed or even disappeared, at the same time, new kinds of organizations are emerging, with their forms becoming more complex and interest communities more diverse, demonstrated in the following aspects:

Firstly, households have become the basic units of social and economic activities in rural areas, organizations at the primary level in the countryside have undergone profound changes and rural economic organizations have become diversified. Since the Third Plenary Session of the Eleventh Central Committee of the CPC, with the implementation of household contract responsibility system, households become the primary units of rural economic activities, increasing their role in rural economy, social affairs and even political activities. Along with the reform and development, partnership businesses, joint-stock businesses, private businesses and self-employed businesses have grown out from individual household production, and a lot of grassroots rural economic organizations have emerged and played an important role in promoting the development of the market economy in China's rural areas. In response to the economic development, in 1987, the pilot projects of self-governance of villagers at the village level was carried out, and in 1998 the Organic Law of Villagers Committees was promulgated, so that the community level democracy in rural areas was spread out nationwide, and based on which, village committee are directly elected and members of rural Party branches are recommended publicly and elected directly. This has further promoted to the democratic elections at township level. As a result, profound changes have taken place in rural community-level organizations.

Secondly, enterprises have become the main economic entities of socialist market economy, and types of enterprise become diverse. With the shaping of thc socialist market economy, enterprises have become independent economic entities. Due to the changes in the structure of ownership, economic entities of diverse ownership coexist and types of enterprise become more diversified. In the primary stage of socialism in our country, in addition to the state-owned and collective-owned enterprises, other types of enterprises, including self-employed, private, joint-stock, mixed ownership, shareholding, foreign funded, have also appeared. Within the state-owned and collective-owned enterprises, there appear such sub-types as state-holding and collective-holding enterprises. At the same time a large number of economic intermediary organizations, such as stock exchanges, law firms, real estate agents emerged. Various types of enterprise have become relatively independent economic organizations, and the original state-owned enterprises and collective enterprises are gradually stripped of the burden of social services, becoming more independent.

Thirdly, the ownership structure has undergone profound changes, giving rise to a variety of economic interest communities and a pattern with diverse forms of ownership coexisting. Statistic data show that, in 1978, the value created by public sectors of the economy in China accounted for 99 percent of its GDP, 77. 6 percent of the industrial output of the public economy was produced by state-owned enterprises. ① Public economy was in an absolutely dominant position in the country's economy and single ownership took a high degree in the structure. This situation determined that the working class and its internal structure were relatively simple. Since the Third Plenary Session of the Party's Eleventh Central Committee, with the improvement of the basic economic system in which public ownership is the mainstay of the economy and economic entities of diverse ownership develop together in the primary stage of socialism, the non-public economy has made great progress, so does the diversification of forms of realization of the public ownership and the ownership structure. Currently, the non-public economy has accounted for one fourth of the GDP, and except for a few industries, most areas have been open to share-holding, private, self-employed, Chinese-foreign joint ventures and foreign funded enterprises. Non-state and non-public owned economies have developed in an unprecedented speed and their shares in the economy have risen rapidly. Of the total social investment in fixed assets in China in 2004, the proportion of investment of state-owned enterprises was 35. 5 percent, a decrease of 46. 4 percent compared to that of 1978, ② whereas shares of self-employed, private, shareholding, foreign and Hong Kong, Macao and Taiwan enterprises increased significantly; so do other areas such as agriculture, transportation, services. These changes have substantially brought about fundamental changes in economic relations characteristic of coexistence of multiple interest communities.

Fourthly, interest groups become important units in socialist economic relations and various interest communities are emerging. Interest groups bound together by

---

① See Xu Wentao, *A Study on the Changes of Structure of Ownership in Contemporary China*, Southwest University of Finance and Economics Publishing House, 2002, p. 81.

② Calculated according to *China Statistical Yearbook*(2005), China Statistics Press, p. 185.

certain economic interests mushroomed and have become basic units in social life in the primary stage of socialism. One of the important features in the structural differentiation and combinations of classes, strata and interest groups is the mushrooming of interest groups and the diversification interest stakeholders, which will necessarily lead to interest differences between them. Under the planned economy, the stakeholders were unitary and the boundaries between the working class, the farmer class and the intelligentsia were clear-cut. In contrast, under the socialist market economy, stakeholders become diverse and differences between them are more obvious, reflected not only in the originally existed differences between workers and peasants, manual and mental workers, urban and rural areas, between regions, but also within the ranks of working class and the farmer class, in which new strata and new interest groups appears. And the differences between classes, strata and interest groups and between industries, occupations continue to exist and even show a trend of widening. Consequently, various social groups developed rapidly. As of the end of 2004, there were 153,000 registered social organizations in China, of which, 1673 were national or cross-provincial (autonomous regions and municipalities), 20, 563 were provincial or cross-district and 50424 were county level ones, in addition to 16 foreign chambers of commerce. ① Also rapidly and widespread developed are intermediary agencies and non-governmental organizations in industries, social services and social welfare and such sectors as information, arts and culture, education, sports, health and scientific research. There are also different professional and hobby associations. In recent years there appeared numerous unregistered organizations such as association of fellow provincials or townsmen, alumni association, research association. Meanwhile, some illegal organizations also show a sign of gaining ground. For instance, the cult Falun Dafa Research Society was once rampant, and some Mafia-like, criminal and other forces are in the rise in some places.

Second, the widespread appearance of interest individuals based on private interests and diversification of individual interests under precondition of fundamental identity of the interests.

The socialist market economy fully recognizes the reasonable interests of individual and integrates the realization of individual interests with social interests,

---

① See Statistical Report of China's Civil Affairs Development(2004), published by the Ministry of Civil Affairs of the People's Republic of China on May, 10TH 2005.

giving birth to widespread interest individuals. The substantial changes in employment make the disparity of interests between individuals become larger. Among the total employed population in cities and towns in 2004, employees in state-owned units accounted for 25.3 percent, the rest were employees in collective, private, self-employed, foreign and Hong Kong, Macao and Taiwan enterprises. ① In contrast, before reform and opening up, the employed population was mainly concentrated in the state-owned and collective units, respectively accounted for 78.3 percent in state-owned units and 21.5 percent in collective units, and only 0.2 percent was employed in other units. ②The diversified employment structure makes the differentiation within the classes and strata and the increasingly diverse of interest individual.

Third, the diversification of forms of distribution also contributes to the widening gaps between classes, strata and interest groups.

Since the Third Plenary Session of the Eleventh Central Committee of the CPC, with the adherence to the principle of giving priority to efficiency with due consideration to fairness and the establishment of the distribution system in which distribution according to work is the main form that coexists with other forms of distribution, the market mechanism is playing an increasingly important role in distribution of income. As a result, the income gap between social members is widening, which is reflected as follows:

Firstly, the income gap between members of society is widening. The income gap between high and low income earners is prominent, forming the high, middle and low income brackets. Before reform and openingup, egalitarianism was very serious in China's social income distribution. According to the National Bureau of Statistics, in 1978, China's Gini coefficients in the urban and rural areas were respectively 0.16 and 0.21. ③ Since reform and opening up, with such factors as capital, technology and managerial expertise participating in distribution, leading to the diversification of income sources. Wealth income and factor income are becoming a more important part of personal income, and the level of education has also become an important factor. Consequently, income disparities between social members become larger in a full scope and at multi-levels, and the high, middle and low

---

① Calculated according to *China Statistical Yearbook*(2005), China Statistics Press, p. 117.

② Ibid., pp. 126, 132, 136.

③ See Zhao Manhua(compiler), *A Study of the Urban-Rural Income Gap in China*, Economy and Management Publishing House, 1997, p. 75.

income brackets are taking shape.

Secondly, the income gap between urban and rural residents is widening. Since reform and opening up, although the income ofthe farmers has considerably increased, the urban-rural dual structure has not completely changed, leading to the continued widening of the income gap between urban and rural residents. Their income ratios in 1978 and 1984 were 2.57: 1 and 1.83: 1 respectively. ① The reason for the narrowing in 1984 is the implementation of the household contract responsibility system, which increased the farmers' incomes. Since the late of 1980s and early 1990s, the gap had been widening constantly. The ratio reached 3.24: 1 in 2003 and 3. 21: 1 in 2004. ② Experts believe that, if social welfare, costs of production, physical assets and other factors are counted in, the income gap between urban and rural residents reached as high as 5 – 6 times. In contrast to the relatively rapid increase of urban residents' income, farmers in some areas have too heavy burden and too slow income growth. From 1997 to 2003, the per capita net income of the farmers were less than 5 percent for seven consecutive years, with the highest in 2002 by 4.8 percent and lowest in 2000 by only 2.1 percent. Although a series of measures have been taken in 2003 aiming at increasing farmers' income, which made the income growth of farmers in 2004 reached 6.8 percent, the highest since 1997, the widening trend of income gap between urban and rural residents has not been reversed, with the increase and actual growth rate still lower than those of urban residents, whose income grew 7.7 percent in 2004. ③

Thirdly, the income gap between rural residents is widening. Affected by the development of non-agricultural industries, the income gap between households engaged in agricultural and non-agricultural activities is growing, resulting in the appearance of disadvantaged group in rural areas. According to two surveys carried out by the Institute of Economics of CASS, during the period of 1988 – 1995, the Gini coefficient in Chinese rural areas rose from 0.338 to 0.429. ④ Although the rise in food prices to some extent reduced the gap, it is often offset by the increase of non-farming income. According to the National Bureau of Statistics of China, since

---

① See Ma Conghui, *A Study of Resident Income Distribution under Conditions of Open Economy*, China Financial and Economic Publishing House, 2004. p. 277.

② See *China Statistical Yearbook*(2005), China Statistics Press, 2005, p. 335.

③ *Ibid.*

④ See Li Shi, *et al.*, *A Empirical Analysis of China's Resident Income Distribution*, Social Science Academic Press, 2000, p. 23.

1995, the Gini coefficient of rural household net income has remained around 0. 34, showing no signs of narrowing. [1]

Fourthly, the income gap between urban residents significantly expanded. Income disparities between workers of different educational levels, industries, work units, etc., are widening, leading to the emergence of urban disadvantage group. In 1978 the maximum and minimum wage ratio in terms of industry was 1. 38: 1; in 2003, among 19 major industries, the average wage of the best-paid industry was 4. 63 times of that of the lowest-paid industry. In 1995, in rural areas, the Gini coefficient of personal disposable income increased by 43. 5 percent compared to that of 1988. And since 1995, this income gap had kept widening. by 1999, only in four years period, the Gini coefficients of monetary income and of disposable personal income of China's urban residents increased respectively by 20 percent and 11 percent. [2] Urban poor population are composed of the following seven groups: (1) workers who get very low wage or even no wage at all and can only maintain the basic needs of their families due to bad performance of their work units, making up about 30 percent of the poor population; (2) unemployed or laid-off employees, accounting for about 20 percent ; (3) some retired workers, accounting for about 17 percent; (4) residents long engaged in low-paying jobs, accounting for about 10 percent; (5) recipients of social relief and entitled groups, accounting about 5 percent; (6) residents whose actual fall below the poverty line due to price increases, accounting for about 10 percent; (7) those who fall into poverty because of other reasons, accounting for about 8 percent. According to the surveys, there are five million impoverished disabled people in China, of which three million are in extremely needy condition.

Fifthly, the income gap between residents of different regions is widening. This gap is mainly derived from imbalance of regional economic development. In the 31 provinces (autonomous regions and municipalities), in the first half of 2004, the top five per capita income provinces (municipalities) are Shanghai (8513 yuan), Beijing (7836 yuan), Zhejiang (7771 yuan), Guangdong (7264 yuan) and Fujian (5879 yuan), with a half year per capita income of 7, 453 yuan. The lowest five provinces (autonomous regions and municipalities) are Ningxia, Qinghai, Gansu,

① See Li Ying, *A Study of Income Disparities of Chinese Rural Residents*, China Agriculture Press, 2005, p. 43.

② See Li Shuang (compiler), *Studies on the Income Disparities of China's City and Town Residents* China Planning Press, 2002, p. 6.

Heilongjiang and Xinjiang, with a half-year per capita income of 3,661 yuan. The income of the top five is double that of the lowest five,① showing a significantly expanding gap between regions and a relative concentration of poor population in western region.

Sixthly, the disparity between rich and poor social members is increasingly prominent. The disparity between rich and poor in our society tends to widen, giving birth to the affluent and the poor strata and highlighting the problem of poverty.

With regard to the problem of the widening gapbetween rich and poor, some people believe that polarization has already exists in China. The fact is, there is no overall polarization of class antagonism nature in China today. The polarization expounded by Marx and Engels refers to a situation in which a few people possess a large amount of means of production and therefore possess the surplus value created by others, whereas the majority of workers have nothing except for selling their labor, so that wealth is concentrated into the hands of the few people with most people being absolutely or relatively poor. In the international scope, the income Gini coefficient of 0.4 is the alerting point of polarization. According to statistics, China has exceeded that point. Although the polarization discussed by Marx and Engels does not appear in China, the stratification of high, middle and low income earners is obvious and the gap between rich and poor continues to widen.

Polarization is a concept used to define the disparity of rich and poor and to describe the nature and status of class antagonism. Marx believed that, in line with the general law of capitalist accumulation, with the promotion of capital accumulation, polarization will occur in a society with one pole being the accumulation of wealth of the capitalist class and the other pole the accumulation of poverty of the proletariat. Under the conditions of private ownership, polarization is created by differences of ownership of means of production: the capitalists become affluent because of their possession of large amount of wealth whereas the proletariat, without means of production, sinks into the mire of poverty. So the private ownership of means of production is the condition of social polarization that takes the private ownership of means of production of the whole society as its basis and premise, therefore we cannot equate polarization with large disparity of income or wealth, nor can we take local and individual cases of polarization as overall class division or antagonism. The two things are related but not equal. Income and wealth not

① See Li Peilin, "Reasonably Adjust the Social Structure", in People's Daily, Nov. 30th 2004.

necessarily has a direct or absolute link with ownership of means of production. The disparity of wealth and income may be, but not necessarily, related to business operation and management of and participation in the process of production, whereas the polarization of class antagonism nature is without doubt linked to private ownership.

China is a socialist country with the public ownership as the mainstay, which has fundamentally eliminated the private ownership of means of production, so polarization caused by the overall private ownership does not exist. However, due to the existence of multiple forms of ownership and forms of distribution, coupled with the laws governing the market economy and other complex social factors, large disparities of income and wealth emerge, so are wealthy strata and interest groups and relatively poor strata and interest groups, and polarization even has appeared in a limited or partial scope. But this does not necessarily mean the overall polarization of the whole society of class division nature. However, if we do not guide the private economy and the distribution according to capital while consolidating and promoting the public economy as the main form of ownership and enhancing the system of distribution according to work, the tendency of polarization can become a social reality.

Fourth, the structural changes in social classes, strata and interest groups have caused significant changes in their proportion and relationship as follows:

Firstly, profound changes have taken place within the working class in terms of internal structure, role and status, resulting inthe diversification of contradictions within the leading class in China. Secondly, new differentiation, combinations and changes have taken within the farmer class, making the contradictions and relations among the people in the rural areas becoming more complex. Thirdly, the rapid development of non-public economy, especially the private economy, has given rise to the existence of contradictions between the stratum of the private entrepreneurs with high income and enormous wealth, especially those who are also employers, and their employees, and contradictions between managerial personnel and employees. Fourthly, in addition to the working class, the farmer class and the intelligentsia, a number of new strata emerge, including entrepreneurs and technical personnel employed by non-public scientific and technological enterprises, managerial and technical staff employed by overseas-funded enterprises, the self-employed, private entrepreneurs, employees in intermediaries, free-lance professionals and members. They are all builders of socialism with Chinese characteristics, but they have some differences from and contradictions with the workers, farmers, intellectuals, as well as the officers and men of the PLA.

Fifth, structure of employment and the problem of unemployment have an influence on the changes in classes, strata and interest groups.

In the process of establishing the socialist market economy, the coexistence of employment transformation and problem of unemployment has influenced the changes in classes, strata and interest groups. The shift tendency of employment toward non-agricultural and non-traditional industries has caused new divisions between classes, strata and interest groups.

Firstly, shift from agricultural to non-agricultural sectors, making a considerable part ofthe farmer class into working class and members of other strata. China has a large rural population, making employment shift toward non-agricultural sectors a difficult task. The vigorous developing of urban and rural SMEs, especially labor-intensive service-oriented and manufacturing ones, are also important forms of absorbing more labor and creating more job opportunities. As of the end of 2003, a total of 16, 950 rural laborers has been transferred, 40 percent of which to secondary industry and 60 percent to tertiary industry. ①

Secondly, the decline of the proportion of state-owned economy in the whole economy and the transfer of some part of it into non-state owned economy has caused changes of strata and interest groups within the ranks of the working class. According to statistics, from 1996 to 2000, employees in state-owned enterprises reduced 31. 42 million, down 27. 9 percent; those in the collectively-owned enterprises reduced 15. 17 million, ② down 50. 3 percent; at the same period, four million, 6. 48 million and 4. 27 million new jobs were created respectively by foreign-funded enterprises, private enterprises and self-employees, most of which were occupied by new workers, new college graduates and migrant workers, with only a small part by laid-off workers in the city. And a total of 58. 89 million new jobs were created by private enterprises and self-employees from 1991 – 2002, accounting for 65 percent of the entire new jobs created in the period. ③

---

① See Rural Investigation Corps of National Bureau of Statistics, Research on Rural Economics of China (2004), China Statistics Press, 2004, p. 97.

② See Zhang Houyi, Ming Lizhi and Liang Chuanyun (compilers), *Report on the Development of China's Private Enterprises,* Social Science Academic Press, 2002, p. 12.

③ See Huang Mengfu (compiler), *Report on the Development of China's Private Economy (2003),* Social Science Academic Press, 2003, p. 6.

Thirdly, new types of jobs were created, triggering the emergence of new social strata and interest groups. Employment in non-traditional ways, which meet the demands of some small enterprises and employees with its flexible working hours and places, represents the direction of employment in the future. Non-traditional employment refers to employment in small, micro or family enterprises, self-employment and employment in independent or social services, etc. with flexible ways of employment such as temporary employment, hourly or seasonal work, short term contract, labor dispatching, subcontract or employment based on project, etc. The encouragement of them has also created a number of new strata and interest groups.

Fourthly, the grim employment situation has produced a large number of unemployed people and a disadvantaged group of unemployment. Since reform and opening up, the structural changes in social members has undoubtedly brought about huge positive influence on our economy and social progress, but at the same time it has also caused some new problems and new phenomena needing our careful research and clear solution. Under these circumstances, it is of theoretically and practically significance to have a correct understanding of the changes in the structure of our social members and the classes, strata and interest groups, to properly handle their relations in the cause of our socialist modernization, to consolidate the Party's status as the governing party, and to expand the Party's class and mass foundation, so as to build a socialist harmonious society and promote socialist modernization.

IV. The trends and significance of changes in the structure of social members

Since reform and opening up initiated in 1978, the Chinese society is transforming from the old planned economy toward a socialist market economy at the primary stage of socialism; from a mainly natural economy to the market economy with exchange of commodities as its main form in rural areas; from an agricultural society to an industrial society; and from a closed or semi-closed society to an open society. This profound social transformation has triggered structural changes in social members toward a modern and rational direction, which are demonstrated in the following aspects:

First, the proportion of agricultural laborers is shrinking. Since reform and opening up, the number of agricultural laborers in China is reducing significantly, with its share in the whole employed population down from 70 percent in 1978 to 47 percent in 2004. [1] Most of them have become employees in township enterprises, migrant workers, entrepreneurs, or self-employed workers.

Second, the middle-income stratum has emerged and is expanding. Since 1978, the middle-income earners in our society has been rapidly increased

Third, the stratum of non-public, especially private, enterprise owners and managerial personnel is emerging and growing. As of the end of 2004, there were 3.651 million private enterprises in China, with the number of investors reaching 9.486 million and 4.0687 million employees. [2]

Fourth, new modern social strata are in the shaping. In addition to the working class, the farmer class and the intelligentsia, a batch of new social strata and groups are taking shape, including entrepreneurs and technical personnel employed by non-public scientific and technological enterprises, managerial and technical staff employed by overseas-funded enterprises, the self-employed, private entrepreneurs, employees in intermediaries, free-lance professionals and members of other social strata.

In short, with the gradual improvement the new social order, the structure of our social members is developing toward a reasonable, balanced and modern direction. On the other hand, although its overall framework is basically in place, its structure is not stable yet. Besides, there are also many institutional factors that affect its transition to the reasonable direction.

At the present stage, the structural changes in classes, strata and interest groups in our society are the outcomes of reform and opening up and mark the economic and social development, which in turn will have a multiple, profound and lasting influence on the deepening of reform and opening up, the development of our economy and overall progress of our society, which can be summarized as follows:

In the first place, it is conducive to the balanced economic and social development. The old structure, formed under the highly centralized planned economy with an egalitarian nature, was ineffective in bringing into play the enthusiasm and creativity of workers. In contrast, under the conditions of the market economy, the differentiation and changes in classes, strata and interest groups, reflecting the actual changes in income, status, etc., and principle of "giving

---

① See *China Statistical Yearbook(2005)*, China Statistics Press, 2005, p. 118.

② *Ibid.* p. 148.

priority to efficiency with due consideration to fairness," not only embodies social fairness, but also ensures efficiency. Under certain conditions, it is conducive to mobilizing the enthusiasm of all social classes, strata and interest groups. By maintaining certain social disparity, it strengthens competition and incentives to enable the social members to glow with their own vitality and power, thus contribute to economic and social progress.

In the second place, the new structural changes in social members of our society are conducive to social stability. Social stability and harmony is a prerequisite for economic and social development, and no country or nation can develop amid severe instability or unrest. Changes in the structure of social members can both be positive or negative to society depending on its nature. If these changes conform to the requirements of development of the productive forces and general trends of the society, they will be conducive to long-term peace, stability and harmony of society, rather than intensification of social contradictions, and verse versa. Changes conforming to social trends of the society will bring about new adjustments of relationship between social classes, strata and interest groups and new social mobility. Reasonable adjustment and mobility of social members are important symbols as well as "safety valves" and "oscillation absorbers" promoting social progress, stability and harmony.

In the third place, the new structural changes in members of our society are conducive to our endeavor of modernization. For a modern society, a modern structure of social membership is imperative. The modernization process of the world shows that, a country without a social structure corresponding with its modern society cannot keep harmonious and stable; instead, it has a latent risk of socio-economic crisis and instability.

In the fourth place, the new structural changes in members of our society will promote the all-round and free development of the people. The increasingly multiple and open social structure, the changes of roles of social members and more easy occupational mobility will provide freedom of choice and broader social space for them, which will promote the flow of talents and the free and overall development of the people.

Since reform and opening up, profound changes have occurred in China's social structure, which has become more multiple, diverse and free-flowing; so do the economic, political, cultural and other relations between its classes, strata and interest groups. A correct understanding of these changes and the status and characteristics of classes, strata and interest groups and relations between them and their developmental trends, their role in the socialist market economy and socialist modernization, will help us draw correct conclusions in these respects, thus to strengthen our understanding of our country, and based on it, to formulate correct lines, principles and policies.

Chapter 11

Interest Groupsin the Primary Stage of Socialism and Contradictions among These Groups

Under the condition ofthe market economy in the primary stage of socialism and the premise of scientific division of classes, the original and new born strata (about their changes, see Chapter Ten), the key to correctly understanding and handling the differences and contradictions among the interest groups is to identify these groups and their differences and contradictions.

I. Interest Groups in the Primary Stage of Socialism and Criteria for their Identification

Theoretically, class contradiction is no long the principal contradiction in the primary stage of socialism. So only by correctly understanding the interest groups and their relations and properly coordinate their differences and contradictions of interests under the condition of adhering to class analysis, can we give full play to the motive forces of interests to mobilize the enthusiasm of all interest groups. Under the new historical conditions and the premise of adhering to the division of working class, the farmer class and the intelligentsia as part of the working class, it is very necessary to identify the interest groups and differences and contradictions between them according to materialistic conception of history, method of class analysis of Marxism and the theory of interest group identification, and on this basis, to make proper policies and strategies, so as to mobilize the enthusiasm of all sides.

What, then, is an interest group in primary stage of socialism? An interest group refers to an interest community formed on the basis of relatively common interests through socio-economic relations. The members of an interest group have relatively identical interest objectives and values while between different interest groups there are certain differences and contradictions. The existence, development, differentiation and combination of interest groupsin the primary stage of socialism are subject to the constraints of economic relations and the influence of various complex factors in this stage, such as society, history, ethnicity, mentality, locality, tradition. It is precisely the ownership, division of labor, forms of social labor and other complex social and historical factors that fundamentally determine that there are interest differences and contradictions between interest groups, which, in turn, objectively determine the historical necessity of the existence of interest groups and criteria for their identification.

Given the necessary existence of differences of interest groups in the primary stage of socialism, what criteria should we use to identify them? Basically they are as follows:

First, determining the essential attributes of the interest groups based on their ownership of means of production. In the primary stage of socialism, the Marxist theory of identifying classes by ownership of means of production is still of methodological significance. The differences of status and role of people in the relations of means of production in the primary stage of socialism determine their economic interest groups. In the ownership relationship with the public sector remaining dominant and diverse sectors of the economy developing side by side, great differences exist between different sectors: within the public ownership, there are the differences of state-owned economy and collective economy; within the same economic sector there is the separation between the ownership and management of the enterprises; between the enterprises in the same sector of ownership, there is the differences of degree of independence; and there are also different forms of realization of ownership in the same sector of ownership. All these differences determine that, the social members, who are inevitably integrated with one of the sectors of ownership, will necessarily fall into different interest groups with different interests, and that different production units constitute different relatively independent economic interest groups. So it is a premise to analyze the interest groups starting from the relationship of ownership.

Second, identifyinginterest groups on the basis of distribution and other relationships in the primary stage of socialism. In this stage, the differences of interests are prominently reflected in distribution: different forms of distribution and different forms of interest realization also determine the existence of different interest groups with certain differences in economic aspect. In the primary stage of socialism the distribution pattern in which distribution according to work is the main form that coexists with other forms of distribution determines the differences of distribution between interest groups. For example, the group that earns their income in accordance with the principle of distribution according to work are different from groups realizing their income according to other forms, such as capital, management, factors of production; even within the same distribution form there are differences of interests. This determines the existence of different interest groups. In addition, relations between people in the production, exchange, consumption and other links also contribute to the existence of different interest groups. For example, in the process of production, there are groups of managerial personnel, technical personnel, salespersons, and so on; in the process of exchange, there are also commodity producers, sellers, buyers and so on.

Third, under the precondition of identifying interest groups on the basis of economic relationships, we can also take into account the differences of social status caused by occupations and other economic and social factors. Same or similar occupations can bring about generally similar economic and political interests, thus contributing to the formation of different interest groups.

In short, in identifying interest groups, we must insist on the criteria of ownerships, possession of products, roles, statusof the individuals in social and economic relations, in addition to other social factors. These criteria show that different interest groups have their different demands, interests and contradictions.

II. Causes for the Existence of Different Interest Groups in the Primary Stage of Socialism

Under the conditions of market economy in the primary stage of socialism, the interest relations among the people are composed mainly of the inter-group relations of different interests. In this stage, with the existence of the working class, the farmer class and the intelligentsia as part of the working class, it is an objective existence that there are the differences of interests and values and thus frictions and contradictions within these classes and strata, in addition to their complex interest structure. What, then, are the causes for the existence of these complex and diverse interest groups in the primary stage of socialism?

First, the productive forcesin primary stage of socialism are relatively backward, and the material and cultural wealth cannot sufficient meets the growing needs of the people. The considerable gap between the limited wealth and the distribution is the fundamental material reason for the existence of the interest groups.

Second, there remains a lot of residue of the old society, which constitutes extensive social basis for the existence of different interest groups. The primary stage of socialism is just born from the womb of the old society, which, under the complex international and domestic circumstances, still maintains complex social relations with the class exploiting society and its remnants and traces. The great social differences caused by the old division of labor still exist, so do the classes, strata, fixed at relatively independent careers and the old mentality and morality. All these give their contributions to the social and historical basis for the existence of complex interest groups in the primary stage of socialism. For example, the old divisions between urban and rural, workers and farmers, and manual labor and mental labor, determine the existence of the interest groups of urban and rural residents, the working class and the farmer class, the manual and mental workers and so on; the groups of self-employed workers, the private entrepreneurs, etc., by their very nature, also have the traces of the old society

Even the new criminals, reactionary exploiting class elements and other anti-socialist elements who are gestated from the residue of the old society, under certain conditions, may form interest groups hostile or antagonistic to socialism. The division of labor in the primary stage of socialism place people in relatively fixed occupations, so that people have different status and different material and cultural benefits, thus giving birth to different interest groups. Besides, the quality and physical differences of the laborers also result in different interest groups. For instance, singers, artists and the like are workers having special professional skills. Another instance includes the interest difference between skilled and unskilled workers, and so on.

Third, multiple ownerships and the diversified forms of distribution, as well as the complex relationship in the market economy is the most direct economic roots in the existence of different interest groups in the primary stage of socialism. The relationships in the market economy in the primary stage of socialism determine that relations between interest groups in this stage are complex. The ownership pattern with public ownership playing a dominant role and diverse forms of ownership developing side by side, and the distribution pattern in which distribution according to work is primary and a variety of modes of distribution coexist determine the existence, formation, evolution and development of different interest groups and their complex structure.

There are of course other social causes for the existence of interest groups in the primary stage of socialism, which are not discussed here.

III. The Composition of the Major Interest Groups in the Primary Stage of Socialism

On the premise of recognizing the general division of the working class, the farmer class and the intelligentsia, we can make further divisions of the interest groups in the primary stage of socialism as follows:

By differences of division of social labor, we can divide the social members into urban residents, rural residents; manual laborers, mental laborers (intellectuals), etc.

By class differences caused by fundamental differences of relationship with means of production, our social members can be divided intothe interest groups of industrial producers, agricultural producers, intellectuals within the working class, the interest groups of private entrepreneurs, self-employers, etc. in the non-public sectors of the economy.

Byforms of ownership and realization, the social members can be divided into interest groups of employees in state-owned, collective-owned units, in township enterprises, in private sectors, in mixed ownership sectors, in joint-stock enterprises, in shareholding enterprises, etc. In addition, there are also interest groups of self-employers, owners or managers of private enterprises and foreign-funded enterprises, etc.

From the prospective of enterprises with relatively independent status in the market economy, there are interest groups of factories, shops, all kinds of companies, etc.

The social members can also be divided on the basis of forms of distribution into the different interest groups, including the civil servants and workers in public institutions, workers based on labor contract system, on leasing management and on the household contract responsibility system, employers and employees in private enterprises, contractors and producers in contracted enterprises, etc.

By occupations and social status in economic activities, they can be divide into interest groups of workers, farmers, individual industrialists and businessmen, engineers and technicians, medical workers, teachers, managers in private sectors, agricultural producers, households involved both in industry and farming, workers in government bodies, managers in public enterprises, etc.

By their economic relations in the socialist market economy, the social members can be divided into interest groups of producers, sellers, consumers, and so on.

By their income and wealth gaps and the tendencies caused by these gaps, the social members can be divided into interest groups of the wealthy, the relatively wealthy, the well-off, those just having adequate food and clothing and the poor. The wealthy group refers to the group of person having assets worthy of millions even hundreds of millions yuan. According to sampling surveys, surveys of typical cases and related data of the National Bureau of Statistics of China, currently the highest income groups are primarily composed of the outstanding scientific and technological personnel, self-employees, private entrepreneurs, enterprise contractors, managers of leasing operation, as well as popular singers, movie stars, sports stars, etc. The relative wealthy group refers to those who have hundreds of thousands of assets each, live a relatively affluent life, have their own houses, cars, and can afford their children's higher education fee and can enjoy vocations. They include managers in foreign-funded or private enterprises, individual industrialists or businessmen with high incomes, engineers and technicians in advantageous industries, entrepreneurs in public-owned enterprises with good economic returns, etc. Well-off group refers to people who have tens of thousands of assets each and live a relatively comfortable life, including teachers, state officials, ordinary intellectuals, workers of enterprises with good economic returns, and so on. The group with adequate food and clothing refers to the group whose members have just enough income to basically meet their needs for food and clothing, including workers in the city and agricultural laborers in rural areas. The poor group refers to people living below the poverty line and cannot get enough food and clothing.

The above is a broad and extensive division. In general, the components of the interest groups in the primary stage of socialism are as follows:

First is the interest group of material producers within the working class. The working class is composed of three parts, i. e., the workers of material producers, the managerial personnel in public-owned enterprises, state organs, etc., and intellectuals engaged in the managerial, cultural, educational, science and technology work. By material producers we mean workers directly engaged in productive labor, including workers in state-owned, collective-owned, mixed-owned economies and in enterprises of joint-stock system, cooperative system, shareholding system, in private enterprises and the self-employee and so on. The group of material producers, based on their occupations, can be further divided into subgroups workers in the fields of industry, transportation, capital construction, commerce, services, agriculture, forestry, animal husbandry and fishery and other. The migrant workers, who derive from the farmer class and enter the urban areas, are also part of the working class.

Second is the interest group offarmer class. Farmers account for the majority of China's population and most of them are agricultural laborers under the household contract responsibility system. Although since 1979 this system has been implemented in rural areas, and the mode of operation has changed with it, the farmers still belong to the interest group of the farmer class in the collective economy. And based on the divisions of labor and occupations, they can be further divided into farmers directly engaged in farming under the household contract responsibility system, farmer- entrepreneurs, farmer-administrators at the community level, farmers engaged both in industry and farming, and so on.

Third is the interest group of intellectuals. In China, intellectuals, as part of the working class, are those engaged in such mental work as management, science and technology, culture, education, ordinary staff in Party and state bodies and so on.

Fourth is the interest group of social leaders and business managers. In the primary stage of socialism, although the leaders of Party and government bodies at all levels and the directors and managers in public enterprises mostly belong to the strata of intellectuals as part of the working class, they still form a special interest group different from ordinary workers, farmers and intellectuals due to the importance of their work, their posts and the political and economic positions as well as the responsibilities they shoulder. The subgroup of social leaders and business managers has dual natures: on the one hand they are representatives of the interests of state or the collective, they should not gain any personal interest from it; on the other hand, as laborers seeking means of livelihood, they have interests and demands of their own. In practice, we should clearly distinguish their capacity as social leaders, managers and representatives of state interests from their capacity as subjects of personal interests.

Fifth, the interest groups consisted of entrepreneurs and technical personnel employed by non-public scientific and technological enterprises, the self-employed, employees in intermediaries, free-lance professionals, and so on. In the current stage, the components of this stratum are complex, but their incomes are usually higher than the incomes of those working in public economy or the Party and state organizations.

Sixth isthe interest group of owners or managers of the private economy. In the primary stage of socialism, the existence of non-public economy will necessarily give birth to its owners and managers. Along with it, there will be de facto wage-labor relationship between the employers and managers and the employees or workers, and the incomes of the former will inevitably include the surplus value created by the latter.

Seventh isthe interest group consisting of managers, agents and operators of foreign-funded enterprises and private enterprises, which has been formed since China's reform and opening up after large amounts of foreign investment were introduced.

Eighth is the interest group of the poor. The poor group, a marginalized group of cross-class and cross strata that are taking shape in our society, refers to those who are disadvantageous in wealth creation and accumulations and weak in competitiveness and ability of life, including: the disabled, laid-off workers, some aged citizens, poor people in cities and towns, some citizens suffering disasters, some retired workers, some migrant workers, poor people in rural areas, and so on.

The components of the poor interest group are:

Firstly, some of thefarmers directly engaged in agricultural production. Many causes have resulted in the existence of the poor farmer group, including the exhaustion of the productive forces released by the household contract responsibility system since 1980s; the slowdown of the development of township enterprises in the 1990s; the decline of the prices of food and other agricultural products (according to estimates, in the later years of the 1990s, food prices fell by more than 30 percent, which severely affected the income of the farmers).

Secondly, the migrant workers as surplus labor forces entering into the city.

The implementation of household contract responsibility system in rural areas made the agricultural productivity released. As a result, rural surplus labor forces entered the city, forming the tides of migrant workers numbered thousands of millions annually. Although they constitute an important force in urban construction and actually become the mainstay of some industries such as construction, mining, they do not have the equal status and treatment as the formal employees in the enterprises, and often take up low-paid jobs under hard conditions that are shunned by urban residents; in some cases their personal rights are not guaranteed. All these make them become a considerably poor group.

Thirdly, the urban poor group with the laid-off workers and joblessas the main body.

Since the 1990s, with the adjustment of industrial structure and enterprise reform, the issue of unemployment in China has become increasingly prominent. A person becoming unemployed in the city means losing his basic source of livelihood except for the social relief fund, so is greatly disadvantaged compared with those having incomes. China now has an urban poor group with laid-off workersand the jobless as the main body.

Poverty, especially poverty in China's urban area, is a major pressing problem. According to the statistics of the Ministry of Civil Affairs, currently, there are 14, 971,069 people, that is, 3.9 percent of urban population, or 4.6 percent of non-agricultural population, live under the minimum living standard for urban residents. In other words, there are four to five poor persons in every one hundred urban residents in China. Among them, workers, laid-off workers and retired workers accounted for 54 percent, the unemployed for 17 percent, and "three no people" (no source of income, no ability to work, no family supporter) for six percent, and the rest for 23 percent.[①] The numbers of poverty-stricken population increase progressively from eastern to middle and to western regions.

The main reasons for the urban residents falling into poverty include: curtailment of income due to the poor performance of the enterprises; low employment and re-employment; major disease or disability of family member or other misfortunes; ineffective implementation of labor and social security policy; rapid increase of the cost of education, and so on.

IV. Main Features of the Pattern of Interest Groups in the Primary Stage of Socialism

Under the condition ofthe market economy in the primary stage of socialism, there exist differences and contradictions among interest groups that cannot be ignored on the basis of fundamental identity of interests, which determine their following basic features.

1. Transitional nature

At present, China is in a reform stage of transition fromthe planned economy to

① In *China Reform Daily*, March, 13th 2002.

the market economy. With the changes in economic and political structures, the original interest structure is changing accordingly, resulted in the drastic readjustment and reorganization of interest pattern. For instance, the groups of entrepreneurs (managers) and the self-employed have become important components in the interest structure; the group of employers in the private economy has occupied a considerable position in the structure; many intellectuals have taken leading posts at all levels, injecting fresh blood to the groups of social leaders and managers, and so on. The interest structure built on the old system was not conducive neither to the dynamism of interests or to the mobilization of initiatives of all sides. The current differentiation and combination of interest structure will gradually lead to the shaping of an optimized pattern that is going to give full rein to the dynamism of all interest groups.

2. Diversity

Another outstanding feature ofthe interest pattern under the market economy in the primary stage of socialism is the diversity of interest group awareness and behaviors. Interest group awareness refers to mental reactions of different interest groups to all the aspects of social life in response to the stimulation of group interests. Interest awareness is composed of sense, concern and understanding of an interest group. The complexity of the interest pattern determines the diverse types of awareness of the interest groups: firstly, longing for socialist modernization, support for reform and opening up and for socialism with Chinese characteristics are the common sense of the various interest groups. Secondly, different interest groups have different goals and benefit-seeking behaviors. Finally, comparison mentality and benefit-comparison behaviors between interest groups are commonplace. This kind of comparison comes from the competition for benefits in their pursuit of interests, because every group has the shared mentality to seek greater interests, although they interest motives may vary. There are two types of benefit comparison: one is positive comparison, that is, through proper comparison, higher enthusiasm are triggered; another one is negative comparison, which views the differences of positions of interest groups in the interest structure in a static way, make comparison only with the higher ones instead of lower ones, and concerns only about short-term interests instead of long-term interests, money and so on instead of contribution, so that it mistakenly believes that theirs is the group getting the most unreasonably low income. Different types of interest awareness will inevitably lead to a different type behavior orientation, a human behavior motivated by the sense of profit-seeking. Different interest groups have different types of interest orientation, due to which, interest frictions, conflicts, contradictions occur, along with the complex interest relations among interest groups. Instances include contradictions between workers and farmers because of the scissors gap between the prices of industrial and agricultural products, contradictions between the employers and employees in the private enterprises, contradictions between entrepreneurs and managers and the employees, contradictions between social leaders and the ordinary people.

3. Differences

The contradictions among interest groups frequently and commonly manifest themselves in distribution, specifically in gaps of incomes. It is necessary to allow appropriate interest gaps between groups so as to form a pattern in which reasonable discrepancies of income are recognized so that enthusiasm of different interest groups can be aroused. However, if the discrepancies are widened unreasonably, the differentiation and structure of interest groups will result in the expansion and intensification of interest contradictions. In the process of China's reform, when the traditional economic model has been broken while the new one is still in the shaping, some distorted and complex economic relations have emerged. On the one hand, in the area of distribution, the egalitarian practice of having everyone "eat from the same big pot" still exist in some places; on the other, the problem in which some people get unreasonable non-labor incomes is exacerbating to some extent. For example, some people illegally get high incomes by taking advantage of the defects in our economy and macro-control to take such practices as bribery, abuse of power, fakery, cheating, etc. This has led to many distorted and tense relations, even interest contradictions and conflicts among interest groups. In our effort to develop the socialist market economy, the widening gap between incomes and between rich and poor has become a prominent social problem.

4. Prominence

The backwardness ofthe productive forces and underdeveloped market economy make the material means of livelihood cannot meet the needs of the people, which, coupled with the not so reasonable distribution policy, causes the interest contradictions among the people extremely prominent and acute.

5. Clear Demarcation

In the primary stage of socialism, the patternof interest groups are complicated, and boundaries between them are clear-cut, so do the demands of the groups and contradictions between them. For example, Chinese intellectuals have a clear political intention to establish a socialist democracy and strong demands to improve their living and working conditions; whereas the attention of ordinary workers is put more on material interests such as wage, prices and social welfare.

6. Concentration

More often than not, the interest contradictions in the primary stage of socialism manifest themselves in contradictions betweenthe leaders and the masses. When a social interest conflict break, a considerable part of the masses express their discontent to the direct leaders of their work units or places, showing that the contradictions are mainly manifest themselves as those between the leaders and the masses.

7. Acuteness

The tension of interest relations tends to cause some conflicts, which, if not handled properly, maycause unrest. In the primary stage of socialism, intensified interest relationships often develop into face to face conflicts. For example, because of the problems of unemployment, housing, wages, prices, and so on, some people adopt measures of direct confrontation such as strikes, collective petitions, demonstrations, assault on government organizations; fierce disputes and conflicts may also break out within the masses because of property disputes, asset allocation, land use, and the like. If we lax our vigilance against this kind of mass incidents or handle them improperly, they may lead to greater social unrest affecting the political stability and social harmony.

Chapter 12

Major Changes in China's Working Class in the New Era

After the establishment of the People's Republic of China, the working class has become masters and leading class of the country and the basic force we rely on in promoting the productive forces and the cause of building socialism with Chinese characteristics. In the process of China's socialist development, the rank of the working class has expanded rapidly with their educational level becoming higher generally. New generations of workers have grown up in large quantity, and major changes have taken place in their composition, quality, quantity, mode of production, lifestyle, and so on; so do the quantity and quality of the intellectuals as part of the working class. With the continuous progress of China's socialist reform and opening up in particular, the status of China's working class has changed significantly: It has expanded steadily with its continuously improved quality and strengthened advanced nature. In the long term, these changes are conducive to its overall raising of quality, the full play of its holistic advantages and the consolidation of its position and role. A scientific analysis of the new changes in the working class, a correct understanding of its position as masters and leading force of the country is of great significance for strengthening its position, for developing socialist productive forces, for consolidating the class and mass bases of the CPC as the governing party, and for building a socialist harmonious society.

I. Main Features of the Changes in the Working Class in the New Era

Under the new historical conditions, the Chinese working class has undergone major changes andshown many new features.

1. The working class has greatly expanded in number

Since 1978 when reform and opening up was initiated, Chinese working class has expanded rapidly in number. The total number of the workers just after

Liberation was only 8. 09 million. It reached around 95 million in 1978 and about 106 million in 2004. [①] They are consisted of three parts, i. e., workers directly involved in production, intellectuals and cadres of the Party and the government. If the employees in the cities and towns and townships are added together, the total number of Chinese workers will reach about 434 million, accounting for 56 percent of China's labor forces. [②] Presently the annual increase of China's entrants into the labor forces is 10 million, meaning more people joining the ranks of the working class. Its distribution is diverse: (1) the working class in public enterprises is increasing in number. The increase of the overall strength of the state-owned and collective-owned enterprises has been constantly adding new forces to the working class. (2) The rapid expansion of the ranks of intellectuals has added fresh blood to the working class. (3) With the rise of the tertiary industry, employees in the service industry have increased significantly. (4) The development of township enterprises has give rise to a new group of farmer-workers, who are both workers and farmers and leave the farmland but not their hometown. By the end of 2004, employees in township enterprises reached 138. 66 million, of which, 20. 24 million worked in private enterprises and 20. 66 million in individual enterprises. [③] (5) A large number of surplus labor force in rural areas joined the ranks of the working class. Since reform and opening up, especially in the last decade, the number of migrant workers has increased steadily. According to statistics, about 200 million farmers have shifted to non-agricultural industries and the number of migrant workers reached 99 million. Among the 38. 93 employees in construction industry, 31. 37 million are migrant workers. [④] At present, there are 250 million surplus labor forces in China's rural area, among which, 99 million are migrant workers in various industries without fixed occupations. Migrant workers, from the first day they left the rural area, had indicated that they represent the main body of the huge population of employees in China. Currently, 90 percent employees in construction industry, 80 percent in coal mining industry, 50 percent to 60 percent in textile industry and 50 percent in services industry in the city are migrant workers. (6) With the development of non-public economies, employees in private enterprises, joint ventures, mixed-ownership enterprises and other non-public enterprises great increased with more than 100

---

① See *China Statistical Yearbook*(2005), China Statistics Press, 2005, p. 127.

② *Ibid.*, pp. 120 – 121.

③ *Ibid.*, p. 121.

④ *Ibid.*, pp. 125 – 126.

million employees currently. ①(7) New blood is constantly added into the ranks of cadres of the Party and state organs at all levels.

2. The overall quality and strength of the working class has been raised

With theprogress of modernization of China's productive forces, the continuous introduction of high-tech and the increase of technology content in various industries, the overall qualities of Chinese workers, such as level of science and technology and skills, have greatly improved. The development of modern productive forces has trained and fostered modern Chinese working class and its qualities, which are mainly manifested in the improvement in two aspects: one is their level of education and the other is their scientific and cultural qualities.

With the development ofChina's education, the educational level of the Chinese working class is gradually increasing. Those who have received senior middle school education account for 70 percent, those with primary school education account for only 3 percent. The details of it is: those are illiterate or quite illiterate account only for 0. 5 percent, those with primary school education 2. 5 percent, junior high school education 25. 9 percent, senior middle school education 23. 1 percent, special secondary school or secondary vocational school education 19. 4 percent, college or above education 19. 4 percent. The average length of schooling of the workers is 12. 19 years, an increase of 0. 74 years compared with the figure in 1992. ② With the improvement in the level of education, coupled with other factors, the overall qualities of the working class in science and technology, morality, culture, politics, etc., have also greatly improved.

The proportion of professional and technical personnel in the working class is getting larger and employees having professional titles have increased substantially. Since reform and opening up, the number of professionals in every ten thousand workers increased from 583. 1 to 1903. 7 people, an increase of 2. 26 times. ③ The total number of intellectuals is 40 million. Meanwhile, with the fundamental improvement of living and medical conditions due to the development of the productive forces, the physical quality of the Chinese working class has also been greatly enhanced. The working class in its original sense is also constantly improving

① See *China Statistical Yearbook(2005)*, China Statistics Press, 2005, pp. 120 – 121.

② See Zhao Ziping, "Keep Pace with the Times to Have a Correct Understanding of Domestic Conditions," In Outlook Weekly, no. 40, 2001 .

③ *Ibid.*

its scientific, cultural and moral qualities, so that the industrial workers and intellectuals increasingly merge to become the main body of China's advanced socialist productive forces.

3. The increase of proportion of intellectuals in the working-class has added fresh blood into it.

As part of the working class, the proportion of intellectualshas become larger, including cadres in Party and state organizations at all levels, technicians, researchers, managers, medical workers, teachers, and have become backbone of the working class and the main representative and pioneers of advanced productive forces. They have injected fresh blood to the working class and improved its overall quality.

4. The origins and composition of the working class are more diverse, and its internal structure more pluralistic.

Changes in the socio-economic structure led to diversification of the internal composition of the working class. Since 1978, with change from single public ownership into the ownership pattern with public ownership playing the dominant role and other forms of ownership developing side by side, workers began mobilizing from public to non-public enterprises, including individual, private, shareholding and mixed ownership. Meanwhile, because of the adjustment of industrial structure and other reasons, the origins and composition of the working class are more diverse. In terms of industries, proportion of workers employed in traditional industries declined to 169. 2 million, accounting for 42. 4 percent of the whole; while those in the tertiary industry increased to 230. 11 million, accounting for 57. 6 percent.[①] In terms of the ownership of enterprises, the proportion of workers in public enterprises decreased while in enterprises of other forms of ownership increased, particularly in private ownership.[②] Specifically, the number of workers in state-owned enterprises is 67. 1 million, accounting for 16. 8 percent of the whole; in township or collective-owned enterprises, 138. 66 million, accounting for 34. 7 percent; in private and individual enterprises, 96. 05 million, accounting for 24. 1 percent. In terms of occupational division of labor, workers directly engaged in industrial production are

---

① See *China Statistical Yearbook(2005)*, China Statistics Press, 2005, p. 118.

② *Ibid.*, pp. 120 – 121.

88.65 million, accounting for 22.2 of its whole, in communication and transport industries, 20.84 million, accounting for 5.2 percent; in financial industry, 3.4 million, accounting for 0.85 percent; in social management, 21.69 million, accounting for 5.4 percent; in science and technology, education, culture and medical sectors, 22.21 million, accounting for 5.6 percent. ①

5. The levels of income and living standard of the working class have obviously increased

Generally speaking, since reform and opening up, the income of China's working class have increased greatly and their economic status has substantially risen, so do their family property and living standards. During the 20 more years of reform and opening up, allowing for price rises, the average wage of the workers grew by 4.4 percent annually, ② while their income other than wages increased by 23.5 percent annually, ③ and the property and intellectual property incomes have gradually become new sources of income for some workers. With more and more workers having various types of property, the Chinese working class began to say goodbye to the "propertyless" proletariat in the old sense.

6. Income gap and differentiation appear within the ranks of working class, as well as group of poverty due to unemployment and laid-off

The emergenceof diverse forms of ownership and distribution and the discard of the egalitarian practice of everyone "eating from the same big pot," the income gap between worker widened, and differentiation occurred along with it. These are manifested in different regions, types of ownership, industries, and occupational division of labor, etc. For example, there are income differences between workers in state-owned and collective-owned enterprises, between workers in enterprises of the same type of ownership but different industries, between employers and employees, between those engaged in management and those in production front in public owned enterprises, and so on. According to statistics, in foreign-funded enterprises in China, the average income of managers is about 15 times that of ordinary Chinese employees. Likewise, there are gap of incomes between manual laborers and mental

---

① See *China Statistical Yearbook*(2005), China Statistics Press, 2005, p. 125.

② *Ibid.*, P. 151.

③ Shandong Province Research Center for Deng Xiaoping Theory, "Correctly Understand the Working Class' Status of Masters in the New Situations," In China Daily, Dec. 6th 2001.

laborers and managers, between workers in different forms of ownership, in different working conditions and different levels of income. Some workers have become shareholders of their enterprises, thus becoming group with considerable property among the working class, and so the income gap between them and ordinary workers is also gradually widening.

Within the ranks of the working class, the egalitarian practice of having everyone "eat from the same big pot" was broke with and the income gap was widened. But at the same time, there appeared the inequality of opportunities and also the disparity between the work they did and the payment they got for it. The most immediate problem is the unemployment and laid-off workers. According to the statistics made by some experts, during the Eleventh Five-year Plan period, there are about 13 million people got unemployed or laid-off in cities and towns every year. Coupled with the not well-established social security system, the daily life of these people and their family often fall in difficulty and thus become a relatively poor group. In the process of socialist reform, the living standard of a part of the workers declined; the basic living of some workers in difficult enterprises can hardly get guaranteed because of the unsatisfactory progress in social security; some laid-off workers cannot get re-employed; in some enterprises, wage and medical expense arrears are common; the proportion of workers suffering occupational diseases and industrial injuries is still high; the system of labor contract has not thoroughly implemented, so that rights and interests of the workers are infringed. These issues have directly affected the creativity and enthusiasm of the working class. Reform will necessarily involve structural adjustment of industries and interests, which will pose challenges for some workers and a tremendous pressure for China's working class as a whole.

7. Competitiveness within the working class intensifies; there is more freedom in job finding and more frequent in job-hopping and workers are younger than ever before.

Under the socialist market economy, competition consciousness of the working class as a whole is growing, but at the same time their internal competition becomes intensified. Reform and opening up has broken with the idea that "workers belong to their work units." Therefore, competition and job mobility become more intensified, giving more occupational freedom to workers, who can flow between units of different types of ownership or become self-employed. The proportion of workers in state-owned enterprise declined whereas those in non-public owned enterprises rose. In

1978, employees in state-owned and collective-owned economy accounted for 23.7 percent of the total employed population in the country and there was nearly no non-public economy. In 2004, employees in non-public sectors only accounted for 25.6 percent of the entire workforce.① The new type of employment of finding jobs on one's own and two-way selection make workers become owners and dominators of their own labor and masters of the country in the true sense. The relationship between workers and enterprises is established more on the basis of labor contract and regulations. As a result, employees become much more active, enthusiastic and progressive in economic activities. According to surveys, 50 percent employees, mainly young workers, changed jobs at least once. The average age of the employees is 36 years old with the ranks of the working class younger than this.② In short, although facing increasing pressure, China's working class' sense of competition has become higher and their ability in the competition is stronger.

8. The leading position and lawful rights and interests are guaranteed by the law, and their status as masters of the society was further consolidated.

China's constitution clearly defines the nature of the country and the leading position of the working class in the country's political life. With the improvement of the socialist legal system, laws and regulations protecting workers have basically been in place. The establishment of modern corporate system makes the workers have the right to know, to propose, to supervise and to participate in the enterprises. With the deepening of reform, the social status of Chinese working class as a whole has been greatly improved. The modern corporate system and shareholding system have legally clarified the role of the workers' congresses and the rights and interests of the employees. The clarification of property rights of the public enterprises has provided more space for workers to play their status as masters. In terms of political affiliation and strength, the numbers of Party members in the working class increased from 1.1 million in 1956 to more than 22 million,③ and many of the workers have been promoted to the leading posts of the state organizations, enterprises and

① Calculated according the related data in *China Statistical Yearbook(2005)*, China Statistics Press, 2005, p. 120 – 121.

② The Bureau of Theory of the Publicity of the CCCPC, *Twenty Five Theoretical FAQs of Cadres and Masses*, Xuexi Publishing House, 2003, p. 69.

③ Research Team of Beijing Municipality Center for Deng Xiaoping Theory, " A Historical Examination of The Composition of Membership of the CPC," in Beijing Daily, Oct. 21st 2002.

institutions.

9. Group differentiation of the working class

From the point of view of interest groups, China's working class can be divided into the following five interest groups:

(1) Group of ordinary workers, referring mainly to workers in the front of production in the enterprises of various types of ownership, including the ordinary skilled workers and middle and lower management personnel, whose incomes are low and own only labor resources.

(2) Group of senior employees and high-tech personnel, consisting mainly of senior employees and the scientific and technical personnel in high-tech enterprise with high incomes, who work in finance, insurance, securities industries or in foreign, Hong Kong, Macao or Taiwan-funded enterprises and participate in production and distribution with technical factors.

(3) Group of civil servants working in the Party and government bodies and employees in institutional units.

(4) Group of poor workers, referring mainly to the workers in difficult or bankrupt enterprises whose livelihood are not guaranteed; the laid-off workers who are difficult to get reemployed; workers whose wages and medical expenses have long been in arrears. This group is the result of social transition, whose lives meet difficulties to a varying degree.

(5) Group of migrant workers. They are the new members of the working class. Workers from the rural areas to the city usually do heavy, dirty, hard and dangerous work. They are hard working, but without any resources, so belong to the lower strata with low income in the social life of the city. According to statistics of the All-China Federation of Trade Unions, the number of migrant workers is about 99 million with an annual growth of five million.

In summary, in the new era, the status of Chinese working class as masters of the country remains unchanged with the reasons as follows:

(1) From the perspective of economic base, with the public ownership playing the dominant role, the position of the working class who combine themselves with the means of production has not changed. (2) In the superstructure, the working class is in the leading position with its party, the Communist Party of China, governing the country. (3) In terms of ideology and culture, the working class' world outlook, moral outlook and culture are in the dominant positions.

II. Major Problems Facing the Working Class in the New Era

In the primary stage of socialism and the process of reform and opening up, the working class is faced with new challenges and problems that cannot be ignored.

First, the status and role ofpart of workers in the working class engaged in activities of production, operation and management of enterprises have undergone some changes, so that their sense of ownership somewhat softened and their labor consciousness weakened. The modern corporate system reform in state-owned and collective-owned enterprises has paid more importance to the directors and managers, stipulated their legal person status, which somewhat have changed the status and roles of the working class in enterprises. Some ordinary workers have less enthusiasm to participate in the operation, payment, decision-making, technical innovation, etc. of the enterprises. Their democratic participation and sense of ownership weakened, because they regard themselves just as ordinary laborers. So, in the process of the public enterprise restructuring, the leading position and status of masters should be highlighted through institutions in the new system. Similar changes have also taken place in the enterprises of mixed ownership and it is more so in private enterprises, where workers are employees under domination. In short, because the system and mechanism of supervision of the workers has not been fully established, the status and role of workers in the process of production, operation and management declined, workers regard themselves only as ordinary laborers with little sense of ownership. This is specifically manifested in the following aspects:

Firstly, in some places and enterprises, workers pay more labor than before, but their income do not increase obviously; Secondly, in some economically underdeveloped regions, the wage levels of the employees and workers in township enterprises and that of the migrant workers are lower even than the minimum wage standard of their localities; Thirdly, some workers cannot fully get their social security and social assistance in retirement, pension, health care, housing, etc.; Fourthly, there are a considerable amount of laid-off and unemployed workers; Fifthly, the political status and occupational reputation of workers need to be further strengthened. For example, the proportion of worker deputies to the fifth, sixth, seventh and eighth national congresses were respectively 26.7 percent, 14.9 percent, 12.4 percent and 11.2 percent.①

---

① See Sun Zhe, *A Study of the System of National People's Congress*, Law Press ·China, 2004, pp. 254 – 255.

Second, their class mission consciousness and collective consciousness has weakened while their cliquism somewhat become intensified. Under the socialist market economy, with the role and status of the directors, managers and technicians being strengthened and the importance of management and technology highlighted, although the Party and the government has been putting the working class as a whole on high position, some workers still feel a sense of loss of ownership, and some workers to some extent have weakened their class mission and social responsibility, as well as their responsibility as members of an advanced class. Also, differences between managers and ordinary employees, competition among workers themselves, etc., all affect the class consciousness of the working class as a whole, so that some workers concern more about personal interests than that of the enterprises and the country. In addition, the gradual replacement of labor-intensive industries by modern IT and high-tech industries has made the role and position of the workers as individuals, which has increased the isolation of the working class and weakened their collective consciousness. Furthermore, due to diversification of types of ownership, modes of distribution, gap of income and life styles after reform and opening up, the working class has differentiated into different interest groups. Besides, the economic and social status of part of the workers has showed a significantly downward trend. According to the Social Mobility in Contemporary China published by CASS, the working and life conditions of some industrial workers is worthy of the Party and government's attention. Despite all these, it should be noted that these are temporary problems that can be resolved. The position and role of the working class will by no means be reduced or fundamentally shaken, let alone be denied. With the resolution of these problems, the deepening of reform and opening up and the gradual improvement of social security system, the Chinese working class will certainly be more adaptable to the development of the modern productive forces, their overall quality will improve and their role in the social life of the country will be consolidated, so do their status as the masters of the country and their sense of historical responsibility and mission.

III. Correctly Understanding the Changes in the Working Class in the New Era

We should correct some wrong ideas about the newchanges in and new challenges facing the working class.

The first wrong idea is, "Since a largenumber of workers have been laid off, a considerable part of workers no long belong to the leading class. "

It is wrong to think that because a large number of workers have been laid off, the working class is no longer the leading class. Firstly, the leading position of the working class in our country is determined by the nature of our socialist system. From the point of view of economic system, China's economic base takes the public ownership as mainstay and diverse forms of ownership coexist; as long as the public ownership as the mainstay is maintained, status of the working class as the masters of the country will not be changed. From the point of view of political system, our state is a people's democratic dictatorship led by the working class. This determines that the leading position of the working class in the country's political life is irreplaceable. Secondly, the leading position of the working class is embodied by its vanguard, the Communist Party of China. As long as the Communist Party of China maintains its class and advanced nature, and its status as the governing party, the leading position of the working class is unchangeable. Thirdly, the laid-off workers make up only a part of the working class, which will not reduce the working class' status and role as a whole. We cannot equate individual workers with the whole working class, vice versa. Working class is an evolving, concrete, and historical category, both the connotation and extension of which are ever changing and developing with the times. The working class is not the equivalent to the laid-off workers, nor to the workers in the production front of material production. The status and role of the working class refers to the class as a whole, which is relative to the relationship between classes and state power, not relative to the status of individuals or part of the workers. Working class is an aggregate or holistic concept that does not refer to specific individuals. Besides, the laid-off of a small number of workers is the result of structural adjustment and production development thus is the necessary for the development of the productive forces and economy. In our reform of replacing the planned economy with the socialist market economy, it is imperative to establish a modern corporate system, in which, sectors failing in meeting the new requirements of the advanced will be gradually eliminated, vice versa. This adjustment is in accord with the overall and fundamental interests of the working class. During this process, some workers who cannot meet the requirements of the advanced productive forces have to transfer their work for re-employment, thus be laid off. In fact, making industrial adjustment and economic system reform to meet the requirements of the advanced productive forces is in accord with the overall interests of the working class, including the temporarily laid-off workers. Throughout the development of socialist market economy, the inevitable layoff of some workers will not affect the leading position of the working class in general. Lastly, the Party and the government have been actively taking policies and measures to care for, support and assist the laid-off workers to help them overcome difficulties and get reemployed. And socialist labor and social security system is under building to safeguard the livelihood and interests of the workers.

The second wrong idea is: "Under modern corporate system, the directors or managers in the state-owned enterprises are the legal persons of the enterprises, and owners of the private enterprises are the bosses, so the workers are no longer the masters of the enterprises."

This idea is also wrong. By saying that the working class is the leading class does not mean that workers should directly manage state or enterprise affairs. The status of masters of the working class mainly manifest themselves in the following aspects: Firstly, in the public sector of the economy, the leading role of the working class is realized through the line, principles and policies of the CPC as the governing party, through the political superstructure and through the government's governance of the enterprise in accordance with the laws of the market economy and the overall interests of the working class. This applies also to the private sector and other forms of ownership. Secondly, the status of the working class as masters of the enterprises and society are mainly manifested in their enjoyment of various rights and interests based on the law. In the state-owned enterprises, the major channel for workers participating in the democratic management is the assembly of the representatives of the employees. According to the Company Law of the People's Republic of China, workers have the rights to information, proposals, supervision and participation. The trade union has the right and obligation to safeguard and fulfill the lawful rights and interests of workers.

The third wrong idea is "The employees in private enterprises are no longer part of the working class."

With the diversificationof ownership, the working class has undergone great changes in employment. The workers in non-public enterprises have outnumbered those in public enterprises. Is it that the increase of workers in non-public economy necessarily weakens the Party's class base and that workers employed in this sector no longer belong to the working class? The answer is no. The vanguard nature of the working class is determined by the advanced productive forces represented by it rather than by the ownership of enterprises. The vanguard nature of the working class demonstrated by Marxism is connected with the industrial production under capitalist private ownership. Workers both in public and non-public economies all belong to the working-class with vanguard nature.

The fourth wrong idea is that the emergence of new social strata will weaken, even replace the position of the working class.

Sincereform and opening up, classes, strata and interest groups in the Chinese society have undergone great changes, with a series of new social strata emerged, including entrepreneurs and technical personnel employed by non-public scientific and technological enterprises, managerial and technical staff employed by overseas-funded enterprises, the self-employed, private entrepreneurs, employees in intermediaries, free-lance professionals and others. These are also builders of socialism with Chinese characteristics, but they do not constitute a new class in full sense. On the other hand, the nature of these new social strata cannot be compared with the class nature of the Chinese working class having "a strong sense of organization and discipline and is firm and wholehearted for revolution," and "is the basic force that pushes the advanced productive forces forward in China." The peasant class and other laboring people, closely united with the working class, constitute a major force that pushes the country's productive forces forward, whereas "other strata are all builders of socialism with Chinese characteristics," which cannot replace the leading class of the working class.

The fifth wrong idea is that workers engaged in traditional industries represent the backward productive forces and the backward part of the working class, "whereas the intellectuals are the representatives of the advanced productive forces and the most advanced part of the working class."

This idea does not fully comply with Marxist scientific analysis of the nature of the working class. Firstly, the working class is a new class rising with the socialized production and is the representative of the advanced productive forces, so its advanced nature is closely linked with the industrial production. Currently the world economy is transforming from traditional toward modern industry. In this process, the working class, a class always advancing with the development of social productive forces and inseparable with the modernization of society, as a whole, is always the representative of the advanced productive forces. Secondly, the productive forces in China is relatively backward with industrialization and modernization carrying out together, that means, while retaining traditional industries, we are vigorously accelerating high-tech industry, thus taking a new type of industrialization. In this process, China's workers in traditional industries, as the representative of advanced productive forces, are still the backbone of the class. And in the construction of socialist modernization, the workers in the forefront of traditional industries constitute also the backbone of the socialist leading class. Workers combining themselves with traditional industries, like the intellectuals combining themselves with high-tech, are also the representatives of China's advanced productive forces. Thirdly, with the development of high technology, knowledge economy and the information society, it is an inevitable outcome of social development that both the number and the role of intellectuals as part of the working class are increasing. This will not weaken the force of the working class, instead, it will greatly enhance it, and the improvement of the status of intellectuals means the improvement of the status of role of the working class.

The sixth wrong idea is that "in the era of knowledge economy and information society, it is the intelligentsia grasping the high-tech, not the rest part of the working class, are the representatives of the advanced productive forces."

This idea is extremely wrong. Firstly, the working class is a whole, so is the statement that the working class is the representative of the advanced productive forces. The fact that the intellectuals as part of the working class grasp the advanced technology precisely demonstrates the advanced nature of the working class. Secondly, the working class, including the industrial workers engaged in material production, is improving in terms of level of knowledge and quality of modern science and technology. Thirdly, high-tech itself does not mean advanced productive forces, for the former to be transferred into actual productive forces, it must be infiltrated into the factors of the latter, the process of which is inseparable from the workers in the forefront.

The seventh wrong idea is: "The migrant workers are not part of the working class yet," and "incorporating the migrant workers into the ranks of the working class will reduce the quality of the class."

"Migrant workers" arethe outcome of China's social transformation, which is a new group that is transiting into and enlarging the ranks of the working class. The group of the migrant workers has gradually become part of the working class, so we should improve their status and treatment through policies to promote their integration into the working class. The migrant workers are workers with identity as farmers. Theoretically they engage in labor exactly as the same as other workers; in terms of income, they also receive wages just as other workers; in terms of lifestyle and values, the migrant workers entering the cities from rural areas have changed much. According to the latest statistic of the Ministry of Agriculture, there are about 9900 migrant workers, accounting for around 13 percent of the rural labor force, ① who constitute the mainstay in China's construction, textile, mining and service sectors and is an important part of China's industrial workers, thus have changed the structure of Chinese working class significantly. At present, migrant workers are working in most of the traditional and emerging industries. Associated with large-scale socialized production, either in terms of nature or number, migrant workers already have and will continue to be fresh blood to Chinese working class. Their rise have accelerated the adjustment of industrial structure in rural areas and urbanization in China, so they make contributions to the narrowing of gaps between workers and farmers, urban and rural, mental labor and manual labor, and to social stability and harmony and to all-round development of society and man as well.

IV. We Must Adhere to the Fundamental Principle of "Persistently Rely on the Working Class Wholeheartedly"

Since the initiation of reform and opening up, the reform toward socialist market economy have greatly changed the ownership structure, distribution structure, employment structure, interest structure as well as the economic relations of the whole society. Differentiation and combination occurred in our social classes, strata and interest groups, posing new challenges to the status and role of the working class. Whatever the changes, however, the mainstay status and leading position of the working class in our social life basically remain unchanged.

China adopts the basic economic system with public ownership playing a dominant role and diverse forms of ownership developing side by side, which, although has led the change of jobs of some workers, has not changed the status of the working class. On the contrary, the development toward the socialist market economy and readjustment of industrial restructure, in the long run, are favorable to improving the overall quality and advantage of the working class. Chinese working class is always the basic force promoting the development of China's advanced productive forces, the leading class of our socialist country and the representative of

① In *China Daily*, Jan. 16th 2003.

China's advanced productive forces and relations of production. The nature of our state and the historical status and role of the working class determine that we must unswervingly adhere to our fundamental guiding principle of wholeheartedly relying on the working class.

Theissue of status and role of the working class is essentially the issue of status and position of the working class in the social life of the country, especially in economic and political life and governance of the country, and in the relations among the social classes, strata and various interest groups. In the semi-feudal society, the Chinese working class, in the position of being ruled, oppressed and exploited, was the revolutionary force playing the historical role of overthrowing the old regime and old society. In 1949, after the CPC took the governing power, the Chinese working class rose to be the ruling class and leading class. In 1956, with the completion of the socialist transformation and the establishment of the socialist system, the working class, liberated from the old relations of production and become masters of new one, took the mainstay position in the social and economic life and the status as masters in politics and economy in China.

First, the status and role of the Chinese working class is determined by China's basic socialist economic system. Our basic system, with public ownership as the mainstay and diverse forms of ownership coexisting, fundamentally ensures the dominant position and leading role of the working class. Despite our adoption of socialist market economy, public ownership remains the mainstay of the economy; public economy, especially state-owned economy occupies a pivotal position in our whole economic life, in major trades that have a close bearing on the country's economic lifeline and key areas. With the improvement of modern corporate system and oversight functions of the assembly of the representatives of the employees, the status of the working class as the master will be further strengthened. Under these circumstances, the non-public economy as an important component of the socialist market economy is impossible to change the status of the working class as masters of the country.

Second, the status and role of the Chinese working class is determined by China's fundamental political system of socialism. From the point view of political system and superstructure, the country's basic political system has not changed, that is, a people's democratic dictatorship led by the working class and based on the worker-farmer alliance, whereby, the working class is entitled to enjoy the various rights of managing the country and society as masters of the country.

Third, the status and role of the Chinese working class is determined by its advanced nature. Chinese working class is the outcome of social production, which is the representative of and the basic force for developing China's advanced productive forces. Our Party should always implement the important thought of "Three Represents" and therefore must rely on the working class wholeheartedly. The class nature and advanced nature of China's working class determines that it has strict sense of organization and discipline as well as revolutionary firmness and thoroughness, excellent moral and cultural qualities, high labor skills and creativity. To build socialism with Chinese characteristics, we must always rely on the working class.

Fourth, the status and role of the Chinese working class is also determined by its components. As a component of the working class, the Chineseintellectuals have enlarged the ranks of the working class. As the part representing the advanced productive forces, culture, managerial expertise and technology, the intellectuals have raised the overall quality of the working class and playing an increasingly important role, especially in the fields of science and technology, management, economic production, culture, education, etc.

Lastly, the status and role of the Chinese working class is determined by the nature of the CPC as the governing party in China. As the vanguard of the working class, the CPC is the party of the working class and is composed of the advanced elements of them. As the firm class base of the CPC and the leading class, the Chinese working class demonstrates its role through the CPC's governance of the country. The sustained vanguard nature of the CPC and its governing position will consolidate the leading position of the working class.

On the other hand, with the deepening of reform and opening up, the leading position and status of mainstay and masters of the country of the working class may change in forms, even become weakened in some times and aspects, but will remain unchanged in terms of connotation and essence. Overall, the mainstay role and social status of the working class is essentially more important than ever before, which we must always uphold and give full rein to it. At present, China has entered the new period of building a moderately prosperous society in all respects and accelerating socialist modernization. With the progress of our economy and society, the working class itself is growing constantly and changing substantially, not only in quantity, but also in its internal structure, education, experience, cultural and technical qualities, ideas, work forms, etc. These changes have not changed the status and role of it in China.

V. We Must Strength the Leading Position and Status of the Working Class

First, we must implement the principle of "relying on the working class wholeheartedly" to strength its leading position and role.

Chinese working class has always beenthe basic force for promoting the development of China's advanced productive forces, the class base of the CPC as the governing party, the strength which our reform and opening up and socialist modernization rely on, the main creators of social and cultural wealth, and the social base and core force of the political power of our socialist country. The CPC must always maintain its nature as the vanguard of the working class, always wholeheartedly rely on the working class and give full play to its role.

Second, we must safeguard the lawful rights and interests of the workers, meet their reasonable demands and raise their income level and living standards.

Politically, we mustensure that the workers can fully enjoy their rights as masters, their opinions are listened in major legislation and policy making to fully reflects their wishes and demands; institutionally, we must, based on laws, regulations and policies, establish and improve the systems such as assembly of representative of employees, equal consultation, collective contract and labor dispute arbitration mechanism, so as to protect their rights to information, participation and supervision to effectively achieve oversight of the working people over the Party, the government, enterprises and social undertakings. To safeguard the interests of the working class, we must, in the first place, create more job opportunities for and constantly increase the income of the workers. In the second place, we must gradually improve our social security system with coordinating labor relations as the focus to gradually build a socialized and institutionalized social system with Chinese characteristics, to help, in particular, the unemployed and laid-off workers and other disadvantaged groups. In the third place, we must protect the reasonable economic interests of the working class. Lastly, we must establish and improve trade unions and make them to play an active role, and through it, to organize, educate and safeguard the lawful interests of the working people.

Third, we must enhance the leadership of the Party to comprehensively raise the quality of the working class.

Lenin believed that we have to bring advanced consciousness to the working class from outside. We should enhance the leadership of the Party, the ideological and political work, and the education and training to guide and help the workers learn more economic, legal and modern technology, so as to comprehensively raise their overall quality. We should study the important thinking of the three generations of leading core of our party, get a deeper understanding of the history of worker's movement and work of trade union led by our party, strength the Party's leadership in the movement, so as to protect, mobilize and give full play to the workers' enthusiasm and creativity.

Fourth, we must expand socialist democracy to provide more channels and ways for the worker's political participation and management, with a view to consolidate the status and role of the working class through democracy and rule of law. The working class is the main creator of social material and cultural wealth and the class base of our party's governance, so we must establish a socialist democratic politics, gradually establish a whole set of regulations, systems and methods for the participation of the working class in our politics and governance, so that the protection of the leading status of the working class can be safeguarded by democracy and the law.

Fifth, we must improve the trade union organization to give full rein to its positive role.

"Getting organized" is the most effective weapon for the working class to achieve its interests and the basic way to play its role. Under the new historical conditions, it is necessary to further organize and unite the working class. We must put more efforts to trade union work and improve their organizations, and make them to play a role in uniting the workers. We should continuously enhance the attractiveness and cohesiveness of trade unions in educating the workers and protecting their legitimate rights and interests. We should pay more attention to the role of trade unions, establish trade union organizations in non-public enterprises to fight all thoughts and actions that are detrimental the interests of the workers. In short, we should promote the development of workers' movement in China, so as to better give play to the roles of trade unions as a link between the Party and the workers, an important social pillar of the state, the representative and defender of workers' interests, and so on.

Sixth, we must strengthen our work in the masses torecruit advanced elements in the working class into the Party.

The workers cannot spontaneously recognize their historical mission or accept

Marxist theories, so our party should always do well in mass work and constantly educate the mass about their historical mission, status of masters and sense of responsibility, to guide them in improving their political quality. We should attach more importance to training and recruiting activists among the workers in enterprises and the forefront of production and those among the intellectuals into the Party, in order to expand the Party's backbone force.

Chapter 13

Changes China's Farmer Class in the New Era

Chinese farmers, a class making up the largest proportion of China's population and natural ally of the Chinese working class and one of the basic laboring classes in the primary stage of socialism, constitute an important force in building socialism with Chinese characteristics and in the development of socialist productive forces, and they are also the main creators of Chinese socialist material and cultural wealth. Chinese farmers provide the Chinese people of all ethnic groups with basic means of subsistence, including grains, fruits, milk, meat, vegetables, etc., to meet people's daily needs; they produce a large amount of raw materials for industrial production and for export. Chinese farmers constitute an important force in safeguarding the stability of China's state power. China's socialist modernization is a transitional process from agricultural economy to industrial economy, during which, the efforts and participation of farmers are inseparable. China has a population of 1. 3 billion with 60 percent of them being farmers, so the stability of farmers and rural areas and the prosperity of agriculture is the foundation for consolidating our state power.

In the process of reform and opening up, differentiation and combinationoccurred within the farmers along with the development of the socialist market economy. How to correctly understand these changes, how to analyze new strata and interest groups emerged in it and how to handle the interest relations among them is a new test for the CPC as the governing party.

I. History of Changes of the Chinese Farmer Class since Modern Times

Before the founding of New China, Chinese farmers can be divided into poor peasants and farm laborers, middle farmers (upper-middle peasants, the lower-middle peasants) and other strata, with poor peasants and farm laborers as its mainstay and the main ally of the working class. Comrade Mao Zedong made a scientific analysis of the economic status, political attitudes and strata of the Chinese farmers in his "Analysis of the Classes in Chinese Society" and made it clear that Chinese peasantry (the farmer class) is the natural ally of the Chinese working class and the Chinese revolution.

The founding of new China, the completion of the "three socialist transformations" and the establishment of the socialist system brought about tremendous changes in China's farmer class. Before the transformations, the poor peasants and farmer laborers had their land from land reform, and the farmers transformed from an oppressed class into a self-sufficient agricultural laborers. After collectivization in the countryside, Chinese farmers became agricultural workers under collective ownership and masters of the land and the country; as an opposite class of the poor and laborer farmers, the landlord class as an exploiting class was eliminated. Along with it, the original distinction of strata between the poor peasants, farmer laborers and middle farmers (the upper-middle peasants, lower-middle peasants) disappeared.

Since the Third Plenary Session ofthe Eleventh Central Committee of the CPC, reform in the countryside and the implementation of the household contract responsibility system had fundamentally changed Chinese rural areas and the agricultural laborers under the collective ownership: the agricultural laborers originally under the collective ownership became laborers under household contract responsibility system; the development of township enterprises transferred part of the rural surplus labor force into farmer-workers who leave the farmland but not their hometown; part of the agricultural laborers became managers or shareholders with the permission of the development of rural individual, private and shareholding enterprises; some farmers become employees in these enterprises, forming the group of employees in rural areas, some others become managers of rural collective enterprises or non-public enterprises, forming the group of managers; the managerial personnel in townships, towns, villages and the corresponding Party and government organizations form the group of social management of rural area; there are also the rural intellectuals in the schools, hospitals, station for popularizing agricultural technique, etc.; a lot of rural surplus labor enter into the city, forming the group of migrant workers, as fresh blood to the ranks of the working class, and so on. All these strata and interest groups are formed in the differentiation and combination under the new conditions of reform and opening up.

II. Differentiation of the Farmer class in the New Era in China

In general, in the primary stage of socialism, under the conditions of reform and opening up and development of the market economy, farmer class in China has undergone new differentiation and combination, giving birth to a number of new strata and groups as follows:

First, the group of agricultural laborers who contract land for operation. They transferred from original agricultural laborers under the collective ownership and now contract some land for farming, planting, animal breeding, etc. They are not farmers in the traditional sense and the planned economy, because the former are individual manual agricultural laborers under conditions of natural economy with each household being a productive unit, while the latter are agricultural laborers under planned economy with Dazhai (a model production brigade in the people's commune system—trans.) mode of distribution system based on work points. The agricultural laborers who contract land for operation are the interest groups who, under the preconditions of the collective land ownership, carry out agricultural production on the basis of household contract management with income from agricultural labor as the main source. They enjoy certain rights of disposition and use of the land under long-term-unchanged contract, and can freely decide their production and sale of their products, although the land is still collective- or state-owned. Among this group, some have become specialized households in farming, planting or breeding with considerable contracted land, agricultural means of production like agricultural machines, etc., as well as tidy income, asset property and other means of production. And some of them have become modern agriculture operators, who are both operators and producers and workers that are educated, innovative and knowledgeable about advanced agricultural technology. They are of a high-quality and innovative group representing the advanced agricultural productive forces and are the main driving force of China's agricultural modernization. On the other hand, there is still a group of agricultural laborers in the traditional sense, mainly women, who are older in age, low in education, backward in ideas, weak in ability and low in income.

The group of agricultural laborers who contract land for operation constitute the mainstay offarmer class in China, the main practitioners engaged in agriculture, forestry, animal husbandry, fisheries, etc., main labor force in rural areas and basic strength of development of agricultural productive forces. But they are annually declining in numbers.

Second, the group of employees in township enterprises and other types of enterprises in rural areas. The reform in rural areas promoted the development of agricultural productive forces and rural market. As a result, numerous rural enterprises were setup, and a large number of surplus labor force emerged, who transferred to the enterprises, becoming farmer-workers in various public- or non-public-owned enterprises in rural areas. They support socialism and the Party and the policies of socialist reform and opening up. Despite their rural household registration and identity of farmers, and close link with the farmer class, they are no longer agricultural producers in its original sense, but rather wage earners working in the second and tertiary industries. On the other side, there are some people who work in a spontaneous, seasonal, migrant, mobile and temporary way. For example, some girls work in township enterprises to earn some money before marriage, but will get married and become farmers again after marriage; some others work in township enterprises or construction industry in slack farming seasons and back farming in busy ones. No matter what the case, a relatively fixed workforce in rural enterprises has formed. These employees, having some relationship with modern productive forces, are quite different from traditional farmers in terms of thinking, behaviors, lifestyles, etc., and they have greatly improved their quality and basically have the good quality of the working class. Therefore, they are an important complement to the working class, constitute driving force for China's agricultural modernization and main body in developing rural enterprises and China's urbanization and rural modernization and are representatives of the new agricultural productive forces, and therefore their roles and status are increasingly important in the countryside.

Third, the group of self-employed and individual laborers. Reform in rural areas have promoted the development of agricultural productive forces. From the lease-holding farm households, a number of self-employed specialized households emerged in aquaculture, agricultural and sideline products processing, farming, etc., and some farmers have become both self-employed operators and laborers. Some employ laborers and some others become large-scale operators. Development of self-employed operation is an important complement to the rural economy and conducive to the development of rural market. The self-employed and laborers constitute an important force in China's rural socialist construction.

Fourth, the group of owners and operators of private economy and other non-public economy in rural area. With the advancement of reform in rural areas and the development of rural market, a great number of non-public enterprises have grown up, including private ones. Non-public enterprises in rural areas are an important part of the socialist rural economy. They take the forms of partnership, shareholding, cooperative, sole proprietorship, or individual on the basis of self-investment, self-management and being responsible for their own profits and losses. The operators of non-public economy, including the private economy, in rural areas are important socialist builders in Chinese countryside and constitute an important force for developing rural socialist market economy.

Fifth, the group of rural intellectuals, consisting of those engaged in education, health care, culture, arts, sports, science and technology etc., such as teachers working at local-run schools, country doctors, rural literary and art workers, veterinarians, agricultural technicians, and so on. They themselves are farmers possessing contracted farmland, and some of them even engage in agricultural production, while mastering advanced scientific and cultural knowledge and mainly engaging in mental labor in science and technology, education and culture, etc. They are farmers with high cultural level and represent the advanced rural productive forces.

Sixth, the group of administrators in the Party and government organizations and social institutions, consisting of administrators of Party and government organizations at towns, townships and village levels, such as township cadres, village cadres. Some of them are civil servants receiving salaries, some are partially off-duty officials receiving subsidies from the state, and some others receive annual fixed subsidies or subsidies for the loss of work time. They themselves are part of the farmer class and links between farmers and the Party and the government, who have natural ties with farmers.

Seventh, the group of managers of township collective enterprises. A large number of rural collective enterprises emerged after reform and opening up, of which, some are solely collective-owned, some are shareholding or mixed owned. The managers of these enterprises are originally either community-level cadres or farmers. They mainly receive wages, some own shares in the enterprises. Many of them are advanced elements of the farmer class.

Eighth, farmers working in other occupations. In China's rural areas, there are a number of small independent or household-based craftsmen and traders such as masons, carpenters, blacksmiths, store clerk, small peddlers. Their work is also a necessary complement to the economy of our socialist countryside.

III. Causes for the Changes in Farmer Class

Since reform and opening up, Chinese farmer class undergone the most drastic changes and differentiation among all classes in the primary stage of socialism. This is due to the following factors: First, the factor of system. Under the planned economy and the solely collective ownership, farmers are laborers under the collective ownership and Dazhai mode of distribution system based on work points. Politically it adopted the people's commune system, a system combining the Party, the government and the economy. In the circumstances, little differentiation, combination and change occurred in Chinese farmer class. After the reform and the implementation of household contract responsibility system, the planned economy was discarded and the people's commune system was abandoned. Individual farmers, under the premise of collective ownership, have considerable rights of disposable and use of the land, in addition to the allowing of diverse forms of ownership and distribution. Under such circumstances, differentiation occurred in farmer class. Second, factor of productive forces. The enthusiasm of the farmers was greatly aroused by reform and opening up, so did the rural productive forces. As a result, a large number of rural surplus labor force entered township enterprises, services and other industries or flowed into the city, which constitutes an important reason for the differentiation of farmers. Third, the factors of the market. The reform in rural areas, the development of the productive forces and township enterprises, the rural surplus labor force and the increase of surplus products—all these have accelerated the rapid growth of the rural market and commercialization. Consequently, the allocation of means of production, resources and labor force developed following the laws of the market economy, which is also an important reason the differentiation of farmer class. Fourth, the development of towns and cities. The development of small towns has provided opportunities and conditions for the development of occupational differentiation and change of identity of farmers. Fifth, the enterprising spirit and lust for getting rich. The change of ideas of the farmers is also an important factor for the differentiation of them. Market thinking, consciousness of competition, lust for better life are all important driving forces of the differentiation in farmer class.

IV. The Problem of Poverty in China's Rural Areas

Since reform and opening up, China's economy is growing rapidly, and the economy in rural areas has achieved a great success. In 1985, China's national agricultural output value was 254. 16 billion yuan, in 1999, it reached 1. 4472 trillion yuan in 1999 and in 2004 it was 2. 07681 trillion yuan. The index of gross agricultural output value in terms of comparable prices was 319. 3 percent. ① But at the same time, there is always the problem of poverty in China's rural areas.

1. The coexistence of relative poverty and absolute poverty

Absolute poverty refers to the situation in which a person lives below minimum living standard of the society and has little material sources and development opportunity. In China's rural areas, in 2003, by the low-income criterion of per capita annual net income 882 yuan, there are 56. 17 million poor people in rural areas, in addition to a large population of hidden poverty. Rural poverty is mainly manifested in two aspects: First, the gap between rich and poor with some farmers living in poverty; Second, the income gap between rural areas in different regions, with most farmers living in poverty being in the central and western regions. The population of absolute poverty and that of relative poverty coexist.

2. The weak ability to resist risks and weak agricultural base

The output of agriculture in China is basically still at the mercy of the elements and mainly by manual labor in a manner of separate operation. Therefore, our rural productivity is relatively backward with a weak economic foundation, poor infrastructure and low levels of science and technology and modernization, therefore its comparative profit is low; moreover, a complete and effective social security system is unavailable in rural areas so that the ability of farmers to resist risks is weak. All these make the poverty of the farmers more severe.

3. Poor educational and cultural conditions

An important manifestation of rural poverty is its unsatisfactory cultural environments, mainly showed in its poor intellectual, moral and value orientation,

① See *China Statistical Yearbook*(2005), China Statistics Press, 2005, pp. 51, 54.

its weak force of restraint of social codes of ethics, educational conditions and other social undertakings.

4. The farmers' increase of income become slow down while their expenditure increase and burden on them is excessively heavy

After 1996 when per capita net income of farmers increased by 9 percent, for seven consecutive years from 1997 to 2003, the annual growth rate of net income of the farmers nationwide had never been higher than 5 percent. The lowest one was 2.1 percent in 2000, and it lightly increased to 4.2 percent in 2001, 4.8 percent in 2002, and 4.2 percent in 2003 (the year when SARS broke out). The average growth rate is only half of that of urban residents over the same period. In 2004, after a series of measures were taken, the per capita net income of farmers increased by 6.8 percent.[①] But the difficult problem of increasing farmers' income fundamentally remained unsolved.

5. Mass incidents in rural areas show a tendency of increase

In recent years, cases of farmers' petitions and unrests have increased and their scale became larger; even massive farmer unrests occurred in several places. The stability of rural areas has an important bearing on the overall harmony of the country.

Main reasons for rural poverty include the slow development of rural productive forces, insufficient investment in science and technology, education, health care, culture and social undertakings, as well as the urgent need of strengthening of community-level Party and political power in rural areas. To eliminate poverty in the countryside, we must attach more importance to agriculture, increase investment in it to speed up the development of its productivity and market economy; increase investment in rural education, science and technology, culture, health care so as to establish a sound and effective rural social security system and public health system; accelerate rural economic development to increase incomes of farmers; reduce the burden on farmers and rescind unreasonable taxes; strengthen rural Party organizations and grass-roots political power; change our mode in rural poverty reduction; build a new socialist harmonious countryside.

---

① See *China Statistical Yearbook(2005)*, China Statistics Press, 2005, p. 359.

V. Gradually Narrowing Gap between Urban and Rural Areas, Balancing Urban-Rural Development to Build a New Socialist Country

Our reform and development should not only focus on the city, but also pay attention to the balanced development between urban and rural areas, to the development of agriculture and the interests of farmers. This has a bearing on both the harmonious development of the entire national economy and social stability and our goals of building a moderately prosperous society and realizing socialist modernization. The key to achieving a moderately prosperous society lies in development of agriculture, rural areas and farmers. The problem of imbalance between urban and rural development is now very prominent and this has become a bottleneck restricting China's economic and social development, crying out for our immediate resolution.

Indicators show that gap between urban and rural development is widening. For example, the total income gap between urban and rural residents is becoming larger. The ratio of income between urban and rural residents was 2.47:1, 1.7:1 and 2.6:1 in 1978, 1984 and 1994 respectively, but it widened to 2.74:1 in 1997, 3:24:1 in 2003, and 3.21:1 in 2004.[①] Allowing for welfare, cost and factors in kind and so on, the actual net income of urban residents is 5-6 times that of the farmers. The widening gap between urban and rural areas has seriously affected the overall development of rural economy and society, which leads to sharp reduction in the area of cultivated land and decrease of grain output in recent years, highlighting the social issues in rural areas. The urban-rural dual system also constitutes an important reason for this issue. This dual structure mainly manifests itself in the imbalance of forms of organization and production, i.e., the coexistence between backward conventional agricultural sector and modern economic sectors, between backward and modern modes of production and lifestyles. The typical example of it is the rigid system of urban and rural household registration. To solve the problems of agriculture, rural areas and farmers, fundamentally speaking, we must address the issue of urban-rural dual structure. The solution to it is the progressive realization of industrialization and urbanization based on China's national conditions. China is

① See *China Statistical Yearbook(2005)*, China Statistics Press, 2005, p.335.

relatively low in terms of degree of industrialization and urbanization. In 2002, our rate of urbanization rose to 39. 1 percent from its previous rate of 18 percent, but still 10 percent lower than that of world average, let along developed countries. In the early 19th century, the total urban population accounted only for 2-3 percent of the total population in the world; it rose to 13-14 percent in the early 20th century and now it accounts for about 50 percent. In 1850, the urbanization rate of Britain was 37 percent, in North America it was 41 percent in 1910, Japan reached 38 percent in 1938. In the developed countries it is now more than 50 percent. By 2020, China's urbanization rate may reach 55 percent, but even by that time our agricultural population will still account for nearly half of our population. Although in the period from 1978 to 2004 the proportion of agricultural output value in GNP has reduced from 28. 1 percent to 15. 2 percent, ① it was still too high. It goes without saying that in the process of urbanization and industrialization, we must advance development proportionally and observe the objective laws. To solve the problems of agriculture, rural areas and farmers and gap between urban and rural, we must take the path of agricultural modernization and industrialization with Chinese characteristics, and must gradually increase investment in them in the building of a harmonious rural society, so as to build a new and modern socialist countryside.

① See *China Statistical Yearbook*(2005), China Statistics Press, 2005, p. 51.

Chapter 14

The New Conditions and Characteristics of Some New Social Strata and Interest Groups

With the development of socialist reform and opening up andthe socialist market economy, a series of new social strata have emerged, including entrepreneurs and technical personnel employed by non-public scientific and technological enterprises, managerial and technical staff employed by overseas-funded enterprises, the self-employed, private entrepreneurs, employees in intermediaries, free-lance professionals and members of other social strata (We will discuss the self-employed and private entrepreneurs in details in Chapter XV). These strata, as the outcome of the basic economic system in the primary stage of socialism, developed in the era of reform and opening up, conform to the requirements of the development of the productive forces and serve the drive of socialism with Chinese characteristics. The long-term existence of these new strata is determined by the following social conditions: the primary stage of socialism is a fairly long historical process; the public ownership is the dominance and diverse forms of ownership develop side by side is China's basic economic system in the primary stage of socialism; the socialist market economy is the basic form of resource allocation in the development of socialism These new strata do not form a class. They are essentially different from bourgeoisie, either in terms of composition or economic basis or political attitudes. Most people of these strata support the Party's line, principles, policies and the socialist system, and actively participate in reform and opening up and socialist modernization; and they are patriotic, dedicated, law-abiding and are widely accepted by society and are builders of socialism. But on the other hand, efforts must be taken to unite, educate and guide them.

I. Entrepreneurs and Technical Personnel Employed by Non-public Scientific and Technological Enterprises

Non-public scientific and technological enterprises constitute a new force in China's high-tech development. With their flexible and diverse forms of ownership, integration of technology and market, the application of scientific and technological achievements as well as the development, production and management of high technology, these enterprises are playing an increasingly important role in the development of China's socialist market economy. The technical personnel employed by non-public scientific and technological enterprises are the backbone of the enterprises. They own shares or options of the enterprises, master key technologies, managerial expertise and innovative ability in research, development and marketing. They form a new group of intellectuals, who are mostly come from educational and research institutions, have received higher education, grasp advanced knowledge and technology, have higher moral and cultural levels, ambitions and pioneering spirit, and are important promoters of the hi-tech industries and productive forces. Those who are at the core of them are the mainstay of the human capital, technological innovation and managerial expertise in this area. They usually are owners of the intellectual property rights of some high-technologies and means of production, or shareholders or even principal shareholders of the enterprises. Working in the high-risk and high-profit area and assuming the capacity as main converters of scientific technology into real productive forces, they enjoy high incomes and returns in accordance with the principle of distribution according to work and to production factors. Entrepreneurs and technical personnel employed by non-public scientific and technological enterprises belong to a social stratum manifesting China's advanced productive forces, and are main workers in high-tech enterprises and important force in building socialism with Chinese characteristics.

II. Managerial and Technical Staff Employed by Foreign-funded Enterprises

Foreign-funded enterprises refer to enterprises established in accordance with Chinese laws and fully or partly funded and thus are proportionally owned, dominated and controlled by foreign investors. Chinese managerial and technical staff employed in these enterprises each has his expertise and at the same time enjoys higher income. While serving the enterprises, they also play an important role in introducing overseas capital, technology and managerial expertise to China. They mainly come from: (1) managerial and technical personnel from state-owned enterprises and institutions; (2) managerial and administrative personnel from Party and state bodies; (3) graduate and undergraduate students from Chinese and overseas colleges; (4) professional and technical personnel demobilized from the

PLA, and so on. The main features of this group are: First, they are generally young and have high level of management, knowledge, technical competence, professional ethics and overall quality; Second, they are mental workers who usually get their jobs through fierce competition, and they usually make more efforts and stand more stress in their work; Third, their thy enjoy higher incomes and standards of living, have their own houses, cars, and their children receive a good education, and they themselves are often customers of high-end services; Fourth, they are the first who have mastered internationally advanced management and technologies; Fifth, in contacts with foreigners, they are more likely to be influenced by foreign trends of thought, culture, lifestyle, ideology, and so on, some of which might be negative.

But they are different from comprador-bourgeoisie in Chinese feudal society, this is because: Firstly, the social environments are different. The comprador-bourgeoisie was the product of the semi-feudal and semi-colonial old Chinese society controlled by imperialists, whereas they are workers under the socialist system; Secondly, the class origin and bases are different. The comprador-bourgeoisie came from the classes of feudal landlords and bureaucrats, while they are from the working class and are members of the working class.

III. Employees in Intermediaries

Intermediaries inthe socialist market economy, which gain their restoration and development since reform and opening up, include services such as notary, quality inspection, measurement, exhibition, accounting, auditing, consulting and others; trading services such as securities, futures, real estate transaction and so on; brokering services such as performances and shows, arts, employment, matchmaking, and others; social and economic organizations such as chambers of commerce, associations, clubs, and so on. These intermediaries are bridges between government and enterprise, enterprises and enterprises, enterprises and consumers, etc., and play multifunctional roles in the market economy, such as services, communication, notary, oversight, and so on. They are civil and commercial in nature and are the products of the socialist market economy. Employees in these organizations constitute a special group, who were originally workers transferred from government organizations or state-owned enterprises, college graduates, overseas returned students, and so on. Their incomes mainly rely on intermediary services or management fees, commission on intermediary services and so on, which are determined both by work skills and by the supply and demand of the market. Their incomes are high in general but vary as well. Apart from a few cases, they are usually excellent in personal quality, ability, professional skills, professional ethics, etc. In short, employees in intermediary organizations, earning their income by providing intermediary services, are laborers for the cause of socialism and are constructive force for improving the socialist market economy and developing socialist productive forces.

IV. Free-lance Professionals

Free-lanceprofessionals, different from the jobless or spare-time employees or the self-employed, refer mainly to intellectuals or other workers who earn their living by exchanging their services or products in the market without working in any government or economic organizations. They are a group of special workers in building socialism with Chinese characteristics, most of which came from the ranks of intellectuals. This group is mainly consisted of intellectuals transferred from governmental, military, enterprise, or institutional organizations, or college graduates or undergraduates, self-taught students, overseas returned students, etc. They usually have good education background, and some of them have studied abroad. They have steady income and are excellent in their work.

Free-lance professionals are often those who want to prove their value in the market economy by choosing free-lance work. Their occupations include: lawyers, actors, artists, freelance writers, medical practitioners, health consultants, athletes, coaches, and so on. They gain relatively high income by meeting people's material and cultural needs through their expertise and knowledge. They conduct their work in accordance with the laws, regulations and policies, accept the management of the government and pay due taxes and thus are recognized, encouraged and protected by the state. Free-lance professionals are special builders of socialism with Chinese characteristics. Although as freelancers with high income, some unhealthy things may appear among them driven by self-interests of the market, they as a whole are beneficial to the society.

V. Main Contributions of the New Social Strata and Interest Groups to Socialist Construction

These new social strata and interest groups are builders of socialism with

Chinese characteristics. They main contributions are as follows:

First, they are creator of social wealth. The new strata and interest groups use their factors of production, knowledge and abilities directly participate in or serve the economic development and the creation of social material and cultural wealth as an integral part of the total social wealth. As practitioners of China's reform and opening up, explorers of mind emancipation and creators of socialist ideology and culture who work mostly in cultural industry and enterprises, as well as important tax payers, they have made their contribution to socialist construction.

Second, they are promoters of the productive forces. In the first place, the new social strata and interest groups are socialist workers that take mental labor as main form and knowledge as main factor, so they are the new components in the productive forces of laborers. In the second place, they, in their work, apply their skills and knowledge into the process of production, turn them into a scientific part, thus add new content to the productive forces. By doing so, they become part of the promoters of the new productive forces.

Third, they are contributors to the steady progress of society. The new social strata and interest groups, through their own business and enterprises, absorb a considerable number of workers, including the surplus personnel in public and other sectors of ownership, as well as surplus laborers in agricultural and other industries, which effectively ease the employment pressure facing our country.

VI. Class Attributes of These New Social Strata and Interest Groups

The above mentioned strata and interest groups formed since reform and opening up belong neither to a nascent nor to any other strata of the bourgeoisie; instead, they are a new part of the working people. This is because:

First, they have a different economic base on which they depend on from that of bourgeoisie and other exploiting classes. These strata and groups form and develop on the basis of the primary stage of socialism in which public ownership is the mainstay and diverse forms of ownerships develop side by side. They exist and develop within this framework, so are conducive to the development of the socialist productive forces. This is fundamentally different from that of the bourgeoisie and other exploiting classes under class exploitation societies.

Second, they exist under a completely different political system from that of the bourgeoisie and other exploiting classes. These new social strata and interest groups form and develop themselves under the people's democratic dictatorship system and conduct their activities in the framework of socialist political system, which isfundamentally different from that on which the bourgeoisie and other exploiting classes depended.

Third, the class origins of them are different from bourgeoisie and other exploiting classes. Emerging from the working class, the farmerclass and intelligentsia, the new strata and interest groups are different from that of the exploiting classes in the old society in terms of class origin and composition.

Fourth, they are different from bourgeoisie and other exploiting classes in terms of political attitudes. At the present stage, the new social strata are serving the socialist system and the promotion of socialist productive services. In our country there is neither mode of production supporting the independent political existence of nascent social strata, nor any political organization representing their individual interests, so their only political choice is to stand with the people to actively involved in the cause of building socialism with Chinese characteristics as their way of making a living.

Fifth, different from the bourgeoisie and other exploiting classes, the new social strata and interest groups are all socialist workers, by no means like the parasitic class in the capitalist society. Although some of their incomes are gained from the surplus labor of others, they themselves create more value from their own labor. Their labor of management, technological development and innovation are important sources of social wealth. In short, they are under different social circumstance comparing with the bourgeoisie and other exploiting classes, they are not nascent bourgeoisie, nor belong to any new social stratum of socialism.

But at the same time, socialist education, guidance and criticism are needed for these new social strata and interest groups.

Chapter 15

The Formation and Characteristics ofSocial Stratum Engaged in Non-public Economic Sectors

Since reform and opening up, with the formation of basic economic pattern with the public sector remaining dominant and diverse sectors of the economy developing side by side, non-public economy has been developing rapidly, forming a new social stratum engaged in non-public economy with an increasingly important role and position, which consists of three parts, i. e., private entrepreneurs, major shareholders or managers of shareholding or other forms of non-public enterprises and the self-employed and or individual workers.

I. Correct Understanding of the People Engaged in Non-public Sectors: An Important Issue in Understanding the Classes, strata and Interest Groups in Present-day China

How to treat the non-public economy and people engaged in non-public sectors that emerge under the new historical conditions is a majortheoretical and practical issue requiring solution in building socialism with Chinese characteristics. To solve this problem, we first of all must have a correct view on the non-public economy.

Non-public economy is a product of China's socialist reform and opening up. In the early 1980s, along with the introduction of the household contract responsibility system, there emerged the specialized households and self-employed workers. With the accumulation of capital and assets and the appearance of large numbers of surplus rural labor force, enterprises with large-scale employment appeared, so did urban small industrial or commercial businesses. The private economy began to develop rapidly in the 1990s. In 1992, After Comrade Xiaoping made his remarks during his tour of the south in 1992, a large number highly educated officials, professionals and managers originally working in Party or government organizations or state-owned enterprises began to set up private enterprises, and as a consequence, a great number of private enterprises mushroomed. Views on the non-public economy were seriously different within the Party and society, with the crux being whether it is capitalist or socialist nature. By emancipating the mind, seeking truth from facts and proceeding from reality in everything, our party gradually deepened its understanding about the nature, status and role of the non-public economy and fully recognized its positive contribution in promoting socialist market economy and productive forces. In 1982, the 12th National Congress of the CPC pointed out that "The individual economy is a necessary and beneficial complement to the socialist public economy." In 1987, the 13th National Congress of the CPC further stated that "The private economy is also a necessary and beneficial complement to the public economy." In 1992, the Party's 14th National Congress of the Party said that "for a long time to come we should allow diverse sectors of the economy to develop side by side. The public sector, which includes enterprises owned by the whole people and enterprises owned by collectives, is to remain predominant, with the private sector, which includes individually owned and foreign-owned enterprises, as a supplement." In 1997, the 15th Party National Congress of the Party pointed out that "maintaining the dominance of public ownership and allowing common development of entities of multiple forms of ownership will be a basic economic system China will adhere to in a considerable historical period." "Non-public ownership is the important component of the socialist market economy." It was stated in the Party's 15th National Congress held in 2002 that "it is necessary to consolidate and develop unswervingly the public sector of the economy" and "it is necessary to encourage, support and guide the development of the non-public sectors of the economy." The change of the wording from "necessary and beneficial supplement" to "important component" and further to "unswervingly encourage, support and guide" reflects the process of our party's long-term exploration and understanding of the status and role of non-public economy, indicating that the Party has gained a mature view on it.

As to how to understand the social nature and political attributes of the people engaged in non-public sectors of the economy, the private entrepreneurs in particular, opinions differed widely. Some said they are workers, some said they are patriots, some others said they are exploiters, still others said they belong to nascent bourgeoisie. On this issue, our party, while adhering to the basic concepts of Marxism, takes the attitude of emancipating the mind, seeking truth from facts, keeping up with the times and making a concrete analysis of concrete problems, to gradually acquire a scientific understanding on the private entrepreneurs. In the 1980s, the Party divided the people engaged in non-public economy in Chinese mainland into two interest groups, i. e., the individual industrial and commercial households and private entrepreneurs, and clearly stated that the former belong to the category of socialist workers; at the same time it took a very careful attitude in judging the social nature and political attributes of the latter. In 1985, Comrade Deng Xiaoping pointed out that under the conditions of reform and opening up, a handful of bourgeois elements may appear, but they will not form a class. ① The first amendment to the Constitution of the People's Republic of China approved in April 1988 states: "The private sector of the economy is a complement to the socialist public economy. The State protects the lawful rights and interests of the private sector of the economy, and exercises guidance, supervision and control over the private sector of the economy."② In 1991, in the Circular of the CPC Central Committee for Transmitting the Report Submitted by the United Front Work Department of the CPC Central Committee Concerning Several Issues about Federations of Industry and Commerce, it is pointed out that, with regard to the private entrepreneurs at present day, we should not simply made analogy between them and the industrialists and businessmen in the past or equate the two. On no account should we carry out socialist transformation of them like what we do in the 1950s. The amendment to the Constitution of the People's Republic of China adopted in March 1999 stipulates: "The State encourages, supports and guides the development of the non-public sectorsof the economy and, in accordance with law, exercises supervision and control over the non-public sectors of the economy."③ In 2000, Comrade Jiang Zemin both in his speech at the National Conference on United Front Work and in the Decision of the CPC Central Committee on Strengthening the United Front Works pointed out that people engaged in non-public economy belong to the "building forces of socialism with Chinese characteristics." In July 1, 2001, in his speech at the meeting celebrating the 80th anniversary of the founding of the CPC, Comrade Jiang Zemin clearly stated: "Since China adopted the policy of reform and opening up, the composition of China's social strata has changed to some extent. There are, among others, entrepreneurs and technical personnel employed by scientific and technical enterprises of the non-public sector, managerial and technical staff employed by foreign-funded enterprises, the self-employed, private entrepreneurs, employees in intermediaries and free-lance professionals." "Under

---

① *Selected Works of Deng Xiaoping*, vol. 3, People's Publishing House, 1993, p. 111.

② *Selected Important Documents since the Thirteenth National Congress of the CPC,* vol. 2, People's Publishing House, 1991, p. 216.

③ Ibid., p. 809.

the guidance of the Party's line, principles and policies, most of these people in the new social strata have contributed to the development of productive forces and other undertakings in the socialist society through honest labor and work or lawful business operations." "They join workers, farmers, intellectuals, cadres and PLA officers and men in an effort to build socialism with Chinese characteristics. They, too, have made contributions to this cause." in 2002, Comrade Jiang Zemin further pointed in the 16th CPC National Congress that these new social strata "are all builders of socialism with Chinese characteristics."① This statement marks the formation of the scientific judgment that private entrepreneurs and other social strata are builders of socialism with Chinese characteristics.

The scientific judgment of our party that the private entrepreneurs and new social strata are all builders of socialism with Chinese characteristics shows distinctive features of the times, accurately reflects the objective reality, has been and will continue to be proved as being scientific.

In the New Democratic Revolution period, the main task of our party is revolution. Therefore, anyone who joined the revolutionary cause, no matter in what way, was called a revolutionary. Likewise, in the period of socialist construction when the focus of our Party has shifted to economic development, all those who actively join the cause of building the socialist country can be called socialist builders. Since reform and opening up, the non-public sectors of the economy has been developing rapidly with more and more people engaged in it. By the end of 2003, individual industrial and commercial households reached 23.53 million with an annual output value of around 874.1 billion yuan, and number of private enterprises reached about three million with an annual output value of about 1896.45 billion yuan.② Under the guidance of the Party's line, principles and policies, they actively participated in and have made great contributions to the great cause of socialism with Chinese characteristics, proving with their practical action that they are the builders of this cause.

First, they have made contributions to the socio-economic growth. The contribution of individual and private sector of the economy to GDP rose from 0.57 percent in 1989 to 22.76 percent in 2002, becoming a new growth point of China's

---

① In People's Daily, Dec. 5th 2000.

② See Huang Mengfu (compiler), *Report on the Development of China's Private Economy* (2003), Social Science Academic Press, 2004, p.4.

national economy. In 2002, the volume of retail sales of consumption goods of the individual and private sectors reached 28 trillion yuan, accounting for 70 percent of the total of that of the country. They have injected much vitality to the market and provided much convenience in improving people's lives and meeting their diverse needs. In 2002, individual industrial and commercial sector paid as much as 190 billion yuan of tax, accounting for 10 percent of the country's total tax revenue; ① it contributed 20 percent of China's GDP with an annual growth rate of 50 percent. In the coastal areas, 50 percent of the tax revenue is paid by private enterprises, and in Zhejiang and Guangdong provinces, the percentage is as high 80 with an annual growth rate of 70 percent. These figures clearly show that the non-public sector of the economy is increasingly making contribution to the prosperity of China's economy.

Second, they have made contributions to our social progress. With the deepening of reform and opening up and development of non-public economy, private entrepreneurs and others directly involve in the construction of science and technology, education, culture, healthcare, etc. After getting rich, many of them devoted efforts to promoting social progress by supporting social and other public welfare. So far, under the Guangcai Program, a program mainly implemented by businessmen in non-public sector, as many as 9765 projects have been implemented, with a total of 52. 3 billion yuan fully funded. It has trained two million people, provided jobs for more than 2. 1 people and helped 4. 59 million people get out of poverty. This program has been set by the related organizations of the United Nations as a new mode of poverty alleviation and development to be promoted to the world.

Third, they have contributed to social stability. With their unique advantages, individual and private sectors of the economy become not only a new source of economic growth, but also an important channel for absorbing laid-off workers from state-owned enterprises, rural surplus labor and urban newly added work force. According to statistics, by the end of 2004, employees in individual and private sectors reached 960. 44 million, which means that, every private entrepreneur averagely creates 12. 7 jobs in addition to himself. ② This is a great contribution to China's social stability and progress.

Fourth, they have made contribution the solidarity of our society. The judgment

---

① See Zhang Houyi, Ming Lizhi and Liang Chuanyun (compilers), *Report on the Development of China's Private Enterprises(*2003*)*, Social Science Academic Press, 2004, pp. 6, 24.

② China Statistical Yearbook(2005), China Statistics Press, 2005, pp. 146, 148 – 149.

that private entrepreneurs and other new social strata are all the builders of the cause of socialism with Chinese characteristics is a major innovation in the development of Marxist theory of scientific socialism, which will produce extensive and profound influence on the service of the Party and state, especially for our party to consolidate and develop the broadest possible patriotic united front for the great renewal of the Chinese nation. Over the years, more than nine thousand private entrepreneurs have been elected as deputies of the NPC and 30 thousand of them as members of the CPPCC respectively at all levels. ①

In short, the new social strata are the builders ofand have made important contributions to the cause of socialism with Chinese characteristics. On the other hand, it must be admitted that, due to its complex composition and varying degree of quality, there are shortcomings, weaknesses among some of the private entrepreneurs, and a few of them even committed illegal activities. So we should also pay attention to this respect. Comrade Jiang Zemin pointed out that there are also shortcomings, weaknesses and even illegal behaviors among people in non-public sectors, so we should make effort to unite, help, guide and educate them. This is the basic attitude of our party toward them. Therefore, we must follow the principle of "unite, help, guide and educate" to strengthen ideological and political work with them, so as to guide them become builders of socialism with Chinese characteristics builders that uphold patriotism, dedication and integrity and abide by the law.

II. Private Entrepreneurs Are Also Builders of Socialism

Private enterprises constitute an important component ofthe socialist market economy. Along with the development of reform and opening up and socialist market economy, non-public sectors of the economy have substantially developed, as has the new stratum of private entrepreneurs. According to the statistics of the State Administration for Industry and Commerce, by the end of 2004, there were about 3.006 million registered private enterprises nationwide, with a total of 7.728 million private entrepreneurs, 33.158 employees and the amount of registered capital totaling 3530.49 billion yuan. They constitute a special stratum in the building of socialism with Chinese characteristics, whose status, role and influence in socialist

① See Chen Xiqing, "New Theories of Social strata and Their Practical Significance," In Tianjin Daily, Jan. 12th 2004.

economic and political life is increasing constantly.

However, at the present stage, private entrepreneurs have not yet formed a class in China, neither a "middle class," nor a nascent bourgeoisie. Throughout history, every society has its basic and non-basic modes of production. The former gives rise to basic class whereas the latter, to some transitional strata and interest groups.

When analyzing capitalist societies, Marx pointed out: "In England, modern society is indisputably most highly and classically developed in economic structure. Nevertheless, even here the stratification of classes does not appear in its pure form. Middle and intermediate strata even here obliterate lines of demarcation everywhere."① In today's China, the pattern with the public sector remaining dominant and diverse sectors of the economy developing side by side determines that, the working class and the farmer class are the two basic classes and there will be some intermediate or transitional strata and interest groups between them.

A special stratum, the private entrepreneurs, has taken shape in our society. Since 1980s, private enterprises have and are still developed rapidly, and the number of private entrepreneurs has increased substantially, as shown in the table 1 below.

Table 1 Basic Data of China's Private Enterprises②

Year	Households (Ten thousand)	Investors (Ten thousand)	Employees (Ten thousand)	Registered Capital (one hundred million)	Industrial output value (one hundred million)	volume of retail sales (one hundred million)
1989	9.1	21.4	174.6	84.5	89.2	33.7
1992	14.0	30.3	201.5	221.2	189.4	90.7
1995	65.5	134.0	822.0	2621.7	2036.1	1006.4
1998	120.1	263.8	1445.3	7198.0	5018.7	3059.3
1999	150.9	322.4	1699.2	10287.3	6521.7	4191.4

First, the private entrepreneurs are the owners and investors of private capital, whose invested capital will combine with labor and thus produce surplus value, so

① Selected Works of Marx and Engels, vol. 2, People's Publishing House, 1995, p. 587.

② See Zhang Houyi and Ming Lizhi (compilers), *Report on the Development of China's Private Enterprises* (1978 – 1998), Social Science Academic Press, 1999, p. 60; Mu Zhirong, *A Study on the Development of China's Private Economy*, Xiamen University Press, 2004, p. 56.

they are theoccupants of surplus value to some extent.

Second, under the condition of public ownership being the dominant sector and the political system of people's democratic dictatorship, with the establishment and improvement of our social security system, nobody can compulsorily or have or expropriate or enslave the labor of others solely by privately owning or possessing the means of production. The relations between the private entrepreneurs and workers are mainly cooperation and shared interests between employers and employees.

Third, under the condition of socialism, the majority of the private entrepreneurs are not only owners of the enterprises, but also operators and managers of them. With theprogress of modernization, operation and management has also become a component of the productive forces and a kind of indispensable important labor activity and an integral part in the total social labor. In this sense, the entrepreneurs also pay efforts and physical and mental labor jus as the employees do. Moreover, most of private enterprises went through many hardships, and they are owners as well as investors, operators, managers and even employees taking risks of start-up and operation, who are different from exploiters or rentiers in the traditional sense.

Fourth, on the whole, the income ofthe private entrepreneurs consists mainly of the incomes from labor, management, venture investment and capital, with capital income being only a part of it. And some of the entrepreneurs are enthusiastic about public service and charity events, such as giving donation to assist education, the disabled and the poor. In 1999, a total of 3, 508 entrepreneurs invested 10. 5 billion yuan and donated 1. 2 billion yuan to help develop education and other undertakings, and a total of 1. 92 million poor people had got rid of poverty because of it. ①

Fifth, some of the private entrepreneurs are advanced political elements. The private entrepreneurs, together with the working people, have make contributions the building of socialism with Chinese characteristics. Some of Party members were originally from rural areas, public enterprises, Party and government bodies, cultural or educational organizations, the PLA or academics, etc. Of the private entrepreneurs, 19. 8 percent are Party members who accept the Party's Constitution, pay Party membership dues, join and work actively in the Party

---

① See Mu Zhirong, *A Study on the Development of China's Private Economy*, Xiamen University Press, 2004, p. 71.

organizations and carry out the Party's resolutions. Many of them keep in mind that they are Party members, uphold the Party's theories and lines and actively support the Party to build organizations and carry out activities in private enterprises, thus play an exemplary role in a certain scope. The stratum of private entrepreneurs is not like the capitalist class in the old society who transferred from the old or foreign bourgeoisie, nor is it the product of imperialist peaceful evolution. On the contrary, some private entrepreneurs are interested in politics and state affairs, have enthusiasm and passion in participating in and discussing state affairs and have engaged in various social activities and play a role in a certain range; some are enthusiastic about public welfare undertakings and charity and have done useful and good things for the masses; and some of them are not only law-abiding citizens and excellent entrepreneurs, but also have applied for the membership of the CPC.

Sixth, in terms of the origin of capital and class, the private entrepreneurs mainly originated in the working masses and their incomes are legitimate. In terms of origin of capital, the majority of their funding is from legitimate business and labor. According to the survey on private enterprises in Zhejiang province carried out by a research team of Zhejiang Provincial Party School, more than 90 percent of the private entrepreneurs was originally socialist workers; 51 percent of the private enterprises were transferred from state-owned enterprises, urban collective enterprises, joint-stock companies, joint-stock cooperative enterprises and associates, etc.; 56 percent of their original capital derived from labor and business, 20.6 percent of it came from friends and families, 16.5 of it were loan from banks, collective organizations, credit cooperatives, private enterprise and so on. In terms of class origin, they were all formerly workers, farmers, demobilized PLA men, cadres and so on, who get rich in the process of reform and opening up through running business in the market.

Seventh, some private enterprises have developed into enterprises of mixed ownership, joint-stock enterprises, or listed enterprises that attract public shares, so that the employees, the owners and the public constitute a stakeholder community of the enterprises, making social capital and private and public capital combine together. In these circumstances, some private entrepreneurs have become shareowners and operators of the social capital.

Eighth, they have contributed to the development ofthe socialist market economy and productive forces.

At the present stage, private entrepreneurs belong neither to the "middle class," nor an independent or nascent bourgeoisie, but to a new social stratum. Nonetheless, it is possible that individual bourgeois elements come out from this stratum. Throughout the whole primary stage of socialism, the private economy will exist and develop rapidly, and along with it, the stratum of private entrepreneurs. Because the socialist government holds the country's economic lifeline and the initiative in class relationship, as long as the socialist system is maintained, and the advantages of the socialist system are made use in handling well the relationship between efficiency and justice to ensure social justice and prevent polarization, it is impossible for the stratum of private entrepreneurs to develop into a particular class. The reasons are as follows: Firstly, they are associated with the dominant mode of production. At China's present stage, the public economy is playing the dominant role and constitutes the basic mode of production, under whose framework the private entrepreneurs in the private sector conduct their economic activities. Secondly, they do not have the economic base that holds the dominant position. Bourgeoisie is inseparable from capitalist private ownership and takes it as its base. Private entrepreneurs don't have economic base playing the dominant role like the public economy. Thirdly, they don't have the natural link with the old exploiting classes. The present-day private entrepreneurs in China are mostly from the working people. And lastly, they do not have the class awareness and demands of an independent class.

III. The Duality of the Private Entrepreneurs

It must be admitted that, some of the private entrepreneurs behave badly and thus bring some negative effecton our construction. For example, because they run business on the basis of private-owned means of production by hiring workers with the purpose of seeking profits, and through it possess the surplus labor of others, driven only by interests, some of the private entrepreneurs may seek nothing but profits, conduct illegal business, make adulteration, bully the competitors, dominate and disrupt the market; some may make bribery and even compete for political power with money, badger games and other means; some may bully employees by violating the law; some may damage social morality by living an extravagant or decadent life, such as "keeping a concubine or mistress"; some may poison the social atmosphere by doing such social evils as pornography, gambling and drug abuse and trafficking; some others may collude with criminal syndicates to play the bully. Although these phenomena are few in number and occur not only in private sector, they, after all, are reflections of the negative side of the private entrepreneurs.

The stratum of the private Entrepreneurs has a nature of duality. On the one hand, their labor of operation and management, a constituent of the "total social labor" in the socialized production, has the property of creating value and the embodiment of their ability of innovation, management, technology and knowledge, so part of their income is labor income. Furthermore, all their factor and capital earnings are partly come from labor. On the other hand, part of their income comes from their possession of the surplus labor of others, which has the nature of surplus value. It should be pointed out that, in a society with the people as masters, there is no such a bourgeoisie that freely possesses the workers' surplus value. Under the socialist system with the state controlling the economic lifeline of the country, the contradictions between the working class and the private entrepreneurs are not of antagonistic nature like that of contradictions between ourselves and the enemy, but rather contradictions among the people with fundamentally identical interests.

With regard to the understanding of surplus value, it is necessary to both adhere to the basic principles of Marx's labor theory of value andto deepen and innovate our research and understanding by combining it with the new realities. Marx believed that the value of the goods is generally created by human undifferentiated abstract labor, and only living labor is the headspring of value. To deepen our understanding of the labor theory of value is by no means to negate it or replace it with factor theory of value.

To deepen our understanding of labor theory of value, we must first of all deepen our understanding of the category of labor. Due to the rapid development of high-tech, labor itself has undergone new changes. Manual labor as the main form has more and more been replaced by mental labor, so does repetitive labor by innovative labor, and along with it, management, operation, etc. increasingly become the components of labor. Even in the capitalist system, other forms of labor, such as management, directing, supervision, etc., also have dual attributes: on the one hand they are associated with socialized production; on the other, the management of and supervision over the workers by capitalists has an exploitative nature. Under the socialist condition of our country, the social background of the emergence of the private entrepreneurs is different from that of the bourgeoisie in the period of primitive accumulation that was gotten by violent plundering and cruel battening on the surplus value created by workers.

The ownership of the means of production of the private entrepreneurs also has a dual attributes: on the one hand, it is privately owned and dominated; on the other, its actual results of operations directly contribute to the development of society. At the present stage, employment relationship do exists in private sector, but it is a special one in that the employers and employees are politically equal.

Generally speaking, the duality of private entrepreneurs in our society at the present stage demonstrates itself in their labor and income. On the one hand, they participate in labor. Many private entrepreneurs apply the knowledge and technology they mastered in scientific operation and management so that the enterprises develop and make profits and thus create wealth for society. So it can be said that they have paid labor, even complex and creative labor. Their income from this part can be regarded as labor income as social builders. On the other hand, they still owned the surplus labor of others. The income of the private entrepreneurs in our country can be divided into three parts, i. e., income from management, operation and technological innovation, venture income and non-labor income. Non-labor income is a concept with a broad sense, including incomes from interest, dividends, inheritance, etc. We should not have a one-sided and static view on the non-labor income of the enterprise owners. Of course, it is undeniable that part of the non-labor income is income from possessing surplus value. Non-labor income should not be taken as the equivalent of exploiting income, which is only a small part of the non-labor income.

Apart from labor and income, the duality of the private entrepreneurs is also manifested in other aspects as follows:

(1) There are loopholes in taxation on private enterprises.

The proportion of the tax collected from private enterprises is relatively low. The share of private sector in the whole economy is increasinglybig, but the increase of tax they paid far lags behind their growth, as is the tax paid-in to their tax payable. (See table below)①

① See Mu Zhirong, *A Study on the Development of China's Private Economy*, Xiamen University Press, 2004, p. 67.

Table 2 Tax Payment Estimation of China's Private Enterprises

Year	Share in GIOV * (%)		Share in TSCG ** (%)		Share in TICTR *** (%)		Tax Paid by PE(million yuan)	Estimated Tax Payable by PE (million yuan)	Tax Payable/ Tax Paid
	SOE ****	PE ******	SOE	PE	SOE	PE			
1989	56.06	0.41	39.10	0.42	67.95	0.06	110	1040	
1990	54.61	0.47	39.59	0.52	68.59	0.10	200	1430	7.2
1991	52.94	0.48	40.19	0.61	68.29	0.16	340	1580	4.6
1992	48.09	0.51	41.29	0.83	66.97	0.20	460	2150	4.7
1993	43.13	0.72	37.52	1.53	63.56	0.26	1050	6480	6.2
1994	37.34	—	31.93	—	63.04	0.37	1750	18370	10.5
1995	33.97	2.22	29.85	4.88	59.74	0.65	3560	34290	9.6
1996	36.32	2.86	27.23	5.89	54.69	1.11	6020	38340	6.3
1997	31.62	3.03	23.28	6.079	56.33	1.32	9050	65830	7.3
1998	28.24	4.22	20.65	10.49	54.05	1.89	16380	136290	8.3
Total							38820	305800	7.8

Notes: * GIOV: gross industrial output value

* * TSCG: total retail sales of consumer goods

* * * TICTR: total industrial and commercial tax revenue.

* * * * SOE: state-owned enterprises

* * * * * PE: private enterprises

(2) Frictions between labor and capital in private enterprises.

To analyze the relations between labor and capital in the private sector, we first of all must analyze its division of profits. According a survey conducted in 2000 over 191 private enterprises, in 1999, the total amount of wages received by all workers was 6.52 million yuan, whereas, based on statistics, the dividend get by the private entrepreneurs is 19.7 times that of the income of the workers. The main body of the employees in private enterprise comprises migrant workers, laid-off workers, college graduates, urban residents, those who resigned from Party and government organizations, etc. The wages and benefits of the workers in private enterprises is generally lower than that of workers in state-owned enterprises, reflected in medical pension insurance and public housing provident fund, in insufficient labor protection, in low wages, long working hours, wages arrear, and even physical punishment, bullying and beating, restrictions of freedom, humiliation of personal dignity, and so on. These often become the cause of the open conflict between labor and management.

We should pay attention to the duality of private entrepreneurs, strengthen our efforts to educate andguide them to become the builders of both socialist material and cultural civilizations.

IV. The Characteristics of Urban and Rural Self-employers

Urban and rural individual self-employers are the first new stratum with a considerable number of people emerged since reform and opening up. They are mainly engaged in the tertiary industry, serving people's needs in daily life and social production. They get paid by self-employment and self-operation and thus are special workers ofthe cause of building socialism with Chinese characteristics.

With the development of the socialist market economy, the number of self-employers is increasing, so is their composition. In terms of occupations, they mainly work in traditional sectors such as small-scale manufacturing, construction, transport, restaurants, repair services, commerce, service industry and such new sectors as computer maintenance, personnel training, etc. In terms of scale, they are usually small; in terms of composition, they are mainly rural surplus labor, former urban laid-off workers, professionals and those transferred from Party or government bodies, state enterprises, institutions of education, science, culture, health and sports, etc. Urban and rural self-employers can be divided into urban self-employers and rural self-employers. Most of them make their living by legitimate and hard work. They are both the operators and laborers, so are similar and belong to ordinary workers in terms of both income and mentality. On the other hand, they are different from ordinary workers in that they own some capital and means of production, because they get higher personal income than the average ordinary workers while directly shouldering social risks and relatively larger occupational pressure due to limited size, capital and low technological contents. Since thc reform and opening up, the rank of the self-employers expanded continuously and their work played an important role in the improvement of people's lives, economy and social stability. It is undeniable that there are also some problems in them, including tax evasion, fake or counterfeit goods, bullying competitors and dominating the market, cheating customers, illegal operation, etc., which need our education and guidance.

Chapter 16

The Characteristics of China's Middle-Income Group at the Present Stage

The Sixteenth Party Congress, bearing in mind the objective of common prosperity and building socialist harmonious society, put forward the strategyof raising the proportion of the middle-income group and increasing the income of the low-income group. This is the first time that raising the proportion of middle-income group was written into the Party's document. It constitutes an important part of building a moderately prosperous society in all respects and will have a far-reaching influence on the harmonious and stable development of Chinese society.

I. The Concept of "Middle Class" in Western Academic Circles

As early as 2000 years ago, in analyzing the society in ancient Greek city-states, Aristotle had pointed out that the most stable social structure is a society that is big in the middle and small at both ends. He believes that a political system created either by the rich or by the poor is often unstable. A system set up by the few rich is inevitably self-benefiting oligarchy; while those by the poor, to an extreme democracy that will lead to despotism of some charismatic leaders. He believes that a large middle class is a buffer zone between rich and poor and an important factor of political democracy and social stability.

Eduard Bernstein (1850 – 1932) is one of the earliest proponents of the idea of "middle class." Regarding the increase of employment of mental laborers in late 19th and early 20th centuries in Western Europe and North America, Bernstein suggested that the development of capitalist society had widened the gap between the working class and the bourgeoisie and the increase of middle-income earners.

In the Western academic circles, middle class refers to people with middle income, consisting mainly of such mental laborers as managers, professionals, salespersons, clerks, secretaries, and so on. They believe that a huge middle class is in the shaping in the Western world.

British sociologist Nicholas Arbercrombie and Stephen Hill made an in-depth analysis of the middle class in capitalist society. ① They divided the middle class into three social groups: First, the upper-middle-class. People of this group have higher knowledge and skills, enjoy relatively autonomous in their work, with less manual labor, more mental labor, high income, independent plan for their own career and future, and have the chance to become senior professionals or managers. The second is the middle-middle-class, who have certain skills but is controlled by upper management. Third is the lower-middle-class, who is consisted mainly of clerks, shopkeepers, secretaries and some skilled workers, and so on. They do work hard but their incomes are low. Arbercombie and Hill believe that only the middle-middle-class is the middle class in real sense. According to Western sociology, three criteria can be used to identify the middle class, there are: economic criterion, political criterion and social criterion.

Western scholars believe that the middle class is the objective outcome of the development of capitalist social productive forces in the course of the development of Western society. Take the United Kingdom for instance. The formation of the middle class in the U. K went through about 300 years. In the early period of its industrial revolution, the "enclosure" created a large number of landless rural poor, who flowed into the city, forming a huge army of the unemployed. The TudorDynasty, in order to maintain social stability, begun to collect the Poor Rate, and later in 1601 introduced the Poor Law, aiming to help the poor and narrowed the gap between rich and poor and solve the problems of living of the urban poor. With the progress of the British capitalist industrialization, the conflicts between the working class and the bourgeoisie became sharp. To ease this kind of conflicts, the British government introduced a series of social security laws and regulations in favor of the poor and lower classes. By the mid-20th century, the implementation of the Beveridge Plan made the social welfare system come into being. In the process of capitalist industrialization, Germany, France, Japan and other countries have introduced and implemented their social security programs one after another. The emergence of the middle class is inseparable from the capitalist industrialization and the establishment and improvement of the social security system.

According to statistics, in the developed Western capitalist countries, currently theproportion of the middle class usually accounts for more than 40% of their total

① See Qin Lianbin, "Is There a Middle Class in China?" in *Chinese Cadres Tribute,* no. 3, 2001.

populations, showing an "olive-shaped" social structure. In the U. S. for example, those with an annual income between $25, 000 to 100, 000 belong to the middle class. In many European countries, the middle-class largely comprises the middle level executives in governmental departments, the middle level managerial staff and employees in state-owned or private-owned monopolistic enterprises and the professionals in other sectors, and so on, which in general account for more than 40% of the entire population and constitute the main body of society. The middle class can be understood from two perspectives: First, from the point of view of the individual, being a member of the middle class means that one's material wealth and social status is at the middle level; Second, from the point view of the social structure, a large middle class means the streamline of the social structure, which is the foundation of social stability.

In recent years, Western academics proposed aconcept "new middle class." They hold that since the end of World War II, in Western developed countries, the traditional middle class between the bourgeoisie and the working class, such as the urban small proprietors, the farmers and others are shrinking, while a new middle class with "high education level, high-tech ability and modern managerial expertise (mainly scientists, engineers, professionals, managers) as the mainstay is on the rise, most of whom still are still employees. They account for the largest proportion in the total population and also the main body for the social stability and development in the Western countries.

With regarding to the formation and connotations of the concept of middle class in the Western academics, as Marxist scholars, we should have our own analysis and option in a scientific manner.

II. The Concepts "Middle Class" and "Middle Strata" Used by Marxist Writers

Marxist classic writers used such concepts as "middle bourgeoisie," "middle class" and "middle strata," which are different from the concept "middle class" used by Western scholars. Marx believes that "Society as a whole is more and more splitting up into two great hostile camps, into two great classes, directly facing each other: Bourgeoisie and Proletariat."[①] Besides, he noticed the existence of middle

① *Selected Works of Marx and Engels*, vol. 1, People's Publishing House, 1995, p. 273.

class in capitalist societies: "...the constantly growing number of the middle classes, those who stand between the workman on the one hand and the capitalist and landlord on the other. The middle classes maintain themselves to an ever increasing extent directly out of revenue, they are a burden weighing heavily on the working base and increase the social security and power of the upper ten thousand."① The concepts of"middle class," "middle bourgeoisie" and "middle strata" mentioned by Marxist classic writers refer to the social strata or interest groups between the two hostile basic classes. In the capitalist society, the two hostile basic classes are the bourgeoisie and the proletariat, with a constantly differentiating middle class comprising the farmers and petty bourgeoisie, such as handicraftsmen, small traders, rentiers, etc. Entering the period of monopoly capitalism, the proportion of urban and rural petty bourgeoisie (mainly farmers) become smaller and smaller while that of the intellectuals and employees is increasing.

III. The Concepts of Middle Strata and Middle- Income Group

The middle class, also known also as middle bourgeoisie, middle-income groups, etc., is a concept used by Western academics in their study of social structure. A striking change in the Western developed countries after they entered into the modern capitalist stage is that, while the number of traditional manual workers (the blue-collar workers) is shrinking, the middle class is in the rising. This class is dominated by intellectuals (white-collar or mental laborers), senior managers, small business owners, etc. Take France for instance. The population of the middle class jumped from 7.673 million in 1982 to 10.173 million in 2000, accounting for more than 40 percent of the working population. Therc are two different opinions about the concept of "middle class" in Chinese academic circles. One holds that we should introduce this concept into our analysis of middle-income strata, because in the primary stage of socialism, the exploiting class no longer exists, and therefore we should not use the method of class analysis. Another opinion is that the method of middle class denies class relations, class differences and class viewpoints, which are contrary to Marxist principles of class and class struggle, so it cannot be used in the structural analysis of our social members in the primary stage of

① *Collected Works of Marx and Engels*, vol. 26, People's Publishing House, 1973, p. 653.

socialism in China.

The author believes that both these opinionsare one-sided. In the premise of upholding Marxist class analysis method, we can use the concept of "middle-income group" (instead of "middle class") in analyzing our social structure. This is because, although in the primary stage of socialism class antagonism and class exploitation in our country has been eliminated, there still exist classes, class differences as well as class struggle in certain limits, so the method of class analysis is still applicable. In the present stage, the economic base on which class exploitation, class antagonism and class differentiation is not in the dominant position. Against this background and the premise of recognizing class division, how should we identify social strata and interest groups of non-class nature? How can we analyze the structure of our social members from sociological and other perspectives? The answer is, we can, on the basis of income differences and method of social statistics, for example, to identify a middle-income group that is basically in the middle position in our society. And we can also divide them by their occupations, divisions of labor, possession of social resources, etc. from sociological perspective. Dividing social structure from different angles can help us to a have a clearer and more comprehensive understanding of Chinese social structure from multi levels and multi dimensions, which will in turn help us to make correct policies and measures in understanding and handling classes, strata and interest groups in China.

Strictly speaking, the concept "middle-class income group" refers not to class. Rather, we can understand it from the following perspectives: First, perspective of quality of life. The quality of life of a family, without doubt, does not just depend on their income but on many other factors, such as purchasing power, social security and welfare, various family burdens, social and natural environments. Second, perspective of income distribution. The middle-income group belongs to the social strata and interest groups whose average income level is around the median income line statistically. The size of this group not only has relations with the economic growth, social conditions and the average income level of the society; more importantly, it is associated with distribution of income. The size and quality of middle-income group can reflect the social structure and distribution structure of the society. Third, perspective of urban-rural structure. The size and quality of middle-income group can clearly reflect the urban-rural structure and differences. Fourth, perspective of industrial structure. In a society with middle-income group as the mainstay, the proportion of employment in tertiary industry usually accounts for over

50 percent of the total employment population. Fifth, perspective of national conditions. Standards for identifying the middle incomers vary in different countries, even in different regions of the same country. In the United States, a middle income family usually refers to a family with an annual income from $ 25,000 to 100,000, which, accounting for about 80 percent of American population, is the main body of its society. In general, the income level of standard for identifying middle-incomers is proportional to the level of development of a country. Sixth, perspective of change. The standard for middle income is always changing. For instance, with the development of China's economy and society, the standard for its middle-income will change. In the next five years, China will have a middle-income population of 200 million. Seventh, the middle-income group is a relative rather than absolute concept. In appearance, middle-income group refers to social strata and interest groups whose income level, living standard, property status, social status, occupation, etc., are in the middle level of the society. Using this concept means that we divide the social strata and interest groups into three levels of high, medium and low. But in actual life, there are no clear-cut unchanging boundaries among them, this is because: In the first place, there is only relative rather than fixed standard for middle-income group. Different countries and different regions in the same country have their different standards, which is relative to the high-income and low-income groups in a country or a region. In the second place, standards for middle-income are dynamic rather than static. It will increase or decrease correspondingly with that of the productive forces and people's income. Furthermore, the size of the middle-income group will also change with the society.

Middle-income group, in general, refers not to any specific social stratum but to several strata with similar features, especially those having or above middle level incomes. In short, the so-called middle-income group is a concept comprising numerous indicators like income level, quality of life, occupation. When using this concept, we should be careful to avoid replacing class division with strata division, which indeed is the attempt of some bourgeois scholars. We must restrain it within the premise of class division. The middle income group is a group with the level of income as its standard, whose income is at the middle level.

Increasing the proportion of middle-income group is conducive to social stability, harmony and progress.

First, increasing theproportion of middle-income group is beneficial to social stability. From the perspective of social stability, only the majority of people in a society live in a relatively well-off middle-income life, can the society as a whole be relatively stable. As a buffer and stabilizer between high-income group and low-income group, middle incomers can ease the contradiction or conflicts between them. A certain size of middle-income group gives hope to the low-incomers, thus, relieve their stress. In a sense, the middle-income group constitutes a group of vested interests who want to maintain good social order rather than unrest. They hold a moderate ideology, which can be a resistance against extreme ideas and an important factor to ensure social stability. If the social structure is polarization with the middle income group being small and the high- and low-income groups big at both ends, contradictions may intensify, leading to social unrest. The numerous uprisings of the exploiting people in history were inseparably linked with serious polarization. Some foreign scholars believe that if the poor and lower-middle class accounts for more than one third or even half of a population, social contradictions in the society will inevitably intensify.

Second, increasing the proportion of middle-income group is beneficial to social and economic prosperity. The majority of social members being middle-incomers will give rise to a large and stable consumer market, which is an important domestic factor for socio-economic development.

Third, increasing the proportion of middle-incomers can help reduce poverty and achieve the goal of building a moderately prosperous society in all respects. Although we have achieved the well-off level, it is still a low-level and imbalanced one with great development and income gaps between urban and rural areas, between regions, between industries, and between members of different social strata, and these gaps even have the possibility of widening. Against this background, increasing the proportion of middle-incomers can help narrow the gaps and achieve a moderately prosperous society in all respects.

IV. The Status and Characteristics of Middle Income Group in China

As mentioned above, the middle income group in China refers to the group whose income, social status, living standard and ideology are at the middle level. They constitute a group in the sociological sense rather than of class nature. Chinese middle income group include those who have a stable income, are able to buy cars and house, and can afford their children's education and modern consumption such as travel, sports, etc.

1. The status quo of middle income group in China

(1) The rapid development of individual sector of the economy results in the increase of middle-incomers. Among them the number of middle incomers increased substantially: they were 0.31 million, 0.81 million, 17.66 million and 61.14 million in 1979, 1980, 1985 and 1998, respectively,[①] and they have become a part of Chinese middle-income group at the present stage.

(2) The rapid development of private enterprises results in the great increase of middle incomers in the private sector of the economy. In 1998, the number of registered private enterprises was 1.201 with 17.10 million employees, among which 0.755 million were urban employees, 1.76 million were investors, and 9.726 million employees;[②] in 2004, the number increased into 3.651 million with 50.173 million employees,[③] becoming an important part in Chinese middle-income group.

(3) The emergence of enterprises built with exclusively foreign funds, Chinese-foreign joint ventures and cooperative firms, etc., gives birth to the some managers and agents, who also become a part of the middle-income group.

(4) The multi-form realization ofthe public economy, including contract system, shareholding system and contractual and leasing system as well as other forms of non-public system, provide opportunities for the increase of middle-income group.

(5) A large number of intellectuals and technicians who grasp hi-tech and relevant knowledge become an important part of middle-incomers.

(6) The development of second and tertiary industries, such as the financing, insurance, real estate, tourism, etc., created and thus increased a number of middle-incomers.

2. The characteristics of China's middle income group

(1) They have a moderate income with salary as the main source.

(2) Most of them do not directly engage in manual labor but in mental labor, and their occupations require high educational level, high-tech knowledge and

---

① See *China Statistical Yearbook(2005)*, China Statistics Press, 2005, p. 121.

② See Zhang Houyi *et al.*, (compilers), *Report on the Development of China's Private Enterprises(1999)*, Social Science Academic Press, 2000, pp. 33, 37.

③ See *China Statistical Yearbook(2005)*, China Statistics Press, 2005, p. 148.

complicated professionaltraining and they enjoy high professional reputation. For example, those require high professional knowledge include scientists, social scientists, teachers in colleges and other types of schools; those need high scientific and technological level include network engineers, software designers, technical personnel in high-tech enterprises, etc.; those need high professional training include lawyers, doctors, writers, translators, journalists, hosts, athletes, designers, etc.; those need modern managerial expertise include the management personnel in sectors such as business, finance, securities, insurance, real estate, etc.

(3) They have a lawful and stable income and enjoy a well-off and upward living condition, and moderately prosperous in terms of consumption level.

(4) They play a certain degree of leading role in terms of cultural and intellectual life with their high educational and theoretical level and morality.

(5) This group was gradually formed in a relatively short period with the development and deepening of reform and opening up.

(6) The proportion of middle income group to the whole population in China is relatively small compared with Western countries. Presently, the middle income group is too small in our social structure, which accounts only for 20 percent, much lower than that in Western countries. Our social structure is pyramid-shaped with the low income group being too big and middle level too small, rather than an olive- or spindle-shaped structure that is conducive to social stability. The causes for this are: there is a huge rural population with low income, whereas profit-driven capital is concentrated into the urban areas, resulting in the widening of urban-rural gap; the incomes of some employees in the state-owned enterprises are low due to economic restructuring; the number of new-born middle incomers is still small.

V. Strategy and Measures for Increasing the Proportion of the Middle Income Group

It takes some time to increase the proportion of middle-income group, which usually forms and becomes stable and proportional with the development of the productive forces. Fundamentally speaking, the most effective strategy is to vigorously develop the economy to "make the cake bigger". Meanwhile, we can also take some measures and policies to advance it.

First, we should implement the system whereby distribution according to work is dominant and a variety of modes of distribution coexist, in particular the principle that other production factors participate in the distribution of income. The so-called middle class in foreign countries is mainly comprised of the owners of capital, technology, management, business and other factors of production. The case is broadly similar in China. To implement the principle of the principle that labor, capital, technology, managerial expertise and other production factors participate in the distribution of income in accordance with their respective contributions will mobilize the enthusiasm of these people. In addition, China's middle-income earners are mostly intellectuals, such as cadres, teachers, experts and scholars, so the full implementation of the principle of distribution according to work, especially the contribution of complex and mental labor, will also help to mobilize the enthusiasm of intellectuals and thus to expand the ranks of middle-income group.

Second, we should strengthen the regulation of income distribution. To increase the middle-income group, we must decrease the proportion of the high- and low-income groups. In doing so, we should pay attention on the fairness in secondary distribution to prevent the widening of income gaps. The decrease of the high- and low-income groups means the increase of proportion of the middle-income group.

Third, greater efforts should be made to support agriculture and increase the income of farmers. The farmer class takes the most population in China, therefore, to increase the middle income group, it is important to strengthen our support to farmers and increase their income.

Fourth, improving the minimum-wage guarantee system to reduce the number of low-income people and enlarge the middle income group.

Fifth, strengthening social security and paying attention to poor groups to gradually raise their income and finally resolve the problem of poverty.

Chapter 17

Correctly Handling Contradictions among the People to Build a Harmonious Socialist Society

To build a socialist harmonious society, we must properly coordinate the interests of all sides and correctly handle contradictions among the people.

I. Some New Problems among the People against Which We should Keep High Vigilance

In present-day China, various relationships are basically coordinated, the political situation is basically stable and the society is basically harmonious. However, we should also be soberly aware that, there are still problems in our society. To put it simple, these problems include: although the economy have developed steadily, people's living standards have improved greatly and they have got substantial benefits, various contradictions among the people become more acute and complex; there are some potential risks that may seriously affect our social stability and harmony, undermine the safe operation and healthy development of the society, and even become a threat to the foundation of the CPC as the governing party and our national security, which by no means can we neglect.

1. The problem of income gap

The income gaps, including gaps between urban and rural areas and between regions continue to widen, which are both the main expression of and underlying cause for the complexity and intensification of all kinds of contradiction among the people.

First, the income gap between some social members continues to widen.

From a long-term perspective, to ensure the progress and harmony of a society, we must combine two principles: one is the maximization of wealth growth, that is, to "make the cake bigger"; the other is the fairness of distribution, that is, to "divide the cake fairly". Only by doing so can we promote social progress and harmony simultaneously. The bigger cake is the prerequisite and the cake is the foundation, so they are the two sides of one coin. The Chines sages believed that "The trouble lies not in scarcity but in uneven distribution." In Chinese record history, there were hundreds of peasant uprisings as the result of unfair distribution or polarization of rich and poor. The peasants would rather rise up than to overthrow the feudal regime than starve to death. The uprising of Li Zicheng, advocating the slogan of "dividing land equally", gathered millions of thousands peasants and finally overthrew the Ming regime. From this we can see that widening income inequality is a major problem affecting social stability and harmony.

Before reform and opening up, one of the major drawbacks in our distribution was the egalitarianism with the practice of having everyone "eat from the same big pot." The discarding of that practice has tremendously aroused the enthusiasm of the people, which has given rise to differences of distribution that boosted people's motivation for work and competition. As a result, our economy gets a rapid growth. It is undoubtedly bad to eliminate differences, but the continued widening gap of distribution between social members has now become a problem of our society and the focus and cause of intensification of contradictions among the people. In addition to the prominent widening income gap between urban and rural residents, there are also income differences between urban residents, between rural residents, between regions, between mental and manual laborers, between workers in different forms of ownership, etc. And off-the-books income and illegal incomes exaggerate the situation.

Apart from distribution differences, development gapsbetween regions, between mental and labor workers and between industries, with the gaps between the urban and rural areas and between regions being the most prominent. Although great progress has been achieved through a series of measures taken by the central government to support the development of rural and backward areas, the imbalance of social and economic development in these respects remains a serious problem. From 1980 to 2004, the economic size of eastern region to the national total rose from 50 percent in to 58. 5 percent in 2004; the ratio of per capita GDP between the western region and the eastern region increased from 1: 1. 92 to 1: 259, and between the central region and the eastern region from 1: 1. 53 to 1: 203. ① A scholar uses the analogue of "four worlds" to describe this differences: The first world is Shanghai and Beijing, with a population accounting 2. 175 percent of the total, is like the

① See Lu Dadao *et al.*, *Report on China's Regional Development*(2000), The Commercial Press, 2001, p. 6.

developed countries with high income; The "second world" comprises Tianjin, Zhejiang, Guangdong, Fujian, Jiangsu and Liaoning, 21 provinces, with a population accounting for 8 percent of the total, is like the middle-income countries; The "third world" is Shandong and other provinces, with a population accounting for 21.76 percent of the total, is like the lower-middle income countries; the "fourth world," the central and middle regions, with a population accounting for 50.57 percent of the total, is like the low-income countries. Just as an Chinese ambassador to a European country figuratively put it: "Half of China, the urban area, is like Europe and the other half, the rural area, is like Africa." The gap between urban and rural areas finds its expression not only in the widening income gap of their residents, but also in the intensifying contradictions of the urban-rural dual structure. For example, many problems arise from the rapid expansion of cities and development of real estate, including: some farmers have lost their means of production for their livelihood; some land was expropriated in an enforced way; some land compensation fund was embezzled; a large number of farmers have lost their land, and so on. The disparity between rural and urban residents become bigger in employment, social security, education, healthcare, culture, welfare, environmental protection and other public utilities. There are 300 million people in rural areas whose drinking water is below the hygienic standards; 150 million *mu* of land has been polluted, and 120 million tons of house refuse was dumped in the open field without any treatment; there is nearly no environmental protection facilities; most farmers have no fixed healthcare, nor subsistence security; the average years of schooling is six years less than the urban residents; land fertility is exhausted, ecological condition has deteriorated, the quality of labor has declined and the wealth and power are concentrated to the city, and the social undertakings and infrastructure in rural area are far lag behind. As a result, the social disparity is widening all round, social justice is imbalanced. How to narrow these gaps, gaps in distribution in particular and urban-rural differences is crucial for us to correctly handle contradictions among the people.

2. Gap between rich and poor and the problem of poverty

Thegap between rich and poor is widening, highlighting the issue of poverty, which is both the expression and cause of the complexity and intensification of contradictions among the people.

One of the important goals of social progress and harmony is social justice and reasonable distribution is an important part of social justice whereas polarization between rich and poor is the biggest injustice. An Indian party, the Indian National Congress (the Congress) is a party with a history of more than one hundred years. It was founded in 1885 and had been in power for 45 years. But due to slow economic growth, the extreme disparity of distribution and polarization — with 50 percent of Indian population live below the poverty line, 70 million people become unemployed and there are more than 100 million child labor — triggered the people's dissatisfaction. The Congress was defeated by Bharatiya Janata Party (BJP) in the election. But, during its eight years in power, although gained obvious economic achievements with the average annual growth of GDP reaching 6 percent and a fast IT industry growth, the BJP failed to resolve the problem of distribution injustice: the gap between rich and poor was bigger than ever, the wealth ratio between south and north was 6: 1, between urban and rural was 60: 1, and the farmers accounting for 65 percent of its population were ignored, 80 percent of its population did not get the benefit from development and as many as 350 million people still lived below the poverty line. Therefore, it was defeated in the election by the Congress, which, using the strategy of "mud" (problem of poverty) to successfully beat the "mouse" (high-tech development), unfurled the banner of social justice, shouted the slogan of improving people's livelihood and resolving the problem of poverty, demonstrated an image of "poor-people-oriented." It finally got the support of the poor and the farmers and back to power.

To keep areasonable level of disparity between rich and poor is crucial for the stable and harmonious development of a country. If the gap is too large to the level of polarization, a series of problems will emerge, social unrest will occur, and the ruling party is bound to lose support of the people and thus its power. On the other hand, it is unrealistic for a society to completely eliminate differences between rich and poor in certain historical stage of development. So we cannot undiscriminatingly say that any gap between rich and poor is bad. The key lies in level of it.

There are three systems measuring income equality.

The first is the Gini coefficient. It is a number between 0 and 1, where 0 corresponds with perfect equality (where everyone has the same income) and 1 corresponds with perfect inequality (where one person has all the income, and everyone else has zero income). There has never been absolute equality in human society. Some people say that in the primitive communist society it was absolutely equal. But this is not accord with historical facts, because workers in the fields would get more food than the elderly, children and women at home. A society will not have the impetus for development if it is absolutely egalitarian without distinguishing between those work harder from those do not, between those are good from those are bad and between those work from those do nothing. On the other hand, there never had been a society of absolute unequality in human history. The most unequal society, the slavery society, was not absolutely unequal. In order to make the slaves maintain the ability to production and reproduction, slave owners must provide them with the subsistence. If a society tends to become absolutely unequal and polarized, social turmoil will happen.

According to the National Bureau of Statistics, China's Gini coefficient rose from 0.341 in 1988 to 0.417 in 2000. According to scholars form China Renmin University, Chinese Academy of Social Sciences and Tsinghua University, China's Gini coefficient was 0.31, 0.38, 0.434 and 0.455 in 1979, 1988, 1994, 1997 respectively, and in 2003, it rose to 0.53, much higher than the internationally recognized warning line between 0.3 – 0.4.① According to the calculation of the World Bank, in 1978, China's Gini coefficient was only 0.16,② the lowest in the world, indicating that China was in an egalitarian country. But during the recent 15 years, the gap between rich and poor has widened in a relatively fast speed.

The second isthe measuring system is Oshima index, or quintile method. It divides the citizens of a country into five equal parts or quintiles: the poorest, the moderate poor, the middle, the moderate rich and the richest. From the shares of these different sections of the citizens in the total income of a country, we can know the inequality of wealth. In China, the poorest 20 percent of the population accounted for 4.27 percent of the total income of all the citizens, while 20 percent of the richest accounted for 50.13 percent.③ This indicates that the country's wealth gap is widening, though it is lower than some countries in South America, Asia and Africa, whose richest 20 percent of the population have more than 60 percent of the total income of all its population.

The third system is income ratio between the high income level and low income level. In China's urban area, the income of the 10 percent of the highest households

---

① See *Research Report on China Economy Development by Renmin University of China*(2004), China Renmin University Press, p.61.

② See Li Shuang (compiler), *Studies on the Income Disparities of China's City and Town Residents* China Planning Press, 2002, p.5.

③ See *China Youth Daily*, Dec. 9th 2004.

was 3.9 times of that of the 10 percent of the lowest income households in 1998, and 5.02 times in 2000; in the rural area, the figures were 4.8 in 1998 and 6.5 in 2000. The deposits of the less than three percent of the high income households totaled 29.32 billion yuan, accounting for 28 percent of the total deposits of all citizens. In 2002, the findings of a research team from the Ministry of Labor and Social Security of China showed that, most Chinese households did not belong to the middle income group but rather to the low and moderate low groups, which respectively accounted for 31.9 percent and 32.36 percent of the all households.

The direct consequences of the large gap between rich and poor are as follows.

Firstly, the problem of poverty. In China, there are nearly 30 million people in rural areas do not have adequate food and clothing, and there are more than 20 million urban residents live below the minimum living standard, with an average annual income of 1,059 yuan, 54.7 percent lower than the national average income level. By the end of 2004, as many as 26.1 million rural residents belonged to the poverty population, with a per capita net income lower than the poverty line of 668 yuan, and the figure would rise to 49.77 million if per capita net income of poverty line is raised to 924 yuan. Secondly, the issue of social injustice. Because the social relations of distribution have not been straightened out, the order of distribution has not been standardized and the social security system needs to be improved, the inequality of distribution has become a problem. Although people accept to a certain degree that some people become rich due to hard and honest work, they are mentally imbalanced, discounted with and have strong resentment towards the income gap caused by the unfair distribution and those who get rich by illegal activities or corruption. Although the incomes of most people have greatly improved, indicators reflecting the wealth gap also rose quickly. A survey conducted among the students in Central Party School of the CPC shows that, according to the participants, the three most serious problems in 2004 in order of seriousness were: (1) income gap (43.9 percent), (2) public security (24.3 percent), and (3) corruption (8.4 percent). Regarding the reforms in 2005, 72.9 percent of the participants cared about reform of the income distribution. We must understand the issue of social justice from the perspective that the essence of socialism is the development of the productive forces, elimination of polarization and the ultimate achievement of prosperity for all. Therefore, resolve the problems of wealth gap and poverty are urgent issues in correctly handling contradictions among the people.

3. The Differentiation and Mobility of Social Strata

As the result of differentiation among classes, strata and interest groups, some new strata and interest groups emerged, and the social mobility become faster and the pattern of interests among the people become diverse: all these are both the expression and deep causes for the complexity and intensification of contradictions among the people, which are demonstrated in the following aspects:

(1) The structure and composition of the working class as a leading class has changed greatly and contradictions within it diversified. In public-owned enterprises, there are differences and contradictions among the leaders, managers, operators and the workers. The workers as producers and masters of the enterprises feel a sense of loss, and feel that their status as leading class becomes merely nominal. In the non-public sectors of the economy, especially the private sector, the ordinary workers as employees obviously differ from, conflict with and oppose to the enterprise owners with a considerable number of workers feel the loss of their original status as members of a leading class. Within the ranks of the working class, due to differences of forms of ownership, distribution and treatment in economic, political, cultural and other social sectors, as well as the faster mobility of workers between regions, enterprises, industries, positions, the income gaps have widened, leading to their differentiation into different strata and groups; even a group has been further divided into subgroups of management personnel, technical personnel and material producers. A part of the workers become laid-off or unemployed due to decline or bankruptcy of their enterprises and they have difficulties in finding new jobs, so that their quality of life deteriorated, some even live in poverty. The following situations are common in some enterprises: arrears of wages and medical expenses of the workers are serious; the proportion of workers with occupational diseases and injuries is high; the labor protection system and labor contract system fail to be implemented; the endowment insurance and medical insurance are not paid in a proper way, resulting in the infringement on the rights and interests of workers, even threat to their lives. In the meantime, some workers, who have more property or assets, have gradually widened their wealth gap with ordinary and poor workers. Mental laborers among the working class, namely the intellectuals, who have taken an increasing proportion as well as income, social status and role in production, also gradually widened their differences from the manual laborers.

(2) Newdifferentiation, combination and changes within the ranks of the farmer

class make the contradictions within rural residents become more complicated. In present-day China, the farmer class is the class experiencing the fastest and most tremendous change: from original collective agricultural workers they have become agricultural workers contracting land; a huge group of migrant workers move seasonably between rural and urban areas, who live as the low level in city life; some farmers have become self-employed and private entrepreneurs; a group of farmer managers appeared in townships, towns and village enterprises; there is the group of leaders and administrators in Party and government organizations in rural area; there is also the group of farmer intellectuals who work in schools, hospitals, agricultural technology promotion stations in rural area.

(3) The non-publicsectors of the economy, especially the private sector, have developed rapidly, forming a rich stratum of non-public or private entrepreneurs. There exist objective contradictions between these entrepreneurs as employers and workers as employees and the contradictions between the managers and the employees. In some non-public or private enterprises, the working conditions are poor, labor protection measures are insufficient, and wage arrears or deductions, overtime work, indignation of workers, child labor and so on are common, so that the relations between the owners of enterprises and ordinary workers are acute.

(4) Apart from the working class, farmer class and the stratum of intellectuals, there emerged new strata and interest groups such as entrepreneurs and technical personnel employed by non-public scientific and technological enterprises, managerial and technical staff employed by overseas-funded enterprises, the self-employed, private entrepreneurs, employees in intermediaries, free-lance professionals and so on. They are all builders of socialism with Chinese characteristics who have made contributions to the development of socialist productive forces and other causes through their honest work and legitimate operation. Between these new social strata and interest groups on one side and the working class, farmer class, intelligentsia, and cadres and the officers and men of the PLA on the other, there are also contradictions.

It is an issue of primary importance to make a scientific analysis of the social structure, to correctly understand the new changes, differentiation, combination and contradictions in classes, strata and interest groups, to analyze the changes in their political attitudes, positions, background and differences, so as to uphold the leadership of the working class, consolidate the worker-farmer alliance, unite all forces that can be united, and correctly handle the relationship between the various classes, strata and interest groups.

4. The problem of employment

The grim situation of employment and large number of employees are both the expression and causes for the complexity and intensification of contradictions among the people

(1) The great stress of employment. Among the population of more than 1.3 billion, 9090 million are aged between 15-64, more than 300 million than the total working forces of all the developed countries putting together. During 11th Five-year Plan, the number of newly added laborers reaches 10 million each year and 13 million get unemployed or laid-off. ① The employment of demobilized soldiers, college graduates and the disabled are added pressure to this problem. In the short term the oversupply of work forces will remain, which will increase the stress of employment and social contradictions.

(2) The problem of unemployment. According to National Bureau of Statistics of China, the registered unemployment rate in urban area in 2003 was 4.3 percent, and it was estimated to be 4.7 in 2004, but actually it was 4.2 percent. In 2006 it is expected to be controlled below 4.6 percent. ② There is a big difference between registered unemployment rate and actual unemployment rate. The 2001 China Social Security White Paper published by the Ministry of Civil Affairs of People's Republic of China points out that, the actual urban unemployment rate in 1993 was five percent, and rose to 8 – 9 percent in 2000, close to 10 percent in 2000. Some experts estimated that currently the figure is nearly 12 percent now. Labor force participation rate of urban population in 1990 was 56.44 percent and decreased to 49.35 in 2002. A survey of unemployment risk made by a professor from China Renmin University using Delphi method shows that, China's unemployment security line is 7.03 percent and 9.73 percent is a point marking China's entry into a period of easy intensification and outbreak of social contradictions.

(3) It is difficult for the transfer of rural surplus labor. China's has a rural labor force of 4900 million, of which the land and township and village enterprises can absorb around 100 million and 133 million respectively, and 99 million are migrant

---

① See Bai Jinhe (compiler), *Research on Several Major Issues in China's Social and Economic Development during the Tenth Five-year Plan,* People's Publishing House, 2001, p. 210.

② See *China Statistical Yearbook(2005),* China Statistics Press, 2005, p. 70.

workers. The rest 150 million are surplus laborers.[①] From 1980 to 2003, the area of China's arable land decreased as much as 100 million *mu*.[②] As many as 34 million farmers have lost their land, becoming farmers of three "Nos" (no land, no job and no subsistence). According to plan, from 2000 to 2030, as much as 54.5 *mu* of arable land will be expropriated, meaning 110 million farmers will lose their land.[③] Some farmers whose land has been expropriated described themselves as "farmers turned landless and jobless urban migrants." And after their land was expropriated, "The rich get the money, the officials get promoted, but the farmers get only IOUs."

High unemployment rate is prone to exaggerate poverty and intensification of social contradiction. The employment rate is a touchstone testing the degree of social harmony and stability. So reducing unemployment and increasing employment isan urgent need for handling contradictions among the people.

5. The problem of mass incidents

Mass incidents are both a kind of expression and obvious cause of the complexity and intensification ofcontradictions among the people.

Maintaininga harmonious and stable social environment is the premise for the Party to realize its ambitious goals in the new era and also the requirements for building the moderately prosperous society in all respects and socialism with Chinese characteristics. Mass incidents triggered off mainly by contradictions among the people have become the outstanding problem affecting our social stability.

(1) Complaints in the form of letters and appeal to the central authorities for help increased significantly. The total number of complaints increases every year, among which group complaints increased substantially. China is currently in the period of high incidence of complaints, which is described by some people as "complaint peak" period. This indicates that our social contradictions have increasingly accumulated. Another feature of the issue is the upgrading the complaints. In recent years, more and more people filed their complaints to higher levels (provincial, central), making the central governmental organs become the focuses, and more and more petitioners gathered in the key areas of Beijing.

---

① See Xu Xianglin, *Study Materials for Cadres on Issues of Agriculture, Rural Areas and Farmers*, The Central Party School Publishing House, 2004, p. 100.

② See Liao Xiaojun, *Research on China's Landless Farmers*, Social Sciences Academic Press, 2005, p. 34.

③ See Cui Lijin, "Bless the Landless Farmers in Zhejiang Province," in *China Comment*(restricted edition), no. 9, 2003.

(2) The number of mass incidents increased, so were their scale. Mass incidents happened more and their scale expanded. During the 10 years from 1994 to 2003, mass incidents and number of people involved rose sharply. In recent years, sometimes several relatively large scale mass incidents simultaneously in the same locality. Since 1998, the scale of mass incidents gradually increased, the number of mass incidents involving more than one hundred people increased from one thousand cases to more than several thousands, and there were cases in which as much as ten thousand people involved.

(3) The composition of the participants was more diverse, their activities were more organized and more violent. The participants were complex in terms of origins; some incidents had their own organizations and had their leaders behind or on the scenes; some made cross-regional activities and supports, showing a more organized feature. Some people blocked the roads, railways and trains, paralyzing the traffic. Such serious cases as violent resistance against enforcement of law, armed fighting that caused casualties were not uncommon, and cases of assaulting Party and government bodies increased.

(4) Most of the participants were ordinary people. Usually their participants were mostly ordinary people, with some of them even being older workers, retired teachers, demobilized soldiers and retired cadres. The ceaseless mass incidents have made some masses alienated from the Party and government, which merits our high alertness and pondering. Take 2001 for example. Among the about 2. 6 million people evolved in mass incidents, those took the first place in number were workers, accounting for 37. 7 percent (one third of them were workers of state-owned enterprises), next were farmers, accounting for 28. 2 percent; third were urban residents, accounting for 11. 8 percent; fourth were the retirees, accounting for 8. 2 percent; fifth were street vendors, accounting for 3. 9 percent; and the rest were teachers, students, civil servants, and so on.

(5) More political factors were behind the mass incidents. Domestic and overseas hostile forces and elements took the advantage of these incidents to create "labor movement", "farmer movement", with the intention to sabotage our national security and social development; The anti-China, anti-Communist and anti-socialist forces overseas have colluded and merged with other forces, including the so-called "pro-democracy activists," the Falun Gong cult, the elements advocating "East Turkistan," "Independence of Tibet," "Independence of Xinjiang," "Independence of Taiwan" and so on, to make use of, to plot and to instigate mass incidents.

Mass incidents, in general, belong to contradictions among the people, but sometimes the rational demands of the masses often intertwine with the unlawful forms of their expressions, plus some criminals and hostile elements taking the advantage, making this issue politically sensitive in handling. Problems triggering off mass incidents are usually problems cropping up in our reform and development and on our way forward, which often intertwined with historical issues. Generally speaking, these contradictions among the people are mainly about economic interests, but with many people involved and more latent risks and antagonism. Therefore they are more difficult to be dealt with; if not properly handled, they could change from local problems into problems affecting overall situation, from non-antagonistic into antagonistic nature and from contradictions among the people to contradictions between ourselves and the enemy.

In short, mass incidents affecting the stability of our society are increasing and taking momentum, the discontentment of some people are accumulating, the opportunities and loopholes that can be taken use of by domestic and overseas hostile forces are increasing, so are the threats to social stability. Although in the short-term it is almost impossible for mass incidents to turn into big scale social turmoil, because it needs time to resolve the contradictions and problems, if we do not make proper efforts, it is possible that cases of mass incidents will increase. China has entered a period during which unstable factors are prone to burst out, mass incidents become an outstanding latent risk affecting social stability and become a new trend of contradictions among the people. In such circumstances, properly dealing with mass incidents is of immediate urgency.

6. The problems of corruption and bureaucracy of a small number of leading cadres

The problems of corruption andbureaucracy of a small number of leading cadres have caused strong discontentment of the people, which constitute both the expression and important causes of the complexity and intensification of contradictions among the people.

The corruption and bureaucracy of a small number of leading cadres that are abhorred by the people are mainly demonstrated in the following aspects:

First, a small number of leading cadres have seriously divorced themselves from the masses and harmed people's interests by living an extravagant life, seeking ease and comfort, being hedonic, even being corrupt, committing jobbery crimes, abusing power for private gain, trading power for money, deliberately breaking the law, and so on. Second, a few leading cadres crave official positions, purchase and sell positions, play nepotism and engage in factional activities, so that corruption is rampant among cadres in some places. Third, some leading cadres infringe on rather than represent the interests of the people by seriously divorcing themselves from the masses, lack enterprising spirit and sense of responsibility, do not have correct working style, be serious in bureaucracy, formalism, subjectivism, make big faults in decision-making, be oversimplified and crude in work.

Althoughnew progress has continuously been made in combatting corruption and the wide spreading momentum of corruption has been checked to some extent, the situation is still grim, and it is quite serious in some localities and departments, so our fight against corruption will be long, arduous and complex. Special efforts should be paid in preventing the emergence of vested interests and the privileged stratum, which is the profound lesson of the failure of the Communist Party of the Soviet Union. Persistence in the struggle against corruption is very important for correctly handling contradictions among the people.

7. Problems arising from the operation of the market economy

Somefierce and acute interest disputes brought about by the contradictions and problems in the operation of the market economy are both the expression and economic causes of the complexity and intensification of various contradictions among the people.

The reform toward the market economy and operation of the market economyitself will inevitably make the economic interests and contradictions among the people become more complicated, including the contradictions between the Central government and local governments, between central and local governments and enterprises, between enterprises of different forms of ownership, between different enterprises of the same ownership, between enterprises and workers, between workers in the enterprises of different forms of ownership, different industries, and different enterprise, and between workers in the same enterprise as well. And economic contradictions in the links of production, distribution and circulation of the market economy become more prominent, including contradictions among producers, sellers and consumers, contradictions among producers themselves, sellers themselves, and consumers themselves, contradictions between unified market and regional segmentations, contradictions between legitimate and illegal operations, and contradictions between fair and unfair competitions. China's inform has always being carried out in the high-speed operation of national economy. To keep high economic growth during the transformation from the old economic system to the new, with the overall economic environment being in a relatively tense situation, will inevitably bring about various related contradictions, such as contradictions among reform, development and stability, between needs and production, between accumulation and consumption, between acceleration of development and improvement of economic returns, between efficiency and equity, between regions, between urban and rural areas and as well as contradictions in financial credit. Currently, contradictions and problems in our economic life are very outstanding, manifested mainly in the following aspects: although grains output increased, the increase of farmers' income is very slow; The total scale of investment is still too big with the rebound of overexpansion of some industries; Resources such as coal, gas, electricity face serious shortage of supply; Pressure of rise of consumer prices is very strong, especially the considerable rise of prices of staple and non-staple foodstuffs including grains, meat, eggs and others, which make the life of the low-income groups more difficult; The contradiction between accumulation and consumption is obvious, which, takes the year of 2005 for example, China's investment rate reached 42. 3 percent, the highest point since 1978, while the consumption rate 55. 5 percent, lowest point since 1978; Deep-rooted problems affecting healthy development have not been solved fundamentally and structural problems still exist, so does the risk of big economic fluctuations. Therefore, to properly handle contradictions among the people, it is imperative for us to coordinate the various relationships among economic interests.

8. Conflicts in ideological and cultural fields

The conflicts among different ideological, cultural and moral ideas constitute both the expression and cause for the complexity and intensification of contradictions among the people.

Contradictions among the people exist not only in economic life, but also in political, cultural, moral, and social fields. The task of our political reform is arduous and has a long way to go, and relationships and contradictions in our political life are diverse. Contradictions in the economic and political fields are bound to find their expression in the ideological and cultural fields, manifested themselves as ideological and cultural contradictions of two different nature, i. e., contradictions among the people and contradictions between the people and the enemy. Generally speaking, contradictions among the people are of non-antagonistic, and constitute the principal type of contradictions in our ideological and cultural field in the current stage. There are two types of ideological and cultural contradictions among the people: the one with a class struggle nature, and other, without; with latter as the dominant type. The complexity of ideological and cultural contradictions among the people lies in the fact that, our struggle with overseas hostile forces in ideological field, and ideological and cultural contradictions between socialism and bourgeois and anti-Marxist forces as well as the remnants of the exploiting classes of the old society, will infiltrate into the ideological and cultural contradictions and take up a considerable part among the people. This determines that contradictions of right and wrong among the people in the ideological and cultural fields, in many ways, are somewhat antagonistic and of class struggle nature, which, if handled improperly, can transform into contradictions between the people and the enemy. The ideological and cultural contradictions among the people manifest themselves as contradictions between right and wrong, old and new, advanced and backward, between science and superstition, innovation and conservatism, between backward culture and advanced culture; and manifest themselves as struggles between ideas, ethics and values of collectivism and socialism with that of egoism, fetish of money; as contradictions between the spirit of hardworking and that of pleasure-seeking and decadent ideas; as conflicts between traditional Chinese culture and foreign cultures; as controversies between different academic schools or points, and so on.

The ideological and cultural front has always been where fierce competition occurs between ourselves and the hostile forces. In order to plunge our society into chaos, the hostile forces often start their plot from confusing public opinions and our ideological and cultural fields to breach a gap and gain their interests in the troubled water by taking advantage of the people's ideological and cultural conflicts and contradictions and some sensitive issues. The lesson of the Communist Parties of the former Soviet Union and the Eastern European countries merit our attention. In the ideological field, for a long time they rigidly and conservatively took class struggle as the key link and strictly controlled the mass media; whereas in the new historical conditions, they came to the other extreme of advocating "openness" and "diversity" and giving up the leadership of and control over the media. As a consequence, their ideological and cultural front and political power were lost. So we must pay attention to ideological and cultural work and adhere to the principle that the Party should supervise the mass media and correctly handle ideological and cultural contradictions among the people as an important issue concerning our harmonious and stable development. Correctly handling ideological and cultural contradictions is a significant issue in the handling of contradictions among the people.

9. Problem of Ethnic Groups and Religion

Contradictions among different ethnic groups and religions are both the expression and causes of complexity and intensification of contradictions among the people.

The differences of social existence and religions of difference ethnic groups and conflicts among them will inevitably be reflected as ethnic and religious contradictions among the people. These include contradictions between the Han and other ethnic groups, contradictions among ethnic groups themselves, contradictions between different ethnic groups in the same area, contradictions among the members of ethnic groups, contradictions among different religions, contradictions within the same religion, contradictions between believers of different religions, etc. The handling of contradictions among ethnic groups and religions is an issue directly related to social harmony and stability. The Communist Party of the Soviet Union, for a long time lacking awareness of the severity, acuteness and complexity of the issue of ethnic groups, pursued Russian chauvinism, arbitrarily changed the division of the ethnic areas and forced a number of ethnic groups to make large-scale migration by ignoring the feelings of and differences between them, which exacerbated their discontentment and centrifugal tendencies. After he came to power, Mikhail Gorbachev went to the other extreme, which finally fuelled local and ethnic separatism, leading to the outbreaks of the long-simmering problems, endless ethnic and religious conflicts and unrests, which trapped the former Soviet Union into an unprecedented crisis of ethnic relations. This is one of the direct causes of the disintegration of former Soviet Union. During this period, the ethnic conflict between Russia and Chechnya intensified in an all-around way. One of the important causes is the CPSU's mishandling of the ethnic problem. Chechnya has an area of 15,000 square kilometers and a population of only about one million. In 1944, as many as 387,000 Chechens were exiled by the government of former Soviet Union to Siberia and Central Asia with the reason of their conspiring with the German invaders. On September 6, 1991, Chechnya declared independence. In 1994, Russia sent troops to Chechnya and the war lasted for two years and with 100,000 people died of it. In 1999, Russia once again sent 100, 000 troops to Chechnya, starting the second Chechen war. Currently, terrorist attack by the Chechen terrorists constitutes a big threat to the security and stability of Russian society. Another lesson is the Communist Party of Poland in dealing with the issue of religion. At first, it handled the issue of religion in a simple and crude way, which seriously hurt the religious feelings of the people; then it made another mistake of relaxing control over the church that eventually developed into a major force in overthrowing the regime of the government of the Communist Party of Poland.

Generally speaking, the ethnic and religious problems in our country belong tothe category of contradictions among the people. However, the Western and overseas hostile forces who collude with international extreme ethnic nationalism and religious forces, Falun Gong cult and ethnic separatists in the country, take advantage of ethnic and religious problems to stir up trouble and carry out anti-socialist activities such as infiltration, separation, sabotage, subversion, anti-socialist political activities. Some local governments have not handled properly these problems, making the ethnic and religious problems become more complicated and incidents occur frequently, affecting the stability of areas inhabited by ethnic groups and ethnic minority frontier areas. Ethnic and religious problems belong to a sensitive issue in contradictions among the people which need our correct handling.

II. The Correct Handling of Contradictions among the People Is an Inexorable Requirement for Building Socialism with Chinese Characteristics

It is precisely the existence of contradictions that we need to pursue harmony, and the pursuit of harmony requires us to handle contradictions. To build a socialist harmonious society, we must effectively coordinate the interests of all sides to resolve contradictions among the people, so that all classes, strata and interest groups have harmonious relations and ease of mind to give full play to their initiative and creativity. Harmony is the opposite of contradiction. To understand harmony, we must first understand contradictions; to build a harmonious society, we must first handle contradictions properly. Marxist dialectics tells us that contradictions exist ever and everywhere; the law of contradiction is a universal and fundamental law concerning the existence of all things, their inner source and their driving force of development. We should learn to use the law of the unity of opposites, that is, the law of contradiction to regard and handle all kinds of contradictions among the people that realistically exist in our country. With regard to contradictions, it is not a question of whether they exist or not, nor of whether they are good or bad. It is a good thing for a contradiction to be resolved, verse versa. After old contradictions are resolved, new contradictions will emerge. Things move forward in the process of ceaseless resolution of contradictions. By a harmonious society we do not mean that there is no contradiction at all in the society, but that we must resolve contradictions and that unity and harmony are realized in the process of resolving contradictions.

There are both domestic and foreign lessons we should learn from in our endeavors of handling contradictions and building a harmonious society.

First, the lessons and experience from Stalin era show that, the correct handling of the two types of contradictions differing in nature is the premise of building a harmonious socialist society.

It is practical and theoreticalquestion of extreme significance to whether recognize or not the existence of contradictions in socialist countries, and if recognized, what is the nature of them and how to handle them. As early as in the era of Stalin, there were two erroneous, though fundamentally opposed, views. The first refused to recognize the existence of contradictions in socialist countries; while the second, though acknowledging the existence of contradictions in socialist countries, exaggerated them to such an extent that all contradictions were regarded as contradictions between the people and the enemy, so that class struggle was arbitrarily expanded. The Soviet Union under the leadership of Stalin paid a heavy price for these errors. When declared that the Soviet Union had entered into the stage of socialism, Stalin first proposed that the "relations of production" "are fully conform to the growth of the productive forces"; It is "the moral and political unity" that had formed the motive forces of Soviet society. These views are metaphysical and run counter to the law of unity in opposites. Since the existence of contradictions in the Soviet Union was denied, how then, the existing numerous contradictions in reality be explained? To this end, Stalin had to theoretically attribute all kinds of contradictions in the Soviet Union to foreign causes and class struggle, and based on it, put forward a "Left" view: The greater progress socialism achieved, the more desperate the remnants of the exploiting class launched their struggle; one frontline of the class struggle was in the Soviet Union, the other in the capitalist countries. All domestic contradictions were contradictions of class struggle nature between the people and the enemy, and whose causes were entirely foreign, i. e., the encirclement of the capitalism and the activities of hostile classes. Stalin's erroneous views were extremely harmful to the Soviet Union. As a result, the existence of contradictions among the people was denied, the two types of contradictions differing in nature were seriously confused, class struggle was put as the top priority, and a series of large-scale purge and repression were carried out while themes of economic growth and all-round development of society and men were ignored. According to statistics of historians, during the great purge from 1936 to 1939, at least several millions people were arrested or executed, which severely damaged the normal life of democracy and legal system, leading to the slow development and stagnation of the Soviet society, and ultimately intensified all kinds of contradictions and become one of the deep roots of the collapse of the Soviet Union.

Second, lessons and experience of China show that, the correct handling of contradictions among the people is the main theme of building a harmonious socialist country.

In China, withthe basic completion of socialist transformation of means of production and the general establishment of socialist system, contradictions among the people had become and outstanding issue. The problems occurred in the Soviet Union and Eastern European countries made the Party begin to study and consider the contradictions among the people. The criticism of Stalin in the 20th CPSU Congress in 1956 caused great ideological confusion and tumult in the international communist movement; and in Poland and Hungary, nationwide unrests occurred. From the winter of 1956 to the spring of 1957, the influence of these unrests spread to China, causing some ideological confusion. Additionally, numerous problems arose from the newly established socialist system in distribution, living conditions, housing, prices, education, employment, bureaucracy, and so on. As a result, a series of mass incidents occurred, and a total of 10,000 workers and more than 10, 000 students launched strikes. The new situations at home and abroad got the Party's great attention and the whole Party was faced with the urgent tasks of summing up experiences and learning from lessons about the proper handling of contradictions among the people. The publication of Comrade Mao Zedong's article On the Correct Handling of Contradictions among the People in February 1957 marked the final formation of our Party's innovative Marxist theory of correct handling of contradictions among the people. Later on, however, we did not completely keep to this theory. We made a series of mistakes of long-term class struggle nature in ideological realm, including the expansion of the anti-Rightist struggle in 1957, the so-called struggle against Right deviations in 1959 and the socialist education movement in the 1960s, which hurt many cadres and intellectuals; and the decade long Cultural Revolution in particular, which seriously confused the two types of contradictions of different nature and brought about chaos to the whole country. It is the Third Plenary Session of Eleventh Party Central Committee with Comrade Deng Xiaoping at the core that the Party decisively set things right, stopped the wrong line of taking class struggle as the key link and reaffirmed and developed the theory of contradictions among the people, making China embark on a new path of stable, harmonious development of socialism with Chinese characteristics.

Third, lessons and experiences from some countries in their risky period of development show that, it is vital important to pay high attention on various social contradictions and to maintain relative harmony and stability of the society.

The modernization experience of various countries shows that, when a country's per capita GDP reaches $1000 – 3000, it enters a high-risk period prone to intensification of social contradictions, because the entanglement of growth and difficulties, development and contradictions will cause dramatic changes to the society. Development will inevitably bring about changes in the interest pattern, in which some people gained interests while others suffered; the rapid economic growth will bring with it some social problems, like unfair distribution, wide disparity between rich and poor, intensified social contradictions, and so on, which, if coupled with economic slowdown and financial crisis, will inevitably cause social unrest and political instability. A good example of it is the so-called "Latin American trap" or "Latin American disease," referring to the social unrests arising from impoverishment and polarization in the process of economic growth. Since the 1980s, many Latin American countries carried out neo-liberal reforms, which in a short-term had achieved some economic success. Argentina gained high growth rates of 10.6 percent and 9.6 percent in 1991 and 1992 respectively. In 2001, the per capita GDPs of some Latin American countries respectively were: Brazil, $ 957; Mexico, $ 6,200; Venezuela, $4,877; Argentina, 7417(decreased to $ 2912 in 2002 due to economic crisis). But some of their growths were achieved with the ignorance of fairness. As the consequence of it, unemployment rate rose continuously, reaching 10.6 percent in 2002. Disparity between rich and poor and polarization were serious problems. In 2004, people lived in poverty reached 227 million; in sharp contrast, the increase of number of millionaires ranked first in the world. In

Brazil, 10 percent of the richest population possessed 40 percent of the nation's household wealth, while 10 percent of the lowest income residents owned less than three percent of it. This led to the intensified social conflicts, instability and ceaseless movements of mass protest, such as Chiapas farmer uprising in Mexico, landless farmer movement in Brazil, *Piquetero* Movement and *Cacerolazo* (pot-banging) in Argentina, and the anti-privatization movements in Peru, Guatemala, Bolivia and other countries. In the 1980s, the ruling Partido Revolucionario Institucional of Mexico abandoned the traditional "revolutionary nationalism" to take the line of "social liberalism. " It fully implemented privatization of the economy and opened up the domestic market. In terms of social policies, it reduced public expenditure in education, healthcare, insurance and other sectors to solve the problem of economic growth. But it failed in properly handling the social contradictions in the transitional process, leading the bankruptcy of a large number of small and medium enterprises, giving birth to a large number of unemployed workers and landless peasants, and along with it, the fall of living standards of ordinary people and great disparity between rich and poor, with the increase both of millionaires and poverty-stricken people (which reached 46 million, accounting for 45 percent of its total population). This greatly shook the foundation of the ruling party, which lost its 71 years long governing position in 2000.

Lessons and experience of various countries tell us:

First, we must attach extreme importance to the correct understanding and handling of contradictions among the people to the building of a socialist harmonious society. Both positive and negative historical experience of our socialist construction has repeatedly shown that whenever we make good distinction between ourselves and the enemy and adhere to the theme of correct handling of contradictions among the people, our socialist cause will thriving; otherwise, we will suffer. At the present stage of high speed economic development, there exist many existing and emerging contradictions and problems. In this context, whether we can properly handle contradictions among the people is of great significance to the building of a harmonious society, and it constitutes a severe test of the Party's governing capacity.

Second, we must always takethe correct handling of contradictions among the people as the theme of our political life, absolutely abandon the erroneous practice of taking class struggle as the key link and always give top priority to development in governing and rejuvenating the Chinese nation. Because of complex domestic and international environment and economic, political, ideological, cultural and other factors, the two types of contradictions differing in nature i. e., contradictions among the people and contradictions between the enemy and ourselves, will exist for a long time; and under certain conditions, contradictions between the enemy and ourselves and class struggle may become intensified, and the two types of contradictions become closely entangled. However, the outstanding and frequent type is contradictions among the people as the principal type of human contradictions at the present stage. Therefore, the correct handling of them is the key to the building of a harmonious society and is the theme of China's economic and political life that we must grasp firmly.

III. The Correct Understanding and Handling of the Antagonism and Intensification of Contradictions among the People

Generally speaking, contradictions among the people are non-antagonistic. But they are possible to become intensified or transform, leading to serious intensification and confrontation, which need our high vigilance to properly deal with.

1. Antagonistic contradictions and the antagonistic phenomena of contradictions

To understand the antagonistic and intensified phenomena of contradictions among the people, we must first of all have a clear understanding of whatare antagonistic contradictions, what are the antagonistic phenomena of contradictions, and make a necessary distinction between the antagonistic nature and antagonistic forms of contradictions. The antagonistic nature of a contradiction means that the two opposites of a contradiction are essentially antagonistic in nature; while the antagonistic form of a contradiction refers that, determined by the specific conditions, a contradiction is resolved by its opposites in form of external conflict. Comrade Mao Zedong pointed out: "... antagonism is one form, but not the only form, of the struggle of opposites. "① An antagonistic contradiction means that the two sides in the contradiction are fundamentally antagonistic and external conflict is the ultimate form of its resolution; if the two sides in a contradiction are not

① *Selected Works of Mao Zedong*, vol. 1, People's Publishing House, 1991, p. 336.

antagonistic, it is not an antagonistic contradiction, although some accidental external conflicts may occur between them. By saying that contradictions among the people are not antagonistic we do not mean that it is impossible for antagonistic phenomena to occur in them.

There are two basic forms of antagonism in contradictions among the people. The first one is direct conflict, referring to emotional or behavioral confrontation arising from direct dispute of interests. If the interests ofone side are harmed or infringed upon by the other side, as in land or water disputes, it will lead to direct confrontation, or even bloodshed. The second one is indirect conflict. Direct conflicts usually occur in the economic field while indirect conflicts occur more in political and ideological fields in political and ideological forms. Indirect conflicts are the expanded, deepened and chain reaction of direct conflicts. The latter may upgrade into the former and expand from economic field into ideological and political fields, and from limited scale to local or regional scale, even to the whole country. When contradictions among the people interrelate with class struggle and contradictions between the people and the enemy, if improperly handled, they may become more acute, even cause social unrest. So vigilance against it must be highly kept.

2. Causes for the intensification of contradictions among the people

First, there are some antagonistic contradictions among the people. Due to the economic, political and ideological remnants of the old society, and the influence and sabotage of external hostile forces, there are not only some contradictions between the people and the enemy but also a few contradictions among the people with antagonistic nature. For example, contradictions between our leading cadres and the masses are non-antagonistic, but contradictions between the few serious corrupt elements within the ranks of our leading cadres and the masses are antagonistic nature. The existence of antagonistic contradictions is the natural cause for the intensification of contradictions among the people.

Second, there are some contradictionswithin the people that are of class struggle nature. Class struggle still exists within certain limits, which will inevitably find their expressions within the people, making some of the contradictions among the people are of class struggle nature. For instance, the struggle against corruption of the bourgeois ideology are apparently has a nature of class struggle, though a considerable part of which belong to contradictions among the people. The existence of contradictions with class struggle nature is the necessary cause of possible intensification of contradictions among the people.

Third, due to changes in subjective or objective conditions, the nature of contradictions may transform: non-antagonistic contradictions among the people may transform into antagonistic ones, contradictions with no class struggle nature into that of class struggle nature and contradictions among the people into that between the people and the enemy. The transformation of contradictions is an important cause for the intensification of contradictions among the people.

Fourth, contradictions differing in naturemay entwine intricately, making the situation more complicated, including: class struggle in certain limits entwines with contradictions among the people that are non-class struggle nature; contradictions between ourselves and the enemy within certain limits entwine with contradictions among the people that are ordinarily and frequently manifested; and antagonistic contradictions that are in a non-dominant position entwine with non-antagonistic contradictions taking the dominant role. For instance, when some of the masses take to the street, generally speaking, the vast majority of them are patriotic, and they belong to the category of the people, but the causes of their demonstration are complex, including sabotage of hostile forces, mistakes in our work that arouse discontent of the masses. Among which, the few hidden scoundrels that deliberately instigate disruption belong to the category of the enemy. The complicated contradictions are the objective reasons for the possible intensification of contradictions among the people.

Fifth, in the face of complicated and intricate contradictions triggered by domestic and international factors, the leading cadres may make mistakes in understanding and handling them, such as losing vigilance, confusing contradictions, making wrong decisions, improper handling. All these can be the subjective causes for the intensification of contradictions among the people.

3. The problem of correct handling of mass incident or unrest

In some cases, confrontation and conflict within the people many develop into mass incidents or even mass unrest. We should first of all make a distinction between mass incidents and mass unrest. Mass incidents refer to small scale events triggered primarily by contradictions among the people and participated in by a number of people in a small range without obvious political purpose, such as illegal assembly, marches, demonstrations, sit-ins, petitions, gathered containment, assaults, armed fighting, traffic blocking, as well as strikes and other activities that severely affect public order. Mass unrests are events of confrontations or conflicts in large scale (local or even nationwide), which are the results of the upgrade and further intensification of mass incident and have clear political demands, slogans and organization. Mass unrests are often triggered by temporary economic or political difficulties or major social problems. Severe mass unrest many turn the nature of social contradictions into hostility and different degree of social chaos, even into direct threats to the political power. Mass incidents, if not handled properly, can develop into mass unrests. These two kinds of event are different from the political plot conducted by a handful anti-Party and anti-socialist elements and from illegal activities of beating, smashing, looting, burning that are undertaken by a few bad guys; and most of the people involved in the events are different from those who fish in troubled waters and violate the law. The handling of mass incidents and mass unrests is an important aspect of the correct handling of confrontation and intensification of contradictions among the people.

From the decadeshistory of socialist countries we can clearly see that, various contradictions among the people not only exist but also can intensified into confrontation, mass incidents, even serious mass unrest. There are many examples of them. During the time Khrushchev was in power, the long-term accumulated contradictions in the Soviet Union was gradually intensified, so that in August 1956, in Tbilisi of Georgia, large-scale mass demonstrations broke out; and later on, large-scale mass demonstrations of workers took place in 1959 and 1962 respectively, which were suppressed by the Soviet authorities with many casualties. According to incomplete statistics of Yugoslav scholars, from 1958 to August 1969, there occurred a total of 1906 workers' strikes in Yugoslavia. In the summer of 1953, tens of thousands of workers took to the streets in the former Democratic Republic of Germany, demanding improved living conditions and major political reforms. In the summer of 1956, large scale labor unrest occurred in Poznan, Poland. This led to bloodshed clash between the masses and the army, and finally the political crisis in the autumn of the year and great change in the top leadership of the country. In the fall of 1956, the Hungarian incident shook the entire socialist camp. In the late 1960s, many social crises happened in Poland. In August 1968, Polish college students launched strikes, triggering a wide range of domestic riots; Eleven years later, large-scale labor unrests and bloodshed took place again in industrial cities of Gdynia and Szczecin, leading to the change of its top leaders. In the mid-1970s, several major strikes occurred again in Poland. In the early 1980s, Solidarity movement throughout the country brought about serious turmoil. The incident of Prague Spring took place in Czechoslovak shocked the world. In China, the unprecedented "cultural revolution" pushed socialist development into an extremely dangerous situation. And the long-term unresolved contradictions accumulated in the Soviet Union and Eastern European countries, coupled with the impact and role of international factors, eventually led to the drastic collapse of the Soviet Union and Eastern European socialist countries.

The direct causes of mass incidents and mass unrests usually include: serious economic, political and social problems; the damage of people's immediate interests or the fall of their living standards due to some wrong policies or measures; unsatisfied material or other demands; among others. One of the noteworthy causes for mass incidents or unrests is the bureaucracy, corruption and malpractices of our leading cadres, which make the reasonable demands of the masses unresolved for a long time, or no effective measures taken. Another reason for mass incidents and mass unrests is the lack of ideological education of the backward masses. Some people, tending to pay attention to immediate, partial or personal interests, make unrealistic demands. In the circumstances, if our ideological and political work lags behind, and the bigotry and erroneous ideas gain the upper hand, the masses may express their discontent toward the Party and government in radical ways. Of course, the fault for lack of education lies also with the cadres. Another important reason for mass incidents and unrests is that, during the initial phase of the incidents, some domestic and foreign reactionary forces step in to disseminate decadent feudal and bourgeois ideology and political views, sow discord, spread rumors and create troubles. The key to preventing this is also lies in the leading cadres, who should expose these elements hidden behind. Other important causes for the mass incidents and mass unrests include the complicated ethnic relations and the factors of instability in religious life. Because of the complex historical, religious, cultural traditions and other factors, frictions and conflicts occur between ethnic groups, between followers of different religions and between the government and the some of the people. The occurrence of mass incidents or mass unrests is always related to some degree with the defects in the economic and political system. In the reform process, the transition from old to new systems, the adjustment of interest and distribution pattern, etc., will inevitably highlight social contradictions. During this process, if wrong or improper guidelines, policies or measures are adopted, mass incidents or unrests may happen. They in general belong to contradictions among the people. However, people's reasonable demands often entwine with their illegal forms of expression, so do historical issues with current problems, in addition to the instigation of hostile elements, under these circumstances, improper handling of them will result in mass incidents or unrests.

In On the Correct Handling of Contradictions among the People, Comrade Mao Zedong calls mass incidents and mass unrests as "disturbances by small numbers of people" and makes analysis of them. He pointed out that "In our society, as I have said, disturbances by the masses are bad, and we do not approve of them. But when disturbances do occur, they enable us to learn lessons, to overcome bureaucracy and to educate the cadres and the masses."[①] We can learn from correct experience, and errors will be turned into fertilizer and bad things into good ones. We cannot declare the matter closed before it is thoroughly settled; instead, we should calmly and prudently distinguish between the two types of contradictions and between mass incidents and mass unrests, because, except for a few elements, most of the participants belong to the people. We should firmly oppose two erroneous attitudes: First, blaming the masses for all the errors, which will encourage bureaucracy of the leading cadres; Second, losing vigilance against the bad elements and failing to see the erroneous tendency of the masses. The correct approach is: ideological and political work are strengthened and the reasonable demands of the masses are met and various contradictions are handled correctly; the people making disturbances are guided into the right track; the few elements who have violated the law are punished according to the law; the disturbances are turned into lessons through which we strive to improve our work and educate our cadres and masses; and a variety of measures are taken to fundamentally eliminate the factors of instability.

4. Causes and characteristics of mass incidents in China

Mass incidents triggered by contradictions among the people are problems arising in the process of economic and social development, which, to a certain degree, are inevitable. The frequent occurrences of them are the result and concentrated demonstrations of combined effects of problems and contradictions surfacing in the process of profound social changes. They constitute latent risks to the building of a socialist harmonious society. Their causes and characteristics are as

---

① *Selected Readings from the Works of Mao Zedong*, People's Publishing House, 1986, p. 793.

follows:

First, mass incidents occur in the context of major transformation and structural adjustment of our society. After 20 more yearsof reform and opening up, China's economy has made great progress, its per capita GDP have exceeded $ 1, 700, which is a remarkable achievement. It also means that China's economic and social development has entered a new and critical phase. At this stage, the profound changes in the economic structure are causing widespread changes in social structure and the widening of income gaps between urban and rural areas, among regions, among industries, and among social members with different resources. Along with it, the interest pattern is changing drastically and interest contradictions become more complicated and prominent. And the increasing diversity of social consumption and its upgrading have increased people's material and cultural needs; but the economic growth, which is a gradual process, cannot immediately meet these needs. Against this background, irrational vying craze and interest conflicts tend to appear. At the same time, people's demands of participation in social and political life are stronger, while it needs a relatively long time for the formation and improvement of the new systems. In this situation, if the development lags behind and the transition of the system and mechanism is not timely completed, the society may become disorder or lose control. In other words, this is a "eventful time" with many complicated problems and contradictions entangled with one another, including the unsoundness of the new system and the defects of the old one; the reform of the distribution system and reasonably differentiation of income with actual income inequality and unfair distribution; incomplete legal system with performing official duties unlawfully and miscarriages of justice; the not-well-organized social management system and mechanism with undutiful or inadequate work, even corruption; reasonable demands of the masses with their unlawful forms of expression; and so on. These problems and contradictions are very difficult to deal with, because they are different from the fight against hostile elements or criminals, which is clean-cut in terms of legal and policy boundaries therefore easier to handle. If improperly handled, the increasingly complex contradictions and problems are prone to cause social instability, even economic stagnation or social unrest and chaos.

China is now at a critical and transitional stage of social development that is prone to social problems and contradictions among the people. With the deepening of reform and opening up, more mass incidents concerning deep-seated interest contradictions among the people are increasing. Issues such as arrears of wages or welfare funds, unlawful land acquisition and demolition, company restructuring, unlawful enforcement, judicial injustice and so on, led to the increasing mass incidents, collective visits to the capital to appeal to the central authorities for help, and even such extreme behaviors as self-immolation, self-mutilation, etc., creating very negative social influence.

Our party, by insisting on the line, principles and policies set by the Third Plenary Session of the Party's Eleventh Central Committee and the principle of "to seize opportunities, deepen reform, expand opening up, promote development and maintain stability," have successfully met various challenges at home and abroad, kept a rapid economic growth, a continuous rise of comprehensive national strength and people's living standards, maintained the political stability and social harmony. This fully demonstrates that the Party's capability of maintaining social stability and building a harmonious society is improving, and its social foundation of governance is solid. In handling mass incidents and ensuring social stability, Party committees and governments at all levels have made relatively good job in the following aspects: Firstly, they have resolved many contradictions and problems and thus prevent the occurrence of many mass incidents; secondly, most of the mass incidents are handled on the spot in a short time; and thirdly, the mass incidents were mostly kept in the local areas without widespread or ceaseless emergence or interactions of or between political, economic and social problems.

Second, most of the mass incidents are caused by contradictions of economic interests. Among which, issues concerning material benefits rank first, next are issues of social management, whereas those caused by corruption, bureaucracy, ethnic, religious, and environmental problems account for less than one percent. Take the top four categories of mass incidents in 2001 for example. Incidents aroused by problems of wages and benefits accounted for 28.1 percent; by company restructuring, merging and bankruptcies that brought about material loss of benefits, 9.5 percent; by land acquisition and demolition, 13.5 percent; by civil disputes, 4.5 percent. It is obvious that these are not political problems, but rather issues related to reform and economic operation mechanism, changes in economic structure, urban development, adjustment of interests, inefficient social management, and so on.

Third, interest demands constitute the main cause of mass incidents. With the deepening of economic reform and structural adjustment, although most of the social members have gotten benefits from it, some of the people have their interests harmed, which gave birth to a number of disadvantaged groups, including workers laid off from state-owned enterprises, the unemployed, the landless or impoverished farmers, urban residents living on subsistence allowances, and so on. At the same time, there are other social groups deserving special attention, including migrant workers, demobilized cadres and teachers laid off from enterprises, citizen-managed teachers, personnel in research institutions transformed into enterprises, urban residents involved in demolition, unemployed college graduates, etc. Some of these groups are prone to become participants or even organizers of mass incidents.

An analysis of the mass incidents in recent years shows that, their participants, demands and forms of expression varied, so were their causes, which included historical issues, practical problems, interest adjustment in the reform, defects in our policies and work, negligence in fulfilling duty, miscarriage in justice, corruption, and so on. But, in general, they belong to contradictions among the people and have a bearing on the immediate interests of the people, and most of the demands are reasonable. Therefore, as long as the leading cadres in our party and governmental departments at all levels be responsible for their duties and fully implement the policies, these problems can be addressed.

Fourth, there are also the following direct causes of mass incidents. Firstly, the damage of interests or fall of living standards of some of the people due to the lack of supporting measures or full implementation of policies in the reform. For example, the policies of basic living security for laid-off workers are not fully implemented in many areas, long-term arrears of wages, pensions, and the like, make the contradictions become more acute. Secondly, discontent originated in the widening income gap. In recent years, China's income gaps between regions, industries and between urban and rural areas are widening, which has become one of important causes of imbalance of social mentality; particularly the wealth gained by illegal means or abuse of power has aroused widespread discontent. Thirdly, bureaucracy and corruption in some of the Party and government departments constitute a threat to our social stability. In the departments or localities where there are good ties between the Party and cadres and masses, mass incidents seldom occur, and contradictions usually can be easily resolved. On the contrary, it is commonly believed that, in departments or localities where radical mass incidents occurred, bureaucracy and corruption had made the relations between the Party and government and the masses become intense, even become the major factor triggering mass incidents.

Despite the instigation of hostile forces and elements and in form of more-organized nature, mass incidents are mostly spontaneous. There is neither opposition party nor real-term underground political organization in China. This is different from the former Soviet Union around 1989 where there were a great number of political organizations. This provides favorable conditions for us to solve various social problems and ensure a stable and harmonious society.

5. Actively prevent the occurrence of mass incidents to maintain social stability and harmony

We should pay high attention to the understanding and handling of contradictions among the people, properly deal with and resolve various social problems to prevent the occurrence of mass incidents triggered by the intensification of contradictions among the people, so as to build a harmonious socialist society. To this end, the following steps should be taken:

First, resolving the contradictions and problems arising in the course of reform and development by deepening reform and accelerating development. Development is the absolute principle. Various contradictions and problems must be resolved in the process of development. We should always keep economic development as the central task and give top priority to development in governing and rejuvenating the nation. We should make the "cake of economic development bigger" so that everyone enjoys more benefit from it. To address the issue of development, we must break the obstacles hindering reform in our institutions and systems. For example, through reform and development to solve the issues of agriculture, farmers and rural areas, expand employment, improve our social security system and give more attention and assistance to disadvantaged groups.

Second, setting up a correct view on performance and a scientific outlook on development. We must bear in mind the fundamental principle that the Party is built for the public and that it exercises state power for the people and establish a correct view of achievements and comprehensively implement the Scientific Outlook on Development. We should correctly handle the relationships between reform, development and stability, between economic development and social development, between the pace of development, the intensity of reform and the extent of bearing of society, and the long-term interests, fundamental interests and short-term interests of the masses. We should pay special attention to safeguarding the immediate interests of the masses to fundamentally reduce and resolve contradictions and thus to reduce the roots of mass incidents.

Third, carrying out comprehensive management to form institutional conditions for correctly handling contradictions among the people. Vigorous efforts should be made to resolve the problems of unfair distribution and income gap and to improve social security system. We should actively and prudently push forward the building of democratic politics to form a democratic and legal system that can fully mobilize the enthusiasm of the masses and ensure the long-term stability of the country. We should institutionally overcome such problems as corruption, low efficiency, bureaucracy, low administrative efficiency, high cost, unfairness and injustice. We should adapt to the reality that the people's sense of civil rights and political participation are increasing so as to minimize the social instability arising from factors of social management.

Fourth, we should make in-depth study of the features and laws governing contradictions among the people under the socialist market economy, explore new ideas of and approaches to actively and effectively preventing, responding to and resolving mass incidents.

Fifth, we should gradually bringthe handling of things concerning the rights and interests of the masses under into the systems of laws and institutions. This is the fundamental way to correctly handle contradictions among the people and mass incidents. For this purpose, currently, we should make efforts in following fields:

Firstly, with regard to such outstanding issues as enterprise restructuring, urban demolition, rural land acquisition, miscarriages of justice, and so on, we should formulate and improve relevant laws and regulations. For example, as to the issue of urban demolition and resettlement, we should formulate unified, strict, clear and transparent rules, to ensure that the demolition and resettlement in urban construction be carried out in a good and orderly way, the legitimate rights and interests of the masses be safeguarded and activities of damaging the interests of the masses be resolutely prevented.

Secondly, we should improve the Administrative Procedure Law and other relevant laws and regulations. In the long run, it is necessary to revise and improve the Administrative Procedure Law, Regulations on Administrative Penalties for Public Security and other laws and institutions, so that the work of dealing with mass incidents is carried out under the system of laws and regulations. With this, we can ensure that the reasonable demands of the masses can be met under legal framework, and that the few elements making instigation with ulterior motives be punished by the law. At the same time, we must also strengthen the people's mediation system by expanding its scope, changing its focus, enhancing its effect and improving its organization, so that some civil disputes that are potential for mass incidents can be solved in the early stage.

Thirdly, we should establish a sound mechanism of social consultation and dialogue. This isan effective way to solve the issues concerning the immediate interests of social members and reduce, alleviate and resolve social contradictions. We can promote the practice of some localities that "turn from 'listening to complaints' into 'going to the public'" and "from passive dialogue to active dialogue," to gradually form a multi-tiered consultation and dialogue system. The existing systems of consultation among government, business organizations and trade unions, including the tripartite consultation, collective negotiation, collective consultation, labor dispute mediation, labor dispute arbitration, etc., has been proven to be effective ways to reduce and resolve contradictions, so they should be enhanced and improved in terms of laws and policies to give them full rein. We should stress everyday dialogue to avoid fastening our attention on the so-called sensitive days, holidays, major celebrations, major political events, and so on.

Fourthly, we should strengthen legislation in this respect so as to enact a special law or regulations relating to mass incidents. We should clearly define the legal connotation, components and objective standards of mass incidents and the responsibilities of various departments. We should strengthen legal education to widely publicize the laws and regulations closely related to people's daily lives, and to guide the masses to express their grievances and resolve their disputes according to the law.

6. Appropriately handle the outstanding problems concerning people's immediate interests.

Firstly, we should give more priority to expanding employment and reducing unemployment in the implementation of the Eleventh Five-year Plan. Governments at all levels should be aware of the actual situation of employment. In the adjustment of economic structure, we should properly deal with the relationship between the development of various industries: while improving state-owned and high-tech enterprises, particular attention should be paid to exploring new market demands, supporting labor-intensive enterprises that are conducive to expanding employment, vigorously develop small and medium size enterprises; promote the development of the tertiary industry centered on community services; encourage the development of non-public sectors of the economy; make full efforts in and specific guide to the implementation of the preferential policies encouraging self-employment of laid-off workers.

Secondly, we should increase input to speed up the improvement of the social security system. We should further expand the financing channels of social security funds, clearly determine and gradually increase the proportion of social security funds in public finance expenditure. On the basis of expanding the coverage and payment of social insurance according to the laws, governments at all levels should allocate some money to ensure that basic living allowance of laid-off workers be paid in full. Based on the principle of "putting people's living first", unproductive projects should be reduced to ensure that proportion of social security in the finance expenditure of governments at all levels increase step by step.

Thirdly, we should accelerate the reform of distribution system and adjustdistribution pattern. The key to the adjustment lies in raising the income of the poor and low-income population. Governmental and other departments should curb extravagance and waste and put on high priority caring the poor and supporting the development of poverty-stricken population and rural areas. The role of tax in regulating income should be given full rein to raise the tax rate on high-income earners and high consumption behaviors, with part of the revenue being used in social security.

Fourthly, the problems facing agriculture, rural areas and farmers should be appropriately resolved to effectively raise agricultural output and farmers' income. Streamlining departments and reducing cadres at county and township levels are important parts in reducing burdens on farmers. The number of cadres at county and township levels should be reduced by drawing on experience of the central and provincial institutional reforms and by adapting to the realities in rural areas. More investment should be put into the infrastructure in rural areas, more job opportunities should be created for farmers and discriminatory restrictions on migrant workers in the city should be abolished. Measures adopted by the central government to alleviate burdens on farmers should be firmly put into effect and any violating behavior should be punished severely.

Seventh, leading cadres of Party Committees and governments at all levels should earnestly improvetheir working style, and oversight and restraint mechanisms should be strengthened. In-depth research, wide consultation and opinion solicitation should be made before any major reform measure is implemented at the central and lower level departments. In implementing a policy, attention should be paid to the collection of various feedbacks so that measures not conforming to actual situation can be revised. Leading cadres at all levels must go deep into reality, concern for the sufferings and listen to the opinions of the public; detailed examination on contradictions and disputes should be made and reports on situation and contradictions at community level should be truthfully made in order to lay a reliable foundation for the central government to make correct decisions, and specific restrictions and punishments should be adopted to those who report only good news while withhold the unpleasant and those who even do not timely resolve problems or prevent their report to higher authorities.

Eighth, we should establish an emergency response mechanism that is quick in reaction, effective in directing, orderly in coordination and efficient in operation in dealing with emergences. Firstly, the unified command and coordinated functions in properly handling mass incidents should be strengthened. Secondly, the primary organizations should be improved and their responsibilities be fulfilled. Local Party committees and governments should take maintaining stability of the region as their basic responsibility, and resolutely implement the relevant arrangements, policies and requirements of the central government. Local leaders should made in-depth study of the characteristics and patterns of mass incidents in light of the actual conditions of their regions, sum up experience to improve the mechanism and methods of handling mass incidents. Leading cadres of localities, departments or units should organize and personally do mass work to the forefront. And system and mechanism of complaints through letters and visits should be improved to play a better role. Complaint reporting handling office, as a unique channel and way for the Party and government to keep contact with the masses and have knowledge of social conditions and public feelings, plays an irreplaceable role. Works related to handling complaint reporting should be brought under a system of laws and its mechanism should be innovated, including the establishment of the system of ombudsman; the judicial relief functions should be improved and channels of resolving disputes and conflicts should be further expanded and the rights of the people, especially the interests of the disadvantaged groups should be fully-protected.

In short, we should establish a sound and effective system and mechanism of handling mass incidents to actively prevent them from rising in number and expansion in scale. Close attentionshould be paid to the aggregate and intensification of various social contradictions and vigorous efforts should be made to resolve them; we should keep high vigilance against and prevent from economic issues turning into political one or the entwining of them. More accurate grasp of the overall situation of social stability should be gained to timely know the problems that may lead to conflicts, so that we can respond quickly to solve the problem in the bud and the initial stage.

IV. Basic Principles and Main Methods of Handling Contradictions among the People

Comrade MaoZedong believed that the correct handling of contradictions among the people "is a branch of science worthy of careful study."[①] So correct principles and methods should be adopted to properly coordinate interest relations of all parties and handle contradictions among the people.

First, the basic principle of handling contradictions among the people is to distinguish between the two different types of contradictions (those among the people and those between the people and the enemy) and handle them in different methods.

Correct distinction of the two types of contradictions is the premise of correct handling of contradictions among the people. Contradictions between ourselves and the enemy are contradictions that emerged on the basis of fundamental opposition of interests, for whose resolution, the method of confrontational struggle, that is, the method of dictatorship must be used. Under the socialist system, they are mainly resolved by using the law. "Qualitatively different contradictions can only be resolved by qualitatively different methods." Generally speaking, the fundamental identity of the people's interests underlies the contradictions among the people, so we should resolutely guard against using the methods for handling contradictions between ourselves and the enemy in the resolution of contradictions among the people.

Firstly, economic methods should be used to resolve contradictions of loss or gain among the people. Loss or gain concerns interests. Comrade Mao proposed that we should use economic approach to resolve contradictions of loss or gain among the people. Comrade Deng Xiaoping advocated dealing with contradictions of loss or gain among the people in accordance with the principle of overall consideration. Economic approach and "overall consideration and proper arrangements" are the main methods of resolving contradictions of loss and gain among the people.

---

① Selected Works of Mao Zedong, vol. 1, People's Publishing House, 1991, p. 311.

Secondly, democratic methods should mainly be used to resolve contradictions of right or wrong, namely, ideological and political contradictions, among the people. Mao Zedong pointed out that, the only way to settle questions of an ideological nature or controversial issues among the people is by democratic method, method of discussion, criticism, persuasion and education, and not by the method of coercion or repression. And he epitomized the democratic methods into a formula "unity –criticism –unity." Comrade Deng Xiaoping said that, in political life within the Party and among the people, we must use democratic means and not resort to coercion or attack. Democratic methods comprise mainly: one, democracy and legal system, and two, ideological education.

Thirdly, comprehensive approach should be adopted to resolve various other contradictions among the people. To settle contradictions among the people, there is no fixed formula or a single prescription for all disease; instead, we must take different ways according to specific conditions. Leading organs and cadres at all levels should, according to specific contradictions, mobilize all forces, pay attention to the working methods, use integrated measures, keep in mind to build harmonious relations, soothe the discontent of the public, deepen understanding and motivate all positive factors by ways of comprehensive coordination, overall consideration, education and persuasion, so that a regular and systematic mechanism can be established for contradictions among the people to be resolved at the community level.

Fourthly, the fundamental ways are deepening reform, developing productive forces and improve socialist democracy and legal system. That means, we should build socialist material civilization and developthe advanced productive forces, promote the progress of socialist cultural and morality and build socialist political civilization and democracy, so as to lay a firm material foundation, a common ideological and moral foundation and democratic and legal foundation for the resolution of contradictions among the people.

Second, taking the fundamental interests of the people as the starting points and goals in all their words and deeds is the general guideline for all departments of our party and government to follow.

To correctly handle contradictions among the people, the Party and government organs must always maintain a blood-and-flesh tie with the people, uphold the mass line and take the interests of the people as the basic starting point and ultimate goals of our line, policies and measures. We must focus on and maintain the most immediate and direct interests of the people and their greatest concern, accurately reflect the interests and demands of the masses from different sectors, and resolutely stop any acts that harming people's interests.

Third, properly handling the relationship between efficiency and fairness is a major task in handling contradictions among the people.

Comrade Deng Xiaoping attached great importance to the problem of wealth gap and unfair distribution. He pointed out in 1993 that, a few people had got so much wealth while the majority of the people didn't, if this situation went on, problems were bound to arise someday. Unfair distribution would lead to polarization and troubles in the future. We should resolve this problem. In the past, we put development first. In retrospect, there are no less problems when we are developed than when we are not."① And he said: "We should use all means, methods and programs to address these problems."② "We should study when to raise this question and how to settle it. I can imagine that the right time might be the end of this century, when our people are living a fairly comfortable life."③ Now it is high time to address this problem. About the relationship between efficiency and fairness, there are many experience and lessons that we can draw on from the long time development of market economy of capitalism. It is without doubt that, the nature of capitalist system itself determines that it cannot fundamentally solve the relationship between efficiency and fairness, although for a short period of time it can deal with the issue, because it cannot overcome the inherent contradictions that determine its inevitable destruction. The market economy is a double-edged sword: On the one side, it can to a certain extent arouse people's enthusiasm, optimize the allocation of resources and raise efficiency; on the other, it brings money worship, individualism and other negative things such as unfair distribution and polarization. In its process of developing the market economy capitalism have enjoyed its benefits and at the same time experienced sufferings from it. The several hundred years of capitalist market economy has given birth to the superpowers like the United States and other developed capitalist countries, and the globalization as well. But it also experienced the following four major sufferings derived from polarization and intensification of social conflicts: The first happened in the period of capitalist free competition.

---

① *A Chronicle of Deng Xiaoping*, Central Party Literature Press, 2004, p. 1364.

② *Ibid.*

③ *Selected Works of Deng Xiaoping*, vol. 3, People's Publishing House, 1993, p. 374.

Focusing only on efficiency and economic growth by neglecting equitable distribution led to the polarization between the working class and the bourgeoisie and the workers' wage decline and absolute poverty. As a result, class contradictions and class struggles intensified. From 1825 on, a major economic crisis broke out every ten years, among which, an unprecedentedly severe global economic crisis broke out in 1873 lasted for 5 years. Crises were often triggered revolution, the turbulent revolutionary workers' movement of the Paris Commune of 1871 was one example of them. The second one was the imperialist period. Through World War I, capitalist countries tried to transfer their domestic contradictions. Capitalism wanted to overcome its inherent contradictions brought about by free competition by way of monopoly, which gave rise to monopoly capitalism, namely, imperialism. Monopoly further exacerbated the polarization and class contradictions of capitalism, the result of which was the outbreak of the October Revolution in Russia. The third one is the global capitalist economic crisis of 1929 – 1933, a fatal blow to capitalism. It further intensified the class antagonism and conflicts in capitalist countries. Their attempt to shift domestic conflicts led to World War II and the subsequent emergence of many socialist countries. The fourth one is the state monopoly period of capitalism after World War II. Further intensification of the internal contradictions and polarization generated an unprecedented social crisis. Some far-sighted capitalist politicians began to mediate the internal contradictions of capitalism by launching capitalist reform. They paid more attention to equity and took a series of measures to ease class contradictions by cutting a part of the high profits gained by capitalists, including levying on high taxes on progressive income and inheritance, establishing sound social security and social welfare systems. These measures led to the formation of a huge middle class and olive-shaped social structure and made capitalism enter a relatively stable stage of development. As can be seen from this that, in its course of development, although it promoted rapid economic growth, capitalism in its early stage of development put too much emphasis on efficiency in the neglect of fairness, leading to polarization, social conflicts and turbulence. The early labor movements, World War I, World War II and the postwar labor movements, almost overthrew capitalist system. After World War II, especially in the 1960s and 1970s, the problem of fairness came to the attention while efficiency being stressed; with this, social contradictions in the capitalist society were temporarily eased. But the problem of high welfare in turn highlighted the issue of efficiency.

The issue of efficiency and fairness isof historical, specific and relative nature, and has different content in different historical conditions and different countries. That means, a thing that is fair in one country is not necessarily fair in another, or fair in one period is not necessarily fair in another, because every period has its own outstanding problems. New problems will arise after old ones have been resolved.

Efficiency and fairness are contradictory to each other, but can be unified under certain conditions. Under socialist conditions, the contradiction between efficiency and fairness can be resolved, because the pursuit of unity of efficiency and fairness is an inherent requirement for socialism. Paying attention to efficiency and striving to maximize the development of the productive forces with less input is an essential requirement of socialism and is in line with the fundamental and long-term interests of the people, and also the premise and foundation for achieving fairness. Efficiency can ensure the steady economic growth and fairness in the true sense at a higher level. On the other hand, higher efficiency can only be achieved after fairness is realized. No efficiency, no higher level fairness; unfairness constraints and affects efficiency. The contradiction between efficiency and fairness is unavoidable. The expense of certain degree of income equality and fairness is sometimes necessary for efficiency; but efficiency will be affected if unfairness comes to a certain level.

We should consider efficiency and fairness in a dialectic way. On the one hand, the market economy can raise efficiency; on the other, it highlights the issue of fairness. We should both oppose emphasizing on absolute fairness that unrealistically takes egalitarianism as fairness by ignoring efficiency, and at the same time guard against polarization that takes efficiency as the only social goal, which will eventually impair efficiency. Therefore we should give priority to efficiency and give enough consideration to fairness. That is, make the market focus on efficiency to consider mainly how to make the cake bigger, while the government put its focus on fairness to mainly consider how to make fair division of the cake; In primary distribution, we should pay more attention to efficiency while in redistribution we should pay more attention to fairness; the principle is to give priority to efficiency with due consideration to fairness.

Giving priority to efficiency with due consideration to fairness is a general principle. The understanding and implementation of this principle should be combined with the realities of different times with the target of optimizing the balance of efficiency and fairness. At the beginning of China's reform and opening up, the priority was to address the issue of efficiency and make the cake bigger without overlooking fairness. At a certain stage of development, the issue of fairness will stand out. Egalitarianism is a kind of unfairness, so is the large gap of income. Currently, egalitarianism and income gap coexist, with the latter more outstanding. The reason why some people are resentful toward the rich and officials and tend to turn a minor problem into great disturbance, in the final analysis, is that their justifiable interests have not been met. Fairness is an essential requirement of socialism and an important yardstick for measuring social progress. Achieving and maintaining fairness and building a harmonious society has a bearing on the fundamental interests of the overwhelming majority of the people. It is also the essential requirement of the principle of "the Party is built for the public and that it exercises state power for the people." Development is the absolute principle and top priority of the Party in governing the country and rejuvenating the nation, and efficiency is a necessity for development. But on the other hand, we cannot pursue development at the expense of fairness. On the contrary, to keep a healthy and sustainable development, we should, under the precondition of maintaining efficiency and growth, fulfill a relative fairness by allowing for a certain degree of income differences. Achieving and maintaining fairness involves not only the economic issue of wealth distribution, but also the political and social issue of the rights of citizens, social status, democratic governance, freedom and equality, public services, judicial justice, etc. We should regard the issue of fairness from political and economic and long-term points of view, and should create a social environment of fairness in terms of legal system, policies and institutions. Fairness necessarily involves distribution, which requires that, in the premise of ensuring efficiency, we should never relax our vigilance against the negative side of the market economy, and pay high attention to the basic role fairness of distribution played in promoting social progress.

In terms of connotation, contribution can be divided into the contribution of means of production and distribution ofmeans of livelihood, namely, distribution of conditions of production and that of the fruits of production. In a market economy, the distribution of the fruits of production is mainly of income distribution. From the perspective of sequence, distribution can be divided into primary distribution and redistribution; from the perspective of type, distribution can be divided into distributions of incentive nature, efficiency nature and social security nature; from the perspective of principle, distribution can be divided into distribution according to work, distribution according to need and distribution according to factors; from the perspective of nature, distribution can be divided into work income and non-work income, direct labor income and management labor income, reasonable and unreasonable income, and legitimate income and illegal income.

Presently the major problems with our income distribution are the irregular income gained by some people and the widening income gap. The impact of these problems is increasingly evident, posing a big threat to our social harmony andstability. The way to solve this problems is, while adhering to the principle of giving priority to efficiency and unleashing all the vitality contained in work, knowledge, technology, management and capital, gradually increase the weight of fairness in distribution to take fairness into more consideration, streamline relations in distribution, regulate distribution order, focus on solving distribution gap caused by irregular income and problems in redistribution, so that a fair income distribution system is established. To this end, the following steps can be taken:

Firstly, we should solve the issue of fairness of distribution in primary distribution to ensure that all social members have equal opportunities. Generally speaking, the existence of differences in primary distribution, which is conducive to the improvement of efficiency, is reasonable. The problem with the primary distribution in our society is, some people have gained a large amount of illegal income by taking advantage of various abnormal factors and unequal competition conditions and opportunities, such as monopoly, corruption, manufacturing and selling counterfeits, smuggling, evading tax by deceit and other means, etc., causing the widening gap in primary distribution. In these circumstances, the government should take steps to solve them. In the system in which the public sector is dominant, only by ensuring equal conditions of production and economic relations and progressive establishment of a good market order for equal competition, can fairness of conditions and equal opportunities in primary contribution be safeguarded. In primary distribution, incentive income distribution is based on the principle of distribution according to work, whereas efficiency income distribution is based on the principle of distribution according to factors. Both take improving efficiency as their premise. Therefore, to fulfill reasonable primary distribution, we must establish a sound market mechanism, coupled with necessary governmental measures, such as fully implementing the principle of distribution according to work, plugging up loopholes in primary distribution, checking irrational incomes, controlling incomes gained by monopoly and banning illegal income.

Secondly, we should solve the issue ofredistribution to ensure the reasonable distribution of income of social security. Primary distribution, in which efficiency is achieved through market mechanisms, will bring a certain degree of income inequality, which requires to be adjusted by the government through redistribution. At present, the prominent problems in China's redistribution include: unsoundness of system, no guarantee for security income, the increasingly widening gap between high and low income groups. Redistribution is dominated by the government according to the principle of fairness to ensure that security income distribution be conducted in full. This requires that the government should strengthen adjustment to properly adjust distribution pattern and effectively solve the problems of widening income gap between regions and among social members, so as to realize common prosperity. In this regard, measures can be taken include economic legislation and policies and tax, financial and administrative means, such as tax reforms, taxation adjustment of different incomes; the increase of transfer payment and public spending; the feedback of industry to agriculture and cities to countryside; support to backward and rural areas; efforts to solve urban and rural residents living in poverty; strict enforcement of the minimum wage system; raising the income of low-income level; expanding middle-income group, etc.

Thirdly, we should establish a sound social security system to solve the problem of fairness of distribution. Establishing a sound social security system through efforts of government and paying more attention on low-income group to ensure their minimum standard of living is the basic measure in security income distribution. It is a remedy for primary distribution and a basic guarantee for fairness of distribution. Social security system consists of social insurance, social relief and social welfare. Social insurance is organized by the government and implemented through legislation to give residents basic livelihood guarantee. Social insurance funds usually are paid by employers and subsidized by the government. The government, following the principle of horizontal equity, collects social security funds from taxation revenue to solve the problems of unemployment, medicine and old-age. Social assistance is the assistance provided by the government to social members who do not have any source of income, or live below the minimum standards, or suffer from major disasters, etc. Social welfare refers to the funding granted by the government in education, healthcare and public undertakings for the guarantee of basic necessities of life or for the improvement of living standards of residents.

Fourth, the long-term guarantee for correctly handling contradictions among the people is the formation of a relatively balanced interest distribution pattern, reasonable structure of social members and an economic-political system favorable to harmony, stability and development of society.

A harmonious society should have a reasonable social structure consisting of three aspects:

Firstly, a relatively balanced distribution structure. Both the egalitarian and polarized distribution patterns are unfavorable to social stability, harmony and development. We should form a relatively balanced income distribution pattern in which a certain degree of differences and fairness are kept. For this purpose, we first of all should ensure the equality of competition conditions and opportunities. It is necessary to stress the fairness of results, but at the same time we should also concern about the fairness of starting point, environments and conditions. The masses accept those who get wealth through honest and legitimate operation and work, but are resentful to disparity of income caused by unequal opportunities, especially to gray income, illegal income and corruption. We should strive to establish a good market order and distribution pattern to ensure equal opportunity to education and completely solve the problems in compulsory education, to provide an equal starting line and fair environment of competition for all social members. At the same time, we should ensure the relative balance of income distribution among social members. To this end, we should build a distribution pattern adaptable to the market economy, in which distribution according to work is dominant and a variety of modes of distribution coexist, incentive-based, efficiency-based and social security-based distributions properly integrated and a sound social security system is in place.

Secondly, a reasonablesocial structure consistent with the income distribution pattern. A "gourd-shaped" polarized society is not conducive to social harmony. We should raise the income of low-income groups and increase the proportion of middle-income group to form a relatively harmonious and "olive-shaped" social structure in which the middle income group constitutes its largest proportion, common prosperity is its goal and the social differentiation and income disparities are controlled within a proper range. In a harmonious society, different classes, social strata and groups should be mutually beneficial, that is, the increase of interests of the members in higher levels is not at the expense of that of members in lower levels, but rather on the contrary; although there are some differences between them, the enthusiasm of them can be fully mobilized to benefit each other; they open to each other and have equal status; they share in the fruits of development.

Thirdly, an economic-political system that is consistent with the primary stage of socialism, the reasonable distribution pattern and social structure, and is conducive to coordinating interest relationship of all parties and to mobilizing the enthusiasm of the different members of society, social harmony and stability. In the market economy at the primary stage of socialism, we must build an economic-political system that take good consideration of individual, collective and national interests, and the interests of different social members, classes, strata and interest groups, and the interest relationships within people, so that to provide an institutionalized guarantee for the over-all consideration of interests, the mobilization of enthusiasm and the synergic improvement of all parties.

Fifth, the improvement the capability of the leading cadres in handling contradictions among the people, building a harmonious society and maintaining social stability is the key link in the correct handling of contradictions among the people.

Leading organs and cadres at all levels should strengthen their investigation and study, make in-depth exploration of the laws and characteristics of contradictions among the people and explore new ideas and new methods for handling contradictions among the people so as to provide theoretical and practical support for the prevention, response to and resolution of all kinds of conflicts. They should analyze the development and changes of classes, strata and interest groups in a scientific way, to have a full knowledge of the conditions and causes of their differentiation and combination, their interest demands and relations, in order to develop effective countermeasures for coordinating all kinds of contradictions; they should be good at social management under the market economy, and build and improve the mechanisms of social consultation and dialogue, the system and mechanism for complaints through letters and visits, and a warning mechanism, preplans and a working mechanism that is quick in reaction, effective in directing, orderly in coordination and efficient in operation in dealing with emergences; they should be forward-looking and foresighted in observing and analyzing problems, be good at finding potential problems from early clues and can solve the problems in the bud; they should study and grasp the laws and characteristics of mass work in the new era, build flexible and efficient coordinating mechanism, and take the issues that are the most difficult, most practical and most related to the people as their focus of work, to conscientiously, responsibly and whole-heartedly resolve them; they should comprehensively take the advantage of the intellectual and moral strengths, strengthen education, ideological and political work to guide the public to express their interest demands in reasonable forms, to safeguard and gain reasonable benefits and to increase their sense as masters of the country and sense of social responsibility.

Appendix

The Global Financial Crisis and the Historical Destiny of Socialism and Marxism (20th September, 2010*)*

The global financial crisis triggered by the subprime mortgage crisisin the U. S. in 2007 and the subsequent overall crisis sweeping the capitalist world has lasted more than two years. Although various measures have been taken, its stubbornly permanent negative impact is lingering on, hitting the world economy and changing world situation. This crisis, along with other worldwide crises, can be taken as a subject of reflection for us to trace back history of about 150 years since the theory of scientific socialism was founded by Marx and Engels in the mid-19th century. The one and a half century long death and life conflict of two forces and historical trends, i. e. , socialism and capitalism, and their ups and downs, has fully proved that, the Marxist classical writers' scientific conclusion is irrefutable truth that capitalism will doom and socialism will inevitably attain victory are historical trends; and it has also convincingly proved the exuberant life of socialism and Marxism and their historical destiny.

I. The Course of World History over the Past Century and a Half Has Irrefutably Proved the Inevitability and Truth of Marxism

Dialectics tells us: everything in the world develops not in a straight line but in a wave-like manner and rises in spiral and zigzag way; so does social history. The world history has irrefutably proved it. This is precisely the logic followed by socialist movement, which is, although experienced twists and turns, setbacks and failures, forging ahead with the times. This historical process exactly proved the indisputable truth of Marxism.

In observing the law of social history, the longer is the time, the clearer we can see, and the more testable the judgments and conclusions about it. After world history entered the development stage of capitalism, the traces, rules and trends of the game of the two major classes of the working class and the bourgeoisie and that of the two social systems of socialism and capitalism, with the development of history, the shift of space and the passage of time, show a clearer picture than ever before. So do the inevitability of socialism and the scientific nature of Marxism.

In retrospect in the 21st century, we can get a clear picture of the four major turning points of socialism in world history. During this process, socialism experienced ups and downs in its struggle, demonstrated its resilience to adversity and now is showing an ascending trend. Despite all the twists and turns, progress and setbacks, successes and failures, the development of socialism proved that, Marxism is correct in its judgment that the historical trend of socialist victory is inevitable; and the historical triumph of socialism over capitalism is by no means all plain sailing, nor it can be achieved in a short time; instead, a fairly long span of time, arduous efforts even blood and lives of dozens or even hundreds of generations are needed. On the one hand, we must see the general trend of historical development, firmly believe that the replacement of capitalism by socialism is an irresistible and unchangeable historical trend; on the other, we must keep in mind that this is a long historical process full of twists and turns, struggles, even temporary setbacks and frustrations. We should oppose both the idea of hopelessness or "quick victory" of socialism. That means that, we must not lose our conviction and faith in it because of frustrations or setbacks, nor can we take chance or hope for its quick success.

The four turning points of historic significance of socialism can be divided into two parts. The first two occurred in first half of the 20th century, before and after World War II, respectively. During this period, socialist movement rose and developed, while capitalism, after going through its rising stage of capitalist revolution, the stages of competitive capitalism and monopoly capitalism, and a series of economic crises and the two world wars, began to decline.

The first turning point occurred in the early 20th century, marked by the October Revolution in 1917. In the mid-19th century, Marxist classical writers established the theory of scientific socialism, replacing the utopian socialism and thus providing a guideline for and opened up a new chapter of workers' movements and socialist movement around the world. Entering the 20th century, socialist movement upgraded from the practice of vigorous labor movements guided by scientific socialism to the practice of socialist system. Lenin successfully led the October Revolution and established the first socialist country. This is the most important world event in the early 20th century, which ushered in a new era in the history of mankind and reached the first upsurge of the socialist movement.

The second turning point occurred in the middle ofthe 20th century, marked by successes of socialist revolutions in a number of countries after World War II in 1945 and the formation the socialist camp. The intensification of conflicts will cause crisis and thus bring about opportunity for revolution. World War I and II broke out in the early and middle of the 20th century respectively, were outcome of intensification of the insurmountable contradictions in capitalist societies. Due to these inherent contradictions, free competitive capitalism led to monopoly and the replacement of free competitive capitalism by monopoly capitalism, which not only failed to overcome the inherent contradictions of free competitive capitalism but exacerbated them. As early as in the stage of free competitive capitalism, from 1825 on, the acute inherent contradictions of capitalism caused economic crises every decade, and the accumulation of which resulted in the unprecedented crisis of capitalism worldwide in 1873. This crisis, coupled with a series of smaller scale ones in 1900, 1903 and 1907, eventually led to the outbreak of World War I. But war can only worsen and aggravate crises. Soon after World War I, in 1929 – 1933, a major crisis occurred in capitalist world, accompanied by a severe recession, so severe that it was once considered as the "doomsday of the world" and "the end of capitalism." War was again resorted to solve the crisis was. But war can only alleviate the contradictions and shift the crises rather than fundamentally overcome them. The further intensification of the contradictions again led to the outbreak of World War II. World War II was the result of conflicts between the imperialist countries, which means that capitalist system was unable to prevent the war. It was the Soviet Union that, by making use of the superiority of the socialist system, mobilizing all people and rallying all anti-fascist forces in the world, defeated German fascists and won the war. The two world wars marked the decline and failure of capitalism. Crises and wars brought about unprecedented opportunities for socialist revolutions. During World War I, Russia took the lead in breaking the weak link of capitalism and establishing the socialist system. Before and after World War II, China and many other underdeveloped countries successfully carried out revolutions, stood up and established socialist countries, forming a the socialist camp. In contrast, the social contradictions and the general crisis of capitalism further deepened, a series of crises erupted in the United States in 1948, 1953, 1957, 1960, 1969, 1973, among others, and spread globally to other capitalist countries in North America and

Western Europe and Japan. The overall strength of capitalism declined because of these big blows. On the other hand, in the declining process of Western European capitalist countries, the United States rose rapidly thanks to its favorable international environment and domestic conditions and the opportunities of the wars. After World War II, just when capitalism was in the doldrums, socialism and socialist movement witnessed a new upsurge.

Inthe twenty more years from the 1980s – 90s to the present, another two major historic turning points occurred. During this period, although socialist movement turned from high to low tide, world socialism represented by socialism with Chinese characteristics began to ride out of downturn. When capitalism entered a rapid development period after depression, the financial crisis initiated in the U. S. has trapped modern capitalism in a situation of further decline.

The third world historic turning point occurred in the late 20th century, marked by the drastic changes in the former Soviet Union and Eastern Europe and the subsequent the disintegration of the socialist camp in the late 1980s and early 1990s. Since then socialism entered a low period, leading to the most significant change and turning point in world situation since World War II. In the first half of the 20th century after World War II, socialism was ascending while capitalism was declining. But when world history entered the second half of the 20th century, the pace of development of the socialist countries slowed down, some even registered stagnation or negative growth, especially the changes in the former Soviet Union and Eastern Europe, resulting in the setback of socialist countries and a very difficult situation for socialism. On the other hand, modern capitalism, drawing lessons on its own development and those of the socialist countries as well, carried out reforms and entered a period of relatively moderate development. But crises didn't cease to erupt in capitalist world. From 1980 to 1990, for example, there were several crises in the United States that were of world influence. Along with the third turning point, a series of new developments and problems emerged in China and the world, which had a far-reaching influence on the development of socialism from the late 20th century to the 21st century. China, starting from a difficult situation, unswervingly pushed forward reform and opening up since 1978 and has successfully paved the development path of socialism with Chinese characteristics.

The fourth important turning point of socialism occurred in the early 21st century, marked by the global financial crisis broke out in 2008. The impact of the crisis on the pattern of world situation and China' endeavor of building socialism with

Chinese characteristics is immeasurable. Just as the Chinese saying goes "Ups and downs are the common sight of life." In just several decades, the success of socialism with Chinese characteristics has provided great impetus for world socialist movement to rise again from low tide. In contrast, the United States and other Western developed capitalist countries have fallen into predicament because of the crisis: the position of the United States as the only superpower has shown a sign of decline and the overall strength of capitalism is downward going. If several decades ago socialism went through a period of low tide while capitalism got the upper hand, then today the situation has dramatically turned round.

The root causeof this financial crisis is the irresoluble problems of capitalist system, so the measures taken till now can only ease it for a short period of time. In sharp contrast to it is the great success of socialism with Chinese characteristics. The essential difference between the socialist market economy and capitalist market economy lies in the ownership of means of production. Capitalist private ownership of means of production determines that the crisis originated in the double contradictions in its commodity production is unavoidable. On the contrary, the socialist market economy with public ownership as its dominant sector determines that it can avoid, if any, can overcome the crisis caused by the double contradictions of commodity production. Because, under the socialist system, although the inherent contradictions of commodity production are unavoidable, the crisis derived from it can be avoided. That is to say, the combination of the market economy and the socialist system make it possible for socialism with Chinese characteristics to prevent and overcome the impact of global financial crisis.

Under the correct leadership of the CPC, the Chinese people have successfully withstood impact of the global financial crisis, reached their development targets and remarkable achievements. We owe all this to the correct leadership and resolute decisions of the Party, and more fundamentally, to the superiority of the socialist system and vitality of socialism, socialism with Chinese characteristics and Marxism.

II. The Success of Socialism with Chinese Characteristics and China's Success in Resisting the Global Financial Crisis Highlights the Great Vitality of Socialism

Marxist classical writers founded scientific socialism and thereby opened a new era for worker's movement and socialist movement. At that time, their focus were primarily put on Western developed capitalist countries. Based on realities at the times, they once imagined that socialist revolution would took place in developed countries that the productive forces were relatively advanced and the working class accounted for the majority of the population; and that socialist victory could only be won if the revolution occurred simultaneously at least in several major developed capitalist countries. But practice and development thereafter went beyond their expectation, which made the founders of scientific socialism began to pay attention to study oriental countries in their pursuit of socialist path. At the turn of the 20th century, when objective and subjective conditions were ripe for a socialist revolution in the backward oriental countries, Marx and Engels timely studied and suggested the possibility of launching socialist revolution and taking socialist road in these countries. They believed that, the non-capitalist oriental countries, under certain conditions, can bypass the Caudine Forks of the capitalist system and assimilate all the positive results created by the capitalist system to achieve a leapfrog development of socialism. They held that the socialist forces were possible to grasp this historic opportunity to open up a non-capitalist development path. Their vision provided a theoretical foundation for the backward countries to launch socialist revolution and embark the path of socialism. Marx and Engels' conclusion that socialist revolution will first win in the Western countries is based on the development law of universal history. According to this law, socialist revolution should took place on the conditions where productive forces are fully mature and the relations of production no longer correspond to the development of the productive forces. In other words, a country should first go through the mature period of capitalism before it enters into socialism. But the outcome was that the success of the socialist revolution and the establishment of socialist system did not occur in the Western developed capitalist countries, but in the oriental backward countries where capitalism was not yet mature but certain historical conditions were ripe. Marx and Engels, through their scientific studies and analyses of the particularity of historical development, raised the issue of realizing socialist system without going through capitalism. Lenin, after analyzing the law of economic and political imbalance of capitalist system in the imperial stage, put forth the scientific conclusion that socialist revolution can have a breakthrough in the weak links of capitalism, and he launched and won the October Revolution. The success of the revolution also proved that the Marxist classical writers' of realizing socialism without going through capitalist road is correct. However, the socialist model or road of the Soviet Union established by Stalin after Lenin's death, despite its temporary achievements, gradually became a highly rigid and highly centralized economic and political system. It ignored the relatively backward productive forces of the Soviet Union in contrast to the developed capitalist countries, the inevitability of the market economy and the actual conditions in the Soviet Union. As a result, the development of the productive forces was seriously restrained, so did the enthusiasm of the people and the superiority of the socialist system. At the same time, a number of countries having won the socialist revolutions, in their practice of building socialism, made the mistakes of copying the model of other countries without adapting them to their own realities of relatively backward productive forces. In the development of the following decades, the development of the socialist countries fell into a difficult situation, because the superiority of the socialist system was gradually depleted by the rigid and inappropriate economic and political systems, coupled with various objective conditions and subjective errors. China's Cultural Revolution and the drastic changes in the Soviet Union and Eastern Europe were precisely the results of this development. The drastic changes in the Soviet Union and Eastern Europe in the 1990s were caused both by the external factors of the capitalist plots of Westernization and differentiation and the internal factors of blunders and rigid socialist systems that divorced themselves from actual conditions and hamper the progress of productivity.

After the victory of socialist revolution, the question of how to build socialism in backward countries must be answered in practice and in theory. The success of the path of socialism with Chinese characteristics presents a good answer to it.

According to Marxist classical writers' theoretical idea of "non-capitalist road", an economically backward country can launch socialist revolution and establish socialist system in a leapfrog manner, that is, without going through capitalist stage. Nevertheless, the natural historical process of the market economy is insurmountable which have experienced by the capitalist countries and had brought about the highly developed productive forces. The Chinese Communists, by summing up the experiences and drawing on the lessons of various socialist countries in their socialist construction, and by combining socialist system with the market economy, launched reform and opening up and has established a economic-political system that conforms to China's productive forces at the present stage. By doing so, it has given excellent answers to the questions "What socialism is and how to build it in a backward country?" By proceeding from reality in all things and going its own way without copying other modes, China has succeeded in creating a path of socialism with

Chinese characteristics.

The financial crisis has brought great chaos and gloom to Western capitalist countries, which has not yet gotten out of the woods. In contrast, socialism with Chinese characteristics under the leadership of the CPC, has withstood the impact with concerted efforts, which once again shows the great strength of mobilization and combat effectiveness of the socialist system. This development once again proved that, socialism is an inevitable trend that cannot be reversed by subjective will of man, in spite of possible twists and turns, low tide and even failures.

III. The Innovation of the System of Theories of Socialism with Chinese Characteristics Has Injected New Content into and Showed the Great Creativity of Marxism

The Chinese Communistshave made innovation in and given new life to Marxism in their great practice of socialism with Chinese characteristics.

The world today is undergoing comprehensive and profound changes, and contemporary China is undergoing extensive and profound reforms. Internationally, theglobal financial crisis triggered by the U. S. subprime mortgage is not only a serious financial crisis, but also a profound economic, ideological, political and overall social crisis of capitalism, which is and will continue to produce grave and long-term impact on the world. In China, in contrast, socialism with Chinese characteristics has obtained great achievements and China's development road and experience has become a symbol of the times and has opened a new path for the progress of human civilization. The major setback confronting contemporary capitalism both gives a rare opportunity and poses unprecedented challenges to contemporary socialism and Marxism and face them with grim situation. That is, opportunities and challenges coexist, with the former outweighing the latter.

World situation and pattern are undergoing profound changes, and world development and world history are both at a major turning point. These significant developments add new variables to the contest between the two forces and ideologies of capitalism and socialism, and at the same time they provide new space and new impetus for the development of socialist movement and Marxist ideology. In retrospect, in the third historic turning point in the 1980s and 1990s when world socialist movement was at an unprecedented low tide while capitalism got the upper hand, the anti-socialist and anti-Communist Party thought went rampant with their proud voices filling the air; along with it, neo-liberalism came into being which was sold everywhere by the Western capitalists.

But 20 years later, the current financial crisis has brought about a new situation: on the one hand, capitalism suffered an extremely hard blow, neo-liberalism went bankrupt and capitalist ideology is being widely questioned; on the other hand, socialism with Chinese characteristics obtained great achievements through reform and opening up and has successfully withstood the financial crisis. Socialism has gotten out of downturn while criticism of capitalism and neo-liberal are receiving harsh criticism. This situation provides an very favorable conditions for the development of contemporary socialist and Marxist ideology and for our party to strengthen its ideological work. Facing this situation, Western capitalists are forced to use double tactics: economically they make use of and try to destruct us by excessive praise; on the other they are encircling us militarily and attacking us ideologically. That means that we are confronted with more severe test. The fast-changing world, the financial crisis and the clashes of various forces clearly show that, financial capital is but the contemporary form of capital; Marxist theory is completely applicable to our times and socialism has a lasting vitality; while today's capitalism, whatever form it takes, cannot escape the fate scientifically predicted by Marxism. Now it is the significant historical mission for the CPC to seize the opportunities to overcome difficulties, make innovations and promote the great development of Marxism.

Is Marxism out of date, or has it run out of vitality? The answer is no. As a scientific theory, Marxism has an exuberant vitality. The reason why Marxist theory is eternal and has a vigorous vitality lies in its practicality. Practice is the source of theory, the criterion for testing truth and the motive force for the continuous development of theories. It is its continuous combination with the ever-changing practice that Marxism keeps its lasting vitality and vigor. The combination and adaptation of Marxism with China's realities have brought about two historic leaps forward and two major theoretical achievements. The first one is Mao Zedong Thought, the practice-proven theoretical principles and summary of the Chinese revolution, the correctness of which has been proved by the practice of socialist revolution and, of course, the socialist construction. The second theoretical leap forward is the formation of the system of theories of socialism with Chinese characteristics. This system, focusing on the theme of socialism with Chinese characteristics, has answered the new questions under the new historical conditions and opened up a new realm of Marxism. In the three decades of reform and opening up and the historical process of giving answers to the questions around the theme of socialism with Chinese characteristics, our party has always been faced and answered in a scientific way the three major questions: What is socialism and how to build it? What kind of party the CPC is and how build it? What kind of development we should realize and how realize it? These three questions boil down to the general question of what Marxism is and how to uphold and develop it. During this process, we have deepened our standing of three laws, i. e., law governing socialist construction, law governing the Party's governance and law governing the development of human society. By doing this, we have given Marxism brand new content and vigorous vitality.

This book is the result of a co-publication agreement between China Social Sciences Press (China) and Paths International Ltd (UK)

This book is published with financial support from Innovation Project of CASS

Title: Social Change in Contemporary China and the Theory of Social Contradictions
-------The Social Class and Interest Group Analysis in Contemporary China
Author: Wang Weiguang
Translated by Huang Yusheng
ISBN: 978-1-84464-267-0

Paths International Ltd
PO Box 4083
Reading
United Kingdom
RG8 8ZN
www.pathsinternational.com

Published in United Kingdom

Lightning Source UK Ltd.
Milton Keynes UK
UKOW03n1242141214

243131UK00007B/47/P

9 781844 642670